SHO 12/15

- 9 JAN 2016

Everything You Ever Wanted to Know About the Tudors But Were Afraid to Ask

TERRY BREVERTON

About the Author

Terry Breverton is the author of *Jasper Tudor: Dynasty Maker*, *Richard III: The King in the Car Park*, *Owain Glyndŵr: The Story of the Last Prince of Wales* and *The Tudor Cookbook*, all published by Amberley. Terry has also presented documentaries on the Discovery and History channels. He lives in the Teifi Valley in Carmarthenshire.

This edition first published 2015
First published 2014

Amberley Publishing
The Hill, Stroud
Gloucestershire, GL5 4EP

www.amberley-books.com

Copyright © Terry Breverton 2014, 2015

The right of Terry Breverton to be identified as the Author of this work has been asserted in accordance with the Copyrights, Designs and Patents Act 1988.

All rights reserved. No part of this book may be reprinted or reproduced or utilised in any form or by any electronic, mechanical or other means, now known or hereafter invented, including photocopying and recording, or in any information storage or retrieval system, without the permission in writing from the Publishers.

British Library Cataloguing in Publication Data.
A catalogue record for this book is available from the British Library.

ISBN 978 1 4456 5053 1 (paperback)
ISBN 978 1 4456 3845 4 (ebook)

Typesetting and Origination by Amberley Publishing.
Printed in the UK.

Contents

Introduction

The time of the Tudors was the beginning of the modern era, which saw a revolution in almost every aspect of life. The sixteenth century opened with the discovery of the great riches of a 'New World'. The Renaissance in Italy spread rapidly north into Tudor society, where it prospered under a period of relative peace compared to the previous bloodshed of the Hundred Years' War and the Wars of the Roses. Life became more prosperous for the average person, with a growing economy and the end of serfdom being accelerated by the sickness known as 'the Great Mortality' or 'the Pestilence'. Not described as 'the Black Death' until 1755, the plague had attacked all classes, killing up to 200 million people across the world, almost half the population. The plague peaked in 1350, and it would take Europe around 150 years to recover. However, it returned sporadically until the nineteenth century. For instance, plague epidemics ravaged London in 1563, 1593 and 1603. Soil exhaustion, overpopulation, wars and epidemic diseases helped cause hundreds of famines in Europe during the fourteenth and fifteenth centuries, which combined with plague to cause social unrest and endemic warfare. Matters were somewhat alleviated under the Tudors, but the advent of the 'Little Ice Age' led to poor harvests and hunger.

Europe saw increased internal and international commerce, new systems of international finance, oceangoing trading fleets and the development of an entrepreneurial bourgeoisie. This gradually built a capitalist, money-based economy, with power accruing to a new merchant class in England. The printing press brought the rapid spread of new ideas and ideals and a questioning of the status quo across the fields of science and theology. New astronomical findings no longer placed the Earth as the centre of God's universe. There was rapid scientific innovation; for instance, gunpowder changed the nature of warfare and the military caste system of society. Great artillery pieces assisted the rise of centralised nation states, as castles could no longer be held by great nobles indefinitely.

Most importantly, the sixteenth century brought the Bible, translated from Latin or Greek, to the masses, and thus brought the spread of literacy. A spirit of inquiry was disseminated through liberal members of the Church, disgusted with the papal excesses of the period. The Roman Church had been the unifying cultural foundation of Europe for a millennium, but came under attack. The first half of the century saw a theological revolution across northern Europe known as the Reformation. The cultural consensus of Europe had been based on universal participation in the Catholic notion of transubstantiation – that the bread and the wine used in the Eucharist are literally the body and blood of Christ – and this was broken, especially in northern Europe. Religious change brought with it massive social and political change.

With the general economy becoming more prosperous at the beginning of the Tudor era (1485–1603), people became more optimistic about the future. There were larger families and the population began growing again across Europe. However, by about the middle of the sixteenth century, a combination of population pressure and inflation, exacerbated by the flow of gold and silver from the New World, saw price rises. These halved effective wages, and changing economic conditions saw many peasants lose their land as the terms of their tenancy became much less favourable. Land became concentrated in the hands of the elites, especially the rising middle and merchant classes. There were clearances of common lands used by the poor to raise animals and crops. Large areas of land were 'enclosed' by hedges, within which were raised profitable stock such as sheep, leading to homelessness and vagrancy, with growing social unrest.

While the poorest and more marginal classes struggled, the middle class was growing and generally becoming more powerful. In English-held Calais, with an active trade with English, Dutch, Baltic and other French ports, the quality of life saw an improvement. Richer people in quickly growing towns began to have leisure time to spend in taverns, and there was a rise in social problems associated with drinking and gaming. People in towns could not safely drink water, which was often unhygienic, so alcohol was consumed to excess by all levels of society before seventeenth-century Puritans began to decry drinking as a sin.

In international affairs, England was only beginning to be regarded as an important nation. Luckily for the new Tudors, the great Continental leaders were more concerned with each other than this island, regarded as poor, peripheral and semi-barbaric. In the first half of the sixteenth century, Francis I of France brought the art and culture of the Italian Renaissance to France and encouraged the new humanistic school of thought. His contemporaries were Henry VIII and the Holy Roman Emperor Charles V, whose Hapsburg territories stretched from Hungary to Spain. The Hapsburgs represented a constant threat to France, with its territories of Flanders in the north, the Imperial duchies and bishoprics in the east, and Spain in the south almost completely surrounding France's land borders. Only during the early years of Henry VII's reign had the French overcome the problem of the Duchy of Brittany to their west.

Dynastic struggles continued across Europe in the second half of the sixteenth century, and Henry VIII's daughter Elizabeth became perhaps the greatest English monarch. With a perilous early existence similar to that of her grandfather Henry VII, hoping for survival, she had assimilated similar pragmatic instincts. Like Henry VII, she was assisted by excellent, trustworthy and experienced councillors and helped heal the nation after the religious excesses of Henry VIII, Edward VI and Mary I. The Elizabethan Age was one of growing national pride, literary and scientific genius, with circumnavigation and exploration leading to the embryonic British Empire.

The Hapsburg Emperor Charles V had divided his lands between his son Philip II, who received Spain and the Netherlands, and his brother Ferdinand, who received the eastern territories of Austria-Hungary and the imperial title. Philip II was the most powerful monarch of the age, controlling an empire that stretched across the world, but he dissipated the fabulous riches of the New World in making war to enforce Catholicism in the Low Countries and elsewhere. Spain replaced France as England's greatest enemy, but by the end of the century she had had declared bankruptcy twice.

While repelling the Spanish invasion threat to England by a combination of seamanship and fortunate weather, any French threat was fortunately lessened by internal dissension. The untimely death of Francis' son Henri II in 1559 saw France suffering under the forces of the Reformation, dynastic rivalry and economic pressure. Its Wars of Religion were as much a political and civil conflict as a religious one, and lasted four decades. The young sons of Catherine de' Medici succeeded, and the last of them, Henri III, was assassinated in 1589. In France Henri IV came to the throne as the first of the Bourbon dynasty, but was a Protestant. Throughout the 1590s Henri fought the forces of the Catholic League, which was backed by Spain. To end the conflict, he converted to Catholicism in 1593, and finally entered Paris in 1594 to take control of the country. However, Spain kept up its war against France.

Against this background, the Tudors were lucky throughout the century. England was little involved, and its monarchs could concentrate upon its internal problems – mainly those of religion, following Henry VIII's Act of Reformation and Dissolution of the Monasteries. For the English people, the weather deteriorated with the advent of the 'Little Ice Age', leading to poor harvests and food shortages. Bread became scarce, with the prices of food, fuel and rents rising while wages were depressed. The situation was far worse in war-torn Europe, however.

Interestingly, a 2012 book by Peter Ackroyd, the second volume in his *History of England*, entitled *Tudors*, begins with Henry VIII. The founder of the Tudor dynasty, Henry VII, deserves far more. Apart from being unfairly traduced in recent years by committed supporters of Richard III, his life is hardly known, yet there is a strong case that he was the greatest of all English kings, in terms of equity and stabilising a war-torn nation. For instance, only under the half-Welsh Henry VII did the original British people of Wales finally accept their conquest after a millennium of struggle against the Germanic Anglo-Saxons, the Danish kings of England and the Norman-French. Instead,

Henry VIII and Elizabeth I are usually all we remember about the Tudors. Indeed, Henry VIII did little to perpetuate the memory of his much more capable father, whose rise from a hidden childhood and exile to overthrowing the Plantagenets is one long adventure. Without Henry VIII's great-uncle Jasper Tudor there would have never been a Tudor dynasty, but he allowed Jasper's tomb to be destroyed in the Dissolution of the Monasteries. Equally, Edward VI's reign is little known, as is the fact that Mary I married Philip II of Spain, who sent the Armada to assist the invasion of Elizabethan England. However, apart from the stories of the monarchs and their courts there is the story of their subjects – little taught but equally interesting – and the second half of this publication is dedicated to the people of Tudor times.

One final note – this period of history is exciting, but limitations of space, in covering over a century of a dynasty, means that there will be some regrettable omissions. It is therefore hoped that the reader will be tempted to explore and discover more about the truly remarkable people both mentioned in, and bypassed by, this book. The reading of history should be stimulating, and it is hoped that this volume achieves that effect.

PART 1

Interesting Facts about the Tudors and Their Children, Courtiers and Advisers

1

British Independence and Tudor Origins

British Independence

To begin to comprehend the Plantagenet civil wars that gave us the Tudors, one has to understand the relationship of England with its unsettled and recently conquered neighbouring nation of Wales. Systematic genocide, as evidenced by DNA patterns, by Germanic, Danish and then Norman invaders, had pushed the original British people westwards out of England over the previous seven centuries. There was thus a British-speaking kingdom in Strathclyde in south-west Scotland, a British-speaking Cumbria (the same root as Cambria, the mediaeval Latinisation of the Welsh Cymru) in north-west England, and the main population had been forced into Cymru (Wales) and the extreme south-west of England, Cornwall. Some Britons escaped from the south-west to colonise Brittany and give it the British language, Breton, similar to today's Welsh. All these British remnants outside independent Brittany had been overcome by the eleventh century except Wales, which, unlike England, beat off the Saxon, then Danish and then Norman Conquests. Strathclyde was overcome by the Scots around 1040, Cumbria (with its Cumbric language still imprinted in landscape features) by William II in 1094, and Cornwall, recognised as still being independent by King Athelstan of England around 930, succumbed to the Normans shortly after 1066.

Thus the only remaining British population in the British Isles was in Cymru, now called Wales as the Saxons named the original inhabitants *walsci*, or foreigners. With growing pressure from the Marcher Lords pushing into Wales, the royal House of Gwynedd in north Wales attempted to unify the princes of the rest of Wales in the thirteenth century. Unfortunately, this led to a direct response from Edward I of England, supported by his great barons and foreign mercenaries. This led to the entrapment and killing of Prince Llywelyn II in 1282, and the ritual execution of his brother Prince Dafydd in 1283, which began ensuring English dominance over Wales. Edward personally supervised Dafydd's ghastly disembowelling while alive, a fate suffered by dozens of Welshmen over the next two hundred years as revolt after revolt flared up.

By the Statute of Rhuddlan of 1284, Wales was divided into two political and administrative areas. The Principality of Wales was under the king's control and was defended by fourteen massive royal castles, the building of which led the king to renege on his debts and bankrupt his foreign moneylenders. The Marcher Lordships, on the other hand, were a collection of independent feudal authorities, run along semi-lawless lines. This led to the building and rebuilding of over ninety large stone castles in the Marches of Pembroke and around the England–Wales border in the fourteenth century. There were also erected hundreds of subsidiary fortresses and fortified houses and churches to try and hold any gains. A large number of walled towns around castles were constructed, essentially copies of the French *bastides*, within which to settle English, Flemish and other nationalities. The native British Welsh were generally proscribed from living in these heavily defended commercial centres.

The new town and its castle became 'symbolical of conquest and the imposition of an alien regime, and the presence within Wales of a privileged burgess element'. There grew among the Welsh a massive resentment of second-class treatment in their own country, the enforced imposition of a new and alien language, the seizing of land and property, and the killing of the last princes and their families. With a constant undercurrent of rebellion, there were hundreds of prophecies of a national leader who would free the Welsh. The bards had always played the vital role in Welsh communications, culture and identity, and, although proscribed and prosecuted, they continued to travel around the country, telling the people and its lords of the coming of *y mab darogan* – 'the son of prophecy'. This would be the national redeemer, a second Arthur, who would give the Welsh back their freedom and drive the Anglo-Saxons, Danes and Normans back to their countries of origin. From at least the sixth century, bards had pleaded for deliverance from the Germanic Saxons and Angles who had taken over England, pressing the Britons back into Wales, and indeed the Welsh words for these pagan 'English' invaders are still derived from 'Saxon', much as the Scottish Gaelic *Sassenach*. In Welsh, the English people are still *Saeson*, speaking *Saesneg*.

With the defeat of the last Saxon king and the incredibly fast Norman takeover of England, Wales then faced a new threat, and the new kings and lords who attacked Wales were rightly dismissed as being 'French' in the Welsh language and by the bards. Norman-Angevin-Plantagenet lords and kings were indeed mainly French-speaking until around the early fifteenth century. The Britons of Wales wanted their rightful lands and power back. On the other hand, foreign kings saw Wales, Ireland and Scotland as new territories to be conquered and assimilated. Interestingly, it was not until Elizabethan times that the English and Welsh became 'British'. Before that intervention by the Welshman John Dee, only the Welsh were known as Britons or British.

Penal laws, anti-English sentiment and prophecies continued in Wales throughout the fifteenth century. War, plague and economic decline led to depopulation in the *bastides* and boroughs of Wales, enabling some Welshmen to settle in them. However, the Welsh towns were still perceived as being

English and privileged. This period saw the emergence of the *uchelwyr* (high men, or squirearchy) class. They gradually gained office as sheriffs and bailiffs, and were so successful that they were generally the local rulers of Wales by end of the fifteenth century. Although many of them had been rewarded by the English Crown, the *uchelwyr* also actively supported Welsh culture and patronised the bards. These men worked for English reward, but remained Welsh-speaking and Wales-directed, which was vital for the Tudor invasion through Wales. It simply cannot be overstressed how important British Welsh resentment and hopes were to the successful Tudor invasion. The reasons for the end of the Wars of the Roses were very deeply entrenched in Welsh history and expectation.

The Wars of the Roses saw the 'baronage of England let loose in a self-destructive sequence of conflicts and practically every family of substance in Wales was drawn in'. Wales and its Marches played a most prominent part, and there was a fresh and aggressively anti-English outburst, which helped reawaken Welsh national feeling. Jasper Tudor and his nephew Henry were well aware that their paternal forebears had been constantly fighting, for over two centuries, for Welsh independence. The civil wars eventually gave the unlikely Henry Tudor an opportunity to be King of England.

The last successful foreign invasion of England was by a British (i.e. Welsh), Breton, Scottish and French army in 1485, not in 1066 as is taught across academia. Englishmen who had joined Henry in exile, and those who joined his banner, probably accounted for less than a quarter of his forces. There had also been a joint Franco-Welsh invasion as far as Worcester in 1405, largely ignored by historical writers. Of other foreign 'invasions', William and Mary were offered the throne by Parliament in 1689 and there was no resistance. There was neither fighting nor invasion.

In 1283, Wales had finally been conquered via treachery, murder, executions and the extermination of its royal family. The country was still restless over the next two centuries, as we shall see in the account of Henry Tudor's ancestors. From 1400 to 1415, there had been six separate invasions by English armies packed with foreign mercenaries in attempts to try and halt Owain Glyndŵr's war of independence. Only from around 1420–21, with the final disappearance of Glyndŵr, had there been an uneasy peace in Wales. Welsh rights to citizenship had been taken away by the Lancastrian usurper Henry IV, the country and its churches and documents burned, and children taken into slavery in England. However, the travelling bards still proclaimed hope for the nation. These bards, with their constant promises of a delivery from English slavery, were crucial to the success of the Tudor invasion of England. During the Wars of the Roses, bardic and Welsh hopes for freedom interchanged between William Herbert of Raglan and Jasper Tudor, finally coming to rest in Jasper's nephew Henry.

There would not have been a Tudor dynasty without the bards, and they ensured that the pure British ancestry of the chosen 'son of prophecy' was known to nobles, yeomen and commoners, all with a deep sense of injustice. When he assumed the kingship, Henry Tudor commissioned research to prove his bloodline back to Brutus and Aeneas, the supposed forebears of the British race. He did not wish to rely upon his mother's claim through the French Plantagenet John of Ghent, but upon descent from the original British kings of Britain. Genealogy had been extremely important in Glyndŵr's acceptance by Welsh lords as Prince of Wales, as it was to be in the acceptance of Henry as king. Only the knowledge of a lost heritage, and a belief in destiny of a British king to come once more, enabled the Tudors to take the throne of England.

Tudor Origins

These are examined in much more detail in this author's *Jasper Tudor*, but we can shortly see that nearly all of Henry Tudor's direct paternal forebears for at least four hundred years had been fighting English invasion attempts. It is important to assess the Tudors not merely upon their records as monarchs, but as a family with a genealogy which was crucial in raising support for their assumption of the crown of England. Henry Tudor's first important British ancestor was Ednyfed Fychan ap Cynwrig (*c.* 1170–1246), seneschal of Llywelyn the Great and then of his son Prince Dafydd. Even before Ednyfed's time, his family had been great servants of the princes of Gwynedd. Because of their service, all the descendants of Ednyfed's grandfather, Iorwerth ap Gwrgan, had been granted the concession that they should in perpetuity hold their lands throughout Wales free from all dues and services, other than military service in time of war. This special tenure was known as that of *wyrion Eden*, 'a conscious development of a feudal model by the Princes of Gwynedd, one which unfortunately opened a competition of lordship which Edward I was in a better position to win' (Chapman, 'Rebels, *Uchelwyr* and Parvenus').

Ednyfed was ninth in descent from Marchudd ap Cynan, Lord of Rhos, the Lord Protector of Rhodri Mawr, King of Gwynedd (*c.* 820–878). Rhodri the Great is called King of the Britons in the contemporary *Ulster Annals*, and King of Wales elsewhere. Having defeated a Danish army, Rhodri was killed fighting the Saxons. Henry's ancestors carried on among the leading nobles of Gwynedd centred on the king's courts, so his family had a lasting link with the rulers of North Wales. Ednyfed was Lord of Bryn Ffanigl, Cricieth, Cellan, Cwmllanerch, Dinorwig, Erddreiniog, Gwredog, Llanrhystud, Llansadwrn, Penmynydd, Penrhyn Creuddyn and Trecastell.

Ednyfed Fychan first came to notice in battle, fighting against the Marcher Lord Ranulf de Blondeville, 6th Earl of Chester and 1st Earl of Lincoln (1170–1232). King John had asked de Blondeville to invade north Wales to attack Llywelyn the Great in 1210, in the Welsh wars of 1209–12. De Blondeville's first wife, Constance, Duchess of Brittany (1161–1201), after many vicissitudes had managed to escape his cruelty, having been imprisoned by him from 1196 to 1198. She was the mother, by a forced marriage to Geoffrey Plantagenet, of Arthur of Brittany, the real heir to the throne of England, whom King John had murdered in 1203. Ednyfed was said to have cut off the heads of three 'Saxon' lords in battle against de Blondeville and carried them, still bloody, to Prince Llywelyn. At this time, the Welsh still referred to the English invaders as Saxon or French.

Prince Llywelyn ap Iorwerth then ordered Ednyfed to change his family coat of arms to henceforth display three helms, or armoured heads. In 1215, Ednyfed became Llywelyn's *distain*, his seneschal, equivalent to his chief councillor. The same year saw Llywelyn take the castles of Carmarthen (Caerfyrddin), Kidwelly (Cydweli), Llanstephan (Llansteffan), Cardigan (Aberteifi) and Cilgerran. Llywelyn also helped the barons in their forcing of King John to sign Magna Carta in 1215. Three of its provisions applied to Wales, and John was forced to surrender Llywelyn's son Gruffydd back to him. In 1216, the other free princes of Wales affirmed their allegiance to Llywelyn at Aberdyfi and he became de facto ruler, Llywelyn I, of the vast majority of the nation.

In 1218, King John's successor, Henry III, negotiated directly with Ednyfed Fychan and confirmed Llywelyn's possessions by the Treaty of Worcester. Ednyfed again represented Llywelyn in a meeting with the King of England in 1232, and helped negotiate the Peace of the Middle in 1234. Now a great landowner across north Wales, Ednyfed seems to have gone on crusade in 1235, and his second wife Gwenllian died in 1236. Llywelyn the Great had a paralytic stroke in 1237, and Ednyfed effectively ran the nation until Llywelyn's death in 1240. Ednyfed continued as seneschal in the service of Llywelyn's son, the Prince of Wales, Dafydd ap Llywelyn.

Although Henry III had formally accepted Prince Dafydd as Llywelyn's successor, there was now constant fighting, as Henry reneged upon his agreement and tried to retake Welsh lands. One of Ednyfed's sons was captured and killed by the English in the war of 1245, and it appears that Prince Dafydd may have then been poisoned, dying at his palace at Garth Celyn, Abergwyngregyn, in 1246. Ednyfed also died in this year, still in service, aged seventy-six. He was buried in his private chapel at Llandrillo-yn-Rhos church on the north coast, only a few hundred yards from his great manor of Llys Euryn. His death was recorded in the *St Werburgh's Abbey Annals* in Chester as being an event of great importance, an extremely rare obituary for a Welshman in an English chronicle.

Ednyfed's first marriage had been to the flame-haired Efa Brân, also known as Tangwystl Goch ferch Llywarch ap Brân. His children by Efa Brân were Tudur, Llywelyn, Cynfrig, Hywel, Iorwerth, Madog, Angharad and Gwenllian. One son, Sir Tudur ap Ednyfed Fychan, also became Seneschal of Gwynedd, and another, Hywel ap Ednyfed, became Bishop of Llanelwy (St Asaph). Ednyfed's second marriage was to Gwenllian, daughter of the Lord Rhys (1132–97). The Lord Rhys, Rhys ap Gruffudd, was the Prince of Deheubarth, also known as the Prince of South Wales, who kept much of Wales independent of the invading Normans for all of his reign. To Ednyfed and Gwenllian were born Goronwy, Gruffudd, Rhys and Angharad. Goronwy also became Seneschal of Gwynedd under Prince Llywelyn ap Gruffudd, and the Tudors of Penmynydd in Anglesey were descended from him.

In these times, Wales was a country still mainly tribal in social and administrative organisation. The remarkably equitable tenth-century laws of Hywel Dda were generally followed in both princedoms and Marcher territories, and the Welsh language, with its four distinct dialects, was used throughout Wales and the Marches. The major princes of Gwynedd (north Wales) and Deheubarth (most of south and mid-Wales, less the conquered south-east and south Pembroke) needed an efficient bureaucracy to run their vast and complicated feudal estates, and began to copy the Norman pattern. Families such as that of Ednyfed Fychan, the *wyrion Eden*, became the leaders of such services, and their members were rewarded with substantial gifts of land. Ednyfed and his many descendants spread across much of Wales in their influence and ownership of manors, in return for military, legal and rent-collecting services to their lords. The most distinguished branch of his clan, later known as the Tudors, settled at Penmynydd in Anglesey. The family constantly widened its connections and influence, by intermarriage with the leading families of north Wales and the Marches, such as the Greys, Scudamores and Mortimers.

Goronwy ab Ednyfed Fychan grew up in an atmosphere of royal favour, which allowed his extended family to remain free landholders in their own right. Goronwy would have been trained by his father to serve and administer at the various royal palaces of Aberffraw, Llys Rhosyr and Garth Celyn. The royal court of Gwynedd was continually moving from one centre to another, its journey known as a circuit, with each commote having its own royal court or *llys*. This was the main centre of administration, each controlling its own regional issues, such as tax collection and justice. The duties of Ednyfed and his sons, being virtual prime ministers of Gwynedd, would have revolved around perhaps twenty of these *llysoedd*, royal courts.

Along with no less than six of his brothers, Goronwy ab Ednyfed acted as a royal administrator to all the *llysoedd*. He would also have been present with his father and some of his brothers at negotiations with various earls and Marcher Lords, discussing treaties. Goronwy married Morfudd ferch Meurig ab Ithel, daughter of a lord of Gwent. After his father Ednyfed's passing in 1246, Goronwy replaced him as seneschal in 1258, serving Prince Llywelyn ap Gruffydd, Llywelyn II, as his main adviser. Goronwy appears upon various occasions as an arbitrator and a witness, and in 1258 he was one of the Welsh leaders who made an agreement with a faction of Scottish lords.

In February 1263, Goronwy, now Lord of Trecastell on Anglesey, led an armed campaign south from Gwynedd to fight powerful Marcher Lords. These Norman barons were only allowed to militarily expand their great estates by conquest into Wales. Goronwy led his troops as far as his wife's homeland of Gwent in the south-east. Seeing that Gwynedd was willing to raise a large army outside its region, the English lords held off a planned invasion. This uneasy standoff meant that the English threat to Gwynedd was lessened for some years. Goronwy was at the side of Llywelyn for the signing of the Treaty of Montgomery in September 1267. By this, Henry III officially recognised Llywelyn ap Gruffudd as the rightful ruler of the Principality of Wales, the only time a British leader would be recognised as such by an English monarch. The treaty required Llywelyn to swear homage and fealty to Henry, but also showed the authority that Llywelyn II and his court wielded.

Henry's only other choice was continuing his extremely expensive full-scale war across Wales.

Goronwy died on 17 October 1268, and at least two elegies were written. In one he is acclaimed as the 'rampart of Gwynedd' and the 'wall of the city'. Like his father, he had been a warrior as well as an administrator. Goronwy's brother, Tudur ab Ednyfed, had been captured during Henry III's inconclusive campaign against Dafydd ap Llywelyn ap Iorwerth in September 1245, being released in May 1247 upon swearing fealty to the king. Tudur had become one of Llywelyn ap Gruffudd's main advisers after 1256, succeeding Goronwy as seneschal until his own death in 1278. Tudur's son Heilyn was held hostage by the king between 1246 and 1263, and submitted finally to Edward I in 1282. The history of Ednyfed Fychan's descendants is complicated, but nearly all fought against the English incursions until 1282, and in all the subsequent rebellions against English rule.

Of Goronwy's sons, Tudur 'Hen' ('the aged') ap Goronwy ab Ednyfed, born around 1245, followed the previous generations of his family, becoming seneschal to Llywelyn ap Gruffudd. Tudur was responsible for the rebuilding of Bangor Priory. While Tudur Hen was seneschal, the French-speaking Edward I of England determined to finally achieve what his Norman forebears and his Marcher Lords had failed to do, deciding to borrow heavily from foreign bankers and conquer the remaining Britons of Wales. Edward I also raised customs duties to help pay for his new wars with Llywelyn ap Gruffudd, and in 1275 negotiated an agreement with the domestic merchant community, which secured a permanent duty on wool. The revenues from the resulting customs duties were handled by the Riccardi, a group of bankers from Lucca in Italy. This was in return for their service as moneylenders to the Crown, which helped finance the Welsh wars. The Frescobaldi, from Florence, had opened an office in London and began financing the wars in the 1270s, eventually taking over from the Riccardi, who were driven to bankruptcy by unpaid loans made to Edward. With Edward's death in 1307, he left a debt to all creditors that amounted to £30,000. Using today's average earnings, this represents an unpaid bill of £417 million. The Frescobaldi debt was also never repaid, driving them, like the Riccardi, to bankruptcy. Edward's conquest of Wales was in effect funded by money literally stolen from the bankers of Lucca and Florence.

A long campaign, with thousands of foreign mercenaries funded by foreign loans and sustained theft from threatened Jewish communities, was failing when Llywelyn II divided his forces, leaving his main army in Gwynedd to travel south to meet Edmund Mortimer. Mortimer, whose father's life had been spared by Llywelyn, had promised support and wished for a meeting. Near Builth in 1282, Llywelyn was lured into a trap with his small bodyguard and all were killed. His nearby army surrendered upon hearing of their prince's death, and all 3,000 were massacred in an event hardly recorded in British history. There are no known survivors. Letters from Archbishop Pecham refer to the event, but some have been destroyed, presumably soon after that time to cover up the Mortimer conspiracy and the killings. Llywelyn's brother

Dafydd, the new Prince of Wales, was captured in 1283. Before this time the death penalty for 'treason' was hanging, drawing and quartering, but the victim was dead before castration and drawing of the entrails.

However, Edward I personally invented, supervised and watched a disgusting new form of execution for Prince Dafydd, who was dragged by horses to his place of execution at Shrewsbury. With flayed skin, Dafydd was hung almost to the point of death, then castrated and his genitals burnt before him, before his stomach was slit for his intestines to pour out. The skill of the executioner was to prolong the pain, and Scotland's William Wallace in 1305 faced the same death by the same king. Like Llywelyn's, Dafydd's body was quartered for display around England, and his head was also spiked for show in London next to his brother's. Edward now took out more massive foreign loans to pay for the 'Iron Ring' of great castles around Gwynedd, which included Rhuddlan, Denbigh, Caernarfon, Conwy, Beaumaris, Aberystwyth and Harlech.

Almost the entire extended families of Llywelyn and Dafydd were incarcerated for life or killed, to exterminate the royal House of Gwynedd. Only the children of one brother of Llywelyn, Rhodri, survived; Rhodri was living in exile at the time. Later, in 1378, Rhodri's grandson Owain Llawgoch was assassinated in France upon the orders of the English Crown after he declared himself Prince of Wales, finally wiping out the royal line of Gwynedd, which dated back over six hundred years. There had been considerable Welsh support for Edward's Welsh wars from 1257 to 1267 and 1277 to 1283, from nobles jealous of Llywelyn II's hegemony. Gruffudd ap Gwenwynwyn was Lord of Powys Wenwynwyn, also known as Powys Cyfeiliog. This was the southern part of the princedom of Powys and was centred on Welshpool. Gruffudd had actively fought for the English, plotting to kill Llywelyn in 1267, and his son Owain has been implicated in Llywelyn's 1282 murder. Owain now altered his family name to 'de la Pole' after his seat at Powys Castle outside Pool. Then known as Y Trallwng (boggy area) in Welsh, and Pool in English, the market town later became called Welshpool.

The nation did not settle under the new ruler. In Carmarthenshire in 1287 there was a revolt led by Rhys ap Maredudd, a member of the Deheubarth dynasty, unsettled because of lack of rewards for supporting Edward during his wars against Wales. Rhys gained support owing to resistance to new English penalties, restrictions and taxes and the aggressive stance of new English administrators and tax collectors. The great-grandson of the Lord Rhys, Rhys ap Maredudd had twice sided with England to fight against Llywelyn, being the only Deheubarth noble to do so. Edward I had given him some lands in gratitude, but had not returned to him his ancestral castle and lands at Dinefwr. Rhys was forced to make Dryslwyn Castle, further down the Tywi Valley, his main residence, embarking upon a substantial building programme there in the late 1270s and early 1280s. Rhys remained loyal, hoping to regain his lands, but in 1283 Edward for some reason forced him to give up Dryslwyn as well.

Rhys at last rebelled in 1287, and this led to his capture of most of the

Tywi Valley, the heartland of Deheubarth, including the castles at Dinefwr and Carreg Cennen. The rebellion was quelled by the autumn, but broke out again in November and was only ended after a ten-day siege of Rhys' final stronghold, Newcastle Emlyn Castle, in January 1288. Rhys went into hiding, but was eventually captured in 1291 and executed for treason at York in 1292. His son, Rhys ap Rhys, was then arrested after his father's execution and was imprisoned in Bristol Castle and then Norwich. He was never released from his incarceration, but is known to have been alive forty-eight years later. Henry IV later followed Edward I's policy of incarcerating Welshmen and their families until their death.

Tudur Hen ap Goronwy, the grandson of Ednyfed Fychan, had fortunately not accompanied Llywelyn to Builth to be wiped out with the rest of his surrendered army. However, he did become one of the rebels during the short-lived insurrection of Madog ap Llywelyn, Lord of Meirionydd, in 1294. Madog's rebellion was noted for a document that he drew up in December 1294 entitled the *Penmachno Document*. Madog signed the document as Prince of Wales, and Tudur ap Goronwy was also a chief signatory, referred to by Madog as 'our Steward', indicating his hereditary importance to the region. It is unclear whether or not Tudur, approaching fifty, fought alongside Madog, who was of a junior branch of the house of the Aberffraw princes of Gwynedd and a fifth cousin of Llywelyn ap Gruffudd. Madog's father was one of those who had opposed Llywelyn ap Gruffudd at Builth, and had died the next year in exile in England. Madog had returned to Gwynedd after the death of Llywelyn in 1282 and had received some of Llywelyn's lands in Anglesey as a reward from Edward I.

In the autumn of 1294, Madog put himself at the head of a well-planned national revolt in response to the punitive actions of new royal administrators across north and west Wales. Swingeing new taxes had been imposed upon impoverished and war-torn Wales to help pay Edward's unsustainable war debts. Madog was aggrieved by the fact that he had been unable to recover his father's lands, which had been confiscated through the courts despite his father having fought for the English. With unjust land-grabs, insensitive officials, the levying of troops in Wales for service in France and the demand for another subsidy from Wales in 1291–2, insurrection spread across the whole nation.

The Madog uprising quickly spread to south Wales in late 1294. Caernarfon Castle and town were taken, along with castles at Hawarden, Ruthin and Denbigh, while Madog besieged Cricieth and Harlech castles for months. Morgan ap Maredudd took Morlais Castle in south Wales, while Cynan ap Maredudd besieged Builth Castle. Caerphilly Castle was besieged and Kenfig Castle burnt. Reginald de Lacy, Lord of Denbigh, tried to end the siege of Denbigh Castle but was defeated and his army routed in November. Flint and Rhuddlan were under siege, other castles were taken and *bastide* towns burnt. Edward led one army to Conwy Castle in December, where he himself was under siege over the Christmas period until relieved by his navy in 1295. Harlech was reduced to just thirty-seven defenders and was on the point of collapse when the main Welsh army was ambushed in a night attack by a second English army under the Earl of Warwick in 1295. The Welsh formed 'schiltrons' of pikemen but were decimated by archers, mainly recruited from Wales and the Marches. Madog barely escaped and surrendered around August in Snowdonia.

There was another harsh response from Edward I in the form of even more humiliating and punitive ordinances, restricting the civil rights and economic and social opportunities of the Welsh. Goronwy Fychan, Tudur Hen's brother, was also deeply involved in the Madog war. The brothers, with Madog's capture and death, could either live as outlaws and forfeit their estates or try to keep the family in power. Both managed to receive pardons. Tudur became a dutiful subject of King Edward, and began serving as a royal official in his clan's heartland of Perfeddwlad, the 'Middle Country' that lies between the rivers Conwy and Dee, between the two traditional kingdoms of Gwynedd and Powys.

However, Edward was still not placated, in 1296 making a speech to Parliament in which he accused the Welsh of countless 'deceptions and plots'. Tudur Hen was one of a deputation of four leaders that informed Edward I, on behalf of the people of north Wales, that his subjects unreservedly pledged their loyalty to his kingship. Wales could not stand another rapacious invasion. Tudur was also present at Caernarfon in 1301 when it was publically announced that Edward's seven-year-old son was to be the first non-native Prince of Wales, symbolising Wales as a conquered English dominion. Tudur now made homage to the first English Prince of Wales, and submitted several petitions to him in 1305. Tudur Hen died on 11 October 1311, being buried in the Dominican friary chapel in Bangor that he had helped rebuild. Because of his low and passive profile since the Madog war of independence, he was enabled to pass on considerable land and wealth to the sons he had with his wife Angharad ferch Ithel Fychan ab Ithel, the daughter of the lord of the nearby cantref of Tegeingl in Flintshire.

Their son Goronwy ap Tudur Hen, Lord of Penmynydd (*c.* 1285–1331), actively served the English Crown as a soldier. He was known to be a captain of twenty archers in Aquitaine. Up until Goronwy, all of the Tudur clan had fought against the English to keep Gwynedd and Wales independent. Aged only nine or ten when his father had allied with Madog, Goronwy had realised that loyalty to the English king was the only way to ensure that his lands, titles and wealth would be secure and safe from attainders. Goronwy remained loyal during Edward II's war with the barons in 1311. The resulting 'Ordinances of 1311' were then forced on Edward II by the disenfranchised magnates of the realm, effectively limiting the king's authority. Goronwy was also present at Newcastle as leader of some of Edward's Welsh troops, and probably saw action at Bannockburn in 1314 during the Scottish Wars of Independence. He served with distinction under the leadership of his distant cousin Sir Gruffydd Llwyd, himself a great-grandson of Ednyfed Fychan. Gruffydd's immediate family had fought upon the side of Edward I during the Welsh wars of 1282–83 and benefited from confiscated lands.

At this time there was a mainly southern rising in 1316, under Llywelyn

Bren, Lord of Senghenydd and Meisgyn in Glamorgan, who later suffered the same grisly fate as Prince Dafydd. His father, Gruffydd ap Rhys, had sided with Llywelyn II. Heavy fines and ransoms on their lands were just some of the means used to bring men to their knees. To worsen matters, the climate was deteriorating and famine was now widespread. Bren was illegally hanged, drawn and quartered in 1218 by the queen's lover, Hugh Despenser, who was later to suffer the same fate. It is important to show how Wales was never at peace throughout the fourteenth or fifteenth centuries, when it was supposedly conquered.

Meanwhile, in north Wales, Goronwy was appointed Forester of Snowdon, succeeding Sir Gruffydd Llwyd for 1318 and 1319. He was now referred to as a member of the King's Yeomen, typifying his new role within Edward II's jurisdiction in north Wales. A 'forester' was effectively a sheriff to enforce the law in a specific locality, and the post carried prestige as a valued member of the king's retinue. When an action was brought in 1331 against the former deputy justiciar of north Wales, William de Shaldford, accusing him of having encompassed Edward II's murder, Goronwy and Sir Gruffydd were among de Shaldford's sureties. Goronwy wed Gwerful ferch Madog, the daughter of the Baron of Hendwr, and died on 11 December 1331, his body being interred and buried at Bangor Friary. His loyal service to Edward II again reinforced the status of his family as being among the most important nobles of the region, and ensured his surviving sons Hywel ap Goronwy and Tudur Fychan ap Goronwy received royal favour.

Ednyfed Fychan's great-great-grandson Hywel ap Goronwy (d. 1366?) became a cleric with substantial power and prestige in the area. Initially Canon of Bangor, Hywel later became Archdeacon of Anglesey. His brother Tudur took over the family lands and may have served in Edward III's armies in France along with many of his Welsh peers. Both were leading figures in north Wales. An apocryphal story related how Tudur called himself Sir Tudur. Upon being summoned by Edward III to explain himself, he answered with such spirit that the king immediately knighted him. The story, attributed to the antiquary Robert Vaughan (1592–1667), may have originated in the sixteenth century, the implication being that Tudur foresaw that his descendants would have the power to confer knighthood. Hywel and Tudur were initially law abiding, but both came to prominence in 1344 in a revolt against more oppressive laws imposed by both the Marcher Lords and English administrators in north Wales. The *bastide* town of Rhuddlan in Denbighshire was razed, forcing the resident English population to flee to England. In 1344, an anti-English riot also took place at the fair of St Asaph.

Henry de Shalford, burgess of Caernarfon, was appointed as attorney in north Wales by Edward III's oldest son, Edward 'the Black Prince'. Soon after, upon 14 February 1345, he was travelling from Denbigh to Caernarfon. De Shalford was attacked and killed near the house of Hywel ap Goronwy in Bangor by a band of men led by Hywel's brother Tudur. The result was panic among the English burgesses in north Wales, especially as many seemingly loyal leading Welshmen, such as Madog Gloddaith, appear to have been implicated.

The acting sheriff of Merioneth was also killed in 1345, as he was holding the county court. Hywel was imprisoned for a time at Launceston in Cornwall, and Tudur in Chester, but they do not seem to have suffered any further punishment. In 1352, they were both known to be back in possession of their ancestral lands in Anglesey. Perhaps the reputation of their family played a part in their acquittal from any major punishment. The king's administrators probably did not wish to alienate such a powerful family, when it was obvious that Wales still was in a semi-anarchic state. There was a stream of complaints in Parliament about the Welsh; for instance, it was claimed that 'unlawful assemblies' were being held at Strata Marcella Abbey 'to excite contentions between the English and the Welsh'. There was despairing correspondence from the burgesses of north Wales in the 1340s, when they assumed that the attitude of Welshmen towards Englishmen was one of imminent revenge. Travelling bards were forever reinforcing the Welsh sense of injustice at the Saxons and French invading their lands, promising an imminent day of reckoning.

The last heir of the dynasty of the princes of Gwynedd now made a bid to recover his patrimony. Owain ap Tomas ap Rhodri briefly returned to England after his father's death in 1363 to unsuccessfully claim his inheritance. In 1369, his English lands were confiscated because he led a Free Company, fighting for the French. His grandfather Rhodri, the brother of Llywelyn II, had survived the carnage by being on his estates in Surrey and staying loyal to Edward I. Owain became one of the most noted warriors of the Hundred Years' War, being thought of by the French and Bretons as only second in valour to Bertrand du Guesclin. He became known across the Continent as Owain Lawgoch (Owain of the Red Hand) and in France as Yvain de Galles (Owen of Wales). Owain fought across Spain, France, Alsace and Switzerland, and was the only real claimant to the title of Prince of Gwynedd and Prince of Wales. In 1378, while conducting a siege at Mortagne-sur-Mer, he was assassinated on the orders of the English Crown.

The Issue Roll of the Exchequer dated 4 December 1378 records the following: 'To John Lamb, an esquire from Scotland, because he lately killed Owynn de Gales, a rebel and enemy of the King in France ... £20.' This, of course, actually referred to the King of England, who claimed the right to the Crown of France. John Lamb had joined Owain's men and become his trusted chamberlain, and cut Owain's throat from behind. Owain was the last true Prince of Gwynedd of the House of Aberffraw, and was seen as a threat to any peace in Wales, being regarded as a *mab darogan* to rescue Wales from its oppression.

Goronwy's sons Tudur Fychan and Hywel ap Goronwy had been noted landowners of various Anglesey estates, not least in Penmynydd, which became identified as the family seat. Tudur also held offices across Penrhyn, Trecastell and Dindaethwy, the latter as *rhaglaw*, a position similar to that of a bailiff or sheriff. Goronwy's son Tudur Fychan ap Goronwy was married twice, with his first marriage producing around seven children, but it was his second marriage, to Marged ferch Tomos, that would have the most profound consequences for the descendants of Ednyfed Fychan. Marged was the daughter of the landowner Tomos ap Llywelyn from Ceredigion, the last male survivor of the royal House of Deheubarth. Tudur had a number of children with Marged, raising five sons who reached adulthood. These sons – Ednyfed, Goronwy, Rhys, Gwilym and Maredudd – had the advantage of a noble birth to landowning parents and as such became men of repute in the region, replicating the niche their ancestors had carved out for themselves. All except Ednyfed seem to have held positions of administrative responsibility in the royal government of north Wales at the end of the fourteenth century.

The boys' maternal grandfather, Tomos ap Llywelyn, had no boys, but there was an elder daughter in addition to their mother Marged, called Elen. Marged and Elen were descended from Llywelyn ab Iorwerth on her mother's side and from the Plantagenet kings John, Henry III and Edward I on her father's side. Elen was married to Gruffudd Fychan II, Lord of Glyndyfrdwy and claimant to the extinct kingdom of Powys Fadog. Their marriage produced a son, Owain ap Gruffudd, born around 1350. Heir to the lordship of Glyndyfrdwy, Owain would later become better known as Owain Glyndŵr and through his mother was first cousin to the Tudurs of Penmynydd, a relationship that had major ramifications for all the children of Tudur Fychan ap Goronwy.

The eldest son of Tudur Fychan was Goronwy ap Tudur (d. 1382), a soldier and administrator. He lived at Penmynydd, the traditional seat of the Tudors, as they can now be called, and was the great-great-great-great grandson of the line of Ednyfed. Goronwy served in France with Edward 'the Black Prince', and in 1368–69 he was at Northampton in the prince's retinue. He was Forester of Snowdon and steward of the Bishop of Bangor's Anglesey lands and in 1382 he was appointed Constable of Beaumaris Castle, one of the very few occasions on which a Welshman was appointed to such an office. Just four days later he died, apparently by drowning, in Kent. His death was mourned by several poets and he was buried in the Franciscan friary at Llanfaes in Anglesey. Goronwy's impressive alabaster tomb was moved to Penmynydd church on the dissolution of Llanfaes. His wife was Myfanwy, the daughter of Iorwerth Ddu of Pengwern, near Llangollen. Their son Tudur was dead by 1400. Their daughter Morfudd married Gwilym ap Gruffudd and his lands therefore passed to the Penrhyn family, although they were eventually to be recovered by Morfudd's descendants, the Tudors of Penmynydd. Ednyfed ap Tudur died around the same time as Goronwy.

The family's close ties of kinship with Owain Glyndŵr and their influential family connections across north Wales ensured that the Tudurs played a central role in the Glyndŵr Rising (1400–20). Two sons of Tudur Fychan, namely Rhys and Gwilym, virtually initiated the rising of their kinsman in 1400, taking Conwy Castle in 1401. For more details see *Owain Glyndwr: The Story of the Last Prince of Wales* (2009 and 2013) by this author. The eldest brother, Goronwy, along with Rhys and Gwilym, had a personal relationship with Richard II, being among his Esquires of the Body, and the latter two brothers now fought for Owain Glyndŵr in his war against Richard II's Lancastrian usurper, Henry IV. Rhys ap Tudur had been at times sheriff and escheator of Anglesey, *rhaglaw* of Malltraeth and forester of Snowdon. Both Rhys and Gwilym were excluded along with Glyndŵr from the pardon granted at the end of the first phase of the revolt in 1400. The brothers next took Conwy Castle on Good Friday 1401, when the garrison was in church. They withdrew after negotiations and were pardoned, but they seem to have continued in rebellion until near the end. After twelve years of fighting, Rhys ap Tudur was hanged, drawn and quartered at Chester in 1412, and Gwilym ap Tudur was killed around 1413. Their lands passed to their kinsman Gwilym ap Gruffudd. Owain Glyndŵr disappeared around 1415, his brother being killed and his wife and children being taken into captivity, where they soon died.

Maredudd ap Tudur (*fl.* 1388–1404), the youngest of the five sons of Tudur Fychan and Marged, was escheator of Anglesey between 1388 and 1391 and was a burgess of the town of Newborough (Niwbwrch) in the same county. He was *rhaglaw* of the Anglesey commote of Malltraeth in 1387–91 and 1394–96. By 1404–05, Maredudd was an esquire of the Bishop of Bangor. Ricardian propagandists make him out to be an 'alehouse keeper', but his pedigree as a local lord dated from at least the ninth century. Maredudd also took part in the Glyndŵr Rising, survived and was pardoned, but most of his family's lands were forfeited to the Crown. Just a remnant of lands at Penmynydd remained in the hands of Goronwy ap Tudur's immediate family. Maredudd married Marged, daughter of Dafydd Fychan of Taefeilir, and their son, Owain ap Maredudd, was born around 1400.

Maredudd now had few options. Wales had been left a desert by continued fighting across its length and breadth, and the consequent depredations. Virtually landless and powerless, he was forced to head for London and try and find favour in court. His son's name was later altered from Owain ap Maredudd to Owen Tudor, one of the very first instances where a surname instead of a patronymic was used by a Welshman. Had Owen taken his father's name as normal, rather than that of his grandfather, the Tudor dynasty would have been called the Maredudd or Meredith dynasty. Details of Owen's birth and the family are missing for a period for decades, as the six invasions of Wales during Owain Glyndŵr's war of independence from 1400 to 1420 led to towns, monasteries and abbeys being despoiled and their records destroyed. If not killed in the rebellion itself, members of the Tudur family were stripped of their estates and debarred from holding office, like many other Welshmen. They were replaced by loyalists and English placemen.

There was no longer any future in Wales for Maredudd or his son Owen. Maredudd had been left with the option of poverty and persecution or accommodation, taking his son to England. Maredudd and his forebears had fought their neighbours for over ten generations, and this legacy would be well known to Owen, his sons Edmund and Jasper, and Edmund's son Henry VII. We can see from the above that the history of the Tudors was one of warfare, of fighting for independence – the sense that the battle was not lost, that a deliverer would come, was imbued in the Welsh people and one of their own, Henry Tudor, took on that mantle of hope. It must be emphasised how Henry VII's family background enabled him to conquer the last Plantagenet king, Richard III, with some help from Richard himself, who in a short period alienated much of his brother Edward IV's Yorkist support.

2

Owen Tudor and Catherine of Valois

In London, Owen Tudor (*c.* 1400–1461) is said to have become the ward of his father Maredudd's second cousin, Lord Rhys. Aged seven, Owen may have been sent to Henry IV's court as a page to the king's steward. Owen is also said to have fought for Henry V at Agincourt in 1415, being promoted to squire, but there are no extant records of the battle participants at lower levels. Squire was a status for boys aged around fourteen to fifteen, whereby they were essentially apprentice knights. Squires were assigned to certain knights, bearing their shields, looking after the armour and horses and accompanying the knight on any battles or recesses. After Agincourt, Owen was granted some 'English rights' and permitted to use Welsh arms in England, which probably indicated his presence in English service in France. Henry IV, during the Glyndŵr Rising, had deprived Welshmen of most of their civil rights. In the ode 'Owen Tudor to Queen Katherine', written in 1579, Michael Drayton suggested that Owen had fought at Rhodes with the Crusaders: 'For Christian Rhodes, and our Religious Truth, / To great Achievements first had won my Youth.'

Owen may have secured patronage at Henry V's court; one source says that this was achieved through the influence of his kinsman Maredudd ab Owain, Glyndŵr's only surviving son. Although Glyndŵr disappeared around 1415, the king kept offering surrender terms until 1421. Even after the disappearance of his father, Maredudd ab Owain Glyndŵr had continued to fight and was connected with the Oldcastle plot in 1417. A last pardon was issued to Maredudd on 8 April 1421 and he entered the king's service in France until Henry V's death in 1422. There was another Maredudd ab Owain, of Cardigan, however, who had fought for Glyndŵr but changed sides and led a contingent of his men for Henry V at Agincourt in 1415. It is more likely that this Maredudd knew Owen Tudor.

The first evidence of Owen in London is on 13 May 1421, when 'Owen Meredith' was given protection in order to go abroad in the retinue of Sir Walter Hungerford. Hungerford played a key role as the king's steward from July 1415 to July 1421, during the wars with the French. This may be another

Owain, but our Owain is also named as 'Owen ap Meredudd' at the time of his imprisonment in Newgate in 1438. If Owen had served with distinction in France, he may well have been rewarded with some official appointment after Agincourt, thus reaching the court and the queen's attention. Hungerford was steward of the king's household again in July 1424. Several historians state that Owen was the keeper either of the queen's household or of her wardrobe, but there is as yet no concrete evidence. If Owen was Keeper of the Queen's Wardrobe when she was living at Windsor Castle, he would have been in control of the queen's tailors, dressers and anything else relating to her wardrobe room. It was also within his remit to handle all inventories of the dresses and to ensure all clothes that were taken on progresses were satisfactorily accounted for when returned. His armed presence would also ensure that any jewel thieves were discouraged.

In his *Cronicl o Wech Oesoedd* (*Chronicle of the Six Ages of the World*), the 'Soldier of Calais', Elis Gruffudd (1490–1552), states that the 'young squire of Gwynedd' became a servant and sewer to Queen Catherine of Valois (1401–37), the young widow of Henry V. A daughter of Charles VI of France, Catherine had an older sister, Isabella of France (1389–1409), who had been married as a child to Richard II. Isabella had thus briefly been Queen of England from 1396 to 1399, from the age of six years, eleven months and twenty-five days, being the youngest queen consort. When Henry IV killed Richard II in 1400, Henry tried to get the widowed Isabella to marry his son, the future Henry V, but she quite reasonably refused. Instead, Catherine, the younger daughter of Charles VI of France, was married to Henry V in 1420. Henry V himself had proposed this marriage, while demanding a large dowry and acknowledgement of his right to the throne of France. Even after his victory over the French at Agincourt in 1415, plans for the marriage had proceeded. In a 1420 peace treaty, Charles of France agreed that Henry should be his heir, and Henry married Catherine in June of that year in France. She was crowned in February 1421 at Westminster, and gave birth to Henry, the future Henry VI in December 1421.

However, Henry V contracted dysentery in France and died in Paris in August 1422 before seeing his only son. Charles VI died a couple of months after Henry V, making the nine-month-old Henry VI king of both England and English-occupied northern France. However, the civil wars known as the Wars of the Roses prevented a full English effort to take control of France, and England's French possessions were gradually lost. Catherine was an attractive twenty-one-year-old widow, mother to the infant king and therefore a wonderful marriage prospect for the upper nobility. It is unknown whether Owen was in her service before Henry V's death, or entered it just after. Elis Gruffudd related how Catherine first saw Owen on a summer's day, when he and his friends were swimming in a river near the court. Intrigued by this handsome man of her own age, she secretly changed roles with her maid and arranged to meet him in disguise. However, Owen attempted to kiss her, and she struggled and received a slight wound on the cheek. On the following day, as Owen served the queen at dinner, he realised her true identity and was ashamed for what he had done. Nevertheless, he was forgiven and the couple eventually fell in love and were married.

Another tradition is that Owen attracted the attention of Catherine at a ball, when he accidentally fell into her lap. Robin Ddu ap Siencyn Bledrydd of Anglesey wrote poems around 1440 to 1470, including a vaticinatory poem upon Owen's death. In this ode, he states that Owen was no traitor, 'although he once, on a holiday, clapped his ardent humble affection on the daughter of the king of the land of wine'. Michael Drayton (1563–1631) repeated the story:

When in your presence I was called to dance,
In lofty Tricks whilst I myself advance,
And in a Turn, my footing failed by hap,
Was it not my chance to light into your Lap?
Who would not judge it Fortunes greatest grace,
Since he must fall, to fall in such a place?

In 1603, the poet Hugh Holland wrote *Pancharis, containing the first book of the love of Owen Tudor for the Queen*, which again tells the story:

Wherefore, as Owen did his galliard dance
And graced it with a turn upon the toe;
(Whether his eyes aside he chanced to glance,
And, like the lovely God, became so blind,
Or else, perhaps, it were his happy chance,
I know not, and record none can I find)
His knee did hit against her softer thigh.
I Hope he felt no great hurt by the fall,
That happy fall which mounted him so high.

After Henry V's death in Paris in 1422, the dowager queen had brought up the future Henry VI, and it is thought that she did not secretly marry Owen Tudor until about 1428 or 1429. Guardians had been appointed to supervise the king's education and training, but because of his infancy the infant king had been apparently committed to his mother's care by the Protector, Humphrey, Duke of Gloucester, late in 1422. Humphrey was the late Henry V's brother, and thus uncle to the new king. On 30 December 1426, Thomas Beaufort, Duke of Exeter, the young king's great-uncle and guardian, died, but no replacement was appointed for eighteen months. Upon 1 June 1428, Richard Beauchamp, Earl of Warwick, assumed the responsibility.

From this date, the queen seems to have had less contact with her son as Warwick trained him for kingship, teaching the child riding, swordplay and the like. Also, it appears that after this date Catherine and Owen concealed their marriage deliberately, with seemingly few knowing about it until after the queen's death. However, even in the account of Owen's later appearance before the King's Council or in later Yorkist proclamations and manifestos, there is no question of the validity of the marriage or of the legitimacy of their children.

The boy king's counsellors had been highly concerned about his young mother remarrying. It seems that a statute or conciliar ordinance was drawn up, forbidding anyone to marry the queen dowager without royal permission. The earliest reference to this appears in *Giles' Chronicle*:

> The lords of the king's council would not agree to her marrying anyone during the king's minority, because she wished to have the Lord Edmund Beaufort, count of Mortain; but the duke of Gloucester and many other lords objected, ordaining that whoever presumed to marry her, against the council's letters would be punished in the forfeiture of all goods and in the death penalty as a traitor to the king.

Elis Gruffudd also claims that the council prohibited Queen Catherine from remarrying, adding that she was resentful about the ban. There is no surviving record of any such conciliar as mentioned in *Giles' Chronicle* or by Elis Gruffudd, but many of the King's Council records for this period have been lost.

In 1428, the queen was twenty-seven years old. Edmund Beaufort was twenty-two, and soon to become the Duke of Somerset. Somerset was to become the great rival of Richard of York and the Earl of Warwick during the forthcoming civil wars. Humphrey, Duke of Gloucester, the fourth son of Henry IV, and his party in the council had needed to prevent this nephew of Henry Beaufort, Bishop of Winchester, the Protector's arch-enemy, from marrying the dowager queen and thereby securing the young king's favour. Supporters of the two factions fought at London Bridge in October 1425, and the bitter Gloucester–Beaufort rivalry was the fulcrum of the following implacable York–Lancaster enmity

There also may have been a legal statute to restrict not just the queen's remarriage, but also her choice of a husband, as mentioned in *Hall's Chronicle*, which states that Owen was imprisoned after Catherine's death because he had married her 'contrary to the statute made in the sixth year of the king', i.e. in 1428. Like the conciliar decree, such an Act does not appear anywhere in print and has possibly been lost. Whatever the truth, it seems that major steps were taken to ensure that the widowed queen did not marry Edmund Beaufort, her late husband's cousin. Edmund Beaufort (1406–55) was the grandson of John of Gaunt, the 1st Duke of House of Lancaster, and his mutual hatred of Richard Plantagenet, Duke of York (1411–60) would lead to war.

In the Parliament of 1427–28, a Bill was introduced setting the rules for the remarriage of a queen dowager. The Bill stated that if the queen dowager remarried without the king's consent, the husband would lose his lands and possessions, although any children of the marriage would still be members of the royal family and would not suffer punishment. Another rule stipulated that the king's permission could only be granted once he had reached his majority. At the time the Bill was written, the king was only six years old. The secret marriage of Catherine to Owen Tudor would thus probably have taken place later than the parliament of October 1427 to March 1428. *Giles' Chronicle* states that Catherine deliberately chose a poor commoner for a husband after the restriction placed upon her remarrying so that the council 'might not reasonably take vengeance on his life'. News of the surreptitious union only became common knowledge after the queen's death on 3 January 1437.

According to Sir John Wynn of Gwydir,

> Queen Katherin being a French woman borne, knew no difference between the English and Welsh nation until her marriage being published ... but the opposition to her union made her desirous to see some of his kinsmen, hereupon he brought to her presence John ap Meredyth and Howell Llywelin ap Howell his near cousins, men of goodly stature and personage, but wholly destitute of bringing up and nurture, for when the Queen had spoken to them in diverse languages and they were not able to answer her, she said they were the goodliest dumb creatures that she ever saw.

Later Tudor chroniclers, like Hall, disparagingly refer to the widowed queen as being young and lusty, 'following more her own appetite than friendly counsel, and regarding more her private affection than her open honour'. Owen was described in *Caxton's Chronicle* as 'Owayn, a squyer of Wales, a man of lowe byrthe', but Polydore Vergil described him as 'a gentleman of Wales, adorned with wonderfull giftes of body and minde'.

The previous information is vital to understanding the mindset of the Tudors at court, the descendants of Ednyfed Fychan. Their fathers' fathers had been fighting the English invader for centuries. Owen Tudor's sons by the queen, Edmund and Jasper, would have known their ancestry via their grandfather Maredudd, and on through the paternal line via Tudur, Goronwy, Tudur, Goronwy, Ednyfed and Cynwrig to Iorwerth. They would have known of eleven generations and their exploits through the bards. There were also another seven paternal ancestors reaching back to Marchudd ap Cynan, Lord of Rhos and Brynffenigl and head of one of the 'eight noble houses' of Wales. There were yet again another twelve paternal ancestors of Marchudd, going back to Llyfeinydd ap Peredur, and ancestors before him. The British lineage of Owen Tudor was of some note, of over thirty generations of Britons.

As A. D. Carr tells us, Jasper and his brother Edmund belonged to

> without a doubt, the most powerful family in thirteenth- and fourteenth-century Wales. They were the leading servants of the princes of Gwynedd and played a key part in the attempt of those princes to create a single Welsh principality. Some were prescient enough to transfer their allegiance to Edward I before 1282; the rest made their peace very soon after and continued to enjoy a significant role in all the royal lands in Wales; at the local level they were often the ones who exercised effective power in the

> name of the king of England. But there remained an awareness of their Welshness, with its concomitant loyalties, which surfaced from time to time in the fourteenth century and which led them to the side of Owain Glyn Dŵr and to the end of that predominance which had lasted since the early thirteenth century. And it was a descendant of one of those rebels against the English crown who won that crown in 1485.

While we have seen that some seeds for civil war were sown over the refusal to allow Beaufort to marry Catherine of Valois, it is also necessary to understand the mood of the Welsh nation. English domination was still harsh. Welshmen still had inferior rights to Englishmen in both England and Wales. Royal agents were constantly looking for new sources of income from Wales. For example, they re-let escheated land, which gave them the opportunity to raise rents. Wales had been impoverished, its buildings had been destroyed and it had been denuded of sources of wealth by over a millennium of fighting invasions, and there was little left to extort. Women had been raped, children taken into slavery, possessions stolen and homes, courts, abbeys and churches had been despoiled and robbed.

Many restrictions were invoked; for instance, both kings and Marcher Lords insisted on sustaining some old Welsh customs such as the virginity fine and *prid* (a four-yearly renewable mortgage of land) because of the better incomes they yielded. Any Welshmen who somehow got to hold office were often subject to harassment or sacking, in that their appointment contravened statutes of Edward I and Henry IV. Welshmen who had lived peacefully for years in towns and villages in England could suddenly be challenged to produce their title for doing so. They might only recover their status as burgesses upon payment of a large fine. Welsh tenants were routinely evicted out of good agricultural land to allow English settlement, as happened in Denbigh and across the Marcher and royal lordships.

Thomas gives us an instructive fourteenth-century court case in Ruthin:

> A Welshman had married an Englishwoman of some landed means, and upon her death, he claimed the right to continue to hold her English lands. He was debarred on the grounds that he was a Welshman, and the land was given to the dead woman's brother and English heirs ... A shrinking labour supply and trade led to English townsmen and burgesses in Wales seeking to enforce their privileges, which led to a sharpening of the racial structure of the borough community, given that burgesses were English and the labourers Welsh. Expensive military commitments led to demands for heavy taxation.

All in all, resentment simmered continually across the land. The Welsh had nothing to lose by rebellion, and they would be fighting to reclaim what was theirs. Against this background, fertile for revolt, the secret children of Catherine of Valois and Owain ap Maredudd ap Tudur ap Goronwy would change history.

3

Edmund Tudor and Jasper Tudor, Earls of Richmond and Pembroke

As queen dowager, Catherine of Valois lived in the king's household and so was able to directly care for the young King Henry VI in his early years. At the king's court, the great lords and councillors could keep her under constant scrutiny – whoever married the king could be a threat to their prospects, being able to manipulate the boy king. They feared a repeat of the influence of the 'commoner' Elizabeth Woodville's family upon her husband Edward IV. However, at some stage after Henry V's death in 1422, Catherine's love affair with her servant Owen Tudor had begun in Windsor Castle.

Upon 6 November 1429, a month before his eighth birthday, Henry VI was crowned at Westminster Abbey by his great-uncle, Cardinal Henry Beaufort, Bishop of Winchester. Catherine had become pregnant at Windsor, and at some point stopped living in the king's household. It may well be that physical relations did not begin until she married Owen around 1429 – for the king's young mother to be pregnant out of wedlock would have been unacceptable. Catherine moved to Hertfordshire to have Edmund and Jasper, half-brothers to the king, born around 1430 and 1431. It is not thought that Henry VI was at that time aware of their births. The bishop's palace outside the church in Much Hadham in Hertfordshire was probably the birthplace of Edmund Tudor. The palace, now Much Hadham House, was originally established as the home of the bishops of London before the Norman Conquest, and had become the home of Owen Tudor and Catherine of Valois. Jasper Tudor was born perhaps a year later at the bishop's palace in Hatfield, now known as Bishop's Hatfield.

This was the palace of the Bishop of Ely, Philip Morgan. Morgan had been Bishop of Worcester (1419–26) and was Bishop of Ely from 1426 until his death in 1435. Ely was the fifth-wealthiest see in England, yet also among the smallest in terms of size or burden, so Morgan was rich, powerful and influential. Bishop Morgan must have known the queen, since he had been chancellor of Normandy, was an experienced diplomat and an expert in French affairs. The Welshman had earlier been elected Archbishop of York from 1423 to 1424. From 1414 onwards Morgan was employed extensively on foreign missions and played a prominent part in peace negotiations with France. From his early background in Welsh churches, Morgan would have been able to converse in Welsh with Owen Tudor, and was probably in the confidence of Owen and the widowed queen.

Morgan had been made a Privy Councillor in 1419, and died at Bishop's Hatfield, Hertfordshire, upon 25 October 1435. He will probably have advised Catherine and Owen, possibly even officiating at their wedding. Until their ennoblement as earls of Richmond and Pembroke, the brothers were known as Edmund de Hadham and Jasper de Hatfield. The queen spent time at Hertford and her presence there is recorded on 20 February and 6 October 1434, and again on 9 May 1436. Edmund's birthplace of Much Hadham and Jasper's birthplace of Bishop's Hatfield were both ecclesiastical manors, the former the summer palace of the Bishop of London. Bishop Morgan of Ely and his servants kept quiet about the birth of Jasper, as was the case with the Bishop of London and his household regarding the earlier birth of Edmund. Owen and Catherine must have known Robert FitzHugh, Bishop of London from 1431 until his death in 1436. FitzHugh was also a distinguished ambassador, and as a civil servant, prelate, councillor and courtier he must have known the queen, or at least something about her private life.

Almost certainly the bishops knew of the births – they would also not have encompassed the queen giving birth at their palaces without a proper marriage. It seems that the two bishops kept secret the marriage, and the existence of Jasper and Edmund, until the accidental birth at Westminster of another son, Owen Tudor. Owen and Catherine had deliberately settled in retreats independent of the main court that were run by servants dependent upon their local masters, in this case the two bishops. Loose-fitting clothing would have concealed pregnancy, and was often used to disguise the birth of an illegitimate child. Possibly some of the main councillors also knew of Catherine's pregnancies and her morganatic marriage. The fact that she could not now marry Somerset would have been a relief to many at court.

In a period of twenty-one months, from April 1430 to 14 February 1432, Catherine may well have given birth to Edmund and Jasper in Hertfordshire without her son's knowledge, as he was in France for that time. She would have had to give some excuse for being absent from her ten-year-old son's coronation as King of France in Notre Dame Cathedral on 16 December 1431. Possibly she may have been excluded on the grounds of her pregnancy, or her indiscretion in marrying a Welsh commoner who did not have the rights of an English citizen, but there is no record of this. Owen and Catherine still kept away from court, and probably had three more children.

Their youngest son, Owen, was born at Westminster Abbey in 1432 when the dowager queen was visiting her son Henry VI. Her waters broke prematurely and she was forced to seek the help of the monks at Westminster Abbey. It may be now that her marriage and children became common knowledge. Owen, also named as Thomas or Edward Bridgewater, was taken from her and raised by the monks according to Polydore Vergil. This 'Owen Tudder' became a monk, and was later given a reward of £2 on 30 July 1498 out of his nephew Henry VII's privy purse. By 1501, however, he was dead, for in that year the churchwardens of St Margaret's, Westminster, paid 6*d* for 'the knell of Owen Tuder with the bell'. There is also mention of a daughter of Catherine and Owen, who Vergil states became a nun, but little is known of her.

Henry may have first learned about his new brothers upon his return from France. Just three months later, in May 1432, the dowager queen's new husband was now granted letters of denizenship as 'Oweyn fitz Meredyth'. Henry IV's laws had limited the rights of Welshmen, and it was still illegal for a Welshman to own a property in England or to marry an Englishwoman. Fortunately for Owen Tudor, Catherine was not English but French. Denizenship was only granted to high-ranking Welsh subjects who had proved their worth to the Crown during the wars against the French, and Owen was still not granted full rights. He was still barred from becoming a burgess, a freeman or representative of a borough. He was categorically restricted from holding a Crown office in any city, borough or market town in the land. He was, however, given permission to acquire land, bear arms, marry an Englishwoman and run a marital household. It was possibly around this time that Owain ap Maredudd became Owen Tudor, or at least began to be unofficially referred to as this. He had previously been referred to in various ways as Owain ap Meredith, Owen Meredith, Owen ap Tudur and so on.

Two years later, upon 11 March 1434, the queen was able to grant Owen the wardship of the lands and the marriage of the heir of John de Conway of Bodrhyddan in Flintshire. Bodrhyddan Hall, near Dyserth, is still in the hands of the Conway family. In 1436, when Edmund and Jasper were about five and six years of age, Catherine again was expecting a child. It seems that she realised that she was dying, possibly from cancer, and went to Bermondsey Abbey to be nursed by the sisters there. In her will, the queen spoke of her long illness. It may be that she was forced to go there by members of the King's Council, still angered by her marriage. In 1436 (or perhaps 1437), Edmund and Jasper were taken away and placed in the care of the Abbess of Barking for about five years, at which time they were considered old enough for their education to be continued by priests. By 1 January 1437, Catherine had written a will and had given birth to a short-lived daughter, possibly named Margaret. Catherine died on 3 January 1437. She had at least four – possibly five – children by Owen, so the couple must have been married before the end of 1432, probably in 1430. Catherine was laid to rest next to her husband Henry V in the Chantry Chapel at Westminster Abbey.

The Regency Council under Humphrey of Gloucester and others deeply mistrusted the Welsh commoner who had impregnated the king's mother, and her death left Owen Tudor without protection. Lacking estates or wealth, he was suddenly at the mercy of the great lords. It seems he decided to escape to Anglesey, and was at Daventry in Warwickshire, when urgently commanded to appear before the king. Deeply suspicious, Owen replied that he 'would not so come without that it were granted and promised him on the king's behalf that he should more freely come and freely go'. A verbal promise of safe conduct from the Duke of Gloucester, on the king's authority, was delivered to him. However, Owen refused to accept its validity, as 'the said grant so made sufficed him not for his surety, less than it were sent him in writing'.

Owen eventually returned to London, but went immediately into sanctuary at Westminster, where the monks had brought up his third son, Owen, since 1432. He 'there held him many days, eschewing to come out thereof', although 'divers persons assured him of friendship and fellowship to have come out'. Unsuccessful efforts were made to entrap him by trying to induce him into a tavern nearby. Henry VI was now sixteen, and Owen had discovered that his stepson was 'evilly informed of him' by his councillors. Several weeks passed before Owen decided to leave sanctuary to defend himself before the King's Council. He declared his innocence of any wrongdoing, stating that he was the king's 'true liege man' no matter what any man should say against him. Owen Tudor was now released from custody, most probably because of the wishes of his stepson Henry VI, who later provided for his stepfather and his two half-brothers.

Owen still did not feel secure and 'returned again into Wales', but he was arrested soon afterwards on the grounds that he had broken the king's safe conduct. Owen had never accepted the safe conduct and thus could not have broken it, but nevertheless he was thrown into Newgate gaol with his servant and priest. The affair lasted for six months between the queen's death in January and July 1437, when the council met to consider and justify the arrest. Owen, probably still grieving from the loss of Catherine, headed once again back to Wales but was overtaken and arrested by messengers of the council. It was determined to punish him properly, but records are missing as to his alleged crimes. It is generally assumed that his second imprisonment was occasioned by the discovery of his marriage. Council records do not specify any particular reason.

However, many may have known of the union during the queen's lifetime, including the lords in Parliament, and it would be extraordinarily difficult to conceal four royal pregnancies and four children. As Monmouth, translating Biondi, stated, 'It is not to be supposed that the Court could be hoodwinked in four great bellies.' Biondi added that although the marriage must have been known, yet it was 'winked at by reason of her husband's birth, which though it was not answerable to her present condition, yet to be tolerated in respect of his forefathers, for nobility doth not lose its privileges for want of fortune and want of worth, which he wanted not'. Owen, together with his chaplain and a servant, were committed to Newgate gaol by the Protector, Humphrey Duke of Gloucester, according to Vergil. All of Owen's possessions were seized. The bard Robin Ddu publicly admonished those responsible for the imprisonment and called Owen 'neither a thief nor a robber ... he is the victim of unrighteous wrath. His only fault was to have won the affection of a princess of France.' Meanwhile, the Duke of Gloucester had been declared innocent due to the verbal promise of safe conduct that he had made to Owen, which now lay broken.

The three prisoners escaped from Newgate in January or early February 1438, but were quickly recaptured by John, 6th Baron Beaumont, with the aid of Thomas Darwent. Thus, upon 24 February, Lord Beaumont paid £80 to the Exchequer, which he had found on Owen Tudor's priest. Beaumont received £13 6*s* 8*d* upon 24 March 1438 for his expenses incurred in recapturing Owen. The three prisoners were placed temporarily into the care of William de la Pole, Earl of Suffolk, at Wallingford Castle, and were soon back in Newgate in March 1438. Owen's circumstances were probably better when transferred to Windsor Castle on 14 July, when he was placed in the custody of the constable, Walter, Lord Hungerford. Walter, 1st Baron Hungerford (1378–1449), had held the office of constable from 1417. He had fought at Agincourt and had been Lord Treasurer of England. However, a week after Owen was sent there the office of constable was granted to Edmund Beaufort, Duke of Somerset. It seems that Owen's service at Agincourt with the strong Lancastrian Hungerford, and his later links in the queen's household with him, were thought dangerous by Yorkists on the council.

Goods and jewels which had belonged to Owen and which were seized at the time of his arrest were handed into the Treasury on 15 July 1438 by William Milrede of London. The inventory, chiefly of silverware, revealed some of Owen's wealth. Perhaps there had been an accusation that this had belonged to the Crown via Henry V's widow. A dozen gilt cups were valued at £32 3*s* 4*d*. Several pieces were broken, but the whole collection was assessed at £137 10*s* 4*d*. Owen remained in confinement at Windsor for a year until he was released in July under a *mainprise* (similar to bail) of £2,000, a massive sum, with a notice to appear before the king on 11 November 1439, or at any time that Henry VI requested. On 12 November he was pardoned all offences committed before 10 October 1439. The *mainprise* was cancelled on 1 January 1440. Owen had requested to appear before the king, and it appears that his stepson sanctioned his acquittal upon all charges, whatever they were. It certainly seems that the council had wished to punish Owen for his secret marriage to the king's mother.

However, Henry VI had reasons to be lenient. He had no parents and no close family. He was just seventeen, and suddenly a stepfather and two stepbrothers, aged eight and nine, came into his life. Henry now granted Owen Tudor by 'especial favour' an annual pension from his own privy purse and welcomed Owen to the king's household. While not at the centre of courtly affairs with the great barons, Owen was safe upon its fringes at last. Owen's elder sons, Edmund and Jasper – and possibly an unknown sister – had been placed in the care of the Duke of Suffolk's sister, Katherine de la Pole, Abbess of Barking in Essex, either from when their mother was sent to Bermondsey or from the time of Owen's first arrest in 1437. They were certainly at the abbey by 27 July 1437, and remained there until at least 6 March 1442.

Katherine de la Pole was to provide Owen Tudor's children with food, clothing, and lodging, and both boys were allowed servants to wait upon them as the king's half-brothers. Perhaps Henry VI had known of the existence of his half-brothers only when his mother told him while she was dying in Bermondsey Abbey in January 1437. It was after her death that Henry would begin to care for them and eventually raise them to the peerage by later giving both brothers earldoms. The brothers must have been well treated, for it cost the abbess 13*s* 4*d* a week to pay for their food and that of their servants, to which we must add the cost of their clothes and other incidentals. Their father had been pardoned, and around March 1442 Jasper and Edmund, aged around eleven and twelve, were taken to court by Henry VI.

While Henry VI gave Owen Tudor estates and monies, he also began to take a special interest in the welfare of Jasper and Edmund. The ascetic Henry arranged for the best priests to educate them intellectually and morally. The brothers also received military training, and later were given military positions. While Edmund and Jasper were growing up in court, the minority of Henry VI had led to factional struggles among the magnate and gentry classes, and the government of the nation began to deteriorate. Richard, Duke of York, was a direct descendant of Edward III, and the Duke of Exeter also had a claim to the crown. The enmity of York and Somerset eventually led to a series of crises. Throughout the reign of Henry VI, the spectacular gains made in France under the reign of Henry V were slowly lost, with English defences being unable to prevent constant attacks by the French. Towards the middle of the fifteenth century England had lost nearly all of its new lands in France, which led to anger across the nation.

In attempt to pacify the French, marriage was proposed between Henry VI and Margaret of Anjou, who was a niece of the French king, Charles VII. Owen Tudor was among the party who brought her from France. Upon 23 April 1445, Margaret of Anjou, just fifteen, married the twenty-three-year-old Henry VI at Titchfield in Hampshire. Henry claimed the Kingdom of France and still controlled various parts of northern France. Charles VII agreed to the marriage of his niece to his rival for France on the condition that he would not have to provide the customary dowry. Instead, he would receive the lands of Maine and Anjou from England. This agreement was kept secret from the English public, and when it was discovered it was to prove disastrous for the Henry and his queen.

Upon 15 and 25 December 1449, Edmund and Jasper respectively were knighted. Although the king had been married for seven years by 1452, he still had no children, and the death of Duke Humphrey of Gloucester in 1447 had removed his last surviving uncle from the scene. Thus, the king's immediate family consisted solely of his wife, Margaret of Anjou, and his half-brothers, the sons of a Welsh commoner and a French queen. The brothers were never imagined as being in line for the throne at this time, by any party at court. York and Exeter had far better claims.

The young king was weak politically and financially, with great nobles jockeying for position in the event of his overthrow, death or lack of heirs. There had been no tradition of a settled monarchy. The subject of the king's powers and finances had been a problem since the reign of Henry IV (1399–1413), the Lancastrian usurper who confiscated great estates, especially from leading Yorkists. During his son Henry V's brief reign from 1413 to 1422 the nobles were busy profiteering from plundering France, but under the boy king Henry VI operating in France was costly rather than profitable. Poor harvests at home and increased rents and taxes led to growing unrest among nobles and commoners. Many 'royal' lands had reverted to the Crown on the deaths of Lionel, Duke of Clarence (1421); John, Duke of Bedford (1435); Queen Catherine of Valois (1437); and Humphrey, Duke of Gloucester (1447). Between 1437 and 1449, Henry VI had granted many parts of these estates into the non-royal hands of his favourites and almost the whole income from what he did retain was enjoyed by members of his household. Nobles and commoners alike saw Henry's favourites prospering while they suffered.

In the years preceding the Jack Cade rebellion of 1450, England saw real animosity of the lower classes towards the king. Years of war against France had caused the country to go into debt, and the recent loss of Normandy led to a widespread fear of invasion. Coastal regions of England such as Kent and Sussex were subjected to attacks by the French. Ill equipped by the government, English soldiers took to raiding English towns along the route to France, with their victims receiving no compensation. Henry's call to set warning beacons along the coastline confirmed suspicions that an attack by the French was likely. These fears and continuous unrest inspired some nobles to attempt to force the king to either address their problems or abdicate his throne in favour of someone much more competent, such as York.

Henry wanted peace with France, but most nobles felt that they should continue to fight for England's claim to the French throne. Plotting in court eventually led to the banishment of the king's closest friend and adviser William de la Pole, Duke of Suffolk. People across the country believed that the king had surrounded himself with advisers who were ineffective and corrupt, especially Suffolk. Suffolk was banished and his headless body was washed up on the shores of Dover, probably tossed off a ship by York's men after being beheaded after a mock trial. Suffolk was said to have been planning a French invasion of England, and to have raped and impregnated a nun the night before he had surrendered to Joan of Arc in 1429. He was hated and few other than the king missed him.

There was bitter resentment against those who were enriching themselves from the profits of Crown lands and thus increasing the need for taxation. Jack Cade's 1450 rebellion, where the Kentish men had risen in arms during the sitting of Parliament, put forward as one of its main grievances a complaint that the king's ministers were preventing the passing of the Act of Resumption for their own selfish ends. Henry VI, urged on by a hated queen, had given away so much of 'the king's own' to favourites that there was almost nothing left for the Treasury. During August 1450, Richard, Duke of

York, heir to the throne and the king's most powerful subject, had left his post in Ireland to force his way into the king's presence with an armed escort. He demanded reform. The future security of the country seemed to be unsure, so in November 1451 Thomas Young, a Bristol lawyer, MP and protégé of Richard, Duke of York, petitioned for York's recognition as heir presumptive, for which he served a term of imprisonment. Shortly after this, Parliament first met. With his kinsmen John Mowbray, Duke of Norfolk, and Richard Neville, Earl of Warwick, York then managed to have Edmund Beaufort, Duke of Somerset, taken into 'protective custody'.

Parliament was due to resume again on 20 January 1451, and over the Christmas holidays the queen worked to improve the confidence of the king against her Yorkist enemies. Somerset was released from the Tower and, to York's despair, was appointed to the prestigious post of Captain of Calais. All the parliamentary reforms did little to rescue the Crown from its debts, which amounted to an incredible £375,000. In current money using the 'economic power' or 'economic cost' indicators, this represents a debt of £121 billion. The kingdom was insolvent.

From August 1450, when Richard of York returned from Ireland, to the First Battle of St Albans in May 1455, when Somerset was killed, the country was dominated by the struggle between these two men. York had achieved little in the 1450–51 Parliament, so by February 1452 issued a manifesto to the people of Shrewsbury which was an unprecedented attack on the government. He followed this up with an unsuccessful coup at Dartford in Kent. In order to boost their flagging prestige, Henry and Margaret went on royal progresses. When the royal party was at Reading in November 1452, Edmund and Jasper were created earls. The Tudor brothers had both probably reached twenty-one years. Henry and his advisers had to decide their future role in life, their relationship to the king, the royal family and the magnate class, while not alienating the lords or people. The two could not indefinitely remain 'in' the royal family but not formally 'of' it. The descendants of Ednyfed Fychan, *wyrion Eden*, were now to be made the premier earls of England, recognised as the king's uterine brothers, with precedence over all men except for dukes. The Tudors were not made dukes as this would have caused massive resentment at court. Even Henry VI's dead uncles, although created earls when they were quite young, had not become dukes immediately.

The pious Henry had carefully supervised the brothers' upbringing since their mother's death, practising the virtues of Christian charity and brotherly love which he held dear. H. T. Evans suggests that it was the Duke of Somerset who was responsible for the 'flash of Athenian acuteness' during the Christmas holidays in 1452, when the two Tudors were ennobled. However, Henry had already implicitly recognised the boys as his kinsmen by the special provision he made for their upbringing. Edmund was created Earl of Richmond and Jasper Earl of Pembroke. Henry bestowed on Edmund the castle and county of Richmount, or Richmondshire, in the North Riding of York. Edmund was also given the mansion called Baynard's Castle, near Paul's Wharf on the banks of the Thames, which had recently been enlarged and beautified by

Humphrey, Duke of Gloucester, the king's uncle. It had fallen to the Crown on Humphrey's death without issue.

Jasper Tudor became possessed of the castle and royal territories in south Wales appertaining to the title of Pembroke, the earldom having been erected into a county palatine in 1138. He was also given an ancient mansion in London belonging to the earldom of Pembroke, then denominated Pembroke's Inn, now known as Stationers' Hall. The brothers were to take precedence above all earls and sit in Parliament next to dukes, by reason of their near consanguinity to the reigning monarch. Edmund and Jasper now adopted the royal arms, differenced only by a border. They were not of the 'blood royal' of England, but they were regarded as members of the royal family and therefore entitled to bear the king's arms. In 1452, Margaret of Anjou travelled to Norwich with the view of raising troops and was accompanied by Edmund and Jasper.

The king instructed William Cotton, Keeper of the Great Wardrobe, to provide Edmund and Jasper with a sumptuous wardrobe of velvets, cloth of gold and furs, as well as saddles and other equestrian accoutrements. On Christmas Day 1452, the king and queen were at the manor of Pleasance, near Gravesend, where they watched 'disguisings'. (Disguisings were entertainments and formal dances where the courtiers were often completely disguised, not partially as in carnival.) The investitures then took place when Henry and Margaret returned to London after celebrating Christmas at Greenwich. Upon 5 January 1453, the brothers were invested in the Tower of London. Upon the following day, the Feast of Epiphany, the king formally created them earls, and the brothers were summoned to Parliament in this new capacity.

It was also necessary to find suitable brides for the new earls and, upon 24 March 1453, they were jointly granted the wardship and marriage of England's richest and most desirable heiress, Lady Margaret Beaufort, only daughter and heiress of John Beaufort, Duke of Somerset. She was the last in the royal line of that family. When Somerset either killed himself or was killed by Yorkists on 27 May 1444, his daughter Margaret was a little under a year old yet was married a few years later to John de la Pole, son and heir of the Duke of Suffolk. Suffolk had taken over from Somerset on his death as Henry's main adviser. On 18 August 1450, the couple were granted a papal dispensation to remain in matrimony, but the same year witnessed the Yorkist assassination of Margaret's father-in-law, William de la Pole, Duke of Suffolk. Among many charges laid against him was one that he had enriched himself at the king's expense by securing the Beaufort inheritance, estimated at £1,000 per annum.

Sometime in February–March 1453, the king allowed the nine-year-old Margaret Beaufort to divorce John de la Pole. The value of the Somerset inheritance included manors, farms and properties stretching through twelve English counties. As well as enjoying the custody of Margaret Beaufort's inheritance, the new earls of Richmond and Pembroke shared several other estates as a result of royal benevolence. When Margaret and the earls visited Norwich in 1453 the city fathers were at pains to entertain them lavishly, and Edmund and Jasper were each given a gift of £5. Taking all the sources of revenue into account, it appears that Edmund's clear income was not less than £925 per annum. In today's money, this equates to £638,800 in the value of real prices, £5,224,000 in labour value and £19,370,000 in income value. As for Jasper Tudor's marriage prospects, increasing bitterness and rivalry between the great baronial families of England reduced his opportunities, and between 1461 and 1485 he was more concerned with staying alive than marrying.

With the dignity of Earl of Pembroke, Jasper had been given the ancient and valuable lordship of Pembroke, a rich prize and a strategic centre in the west, commanding St George's Channel and the southern route to Ireland. Simultaneously, Jasper received the castles, towns and lordships across Pembrokeshire, Carmarthenshire and Monmouthshire. While the Tudor brothers were learning the details of running their own councils and widespread estates for the first time, the French were rapidly taking castle after castle in Gascony in 1453, and the Earl of Shrewsbury was killed while leading a relief expedition in July. Bordeaux surrendered upon 19 October, and the Hundred Years' War, which began in 1337 with Edward III's invasion, ended in all but name. However, the rivalry between the great Northern families of the Percies and the Nevilles led to local warfare in Yorkshire in the summer of 1453.

Other than his Tudor half-brothers, Henry VI had no close blood relatives. His uncles, the dukes of Bedford, Clarence and Gloucester, had all died without legitimate heirs and this left a familial and dynastic void at the court. Henry's government was also still hated as being inefficient and corrupt. His two main ministers, the dukes of Suffolk and Somerset, had been hated by nobles and commoners alike and both were now dead. By 10 August 1453, with the loss of France and domestic problems, Henry VI was reported to have fallen seriously ill, with a complete mental and physical collapse that was to last for more than eighteen months. He fell into imbecility, sitting for days without moving or speaking. The king was unable to speak or even to rise unaided from his chair. Once his attendants had dressed him and placed him in his chair he looked perfectly normal, but when addressed it was clear that he had no comprehension of what had been said. Incapable of speech, he could give no reply and seemed unaware of any activity or person in his vicinity. He may have suffered from catatonic schizophrenia, and it was the first of several bouts of illness which were to leave him permanently feeble.

While Edmund kept away from politics, Jasper seemed to ally with the party of the rising and efficient Richard of York. It was clear that he was a far more capable man than the king, and had wide respect. With the king's illness, immediate steps had to be taken to ensure the survival of the royal government. York was expected to be appointed as regent, and would probably have assumed the kingship, but on 13 October 1453, just six days before the surrender of Bordeaux, Queen Margaret unexpectedly had a son and heir to the crown. It was doubted by the Yorkists that it could have been the king's child, with the queen's favourites Wiltshire and Somerset being posited as fathers. Edmund Beaufort, Duke of Somerset, was Margaret Beaufort's cousin and, like Wiltshire, hated Richard of York. The new Prince of Wales was known as Edward of Lancaster, or Edward of Westminster after his place of birth.

Upon 21 November 1453, Jasper attended a meeting of the council in the Star Chamber at Westminster, together with a large number of peers. They listened to York's complaint of being deprived of the services of his counsellors, and studied his petition for their restoration. Somerset was the only prominent magnate absent and the council agreed to York's request. Jasper supported York's candidature for regent. Also in November 1453, the Duke of Norfolk presented a Bill of complaint to the council concerning Somerset's administration at home and abroad. Upon 6 December 1453, Jasper was in York's company at a small meeting of the council to consider new means of funding the king's household. As Jasper and Edmund were members of the household, Jasper would have known far more about its inner workings than many other lords. Alarmed at the Yorkist attempt to take over the kingship, Margaret and her supporters tried to jolt the king back into sanity. Queen Margaret could see that the only hope of the infant prince's survival lay in the king's recovery, and doctors were urged to try anything to cure him. They put him on different diets, purged him, shaved his head, bled him, rubbed in embrocation and made him drink fermentations, all to no avail.

Edmund and Jasper accompanied York to London in January 1454 with the possible risk of imprisonment facing them. However, York now took control of the council, and he and Norfolk managed to get Somerset placed in the Tower while an inquiry was held into his deeds. With her ally Somerset out of the way, Queen Margaret was forced to set up herself as head of the anti-York court party, and in anticipation of the coming session of Parliament she drew up a document asserting her own right to the regency. In the February 1454 parliament, many peers, including Edmund Tudor, deliberately stayed away rather than commit themselves to either side. He may have been ill, or away in Wales, but as in the later English Civil War we often see brothers taking opposite sides so that at least one will retain the family estates and honours or be left in a position to protect his sibling from punishment.

Despite a possibility of arrest, Jasper was present at the short-lived parliament of February–April 1454, although Edmund was one of the many absentees, being fined 100 marks for his failure to appear. Upon 15 March, Jasper attended a meeting of the council at which it was decided that a commission should be issued to three physicians and two surgeons to attend upon the king's person and prescribe remedies for his illness. Councillors went to the king to discuss who should be regent, but found Henry far worse than they had expected. Thus, on 27 March 1454, Jasper and the other peers agreed that York should become Protector. However, York's appointment was carefully defined and hedged about with several restrictions. The duke's subsequent administration, and the composition and activities of the council during his protectorship, show that his regime was not a factional clique.

Jasper and the lords of Parliament next endorsed the creation of Salisbury as chancellor at Westminster on 2 April, and Jasper attended a council meeting concerned with routine business six days later. York made a genuine attempt to govern well, and to bring some reform, stability and justice to the realm.

Both Tudors were summoned on 29 May 1454 to attend a great council on the following 25 June. However, because of the Percy–Neville feud in the North, the council meeting was postponed until July. Edmund Tudor, like Jasper, Buckingham and Shrewsbury, was no committed partisan of Somerset and the queen's party, and was prepared to participate in the attempts made by York to reform the government of England. Both Edmund and Jasper were present at a meeting of the great council on 13 November when ordinances were promulgated for the long-awaited reform of the expensive royal household. Neither brother derived any material benefit from their liaison with York, and they seemed to sympathise with the duke's intention to stamp out bad government based on graft and corruption. York achieved a great deal in his nine months as Protector, from 27 March 1454 until the last days of the year. However, the king somehow recovered his senses over the Christmas period and York was no longer needed.

While Jasper had been close to Richard of York and the Earl of Warwick during the illnesses of Henry VI, Edmund largely stayed out of politics. However, he was active in Wales, halting Yorkist incursions into Crown lands. This may have been deliberate policy by the brothers; whichever party triumphed, the winner could assist the other to retain his estates. Richard of York found himself being excluded from influence as Henry and Margaret regained their hold on power and, expecting the worst, he withdrew to the North to take council with his supporters and muster his men. York's suspicions were confirmed when Somerset called a great council in Leicester, packed with his own supporters, where presumably he intended to enforce York's submission and possible imprisonment. Instead of attending, York marched south in full force and at full speed to encounter the royal party at St Albans on 22 May 1455.

This was to become the first battle of the Wars of the Roses, known as the First Battle of St Albans. Henry and his followers, knowing the support that the popular York might muster in London, had no choice but to march out to meet Richard's army. Henry's 2,000 Lancastrians included Jasper Tudor, Somerset, Northumberland and Clifford, and together they barricaded themselves in the streets of St Albans. The 3,000 Yorkists, under York, Salisbury and his son Warwick attacked. Warwick took the reserves and broke through into the main street from behind the Lancastrians. The battle became a rout and many nobles on the Lancastrian side were slain, including Somerset, Northumberland, Stafford and Clifford. Henry was captured and York regained his Lord Protector role. The twenty-four year-old Jasper was not harmed – it is unknown whether he was captured and released or if he escaped. He had been friendly towards York, so the former may be the case. Jasper is the only peer to have been present at the first battle of the civil wars in 1455 and the last at Stoke Field in 1587.

Margaret Beaufort was twelve when she married the twenty-four-year-old Edmund Tudor on 1 November 1455. There is a tradition that their son, Henry, was conceived at Jasper's Caldicot Castle, near his castle at Newport, in 1456. Edmund had taken some of York's castles in Wales but was captured by Lord William Herbert and died in captivity in Carmarthen Castle. He left a thirteen-year-old widow who was seven months pregnant with their child. Margaret Beaufort, Countess of Richmond, was taken into the care of her brother-in-law Jasper at Pembroke Castle. She gave birth on 28 January 1457 to her only child, Henry Tudor, the future Henry VII. The birth was difficult. At one point both, Margaret and her child were close to death owing to her young age and small size. After this difficult birth it is thought that she could never give birth again, which made her relationship with Henry particularly close in the years they shared. The child was to have a tumultuous and insecure upbringing, which would affect his adult life.

4

King Henry VII: The Practical King, 1485–1509

Parents: Edmund Tudor, Earl of Richmond, and Margaret Beaufort, Countess of Richmond
Born: 28 January 1457 at Pembroke Castle, Wales
Ascended to the throne: 22 August 1485, aged 28 years 10 months
Crowned: 30 October 1485 at Westminster Abbey
Married: Elizabeth of York (1466–1503), daughter of Edward IV, 18 January 1486
Siblings: None
Children: Arthur, Prince of Wales (1486–1502); Margaret, Queen of Scots (1489–1541); Henry VIII (1491–1547); Mary, Queen of France (1496–1533); Edmund, Duke of Somerset (1499–1500); Katherine Tudor died at birth, followed by her mother 1503. Perhaps Roland de Vielville of Brittany was an illegitimate son, born around 1474
Died: 21 April 1509 at Richmond Palace, aged 52 years and 3 months
Reigned: 23 years and 7 months
Buried: Westminster Abbey

> His body was slender but well built and strong; his height above the average. His appearance was remarkably attractive and his face was cheerful especially when speaking; his eyes were small and blue; his teeth few, poor and blackish; his hair was thin and grey; his complexion pale.
>
> Polydore Vergil, *Anglica Historia*

Henry's upbringing and dangerous life have been described by this author in some detail in *Richard III: The King in the Car Park* and *Jasper Tudor: Dynasty Maker*. Henry's reputation has dimmed since the 1960s and 1970s as new writers have attempted to resurrect Richard Plantagenet as a noble warrior and portray Henry Tudor as a cowardly, miserly arriviste. However, a pragmatic approach demonstrates that Henry was probably the greatest of all English kings, whose qualities unfortunately bypassed his second son Henry but reappeared in his granddaughter Elizabeth. It took incredible courage, when unproven in battle, to lead an invading army with virtually no chance of success across Wales and into England. It took great perception to curtail the power of the great nobles and thereby end the Wars of the Roses, and indeed any reoccurrence of familial royal genocide. The years 1399–1485 had seen violent struggles, with kings being violently deposed six times. Three kings were murdered by relatives, and the vicious usurper Richard III was killed in battle. Henry's treatment of his enemies was remarkably lenient by the European standards of his day and later, a trait remarked upon with amazement by foreign writers. He brought peace.

More than anything, Henry stabilised the nation, leaving a full treasury to ensure a peaceful succession. He practically wore himself out overseeing the administration of the state. Henry was capable, efficient, thoughtful, pacific and effective – qualities hardly seen in any monarch before or since. Unfortunately, his son's historians ensured that all glory accrued to 'Bluff King Hal' rather than his father. Nothing could distract from the glory of that king during his thirty-seven years of rule, similar to the forty-four years of Elizabethan rule. While Henry VIII and Elizabeth I were feted and remembered, Henry VII was ignored – they did not wish to remind the people that theirs was a new dynasty. Historians have argued that Bosworth Field marked the end of medieval England, and the beginning of more modern government. This may be an oversimplification, but Henry certainly had a more efficient administration. He did not favour those without ability, and a new class of excellent civil servants from outside the ruling great houses accomplished the better running of the English state. Henry chose these men personally, and devoted himself to the minutiae of government, personally initialling household account books.

From his birth at Pembroke, Henry Tudor, Earl of Richmond, was under the care of his young mother and under the protection of Jasper, Earl of Pembroke. His uncle Jasper returned to Wales, taking the place of his dead brother in securing the country against the armed incursions of the Yorkist Herbert and Devereux families, who had been the cause of Edmund's death. When Henry Tudor was not yet two there was an indecisive engagement at Blore Heath, and Salisbury escaped with his army to meet with York and Warwick at Ludlow. On the night of 12 October 1459, faced by a much larger Lancastrian force led by the king's standard, the Yorkist leaders abandoned their army. York escaped to Ireland with his son Rutland, while Salisbury, Warwick and York's eldest son Edward, Earl of March, escaped to Calais. Soon afterwards the Coventry parliament condemned them as traitors and confiscated their estates. In June 1460, the three sailed to Kent and took London without a fight. On 10 July 1460 there was another battle outside Northampton, and Henry VI was taken captive again by the Yorkists. In the autumn, York returned from Ireland on a triumphal progress through Wales, and unexpectedly claimed the throne for himself. After a prolonged debate in Parliament, a compromise was agreed whereby Henry VI would retain the crown during his lifetime but, after his death, his son Edward of Lancaster would be disinherited in favour of the House of York.

Queen Margaret rejected this Act of Accord and raised a new army. On 30 December 1460 at Wakefield, York was killed in battle and Salisbury was executed the following day. In January 1461, the queen and her Northern army marched south towards London. On 17 February she defeated a force commanded by Warwick at the Second Battle of St Albans, and Henry VI was reunited with his wife again. London did not want the 'French' queen and her undisciplined army, and Henry refused to let her take the city. The Lancastrians and Scots retreated north. Jasper Tudor had been raising an army in Wales and had fought Edward, Earl of March, at Mortimer's Cross in Shropshire on 2 February but was defeated. His father, Owen Tudor, was executed after the battle at Hereford marketplace. Edward and Warwick met in the Cotswolds and a few days later entered London amid considerable enthusiasm. Upon 4 March 1461, the eighteen-year-old Earl of March was proclaimed Edward IV. Jasper's lands were seized and he was hunted by Edward IV's ally William Herbert. He escaped and spent the next eight years between Scotland, Ireland, Wales, France and Brittany, gathering support for the Lancastrian cause.

His nephew, the four-year-old Henry, Earl of Richmond, was left behind at Jasper's Pembroke Castle. William Herbert was awarded Jasper's lands by Edward IV, and he paid £1,000 to secure Henry's wardship and marriage prospects, intending Henry to marry his daughter Maud. Herbert and his wife, Anne Devereux, had a large family of their own and Henry grew up with his children at Raglan Castle, being well educated by Oxford scholars who were remembered when Henry became king, as was his new 'mother', Anne Devereux. Henry rarely saw his own mother, Margaret Beaufort. A few months after his birth in 1457, she married Henry Stafford and they lived in Lincolnshire and Surrey. Herbert's purchase of her son's wardship was another obstacle. Margaret's husband made peace with Edward IV around 1461 and, while her son was not allowed to return to her guardianship, she was allowed to visit and write to him.

At Towton near York on 29 March 1461, Edward IV won the bloodiest battle of the wars. Henry VI, Margaret of Anjou and their only son, Edward of Lancaster, fled to Scotland. Lancastrian resistance to Yorkist rule continued, particularly from Jasper in Wales and the north of England. When the Yorkists won a further major victory at Hexham in Northumberland in May 1464, and Henry VI fell into their hands in Lancashire in July 1465, there was a hiatus in the fighting.

The exiled Lancastrian nobility were involved in countless plots to return to power. Edward IV captured the Earl of Oxford and his son, and executed them for treason. Jasper Tudor was meant to invade from France, and increasingly began to see Wales as the best place for invasion as it was always hostile to the English monarchy. To many Welshmen, Jasper was a national hero. He was considered a Welshman who could be counted upon to support their rights, and was feted by the bards as the new 'son of prophecy'. In 1468 Jasper arrived in Wales, gathered 2,000 men, and attacked Denbigh Castle, burning the *bastide* town. Harlech had held out for eight years, being the last Lancastrian castle, and with Jasper's defeat by the superior forces of the Herbert brothers it surrendered. Jasper again escaped, possibly by impersonating a peasant. In France, he carried on planning for the return of Henry VI to the throne.

Edward IV's main ally, Warwick, jealous of William Herbert's growing influence, led a rebellion and defeated and then executed the Herberts at Edgcote on 26 July 1469. Edward was captured soon afterwards, but a few weeks later he was released, or escaped, and resumed his rule. There was another Warwick-inspired rebellion in Lincolnshire in March 1470, resulting in the flight of Warwick and Edward's brother Clarence to France. Here, Jasper and Louis XI managed a reconciliation between Warwick and the exiled Lancastrian queen Margaret of Anjou in July. Another invasion was planned. Warwick and Jasper would go through Wales, and Margaret and Prince Edward would follow when it was safe. Henry Tudor was now thirteen years old, old enough to understand the danger he was in after he attended the Battle of Edgecote Moor. Since his guardian William Herbert had been killed by Warwick, Henry was under the sole protection of Anne Devereux. She took him and her Herbert children to her family's home in Weobley, Herefordshire. Henry's mother tried to regain custody of her son after Herbert's death.

When Jasper and Warwick's army arrived in England, Edward IV was not in London and was unable to reach the city before the Lancastrian forces. Therefore, Edward fled to Burgundy on 2 October 1470. Meanwhile, a relative of Anne Devereux had taken Henry Tudor to Hereford and given him to Jasper when he arrived at the city. The reunion of uncle and nephew was undoubtedly emotional for Jasper, an exile from his country for years. Meanwhile, Warwick entered London and freed Henry VI from the Tower. It was also a reunion for Henry Tudor and his mother. Within a few days, he and Jasper had joined Margaret and her husband. They entered London together and spent about six weeks there. On 12 November, Henry Tudor left his mother again to leave with Jasper. Henry VI's short restoration immeasurably increased Jasper Tudor's wealth and prestige. He was restored to his lands and his attainder for treason was reversed.

However, Henry VI was still incapable of governing and Warwick struggled to reconcile competing factions. Edward IV landed in northern England in March 1471 and attracted increasing support as he marched south. His brother Clarence deserted Warwick and, on 14 April, Edward won at Barnet, where Warwick was killed. On the same day, Margaret of Anjou and Edward of Lancaster set foot on English soil for the first time since 1463. Margaret met Jasper, who went to Wales to raise troops, and her army marched to meet him at Gloucester. However, heavy rains had swollen the River Severn, and her army was forced to face the Yorkists at Tewkesbury on 4 May 1471. Edward of Lancaster was killed after the battle, his mother was captured and almost immediately Henry VI was murdered in the Tower of London. The Wars of the Roses appeared to be over. Edward sent Sir Roger Vaughan to trap and kill Jasper, but Jasper intercepted him near Chepstow and had him executed. This is the only blot upon Jasper's career, but Vaughan had been the man responsible for executing his father Owen after Mortimer's Cross.

Upon learning of the defeat, Jasper disbanded his army, took Henry from his custody and rode at all haste to Pembroke Castle. Here they were besieged, but managed to escape to Tenby where they hid in underground tunnels until they could secretly sail to Jasper's brother-in-law, Louis XI. However, storms meant that Jasper and Henry were wrecked in Brittany, then an independent duchy led by Duke Francis II. Jasper Tudor had good reason to fear for both his and Henry's safety. Margaret Beaufort and her husband almost immediately declared allegiance to Edward to protect themselves. Henry was one of the few surviving adult males with a Lancastrian claim to the throne. In just another twelve years, the only surviving adult claimants to the throne would be Richard of Gloucester, who became Richard III; his ally the Duke of Buckingham; and Henry Tudor, in exile. In that year, 1483, Richard III executed Buckingham and Henry was to become the only possible alternative to an increasingly unpopular Richard III. Both Edward IV and Richard III made constant attempts to take Henry and Jasper back to England, but were foiled by a combination of politics, cunning and good fortune.

In Brittany, the fleeing earls were treated honourably. Duke Francis II was desperate to preserve independence from France and recognised Jasper and Henry as powerful diplomatic tools. If Edward would aid him against France, then perhaps he would return the Tudors. Louis XI, if he had them, could offer them to Edward in return for support against Burgundy and the Holy Roman Empire. Also, they could be useful as an 'English front' in any invasion of England. Jasper and Henry remained in Brittany from 1471 until Edward's death twelve years later, staying at Suscinio before being taken to different castles. Both England and France had made representations that their security must be made stronger, being afraid that the other nation would capture the earls. Louis XI of France, resenting Edward's relations with his enemies, sought the release of Jasper and Henry into his custody. The earls had meant to land in France and Jasper had been given a pension by Louis, consequently being a servant of the king and under his protection. There were reports that Edward IV wanted Henry killed and that Louis XI was going to kidnap them.

In late 1476, worn down by ill health and the English ambassadors, Duke Francis II consented to send Henry to England. Henry pretended an illness at St Malo and the tides were missed for sailing. He managed to escape his captors, and Francis realised that he had been duped by his counsellors, having become quite close to Henry and Jasper over the years. When Edward IV died unexpectedly on 9 April 1483, Francis was facing instability in his own lands. He only had an heiress, Anne, and royal families across Europe were trying to arrange the marriage the duke needed to secure the independence of Brittany against France. Richard, Duke of Gloucester, seized the throne from his nephew, Edward V, his brother's twelve-year-old heir. Louis XI and Duke Francis II immediately recognised the possibilities. Richard III's claim was tenuous and he would need to work out some arrangement regarding other claimants. Jasper and Henry Tudor became even more important. In

1483 there was a series of rebellions across southern England, and Richard's ally Buckingham also revolted. Buckingham had been plotting with Henry's mother, Margaret Beaufort, and the Tudors. Henry raised a force but had been delayed and was too late to help Buckingham. Learning of this, he did not land. When the revolts failed, hundreds of disaffected former Yorkists joined Henry in exile.

The subsequent disappearance of Edward V and his brother Richard angered the populace, and it spread across the courts of Europe that Richard killed them. He never responded to the rumours, or showed the princes to the public, as Henry VII was later to do with the Earl of Warwick. There had been uprisings against Richard III just days after his coronation, which highlighted popular dissatisfaction. Margaret Beaufort, now the wife of Lord William Stanley, had become an ally of Edward IV's widow, Elizabeth Woodville, who was in sanctuary from Richard at Westminster. As dowager queen, Elizabeth was eager to reassert her family's claim to the throne. With her sons dead, the eldest of her five daughters, Elizabeth of York, had a claim the throne, but only through marriage to a male claimant such as Henry Tudor. Margaret sent Christopher Urswick, a young priest from her household, to Brittany. Margaret also sent a large sum of money, raised from loans in London.

The 500 English exiles joining Henry in Brittany told him he must reassemble his allies and attack again, before Richard III became more firmly entrenched as king – and before the duke ended his hospitality. In December 1483, Henry gave a speech at Rennes Cathedral to inspire his supporters, promising to marry Elizabeth of York, thus joining the houses of York and Lancaster together. The assembled men swore oaths of loyalty to him. Their next task was more difficult – persuading the Duke of Brittany to lend them more money to assemble yet another fleet. Again, Henry promised to repay the money. He was fortunate that Richard III had decided to retaliate against Breton and French ships because of their assistance to Henry and Buckingham; this had angered the duke, and he agreed to loan Henry more money. So another flotilla was assembled and final preparations made in mid-spring 1484. But, for some unknown reason, the exiles did not sail for England.

Instead, they remained at Vannes in Brittany. Elizabeth Woodville's son by her first husband, the Marquess of Dorset, was in Brittany, as were her three brothers, Lionel, Edward and Richard. Another brother and son had been executed by Richard, as well as the two princes in the Tower. Richard negotiated with the treasurer of Brittany, Pierre Landais, knowing that the duke was ill again. Landais believed Brittany's fate would be better served with an English alliance. Henry heard that he was to be taken to England and, in a small party separate to Jasper, rode in disguise to the French border, just evading the chasing Bretons. They were escorted to meet the new king, thirteen-year-old Charles VIII, in Anjou. The situation at the French court was confused and problematic; in the end, Henry relied upon the king's older sister, Anne of Beaujeu, for assistance. Her role was of vital importance as Henry planned for the greatest battle of his life, Bosworth Field. Charles

VIII began to fear an English–Breton invasion of France. So he encouraged Henry Tudor to hasten his plans to invade England. Richard's queen, Anne Neville, died in March 1485, but this personal matter had to be shoved aside in the face of Henry Tudor's rebellion. It was soon rumoured that Richard would marry Elizabeth of York or her sister Cecily, thus regaining the support of Henry's Yorkist allies. Henry became frantic. He cast about for another prominent Yorkist bride, with little success. Henry pressed Charles to request money from the French Parliament. The French king did so on 4 May 1485 and was successful; he returned with Henry to Paris about a month later. Already, plans to assemble an invasion fleet were being approved. At Harfleur, near the mouth of the River Seine, Henry spent about 50,000 livres to assemble 4,000 men. Of these, 1,500 were discharged soldiers from a base at Pont de l'Arche. The French soldiers were commanded by a nobleman from Savoy called Philibert de Chandée, who later became a good friend of Henry Tudor's. There were also Henry's 500 English supporters who had shared his exile. Henry placed these men under the command of Richard Guildford. Some Scots also sailed from France with him.

On 1 August 1485, Henry and his followers left Honfleur and sailed down the Seine into the Channel. On 7 August, they sailed into Milford Sound near sunset. They landed at Mill Bay, inside the Sound. This was near Pembroke Castle, Henry's birthplace and where he had been brought up. Upon landing, Henry knelt down and whispered, 'Judge me, Lord, and fight my cause.' He kissed the soil, crossed himself, and told his men to follow him – in the name of God and St George. He had chosen to land in Jasper's former earldom of Pembroke.

Before leaving France, Henry had won the support of the most influential landowner in south Wales, Rhys ap Thomas, who brought hundreds of mounted men-at-arms to join Henry's army. No Yorkists tried to stop his march through Wales, and instead joined him – the progress is described in this author's book on Richard III. More Yorkists joined Henry as he turned east and crossed the English border near Shrewsbury. Regardless of his support in Wales, Henry needed more support in England. His stepfather, Lord Thomas Stanley, and Thomas's brother, Sir William Stanley, owned large areas of land in north Wales and in the northern Marches. Both men secretly gave money to Henry, although Lord Stanley's eldest son, Lord Strange, was being held prisoner by Richard III as an insurance of good behaviour. The uncle of the Earl of Shrewsbury, Gilbert Thomas, also gave his support to Henry along with a few hundred men.

Richard III was at Nottingham Castle when he learned about Henry's invasion. He did nothing as he assumed that the major landowners of Wales would see Henry as a threat and group their forces together and attack him. When he realised that he had made a mistake, Richard marched his forces to Leicester. The two armies fought two and a half miles south of Market Bosworth. Henry had a force of about 5,000 men, while Richard's army probably was nearer 12,000. The fighting began early in the morning of 22 August. The two Stanley armies, ostensibly Yorkists, watched the actual fighting at this stage so that the contest was literally a battle between Richard's and Henry's forces. Northumberland's army also watched the battle develop, not becoming involved. Although there are no contemporary accounts of the battle, it is generally accepted that it lasted about two to three hours. Casualties on both sides were heavy.

The redoubtable Oxford led Henry's centre and was not pushed back by the Yorkist vanguard, led by John Howard, Duke of Norfolk. It seems that Norfolk's men were disheartened by the failure of the Stanley and Northumberland armies to join battle. Also, Norfolk's troops had been forced to fight for an unpopular king who had taken the crown from the rightful boy king, Edward V. For this and other reasons, such as the murder of the popular baron William Hastings, many supporters of Edward IV had turned against Richard and did not answer his call to battle. Henry's men were a mixture of foreign mercenaries, Welshmen and former Yorkists. They knew that they had to win or die. Some of Norfolk's troops may have begun to desert, seeing no progress and fearing that a Stanley intervention on Henry's behalf would turn the battle. Henry was seen making a move towards Lord Stanley, almost certainly with the intent to urge Stanley to use his forces on Henry's side. Richard saw an opportunity and charged Henry. William Stanley quickly brought his men into the melee. He had little choice; if Henry was killed, Richard would execute him for not joining the battle earlier. Richard was cut down by Henry's bodyguard, and his forces immediately began to melt away.

Lord Stanley picked up the slain Richard's crown and placed it on Henry's head. Richard's naked body was put over a mule and taken to Leicester to be buried. Henry's success had been largely due to Welsh support, and the emissary for Venice reported to the doge that 'the Welsh may now be said to have recovered their independence, for the most wise and fortunate Henry VII is a Welshman'. And Francis Bacon commented that 'to the Welsh people, his victory was theirs; they had thereby regained their freedom'.

With Henry VII dedicated to not repeating the errors of the Wars of the Roses, his actions in the aftermath of Bosworth were seen as incredibly forgiving by all foreign commentators. The only men executed after the battle were Richard's main adviser Sir William Catesby, a commoner whose death would not offend the nobility, and two minor West Countrymen, probably as a result of a local land feud. Men who fought for Richard but pledged allegiance to Henry were not attainted, except Catesby and a few minor lords who would not accept his rule. Edward IV and Richard III had accrued vast lands by the deaths of Lancastrian nobles, and many of these were now available to Henry. Many he restored to their rightful owners, such as his faithful general Oxford and his uncle Jasper.

Upon becoming king, Henry's immediate problem was the same as that of his Yorkist predecessors – the legitimacy of his claim to the throne. Bosworth Field had not ended the struggle for England's crown, and Henry faced considerable unrest throughout the early years of his reign. Yorkist support continued in Ireland (where Lambert Simnel was crowned Edward VI in 1487) and in mainland Europe, where Edward IV and Richard III's sister Margaret of

York was the influential Duchess of Burgundy. Henry had married Elizabeth of York as promised in exile, uniting the houses of Lancaster and York, but waited to crown her until he was secure upon the throne. Henry wished to be regarded as king in his own right rather than through his wife. The wedding celebrations featured a great artificial green mountain, glittering with precious metal, with an armour-clad king on its summit, sheltered by three trees. The central tree, covered with red roses, belonged to King Arthur and sheltered a fierce red dragon, the symbol of Wales. Wine poured down the mountain for the revellers to fill their cups. Henry intended to demonstrate his right as a 'British' king to all.

Henry's genealogists traced his paternal line back to the British kings of pre-Saxon times, and his mother's line from John of Gaunt had been legitimised many years before. Henry had come to regard himself as the *mab darogan* (son of prophecy) chosen to unite the land, and, like all English kings for the last two centuries, identified himself with the line of the British war leader Arthur. When Elizabeth of York became pregnant Henry expected a boy child, and remembered that Merlin had said that Arthur was the son of a red king and a white queen. Thus Arthur was born in Winchester Castle, the site of the table of the knights of King Arthur (which Henry VIII would later have repainted to show himself in splendour), the legendary place of the court of Camelot. From Arthur's birth in the early hours of 20 September 1486, outriders galloped across the country to spread the great news. Fires were lit across England and Wales, and minstrels sang a new lay: 'Joyed may we be, Our Prince to see, and roses three.' These were the red and white roses of Lancaster and York and the new bicoloured 'Tudor Rose' emblem of Arthur and the Tudor dynasty. Arthur was married with great ceremony to Catherine of Aragon in 1501, cementing the Spanish alliance. His untimely death in the following year gave the nation his brother, Henry VIII, and changed the course of British history – without it Britain would probably still be a Catholic country.

Financial Policy

One of the two main problems with preceding kings, with the notable exception of Edward IV, had been that they died leaving great debts. Henry's rule was devoted to making the crown financially secure. He created a council 'learned in the law' in 1495 to deal with enforcement of already existing taxes, particularly those owed by the nobility, obviously causing resentment through their more efficient collection procedures. Henry bypassed the existing cumbersome Exchequer and innovated the Privy Chamber, a department in the royal household, to control Crown finances. Henry has thus been credited with the creation of the modern Exchequer. F. C. Dietz writes, 'Henry VII completely broke away from the medieval financial system, and laid the foundations for the more modern English revenue system.'

More than that of any other English monarch before or since, Henry personally scrutinised state accounts, initialling every page. He noted descriptions of monies owed and paid out and would even count bags of coins to balance the books. As Penn notes, 'these were the actions, not of a miser, but of a sophisticated financial mind; a king with a complex, all-consuming obsession with the control, influence and power that money represented, both at home and abroad'. For this Henry has been pilloried by recent writers as a 'mean' king, rather than a hard-working man of great intelligence. His intense and personal concern with balancing the books increased revenue from royal lands, customs, forced loans and parliamentary taxation, but led to unpopularity. The king's commissioners were on a constant mission to take as much tax revenue as possible from the upper classes, the main threat to any new monarchy. They devised a system known as 'Morton's Fork', named after his counsellor and chancellor, Bishop John Morton. Those who lived in luxury were seen to have money to spare, while those who lived frugally were reckoned to have accumulated savings that should have been paid to the Crown. Henry only called Parliament seven times during his reign. Instead of creating new methods to raise money, he properly exploited the existing sources. For Henry VII, money equalled security. Rights of wardship, marriages, promotions, death, forced loans, benevolences and trade dues were all tools to gain financial security.

Henry's treasury also benefited from the end of civil war, leading to the Milanese ambassador in 1499 noting that 'the king here enjoys good fortune and has nothing to do but to guard and accumulate his own immense treasure'. Another Milanese report recommended the stability of the kingdom, and credited it 'first [to] the king's wisdom, whereof everyone stands in awe, and secondly on account of the king's wealth'. As Henry now held the lands of both the Lancastrian and Yorkist branches of the royal family due to his marriage to Elizabeth of York, and also possessed Warwick the Kingmaker's inheritance, his income from estates was much greater than that of his predecessors. He also had no siblings to bestow land on – the land given to his only close relative, his uncle Jasper, soon reverted to the Crown upon Jasper's death. However, Henry was intent upon building up the wealth of the impoverished nation. A strong monarchy meant a strong nation state that could prosper in international trade.

Alum was vital to England's great wool and cloth trades because of its use as a dye-fixer. There were only two sources in Europe. There was a mine near Rome owned and operated by the papacy, and vast deposits in the Turkish-controlled eastern Mediterranean. The trade was so valuable to the Holy See that the papacy had declared the trade in alum to be a monopoly, threatening 'excommunication, anathema and perpetual condemnation on anybody trading alum illegally with the infidel'. Henry saw vast profits to be made trading with the Turks, and London was soon at the heart of a secret trading network that benefited both the English treasury and her lucrative wool exports.

The Quelling of the Nobility

Apart from constant financial insecurity, the other major problem facing English monarchs had been the power of the great nobles, especially those on the fringes of the kingdom, in the Welsh and Scottish Marches. Henry forbade nobles to retain their own armies and livery. A small number of attendants was acceptable, but Henry did not want any lord to have more power than the king. At Henry's accession, England was covered with baronial castles filled with armed retainers that could prove focal points of resistance to the Crown's authority. Earlier kings had persuaded parliaments to legislate against armed retainers, but nobles ignored the legislation. Henry VII was far more successful in asserting the state's power. Henry owned most of the gunpowder in the country, and great cannon had negated the power of the great castles of his nobles. The influence of the English nobility, already in decline during the Wars of the Roses, fell rapidly under the Tudors. He continued the Yorkist tradition of promoting government officers from the middle class and kept many of Edward IV and Richard III's councillors. Loyalty and ability were Henry's sole requirements in his most important servants. Patronage now had to be earned, and was no longer an automatic privilege of the upper class. The educated middle class was growing steadily in power and influence, and carefully making its way through the corridors of power.

Henry revived the powers of the justices of the peace, whom he used to administer the king's justice throughout England, hopefully free of local prejudices. In the past local gentry and nobles had often held ad-hoc courts, accountable only to themselves. Earlier kings had often chosen advisers from the highest nobility, but Henry had spent little time at the English court. He preferred to select his councillors on merit.

His reign coincided with the growing influence in England of humanism, and its most famous advocate, Erasmus of Rotterdam, argued that social distinctions should be founded on virtue, not birth: '*virtus vera nobilitas*' (virtue is true nobility). This strategy was followed by Henry VII and his chief minister John Morton, Archbishop of Canterbury and Lord Chancellor. Many of Henry's closest advisers had been with him in exile and were drawn either from the clergy, such as Bishop Richard Foxe, Lord Privy Seal, or from the gentry, for instance Reginald Bray and Giles Daubeney. At the end of his reign, Richard Empson and Edmund Dudley were powerful but unpopular, having been appointed to detect money owed to the Crown and secure its payment. Writers in Henry VIII's time and since vilified these efficient public servants, partly to justify that king's wilful execution of them, and partly because it is, of course, always difficult for efficient tax collectors to acquire a good reputation.

The Council of the North had allowed the great border families of Neville, Dacre, Scrope and Percy to rule as virtually independent princes with their own armies, necessary to maintain the Scottish border. Henry controlled all the Marcher Lordships in Wales and on its borders, but realised that the North needed a strong leader, a servant of the Crown. He trimmed the power of the Council of the North, and in 1485 released Henry Percy, Earl of Northumberland, from comfortable lodgings in the Tower of London and appointed him Lord Warden of the East and Middle Marches. Northumberland had stayed out of the fighting at Bosworth and surrendered to Henry afterwards. He now showed loyalty to his new king. Percy subsequently ran the council as an extension of Henry's government.

Henry VII handed out very few new titles of nobility, preferring to reward servants by making them Knights of the Garter. Henry VII was reducing any threat to himself. In the whole of his reign, Henry only created one earl (compared to Edward IV's nine) and five barons (compared to the thirteen of Edward IV). The titles had very real status in Henry's reign as so few possessed them. The number of peers dropped from fifty-seven to forty-four as more noble families died out than titles were created and granted. Loyal nobles were awarded the Order of the Garter. This bestowed much status on the recipient but it cost Henry VII nothing, whereas the creation of new titles invariably cost the king money as estates were usually granted from royal land. In Henry's reign, thirty-seven nobles received the Order of the Garter. If a title died out, it was not replaced. If the heir was a child, as when Northumberland was killed in 1489, Henry directly managed the estates and incomes until the child came of age. Henry forced important noblemen and gentlemen into entering into bonds and recognisances with him, promising to do the king's will or else to pay large fines. Roughly three in four nobles and thousands of gentlemen entered into bonds, with the sums involved being often extremely high. To disagree with the king could be extremely costly.

Henry used money as a way of maintaining loyalty. The nobles had to pay a certain sum of money if they failed to keep written promises based around what functions they would perform in the areas they controlled. The lesser nobles paid a sum of £400, while the senior nobles paid £10,000. If they did not keep to their part of the deal, they lost the money. If they kept to their promise, Henry benefited. This process even percolated down to men who had been given positions of responsibility. The Captain of Calais had to promise £40,000 to fulfil his duties. Such a practice had been in place before, but Henry refined it so that he could, as much as was possible, guarantee loyalty. If a noble failed in his duties, he could have his fine delayed if he accepted conditions that left him at the mercy of the king.

Henry had two unsuccessful pretenders to the throne during his reign, but the nobles did not rise to support them. The sister of Edward IV and Richard III was Margaret of York, Duchess of Burgundy, and her court in Flanders became a magnet for opposition to the new king. Margaret backed both Lambert Simnel and Perkin Warbeck in their bids for the crown, even going so far as to acknowledge Warbeck as her nephew. The Battle of Stoke in 1487 was the true final battle in the Wars of the Roses, where Henry, Jasper Tudor and Oxford easily defeated Simnel's force of German and Swiss mercenaries and the exiles Lord Lovell and the Earl of Lincoln. Simnel was not hanged, drawn and quartered, the usual punishment; instead he was given a job in the royal kitchens, later becoming a king's falconer. A series of small invasions by Irish and Scottish supporters of Perkin Warbeck was easily squashed, but dealing with Warbeck cost Henry VII over £13,000, putting a strain on his state finances. Warbeck was initially treated well by Henry. As soon as he confessed to being an impostor, he was released from the Tower of London and given accommodation at Henry's court, even being present at royal banquets. After eighteen months, Warbeck tried to escape but was recaptured.

He tried to escape in 1499 with Edward, Earl of Warwick, and was again captured. He read out a confession at Tyburn and was hanged. Again, the normal punishment for treason was hanging, drawing and quartering, a punishment that Henry would not impose during his reign. Henry found Margaret problematic, but there was little he could do since she was protected by her stepson-in-law Maximilian I, the Holy Roman Emperor.

Foreign Policy

Henry looked for ways to cement his new dynasty. He attempted to solve the Scottish problem and dismantle the 'Auld Alliance', the longstanding friendship between France and Scotland, by marrying his eldest daughter Margaret to the Scottish king in 1503. From her we have the line of Stuart monarchs. He also betrothed his youngest daughter, Mary, to Charles, Prince of Castile and later Holy Roman Emperor, but the wedding did not take place. Instead, in 1514, aged eighteen, she would be married to the fifty-two-year-old Louis XII of France, with Anne Boleyn as one of her maids of honour. Henry's eldest son and heir apparent, Prince Arthur, was wed to the youngest daughter of Ferdinand and Isabella, the effective rulers of Spain.

With these marriage alliances, Henry hoped to protect his domestic interests. He had no wish for costly foreign wars – the establishment of his own dynasty was more urgent – but he needed foreign allies. Marriage was less expensive and hopefully more effective. The match with Spain meant that the most powerful European monarchs recognised his claim to the throne. His reign coincided with the rise of this new power in Europe, a Spain united when Ferdinand of Aragon married Isabella of Castile. Spain quickly gained control of much of Italy. England was weak compared to France or Spain, and Henry VII knew this and acted accordingly. Arthur died in 1502, but Henry used his control of Catherine's person to bring pressure upon Spain. He now intended her to wed his second son, Henry.

Catherine of Aragon's elder sister, Joanna of Castile, married Philip the Fair, the son of Maximilian I, Holy Roman Emperor. In 1504, Philip's mother-in-law Isabella died, leaving the crown of Castile to Joanna. Isabella I's widower and former co-monarch, Ferdinand II, tried to lay hands on the regency of Castile, but the nobles, who disliked and feared him, forced him to withdraw. Philip was summoned to Spain, where he was recognised as king. However, en route to Spain in January 1506, Philip and Joanna were caught in a tempest and shipwrecked off the Dorset coast. Henry saw an immediate opportunity, and Philip and Joanna were taken to court for six weeks as 'guests', in fact becoming hostages. To secure their release, Philip was forced to sign a treaty with Henry known as the *Malus Intercursus* (as it was a bad deal for the Spanish). It included a mutual defence pact, the extradition of rebels – including the Earl of Suffolk, who was an exile in the court of Philip in the Low Countries – and an extremely lucrative trade agreement which allowed English merchants to import cloth duty-free into the Low Countries. Suffolk was handed over, Philip and Joanna were allowed to leave, and the wool trade and Henry's incomes prospered greatly. Henry directed his foreign policy away from war and towards enhancing trade, even subsidising explorers, such as John Cabot, in the hope that this might bring in large returns from commerce.

Bosworth Field marked the end of the Plantagenets of medieval England and the stabilisation of a more modern government, seeing a conscious attempt to integrate Wales into England. The historian G. M. Trevelyan pointed out the influence of Bosworth Field and the Tudors: 'Here, indeed, was one of fortune's freaks: on a bare Leicestershire upland a few thousand men in close conflict foot to foot ... sufficed to set upon the throne of England the greatest of all her royal lines, that should guide her through a century of change down new and larger streams of destiny.' The concord between England and Wales was demonstrated symbolically in a great tournament held by Sir Rhys ap Thomas at Carew Castle in 1507. At its end, the champions, representing St George and St David, the patron saints of the two realms, embraced.

In 1509, Henry VII died of a lingering lung disease at the age of fifty-two. The 'founder of the new England of the sixteenth century', Francis Bacon called him 'a wonder for wise men'. Worn out with duty, he left a peaceful country, full treasury and an uneventful succession to his son, Henry VIII. However, the wilful young king would soon undo his father's careful accumulation of wealth. Years of costly wars and extravagant expenditure would soon reverse royal fortunes and create massive debts. It is owing to Henry VII's strengthening of the monarchy that Henry VIII had a long reign with no internal threat to his kingship. In previous times, the great magnates would have colluded to bring war to the kingdom.

5

King Henry VIII: 'Old Coppernose', 1509–1547

Parents: Henry VII and Elizabeth of York
Born: 28 June 1491 at the Palace of Placentia, Greenwich
Ascended to the throne: 21 April 1509, aged 17 years 10 months
Crowned: 24 June 1509 at Westminster Abbey
Married: Catherine of Aragon (1485–1536), 11 June 1509, Greenwich Friary, Kent
Anne Boleyn (*c.* 1500–33), 14 November 1532 (secret), Kent; 25 January 1533 (secret but sanctioned), York Place, later Whitehall Palace
Jane Seymour (*c.* 1508–37), 30 May 1536, Queen's Closet, Whitehall Palace
Anne of Cleves (1515–57), 6 January 1540, Palace of Placentia, Greenwich
Catherine Howard (*c.* 1520–42), 28 July 1540, Oatlands Palace near Weybridge
Catherine Parr (*c.* 1512–48), 12 July 1543, Queen's Closet, Hampton Court Palace
Siblings: Arthur, Prince of Wales (1486–1502); Margaret, Queen of Scots (1489–1541); Mary, Queen of France (1496–1533); Edmund, Duke of Somerset (1499–1500); Katherine Tudor (d. 1503); possibly Roland de Vielville (*c.* 1474–?).
Children: By Catherine of Aragon: Queen Mary I; two unnamed daughters; an unnamed son; two sons who died in infancy, both named Henry, Duke of Cornwall
By Anne Boleyn: Queen Elizabeth I (1533–1603); Henry, Duke of Cornwall (d. 1534); an unnamed son
By Jane Seymour: Edward VI (1537–1553)
Several illegitimate children: Henry Fitzroy (b. 1519); Thomas Stucley (b. 1520); Richard Edwardes (b. 1523); Catherine Carey (b. 1524) and Henry Carey (b. 1526); Ethelreda Malte (b. 1527); poss. Sir John Perrot (b. 1528)
Died: 28 January 1547, Whitehall Palace, aged 55
Reigned: 38 years and 9 months
Buried: Windsor Castle

Henry was only seventeen years old when he acceded to the throne of England. His father had been heartbroken at the death in 1502 of his capable elder brother, Prince Arthur, possibly in the belief that Henry was not of the same calibre. At Henry's accession, England contained only one duke – Edward Stafford of Buckingham – and one marquess – Thomas Grey of Dorset. Henry VII had been careful not to allow powers to accrue to the great nobles, all of whom had become loyal to the king. There were only ten earls and twenty-nine barons, all of whom were trusted by Henry VII. Henry VIII was the first true king of both England and Wales, Wales having been annexed in 1536. Wales was no longer rebellious, as its people believed that the Tudors were the British kings reborn. The great Marcher estates across its borders and Pembrokeshire were now Crown property. Henry inherited increased Crown lands along with more estates from both Yorkists and Lancastrians, with control over territory that had previously been semi-independent of the Crown.

Henry was therefore the first monarch to inherit a comparatively united kingdom. His father had established relationships with the leading countries of Europe and, with no foreign wars for some years, finances were excellent. The country was being run effectively and efficiently, although Wales and Ireland had not yet been properly integrated into the kingdom. Henry obeyed his father's dying wish that he marry his elder brother's widow, Catherine of Aragon, in order to continue the alliance with Spain. They were married six weeks later. Their double coronation in Westminster Abbey was wildly popular, leading to great expectations of prosperity, and Henry came to live a carefree life, leaving government to ministers he could trust.

Henry was handsome, sporting, cultured and a populist contrast to his reserved father. Almost his first act in government was to please the nobility and merchant classes by imprisoning Sir Richard Empson and Edmund Dudley, the architects of his father's effective taxation policy, the very strategy that enabled Henry VIII to come to the throne with a surplus of savings and incomes. They were beheaded the following year, 1510, upon the spurious grounds of 'constructive treason as they had sought to arm their men as Henry VII lay dying'. Their true crime was efficiency in carrying out the late king's orders to run an effective tax system. Henry's wilfulness, ruthlessness and lust for popularity thus was displayed at the very start of his regime.

Unlike his father, Henry had little interest in administration, tending to more hedonistic pursuits. In the beginning he delegated domestic affairs to William Warham, Archbishop of Canterbury; Lord Treasurer Thomas Howard, Earl of Surrey (later 2nd Duke of Norfolk); and Bishop Richard Foxe. After 1514 he left the details of government principally to Cardinal Thomas Wolsey, and Wolsey was followed in this role by Thomas Cromwell. However, upon the international scene Henry began to squander great sums of money. He supported his father-in-law, Ferdinand of Aragon, against the Moors in 1511, and joined Pope Julius II, along with Venice and Spain, in the Holy League against France. This increased the friction between England and France's ally

Scotland, which led to more border fighting and sea attacks. Scotland and England were at peace in 1509, but had a long tradition of warfare, especially when England was at war with France. France was England's oldest enemy, and Scotland's oldest ally.

James IV of Scotland had married Henry's older sister, Margaret Tudor, and threatened war unless England left the Holy League's alliance against France. However, early in 1512 Henry sent 10,000 troops to fight for Spain on the border with France. The expedition was a disaster. Those who did not die from illness returned home with nothing accomplished. To wipe out his perceived disgrace, Henry decided to invade France in person. Wolsey personally ensured that this expedition was well equipped and the troops were adequately fed, and in June 1513 Henry led an invasion army to Calais.

Henry led successful sieges of Thérouanne and Tournai while his forces defeated the French at the Battle of the Spurs, at Guinegate, on 16 August 1513. The name of the battle signified the speed at which the French cavalry fled without fighting. While Henry was in France, James IV of Scotland quickly invaded England with over 20,000 men, and Surrey was sent to meet him at the Battle of Flodden Field upon 9 September 1513. The English were outnumbered, but better equipped and led. The Scots were completely defeated, suffering about 10,000 casualties. The dead included twelve earls and two bishops, and, above all, James IV himself. His heir, James V, was only a year old. Henry's sister Margaret Tudor now became the Scottish regent, and sought to mediate with Henry, but received little support from the Scottish nobles.

The French war brought England no benefits. Henry's allies made peace with France in 1514, and he had to follow suit. In 1518, the English agreed to hand back Tournai. One provision of the peace was the marriage of Henry's eighteen-year-old sister Mary Tudor to the fifty-two-year-old Louis XII. The marriage was short-lived as Louis died only a few months later. Mary then angered Henry by running away with his close friend Charles Brandon, Duke of Suffolk, and marrying in secret in February 1515. They were eventually pardoned, upon payment of an exacting fine, and they would subsequently become the grandparents of the ill-fated Lady Jane Grey.

For his first two decades as king, which he spent married to Catherine of Aragon, Henry concentrated upon foreign affairs, wishing to be seen in the centre of the European stage. The title of Holy Roman Emperor was held in conjunction with the rule of the Kingdom of Germany and the Kingdom of Italy (Imperial Northern Italy). The Holy Roman Emperor was *primus inter pares*, regarded as first among equals among the other Roman Catholic monarchs across Europe. The *Römisch-deutscher Kaiser* (Holy Roman Emperor) Maximilian I encouraged Henry to succeed him, and died aged sixty in January 1519. Henry stood as a candidate for the position, but Charles V was elected from the controlling Hapsburg family. Charles was heir not only to the House of Hapsburg, but also to the House of Valois-Burgundy and the crowns of Castile and Aragon.

Disappointed but still wishing to influence Europe, Henry wanted to meet the new French king, Francis. In June 1520, Thomas Wolsey arranged a summit meeting at Guisnes, near Calais, which became known as the Field of the Cloth of Gold because of the extravagance of the display. Determined to impress the French king, Henry VIII had a temporary palace made and it was decorated with expensive velvets, satins and cloth of gold. In turn, the French king erected tents of gold brocade with precious gems adorning them. Both kings and their men-at-arms met at the camp. Also present were the Queen of England and the Queen of France with her ladies-in-waiting – all riding in litters and sedan chairs covered in sumptuous embroidery. Some other ladies also arrived mounted on richly decorated palfreys. Each camp occupied about two and a half acres of land and included a large pavilion to serve as a great hall, another for a large chapel and numerous gilded tents to house the kings' enormous retinues, which numbered in the thousands at both camps. A temporary gilt fountain was built, with three separate spouts for claret, spiced wine and water. Some idea of the size of Henry's retinue may be gathered from the fact that in one month 2,200 sheep and other animals in a similar proportion were consumed. In the fields beyond the castle, 2,800 tents were erected for less distinguished visitors.

The two kings entered the field with their teams of challengers at their sides, every one fully armed and magnificently dressed. The French king started the jousts and did extremely well, even though the first lance was broken by Henry, who managed to break one on each charge. The French king broke a good number of lances, but not as many as Henry. The following day saw Henry in the field again, fully armoured and challenging all comers. On the Saturday, Henry's armour skirt and horse trapper were said to be decorated with 2,000 ounces of gold and 1,100 pearls, and the Earl of Devonshire was said to have appeared that day wearing elaborately embroidered cloth of gold, cloth of silver and tissue cloth, his retinue wearing the same. The expense of the occasion was enormous for both monarchs, putting tremendous strain on the finances of each country. Henry had travelled with 5,000 people and spent over £13,000, but the twenty-day visit brought no tangible benefit to either country. Just before Henry had sailed to parley with Francis I, he had a meeting with Charles V at Dover Castle and they went to Canterbury to pay homage at the shrine of St Thomas Becket. Their piety served as a cover for talks behind the French king's back, and they later signed a treaty, much to the disgust of Francis.

This period was one of immense change in Europe. Most significant was the reforming work of the German scholar and preacher Martin Luther, who began a prolonged series of attacks upon the papacy and the Catholic Church, including his book *On the Babylonish Captivity of the Church* in 1520. Henry remained a staunch supporter of the Pope and felt compelled to respond to Luther's attacks. Together with Thomas More and John Fisher, Henry wrote *Assertio Septem Sacramentorum* (*Defence of the Seven Sacraments*), which became a bestseller throughout Europe. Henry's prestige was thereby strengthened by vindicating the Roman Church's dogmatic teaching regarding the sacraments and the 'sacrifice of the Mass', and he insisted upon the supremacy of the papacy in unequivocal terms.

In recognition of his support, Leo X conferred on Henry in 1521 the title of *Fidei Defensor*, Defender of the Faith, a title which has been used by all subsequent English monarchs, regardless of their faith, with FD still appearing upon coinage.

Frustrated in his personal foreign ambition, Henry now attempted to have an English pope elected. He nominated his Lord Chancellor, Thomas Wolsey, Archbishop of York, when Pope Leo X died in December 1521. Leo X was Giovanni di Lorenzo de' Medici, a son of Lorenzo the Magnificent, and in that year had excommunicated Martin Luther. Charles V had promised to exercise his influence in Wolsey's favour, but he did little and Wolsey received very few votes. French and Spanish cardinals could not agree, so voted an absentee cardinal from Utrecht, Adrian VI, as a compromise. This new pope died in September 1523, and again Wolsey was a candidate for the papacy. The English ambassadors at Rome were confident that the united influence of Charles V and Henry VIII would secure Wolsey's election, but again Charles deceived Henry and Clement VII was chosen. Clement was the illegitimate nephew of Lorenzo the Magnificent, Giulio di Giuliano de' Medici, and the natural order of familial power was restored.

Henry should have learnt not to trust Charles V but, urged on by the Holy Roman Emperor, and against Wolsey's advice, he invaded France in 1523. This was less than three years after the mutual 'friendship' displayed at the Field of the Cloth of Gold. The English army was soon forced to withdraw back to England, and Francis I of France was confident enough to invade Italy in 1525. However, Charles V defeated Francis at the Battle of Pavia in 1525. Henry now wanted to take advantage of France's weakness and invade again, but lacked the resources because of the failure of his new tax, the Amicable Grant. Wolsey had set off a series of riots in trying to impose this new tax. Francis renewed his attack on Charles V in 1526, and this time Henry allied himself with France. Yet again, England gained nothing. Charles seized much of Italy, including the Pope, Clement VII, and England went ignored in the resulting Treaty of Cambrai, signed on 3 August 1529.

Henry had been almost eighteen when he married his brother's widow, the twenty-three-year-old Catherine of Aragon, in 1509. She had borne him six children, but only Mary had survived infancy. Their last child died within hours of its birth in November 1518. By 1526, when Catherine had turned forty, it was evident that Henry would not have a son to cement the Tudor dynasty in place. He could not see his only daughter succeeding him; the closest thing to a previous female monarch was Matilda, who had nominally been queen for six months in 1141, but her attempt to be crowned at Westminster had collapsed in the face of bitter opposition from London crowds. As a result of her retreat, Matilda was never formally declared Queen of England, and was instead titled the 'Lady of the English'.

Henry even began to believe that his lack of a male heir was God's punishment as he had committed a sin in marrying his brother's widow, even though the marriage had received papal blessing. He knew he could produce healthy children. In June 1519, his mistress Elizabeth Blount, who was only seventeen, had borne him Henry Fitzroy, whom he made Duke of Richmond. Henry began to regard Fitzroy as his likely heir.

The future of England was irrevocably altered by 1527. Catherine of Aragon was probably no longer capable of giving birth to a healthy son. Henry wanted a legitimate heir and, after several mistresses in his sixteen years of marriage, had become besotted with the twenty-five-year-old Anne Boleyn. Her elder sister, Mary, had been Henry's mistress for some years and had probably borne his children Catherine Carey and Henry Carey. However, Anne refused to be the king's mistress, rebuffing physical advances on the grounds that they were unmarried. Henry looked for grounds of annulment, specifically through the allegation that Arthur and Catherine had consummated their marriage, which Catherine always denied. They had been married for a only few months, with Arthur dying six months short of his sixteenth birthday. Thomas Wolsey now negotiated with the Pope to formally annul Henry's marriage.

The new pope, Clement VII, looked as if he might accommodate Henry, but then succumbed to the power of the Holy Roman Emperor, Charles V, who was the nephew of Catherine of Aragon. Clement now procrastinated in every way possible, setting up a commission to review the issue, and the affair dragged on for six years. During this time, the whole of Scandinavia broke with Rome and adopted Lutheranism, beginning in 1527. Infuriated by Wolsey's inability to resolve the matter, Henry had him arrested for treason in November 1530, but Wolsey died before he could be killed. Henry's main adviser was now Thomas Cromwell, who quickly moved matters ahead. Under his guidance, Henry soon became the Supreme Head of a separate Church of England, with the authority to appoint his own archbishops and bishops. Thomas Cranmer, Henry's newly appointed Archbishop of Canterbury, could now pronounce on 23 May 1533 that Henry's marriage with Catherine was void.

However, Henry had already secretly married Anne Boleyn in January 1533, when she was a month pregnant. The Pope refused to accept Cranmer's decision, and in July 1533 Clement VII declared the divorce and remarriage void and prepared to excommunicate Henry. The excommunication was suspended, but it was then reaffirmed by Clement's successor, Paul III; however, he was unable to gain the international support he desired to formalise the sentence. Paul III was Alessandro Farnese, whose sister had been the favourite mistress of Pope Alexander VI. Paul III was a remarkable character whose nepotism advanced his family's wealth and power and who fathered at least four illegitimate children. Henry's decision to set up an independent church was greatly helped, as was the Protestant Reformation in general, by the scandals and abuses emanating from the Vatican over the centuries.

The attempt to excommunicate him forced Henry further away from Rome, and away from reconciliation. He took great pains to demonstrate that his argument was only against the Pope, not the Church. The significant change was that Henry was to be, like the Pope, God's representative, or the

'Head of the Church' in his own dominions. In 1534, the Act of Supremacy made Henry Supreme Head of the Church of England. Sir Thomas More and Bishop John Fisher refused to acknowledge this change, and were executed in 1535. The Act of Succession was passed in the same year, declaring that Anne Boleyn's child would be heir to the throne.

Henry's delight over Anne Boleyn's pregnancy soon faded when she gave birth to a girl, the future Elizabeth I, in September 1533. This was followed by two stillborn children. Henry fell from a horse in January 1536, leaving him unconscious, and the shock brought on Anne's labour. Henry recovered, though the injury led to trouble with a severely ulcerated leg in his later years. Anne lost this fourth child, said to be a boy. Henry had lost all interest in Anne in just two years of marriage, during which she had been almost constantly pregnant. He now maintained that he had been seduced by witchcraft, and Catholics later ascribed to Anne the witch's sign of a shrivelled sixth finger. Charges of her infidelity and adultery were fabricated, and she was arrested, tried and found guilty of high treason, incest and adultery, being executed on 19 May 1536. Two days before her death, Archbishop Cranmer declared Anne's marriage to Henry to be null and void, possibly upon the tenuous grounds that Henry had formerly had a relationship with her sister Mary.

On the day of Anne's execution, the king had a great feast with twenty-six young ladies at his own table, and over the following days gave many more feasts. He grew bigger, having his bed enlarged to seven feet in width. However, his dissatisfaction in private is shown in a double mark he made against a passage in his Book of Proverbs: 'For the lips of a harlot are a dropping honey-comb, and her throat is softer than oil. But at the last she is as bitter as wormwood, and as sharp as a two-edged sword.'

During his short marriage, Henry had become infatuated with one of Anne's ladies-in-waiting, the twenty-eight-year-old Jane Seymour. They were betrothed on 20 May 1536 – just one day after Anne Boleyn's execution – and married ten days later, but Jane was never crowned queen; an outbreak of plague in London delayed the coronation, and then she became pregnant. She gave birth to a boy, the future Edward VI, but died twelve days later in the midst of Henry's celebrations. They had been married for just seventeen months. As she had given him a son and heir, Jane Seymour was the only one of his wives to be given a queen's funeral, and after Henry's death he was laid beside her in St George's Chapel, Windsor.

Henry appointed a commission to report on the state of the monasteries. Thomas Cromwell believed that they were too rich and powerful, with incomes from vast estates, and were likely to lead any resistance to change. Following the quick report upon monastic abuses, Parliament passed an Act in 1536 for the suppression of all small monasteries on the grounds that they were 'uneconomic'. In the north of England, there was a rebellion known as the Pilgrimage of Grace. For those who rebelled, the two Acts of Dissolution had been the final straw after poor harvests, high rents and the enclosure of common lands. The rebellion had begun in Lincolnshire in October 1536 and spread through Yorkshire under the command of Robert Aske. Henry appeared conciliatory and defused the rebellion by promises, none of which he fulfilled, and some months later he had Aske and over 200 of the rebels executed. In 1539, all remaining monasteries were dissolved. The monks were given pensions and many of them married and learned trades. Many monastery buildings became manor houses. Others were dismantled and their stones were used for other buildings.

Cromwell's commissioners met little resistance as they moved from county to county closing the monasteries. The last to fall was Waltham Abbey in Essex in March 1540. Although the Crown benefited considerably from the closure of the monasteries, most of the profits passed to Henry, who was always desperate for money for his foreign exploits. As such, the ultimate beneficiaries were the local landed gentry who, once the monastery was closed and ransacked, acquired most of the land and remaining properties.

Until his break with Rome, Henry had made donations to shrines and dispensed alms generously. He had made several pilgrimages, his last one taking him and Jane Seymour, through Kent via Rochester and Sittingbourne to Canterbury. Here he made offerings at Becket's shrine. He would have noted its wealth. During the Dissolution, the king came into the habit of appropriating treasures from the religious houses he ruined. Among the treasures he laid his hands on was a ruby given by Louis VII in 1179 to decorate Becket's tomb in Canterbury. Henry had this precious jewel, the '*Regale de France*' set in a thumb ring. It took twenty-six carts to move the gold and jewels taken from Becket's tomb. Proceeds from the Dissolution doubled royal income and marked the greatest shift of land ownership since the Norman Conquest. Henry gave around one-third of confiscated lands to the nobility and gentry and retained just a few religious foundations for himself. These were mainly sited on the London–Dover route that he used for his travels abroad and included Dartford Priory and St Augustine's Abbey in Canterbury.

Although Henry VIII had broken with Rome, he kept the Catholic religion essentially intact. However, in 1538 Chancellor Thomas Cromwell did make some minor reforms. In 1538, he ordered that every church should have an English translation of the Bible. He also ordered that any idolatrous images should be removed from churches. Other changes were limited. Henry emphasised this with the publication of the Act of the Six Articles in 1539, which reaffirmed doctrines inherited from the Church of Rome. From 1545, Latin was replaced by English as the language of church services.

Between 1536 and 1543, a compliant English Parliament passed a series of laws that together became known as the Acts of Union. Wales became a united entity and the Principality lands and the Marcher lands both disappeared. The whole of Wales was divided into shires (counties) and each one had a justice of the peace, who was appointed in England. Wales was represented in Parliament under the terms of the Acts of Union, but there was an attempt to remove the Welsh national identity. Welsh MPs were not truly representative of the people in their constituencies and Welsh was not spoken in Parliament. The rich Welsh families who sent their sons to London in an effort to advance themselves ensured that they only spoke English. The law courts in Wales only conducted their affairs in English. By doing this, Henry was attempting to 'make' all Welsh people English and thus tie them to London in terms of loyalty. If, as a young man, you wanted to make your way in London either politically or socially, you had to drop any pretence of being Welsh.

Because of the papal bull isolating him from any protection by the Church, Henry was afraid that the French, the Hapsburgs or both would invade England. The vast estates owned by the monasteries were sold and, fearing foreign invasion, Henry used the wealth to build a network of new castles around the coast. He also now sought a political marriage with a European princess. Through the advice of Thomas Cromwell he settled on Anne, the sister of the Duke of Cleves in Germany. Although Henry admired her portrait, he was horrified when he first met Anne in January 1540. However, by then marriage arrangements had proceeded too far. Henry feared the backlash if he withdrew. Although they were wed on 6 January, the marriage was never consummated and both parties readily agreed to a divorce, which went through seven months later. Henry was generous to Anne because of her compliance, and the two remained good friends.

Within three weeks of the divorce, on 28 July 1540, Henry married the beautiful teenager Catherine Howard, a cousin of Anne Boleyn. Catherine was the third of Henry's consorts to have been a member of the English gentry instead of European nobility. Now aged forty-nine, he was becoming grossly fat and ageing fast. Catherine soon tired of her husband, and was said to have turned to her former lovers. She was soon betrayed and charged with treason. The Royal Assent by Commission Act of 1541 was specially created to more easily prosecute her. It was more than just an Act of attainder, making it high treason for any person who married the king to conceal from the monarch their previous sexual history. She was executed on 13 February 1542.

Henry's final marriage took place the following year, to an older lady, already twice widowed, named Catherine Parr. Henry was now after a companion rather than a lover. Parr served as an excellent stepmother to his three surviving children, Mary, Elizabeth and Edward, who were reconciled for the first time in 1543. Following Charles Brandon's death in 1545, it was rumoured that King Henry had considered marrying Brandon's twenty-six-year-old widow Catherine Willoughby as his seventh wife while he was still married to Catherine Parr, her close friend. In February 1546, the Imperial ambassador, van der Delft, wrote,

> I hesitate to report there are rumours of a new queen. Some attribute it to the sterility of the present Queen, while others say that there will be no change during the present war. Madame Suffolk [Willoughby had been Duchess of Suffolk] is much talked about and is in great favour; but the King shows no alteration in his behaviour to the Queen, although she is said to be annoyed by the rumour.

During these tempestuous marriages Henry had not ignored the international scene, or indeed the state of Britain. He regarded the British Isles as his own empire, and thus had begun to consolidate it in 1536 with the Act of Union, which officially incorporated Wales as part of England rather than as a separate province. He was unable to enact the same legislation for Ireland, although his father had made the Irish parliament subject to the English. A rebellion led by the Fitzgeralds in Ireland in 1534 was summarily dealt with, and in 1542 Henry declared himself king rather than lord of Ireland. Relationships with Scotland soured, and the last connections between them ended when his sister, Margaret, died in November 1541. The following year saw Henry prepare to go to war to conquer Scotland and the Scots gained the upper hand in a number of skirmishes. However, a disorganised Scottish force of some 10,000 was soundly defeated by three thousand English at Solway Moss in November 1542. Soon after, James V took to his bed and seemed to pine away in despair.

Henry now pursued a marriage alliance between his son, the future Edward VI and James's infant daughter Mary. This would unite the nations under an English king. Mary was supposed to marry Edward in her tenth year under the terms of a peace treaty concluded in July 1543, but the treaty was never ratified by the Scots as their pro-French nobles did everything they could to undermine it. Hostilities continued between England and Scotland throughout the 1540s, with Scotland using this as an excuse to argue that the treaty was invalid. The invasions of 1544 and 1545 were led by Edward Seymour, later Duke of Somerset, who captured Edinburgh in 1544.

The ailing Henry invaded France in 1544, carried in a litter at the head of an army of 40,000 men. He captured Boulogne but was forced to return to England to deal with the threat of French invasion. The French had sent a fleet to the Solent and landed a force on the Isle of Wight. In a naval battle the *Mary Rose* was sunk but the French fleet were forced to withdraw against a far superior English force. As a prince, Henry had been Lord Warden of the Cinque Ports, overseeing the coastal ports of Kent and Sussex, which were charged with providing the king with ships and men in return for special privileges. The concept of the Cinque Ports was a forerunner of the Royal Navy. As king, he was later celebrated as the 'Father of the English Navy', building up a major fleet that laid the foundations of England's subsequent naval dominance. In all Henry constructed forty-six warships and thirteen galleys, bought twenty-six vessels and captured thirteen more. In 1547, Henry rented a storehouse to service his fleet at anchor on the River Medway. The dockyard that grew up at Chatham built and repaired many of the vessels that helped seal victory against the Spanish Armada in the reign of Elizabeth I.

Henry concluded a peace treaty with Francis in 1546. The only achievement was the capture of Boulogne, but in the Peace of Ardres of 1546 Henry agreed to sell the town back in eight years' time. Arguably, Henry only strengthened the hand of the French in Scotland. The last Scottish cardinal prior to the Reformation was David Beaton, Lord Chancellor of Scotland and Archbishop of St Andrew's. On 29 May 1546, two Fife lairds killed a porter to gain entrance to St Andrew's Castle and murdered Beaton, mutilating the corpse and hanging it from a castle window. At the time it was widely believed that his death was in the interests of Henry VIII, who regarded Beaton as the chief obstacle to his policy in Scotland, but the English were still unable to reduce Scotland to obedience. These wars cost over £3 million. In order to pay for them, Henry had to sell off even more of the monastic land he had acquired, as well as taxing at an unprecedentedly high rate.

Henry's declining years witnessed factions at court, the renewal of war with France and Scotland, and nascent economic decline caused by the 'Great Debasement'. Henry was only called 'Bluff King Hal' posthumously, whereas the nickname 'Coppernose', or 'Old Coppernose' was well known in his lifetime. He began to debase the coinage from about 1542 onwards, mixing base metals with the silver that was used for coins. By 1544, his extravagant lifestyle and consequent expenditure had accelerated his running short of money. His solution was to officially lower the fineness of the third issue of coinage, from 1544 to 1547, to only one-third silver and two-thirds copper. This debasing was unpopular, and resulted in his nickname as the silver rubbed off the high-relief part of the coin design. Soon the silver coins were almost entirely copper. This expedient allowed the government to buy what it needed but soon led to rapid inflation as people lost faith in the value of the currency and hoarded their old silver coins. From this period we get Gresham's law that 'bad money drives out good'. Sir Thomas Gresham (1519–79) gave early expression to the principle that when depreciated or debased coinage is in concurrent circulation with money of high value in terms of precious metals, the good money is withdrawn from circulation by hoarders. Henry's debasement also made foreign goods far more expensive, as traders on the Continent refused to accept worthless copper for their wares. The disruptive effects of debasement continued for many years, until Mary began a partial recoinage that was completed by Elizabeth.

On 24 December 1545, in his last speech to Parliament, Henry railed against the members of the Church as their Supreme Head:

> Be not judges yourselves of your own fantastical opinions and vain expositions; and although you be permitted to read Holy Scriptures and to have the Word of God in your mother tongue, you must understand it is licensed so to do only to inform your conscience and inform your children and families, not to make Scripture a railing and taunting stock against priests and preachers. I am very sorry to know and hear how irreverently that precious jewel, the Word of God, is disputed, rhymed, sung, and jangled in every alehouse and tavern, contrary to the true meaning and doctrine of the same.

Probably suffering from type 2 diabetes, Henry had become obese. The king had a chronic leg ulcer, first mentioned in 1528 but possibly aggravated by his fall in 1536. The ulcer often became inflamed and Henry did not rest long enough for it to heal. Towards the end of his life the king had enormously swollen, dropsical legs. There is no evidence that Henry VIII was syphilitic, as some have theorised. It is possible, though, that he suffered from some form of depression in the second half of his life, with a particular bout in 1541. In 1514, aged twenty-three, his chest circumference had been forty-two inches, and his waist thirty-five inches. He gradually became larger after 1528, and by 1536 his chest measurement was forty-five inches, and waist thirty-seven inches. However, by 1541, aged fifty, he had become enormous, with a chest measurement of fifty-seven inches and a waist measurement of fifty-four inches. His last set of armour showed a waist measurement of waist of about fifty-eight to sixty inches, indicating a weight of about 300 to 320 pounds, over 20 stone, Especially large horses had to be used to carry him, and by 1545 he had started using a sort of wheelchair, a chair called a 'tramme', to carry him between his chambers and a lift to take him up and down stairs. Henry VIII spent his last eight days in bed and was too weak to even to lift a glass to his lips. His sick room was filled with the stench of his leg ulcers. His doctors and physicians were afraid to tell him that he was dying because the Treason Act forbade anyone from predicting the death of the king. Thomas Cranmer gently told Henry of his imminent death, and he died on 28 January 1547, aged fifty-five. Henry died in pain, not wanting his wife or children at his bedside.

Henry left an empty treasury. When not feasting to excess, he had enjoyed hunting in his leisure time and by 1541 owned eighty-five hunting parks and forests, which needed upkeep. He also had a mania for building and acquiring property, again which required huge running expenses. At his death in 1547 he owned over seventy residences, including fifty-five palaces – more than any other English monarch. Knole had belonged to Thomas Cranmer, Archbishop of Canterbury, but Henry liked it and in 1538 obliged the cleric to hand it over, along with nearby Otford Palace. Similarly, he took Hampton Court from Wolsey. In Kent alone, he inherited the medieval castles of Dover, Leeds and Rochester and acquired Hever Castle, Knole, Otford Palace and Penshurst Place. The king lavished over £170,000 (at least £92 million in today's money) on his residences. He was particularly fond of Leeds Castle, near Maidstone, spending £1,300 on it between 1517 and 1523.

Henry flaunted his prestige by surrounding himself with large numbers of courtiers and servants, and his royal palaces were duly designed to accommodate them. Complete ranges were allocated for courtier lodgings, such as the Green Court at Knole, Sevenoaks. His palaces were furnished with unprecedented splendour: expensive carpets and tapestries showed off his status and wealth. It took ten men to complete the prescribed ritual for preparing the royal bed each evening, and one of their number had to roll on it to check for any harmful objects that might have been hidden. By the end of his reign he had amassed 2,000 tapestries, 800 carpets, 150 paintings, seventeen extremely expensive 'standing clocks' and nearly 1,800 books. He also owned forty-one gowns, twenty-five doublets, twenty coats, eight cloaks, fifteen capes and eight walking sticks. Henry boasted a greater collection of jewellery than any other English king and he heaped clothes and jewels on his wives and lovers, with Anne Boleyn receiving the equivalent of £165,000 in gifts in just three years. When Henry visited Dover Castle in March 1539, he sent ahead nineteen travelling cases containing furs, tapestries, twenty-seven pairs of spectacles and 314 rings, three of them wedding rings. He later presented one of these rings to Anne of Cleves, cautiously keeping the other two in reserve. In 1539, Henry also sent two of his best beds to Rochester and Dartford in time for the arrival of his prospective fourth wife, Anne of Cleves.

Despite the major reforms of his reign, Henry was not a great initiator, relying instead on such men as Wolsey and Cromwell, whom he dispensed with when no longer needed. At times he ruled like a despot, and it is true to say that no other English king could have undertaken such reforms and succeeded. It was through Henry, the first king to be referred to as His Majesty, that the modern English state was created. Under Henry, England went through changes that would eventually lead to the creation of modern sovereignty, a nation not under the control of the Church, although he never intended it. He was a devoted Catholic who rejected the Pope and founded his own religion. He was an educated humanist who executed tens of thousands of subjects. He was the most fortunate king of all. Without his father's hamstringing of the nobility, his reign would have been short.

The Catholic Encyclopaedia points out Henry's hypocrisy:

> Looking at the last fifteen years of Henry's life, it is hard to find one single feature which does not evoke repulsion, and the attempts made by some writers to whitewash his misdeeds only give proof of the extraordinary prejudice with which they approach the subject. Henry's cruelties continued to the last, and so likewise did his inconsistencies. One of the last measures of confiscation of his reign was an act of suppression of chantries, but Henry by his last will and testament established what were practically chantries to have Masses said for his own soul.

6

The Various 'Wives' of Henry VIII

Annulled, Annulled and Killed, Died, Annulled, Killed, Survived
The number of Henry's wives is anywhere between one and six, depending upon one's interpretation of law. The common mnemonic for remembering the order of Henry's wives is 'divorced, beheaded, died, divorced, beheaded, survived'. A more accurate representation is given above and explained in the chapter on Tudor myths. Henry was married for twenty-three years and eleven months to Catherine of Aragon, and less than half that – a total of nine years and one month – to his other five wives. The lengths of Henry's marriages, in order of length, were:

Catherine of Aragon: 23 years and 11 months; Henry aged 17, Catherine 23
Catherine Parr: 3 years and 6 months; Henry aged 52, Catherine 31
Anne Boleyn: 3 years and 3 months; Henry aged 41, Anne 31 or 32
Catherine Howard: 2 years and 6 months; Henry aged 49, Catherine 17–22
Jane Seymour: 1 year and 4 months; Henry aged 44, Jane 26–27
Anne of Cleves: 6 months; Henry aged 48, Anne 24

1. **Catherine of Aragon of the House of Trastámara** (1485–1536), reigned 1509–33
Parents: Ferdinand II of Aragon and Isabella I of Castile
Born: 16 December 1485 at the Archbishop of Toledo's Palace, Alcalá de Henares, Spain
Nationality: Aragonese and Castilian
Married (1): Arthur, Prince of Wales, 14 November 1501, St Paul's Cathedral, London
Married (2): Henry VIII, 11 June 1509, Franciscan church at the Palace of Placentia, Greenwich
Children: Stillborn daughter (1510); Henry, Duke of Cornwall, died after 52 days (1511); stillborn or short-lived son (1513); Henry, Duke of Cornwall, died soon after birth (1514); Mary I (1516); daughter who lived a week (1518)
Marriage annulled: 23 or 25 May 1533

Died: 7 January 1536, Kimbolton Castle
Buried: 29 January 1536, Peterborough Abbey (now Cathedral)

Catherine was the youngest surviving child of the joint rulers of Spain, and as a three-year-old was betrothed to Henry VII's eldest son, Arthur, who was then almost two years old. At almost sixteen the reputedly beautiful Catherine married Prince Arthur, being escorted by the groom's younger brother, Henry. They moved to Ludlow Castle in the Welsh Marches, an area Arthur was to administer, but under six months later both contracted the 'sweating sickness' and Arthur died. Henry VII wished to keep her large dowry, so fourteen months later he arranged for her betrothal to his surviving son, Henry, who was too young to marry at that time.

Marriage to Henry depended upon papal dispensation because canon law forbade a man to marry his brother's widow. Catherine therefore testified that her marriage to Arthur was never consummated as, according to canon law, a marriage was not valid until consummated. Henry VIII took the throne on 21 April 1509, and obeyed his father's wishes by marrying Catherine on 11 June 1509, seven years after Prince Arthur's death. She was twenty-three and the new king was just days short of his eighteenth birthday. A joint coronation was arranged for Midsummer's Day, 24 June. Their marriage of almost twenty-four years was marred by five children not living more than a few weeks, with only Mary Tudor surviving to adulthood.

The king had been happy enough with a string of mistresses, but the destiny of the dynasty depended upon having a healthy son. Around 1524 or 1525, physicians told Henry that Catherine, now almost forty, was unlikely to give birth again. By 1527 he had become infatuated with Anne Boleyn, who would only bed him if married. It is now that the so-called 'Great Matter', of how to end the marriage to Catherine, began. However, only the Pope could annul a marriage, and, as the Church believed in the sanctity of marriage and family, this was a very rare occurrence. Royal families were expected to set the standards that others should follow. Henry used the Bible to justify his request for a marriage annulment. Leviticus 20:16 states, 'If a man shall take his brother's wife, it is an impurity; he hath uncovered his brother's nakedness; they shall be childless.' He seemed to believe that his lack of a male heir was God's punishment for marrying his brother's wife.

He argued that his marriage had been against God's law from the start, despite the Pope's blessing in 1509. He was therefore living in sin and the Pope should annul his marriage so that he could rectify this. As 'Defender of the Faith' since 1521 for his attack on the doctrines of Luther, Henry expected the annulment to be a foregone conclusion. In a speech in November 1528, he passionately argued that Catherine was noble and virtuous, and that in other circumstances he would marry her again. However, he now lived in 'detestable and abominable adultery'.

Cardinal Wolsey was certain that the Pope would annul the marriage, as he was in a vulnerable position and needed the support of every Christian monarch. The Muslim Turks were advancing across the Mediterranean towards Rome. Wolsey fell out of favour for his failure. Catherine had appealed against any annulment directly to the Pope, who she felt would listen to her case since her nephew was Charles V, the Holy Roman Emperor. The political and legal debate continued for six years. Catherine was adamant that she and Arthur did not consummate their marriage and therefore were not truly husband and wife. Catherine needed not only to retain her position, but also to secure the future of her daughter, Mary.

In 1533, Anne Boleyn became pregnant. Henry had to act, and his solution was to reject the power of the Pope in England and to have Thomas Cranmer, Archbishop of Canterbury, grant the annulment. Catherine was to renounce the title of queen and would be known as the Princess Dowager of Wales, something she refused to acknowledge through to the end of her life. Catherine and her daughter were separated and she was forced to leave court. She lived for the next three years with just a few servants but seldom complained of her treatment and spent a great deal of time at prayer. When the king asked her to surrender her jewels since they belonged to the Queen of England, a position she no longer held, Catherine replied, 'I will not give them up to a person who is the scandal of Christendom and a disgrace to you.'

In 1535, Catherine was transferred to the decaying Kimbolton Castle. She wore a hair shirt and stayed in one small room, leaving only to attend Mass, and was forbidden from seeing or writing to her daughter, Mary. Henry offered them both better quarters and each other's company if they would acknowledge Anne Boleyn as his new queen. Neither did. She fell ill in late December 1535 and died, aged fifty, on 7 January 1536 at Kimbolton. The cause of her death may have been 'a melanotic carcinoma', but was diagnosed at the time as 'slow poisoning'. In December 1535, probably suffering from cancer and sensing that she was dying, Catherine made her will and wrote one final letter to Henry VIII, still regarding herself as his rightful wife and queen:

> My Lord and Dear Husband, The hour of my death draweth fast on, the tender love I owe thou forceth me, my case being such, to commend myself to thou, and to put thou in remembrance with a few words of the health and safeguard of thine soul which thou ought to prefer before all worldly matters, and before the care and pampering of thy body, for the which thou has cast me into many calamities and thineself into many troubles. For my part, I pardon thou everything, and I desire to devoutly pray God that He will pardon thou also. For the rest, I commend unto thou our daughter Mary, beseeching thou to be a good father unto her, as I have heretofore desired. I entreat thou also, on behalf of my maids, to give them marriage portions, which is not much, they being but three. For all mine other servants I solicit the wages due them, and a year more, lest they be unprovided for. Lastly, I make this vow, that mine eyes desire thou above all things. Katharine the Queen.

2. **Anne Boleyn (Bullen)** (*c.* 1501–36), reigned 1533–36
Parents: Thomas Boleyn, later Earl of Wiltshire and Earl of Ormonde, and Lady Elizabeth Howard

Born: *c.* 1501–1507, probably at Blickling Hall in Norfolk
Nationality: English
Married Henry: 14 November 1532 (secret), Kent; 25 January 1533 (secret but sanctioned), York Place, later Whitehall Palace
Coronation: 1 June 1533
Children: Elizabeth I (1533); three miscarriages
Arrested: 2 May 1536
Marriage annulled: 17 May 1536
Executed: 19 May 1536
Buried: Chapel of St Peter ad Vincula, Tower of London

Her father, Thomas Boleyn, inherited Hever Castle in 1505. He was a diplomat, and achieved for Anne a position in the household of Archduchess Margaret of Austria in Brussels. He then arranged for her to follow Henry VII's daughter Mary Tudor on her way to France to marry Louis XII. Anne briefly served as a maid of honour to Mary Tudor and then to queen consort Claude of France, whom she served for seven years. As a young girl Anne made a great impression at the French court, and Francis I wrote, '*Venus était blonde, on m'a dit: L'on voit bien, qu'elle est brunette*!' ('Venus was blonde, I've been told: Now I see that she's a brunette!')

Fluent in French, Anne was recalled to England to marry James Butler, and joined Henry VIII's court in 1522. The marriage was cancelled and Anne attracted suitors, falling in love with Henry Percy, heir to the dukedom of Northumberland, but he was already betrothed. The couple planned to marry but Thomas Wolsey prevented it, earning Anne's enmity. The poet Thomas Wyatt also fell in love with her, and wrote poems about her refusal of his advances. Henry VIII had several mistresses during his marriage to Catherine of Aragon, one of whom was Anne's married sister Mary. Henry may well have had a son and daughter with Mary Boleyn. Anne refused to become his mistress, repeatedly declaring that she would not sleep with him unless they were married.

For seven years Henry courted Anne, trying to divorce Catherine, who was now too old to give him a son and heir. In the early 1530s, the Venetian ambassador Savorgnano called Anne 'a young woman of noble birth, though many say of bad character, whose will is law to him, and he is expected to marry her should the divorce take place, which it is supposed will not be effected, as the peers of the realm ... and the people are opposed to it'. In 1532, a new Venetian ambassador called her

> not one of the handsomest women in the world. She is of middling stature, with a swarthy complexion, long neck, wide mouth, bosom not much raised, and in fact has nothing but the king's great appetite, and her eyes, which are black and beautiful – and take great effect on those who served the queen when she was on the throne. She lives like a queen, and the king accompanies her to Mass – and everywhere.

Henry gave her great power at court, being able to grant petitions, receive diplomats and give patronage. A French ambassador noted in 1531 that it was necessary to have Anne's support if you wanted to have any influence at the English court.

In September 1532, Henry made Anne the Marquise of Pembroke in her own right, something not normally possible for a woman to obtain. This gave her the appropriate peerage for a future queen, and it was after this that their relationship was consummated. She needed such a title of status in readiness for meeting Francis I of France. Anne was not yet Henry's wife and queen, so she required some status befitting of England's future queen. Upon 1 September, Anne dressed in jewels and ermine-trimmed velvet for the lavish ceremony at Windsor Castle. She was England's queen in all but name. Accompanied by her cousin Mary Howard and the countesses of Derby and Rutland, she knelt in front of the king and the dukes of Norfolk and Suffolk. Stephen Gardiner, Lord Chancellor and Bishop of Winchester, read out the patent which gave her the title of Marquess of Pembroke in her own right, a title that would pass on to her offspring. Henry then crowned her with the gold coronet of a marquis and placed on her a crimson velvet mantle. Anne also received her own lands, worth over £1,000 per year.

After nearly six years of abstaining from sexual relations until she could be certain it would lead to marriage, the couple probably slept together at the end of the state visit to Calais, or in Dover Castle shortly after their return to England in November 1532. There was a secret marriage service at Dover, and then an official marriage in London on 25 January 1533. Anne was pregnant and she and Henry were sure that it would be a boy. Any child born before she was queen would not be able to succeed to the throne, so they had to marry quickly – before Henry's existing marriage was annulled, in fact. Thus it was a bigamous, and hence illegal marriage. Thomas Cranmer, the new Archbishop of Canterbury, declared the marriage with Catherine null and void and the new marriage good and valid upon 23 and 25 May 1533 respectively.

Royal etiquette demanded that a pregnant queen 'take to her chamber', isolating herself from male company and the world outside for a month or a month and a half prior to her child's birth. However, Anne took to her chamber only ten days before Elizabeth's birth in September. By taking to her chamber at the end of August, Anne may have been expecting a delivery at the end of September. She and her women and doctors would have assumed she had first fallen pregnant at the end of December or the beginning of January. *Hall's Chronicle* and the account of the break with Rome by the Jesuit priest Father Nicholas Sander both suggest a different date for the royal wedding of 14 November 1532.

The well-informed Hall wrote, 'The king, after his return [from the state visit], married privily the Lady Anne Boleyn on Saint Erkenwald's Day, which marriage was kept so secret that very few knew of it, till she was great with child, at Easter.' Father Sander, who depicted Henry as an incestuous monster and Anne a heretical witch, had no reason for supporting the view that they waited until marriage before sleeping together or that Elizabeth I, whom Sander loathed, had been conceived in wedlock, unless he believed it to be true. If they were married on 14 November 1532, then it is most likely that they were married in Dover Castle, within a day or so of their return from France.

Even the second ceremony was secretive, taking place on 25 January at Whitehall. Of course, Henry was still married. In the sixteenth century, two ceremonies, even two weddings, were not unusual. Eric Ives believes that there was a 'commitment' ceremony in November, quite possibly a binding pre-contract, a watertight legal declaration of intent to marry each other. After such a ceremony had taken place, sixteenth-century canon law stated that it was permissible for the couple to commence sexual intercourse with one another. Engagements were thus treated with suspicion by future brides. It was on grounds of such pre-contracts that Henry VIII's subsequent marriages to Anne of Cleves and Catherine Howard were declared invalid. With the pre-contract formally ratified in November, Henry and Anne began sleeping together and conceived Elizabeth, and the full nuptial Mass took place at Whitehall on 25 January.

David Starkey has argued,

> Anne had been doing her research. She had already ... informed herself widely on the debate about the divorce. Now she wanted to make sure that her own title as queen was unimpeachable. This meant that everything would have to be done in the proper form set out in the bible of ceremony known as the royal book ... It was these stipulations, at least as much as the pressure of contemporary events, which governed Anne and Henry's actions over the next few months ... The circumstances of the Calais interview reinforced all this. She had re-entered the world of the French court; she had danced with the French king and talked privately with him. Now she was sailing to English soil, where soon she would be crowned. It was just as the royal book prescribed. What more natural therefore than to marry Henry as soon as they landed?

Henry and Anne would then have a second marriage service at a later date, just as foreign royal brides of the Middle Ages had done.

In February 1533, matters hastened; Anne must have suspected that she was pregnant. On 11 April, Henry ordered his council to accord Anne royal honours, and Catherine of Aragon's demotion to Dowager Princess of Wales. The following day, the pregnant Anne attended Mass in the Queen's Closet at Greenwich Palace 'with all the pomp of a queen, clad in cloth of gold, and loaded with the richest jewels'. It was a dramatic public statement by Henry of her new status as queen.

Eustace Chapuys, the Imperial ambassador, recorded,

> On Saturday, Easter Eve, dame Anne went to mass in Royal state, loaded with jewels, clothed in a robe of cloth of gold frieze. The daughter of the duke of Norfolk, who is affianced to the duke of Richmond, carried her train; and she had in her suite 60 young ladies, and was brought to church,

and brought back with the solemnities, or even more, which were used to the Queen. She has changed her name from Marchioness to Queen, and the preachers offered prayers for her by name. All the world is astonished at it for it looks like a dream, and even those who take her part know not whether to laugh or to cry.

The King is very watchful of the countenance of the people, and begs the lords to go and visit and make their court to the new Queen, whom he intends to have solemnly crowned after Easter, when he will have feastings and tournaments; and some think that Clarencieux went four days ago to France to invite gentlemen at arms to the tourney, after the example of Francis, who did so at his nuptials. I know not whether this will be before or after, but the King has secretly appointed with the archbishop of Canterbury that of his office, without any other pressure, he shall cite the King as having two wives; and upon this, without summoning the Queen, he will declare that he was at liberty to marry as he has done without waiting for a dispensation or sentence of any kind.

Thus at Easter 1533 Anne was publicly proclaimed as queen, but not until May did Cranmer annul Henry's marriage to Catherine of Aragon. Anne was formally crowned in June in a great ceremony at Westminster. She was the last queen consort of England to be crowned separately from her husband, on 1 June 1533 in a magnificent ceremony at Westminster Abbey, just a week after the annulment of the marriage of Henry and Catherine. The public's response was moderate – Catherine of Aragon was widely liked. In late August 1533 Anne took to her chamber, and on 7 September gave birth to the future Elizabeth I. Henry was disappointed, but said that a son would surely follow and professed to love his second daughter.

Pope Clement announced a provisional sentence of excommunication against Henry and Cranmer, condemned the marriage to Anne and, in March 1534, declared the marriage to Catherine legal and again ordered Henry to return to her. In return, Henry required his subjects to swear the oath attached to the First Succession Act, rejecting papal authority in legal matters and recognising Anne Boleyn as queen. In late 1534, Parliament declared Henry 'the only supreme head on earth of the Church of England'.

Anne presided over a magnificent court, spending lavish amounts of money, and numerous palaces were renovated to suit her extravagant tastes. She quickly came to be blamed for the tyranny of Henry's government and was referred to by some as the 'king's whore' or a 'naughty paike [prostitute]'. Her failure to produce the expected son and the executions of Sir Thomas More and Bishop John Fisher further hurt her image. Unpopular with the people, Anne suffered a stillbirth or miscarriage around Christmas in 1534 and Henry drew away from her, much as he had dropped his former mistress, her sister Mary. He discussed with Cranmer and Cromwell the possibility of divorcing her without having to return to Catherine. They reconciled and spent the summer of 1535 on progress around the kingdom. By October, she was again pregnant.

Catherine of Aragon died in January 1536, and rumours quickly spread that she had been poisoned. These began after the discovery during her embalming that her heart was blackened, which today indicates cancer. Anne knew the danger if she failed to give birth to a healthy son. With Catherine dead, Henry would be free to marry anyone else without any illegality. Apart from his mistresses, the Shelton sisters, he was romancing Jane Seymour, and gave her a locket with a miniature portrait of himself inside. Seymour, in the presence of Anne, began opening and shutting it, and Anne ripped off the locket with such force that her fingers bled. Next, Henry was unhorsed in a tournament and knocked unconscious for two hours, an incident that Anne believed led to her miscarriage five days later. She also saw Seymour sitting on Henry's lap and fell into a rage shortly before another miscarriage, which was thought to be male. Anne knew she had to produce a male heir. She knew of Henry's mistresses, but also that he would never repudiate and divorce the mother of his son. The Imperial ambassador Chapuys commented that 'she has miscarried of her saviour'. In was 29 January, the day that Catherine of Aragon was buried at Peterborough, which must have seemed a sign to Henry. Anne may have had two stillborn children after Elizabeth's birth and before the male child she miscarried in 1536. According to Anne's attendants, Henry said to her, 'I see God will not give me male children' and that he would have 'no more boys by *her*'. As Anne recovered from her miscarriage, Henry declared that he had been seduced into the marriage by means of 'sortilege', indicating deception or a spell. Stories abounded, accusing Anne Boleyn of bewitching Henry. She was to have had 'the devil's marks' all over her body, which may have been moles, if they existed at all. Other rumours were that she had a sixth finger, a third breast, warts and a large mole or goitre on her neck. His new mistress, Jane Seymour, moved into royal quarters.

Thomas Cromwell, Anne's greatest enemy, immediately began fabricating evidence to get rid of Anne and facilitate Henry's marriage to Jane Seymour. Anne gave more money to the poor of England in her three years as queen than her predecessor Catherine of Aragon did during almost twenty-four years. When Cromwell wished to transfer the money that came out of the Dissolution of the Monasteries to Henry's treasury, Anne protested as she wanted the money to go to the poor and educational resources. On her summer progress in 1535 she spent more time than Henry inquiring after how she could help the people, trying to become popular. She sewed clothing herself to distribute to the poor and personally tended to the ill on her travels. Anne also convinced Henry that the Bible should be translated into the vernacular and thus be available to the common people and not just clerics.

Anne's brother George and her friends Mark Smeaton, Sir Henry Norris, Sir Francis Weston and Sir William Brereton were arrested and taken to the Tower. Mark Smeaton was not a nobleman, so was persistently tortured until he agreed with the statement that he had had a sexual relationship with the queen. In return he was not hanged, drawn and quartered but merely beheaded. Sir Henry Norris denied everything and repeated that Anne was innocent. The main reason for his arrest was that Cromwell could confiscate his extensive estates. Anne's brother George was charged with committing adultery with the queen. Anne was arrested on 2 May 1536 and taken to the Tower. Cromwell managed the show trial. Norris, Brereton and Weston all pleaded innocent but were found guilty. Anne and George Boleyn were tried three days later separately, with Anne facing the charges of adultery, incest and high treason. George Boleyn, Sir Henry Norris, Sir William Brereton, Sir Francis Weston and Mark Smeaton were all beheaded on 17 May.

On this same day, the day before her scheduled execution, Archbishop Cranmer declared Anne's marriage to Henry to be null and void. Henry allowed Anne to escape the allotted sentence of being burnt alive. Anne was told she was instead to be beheaded with an axe on the morning of 18 May, and was then kept waiting until noon before being told she was to die the next day by the sword. Henry had summoned an expert swordsman from Calais. 'I heard say the executioner was very good and I have but a little neck,' Anne said the day before her execution, and, laughing, she put her hands round her throat. Anne had witnessed botched beheadings so had been terrified of the axe, but Jean Rombaud was so skilled that he once beheaded two criminals with a single stroke. On the morning of 19 May 1536, Anne Boleyn walked to the scaffold on Tower Green. She addressed the crowd and implied her innocence before being beheaded. Henry had not bothered to organise a funeral or a coffin for the woman he had loved, and an empty arrow chest was found for her head and body. She was buried in an unmarked grave in the chapel of St Peter ad Vincula. Her last words were, 'Oh God, have pity on my soul. Oh God, have pity on my soul.' The executioner was paid £23 to reduce Anne's suffering to a minimum and he took her head off in one stroke of his sword. In prayer, Anne's lips were still moving after her head fell into the straw.

Henry VIII stayed at Waltham Abbey whenever he went hunting in Waltham Forest. He had set out from Greenwich to Waltham Abbey with both Catherine of Aragon and Anne Boleyn in May 1528. The next time Henry visited Waltham Abbey was in July 1529, but this time he was accompanied by Anne Boleyn alone. He also took her there on progress in 1532, during which time they stayed for five days at the abbey. On 19 May 1536, Henry VIII went to Waltham Abbey alone. He was having breakfast under the shade of a large tree when he heard the sound of a cannon being fired. This informed him that Anne Boleyn had been executed. According to Moray's *History of Essex*, the king then cried out, 'Away! Unkennel the dogs!' From 30 May, Jane Seymour became queen consort, being proclaimed Queen of England on 4 June 1536, just sixteen days after Anne's beheading.

3. **Jane Seymour** (1507/9–37), reigned 1536–37
Parents: Sir John Seymour and Marjery Wentworth
Born: *c.* 1507–09, probably at Wulf (Wolf) Hall in Savernake Forest, Wiltshire
Nationality: English
Betrothed to Henry: 20 May 1536

Married Henry: 30 May 1536, Queen's Closet, Whitehall Palace, London
Children: Edward VI (1537)
Died: 24 October 1537, Hampton Court Palace
Buried: 13 November 1537, St George's Chapel, Windsor Castle

Jane Seymour was one of ten children, becoming maid-in-waiting to Catherine of Aragon and then Anne Boleyn. She remained in royal service from 1529, and claimed royal blood through descent from Edward III. The exact date on which she met the king is not known, but before her he had made another of Anne Boleyn's ladies-in-waiting his mistress: Margaret ('Madge') Shelton. Shelton was Anne Boleyn's first cousin, a girl 'very gentle of countenance' and 'soft of speech'. She was governess to Princess Elizabeth and her husband was captain of the child's guard. The affair lasted about six months in early 1535. Chapuys, the Imperial ambassador, also mentions another affair in autumn 1534. The woman's name is not known but it may have been Margaret's sister Mary. In autumn 1535, the king was on progress to Southampton with Anne Boleyn and stayed at Jane Seymour's father's home, Wulf Hall in Wiltshire, with the travelling court. He would have known Jane since around 1529, but it appears that now their relationship began. Anne drove her rival from court, but Henry was angry and threatening, and carried on the affair.

To the rest of Catholic Europe, Catherine of Aragon had always been Henry's wife. With her death in January 1536, Henry was officially widowed. He was thus free to marry again, as his union with Anne was not recognised. Just a few weeks later, Anne miscarried a male child and was widely believed to be incapable of delivering a male heir. Jane Seymour came from a respectable noble family which took its opportunity. Jane's father had been knighted in the field by Henry VII at Blackheath. He accompanied Henry VIII on his French campaign in 1513 and also the infamous Field of Cloth of Gold in 1532. Jane's father was over sixty, and it was her older brothers Edward and Thomas who stood to profit most from her rise to power. They seized – and relished – this unexpected opportunity to advance their fortunes. Jane was not particularly beautiful, but was courteous and kindly. Her family was joined by supporters who had been slighted by the Boleyn faction. On 18 April 1536, Cromwell vacated his apartments at Greenwich Palace so the Seymours could move in. Now the king could visit Jane discreetly, without anyone knowing. Cromwell's was Henry's chief adviser and Anne Boleyn's fall became inevitable.

Before Anne's execution Henry was careful to obtain a divorce, which to his eyes meant that his marriage to Jane was the first legal union of his life. On their first splendid procession through London as husband and wife they passed the Tower, where the late queen's body lay stuffed in an arrow chest, her head tucked beneath her arm. Henry also planned an equally lavish coronation, but it was prevented by an outbreak of plague. While Anne had been witty, flirtatious, stylish and passionate, and educated at the notorious French court, Jane was the pious and dutiful daughter of an old English family. When she argued for Henry to reinstate his daughter Mary, the king replied that she would do well to think of herself and the children they would have; Jane replied, with submissiveness, that she was thinking only of the king's happiness.

Jane also ordered her ladies-in-waiting to dress conservatively, wanting no one to tempt the king just as she had done. She also became mother to the princesses. Mary and Elizabeth benefited from Jane's kindness, although both had been bastardised by Henry's actions regarding their mothers. The first harsh words Henry was recorded as speaking to Jane were over religion. She sought clemency for the leaders of the Pilgrimage of Grace rebellion and said that it was perhaps God's rebuke over Henry's Dissolution of the Monasteries. Henry reminded her that the late queen had died as a result of meddling in his affairs. Luckily, Jane became pregnant a few months later, in early January 1537. Her coronation was now planned to be after the child's birth, probably late October. Henry was optimistic and, as usual, the astrologers and doctors predicted the birth of a son. Jane's labour lasted three days, and on 12 October a boy was born. Henry wept when he took this longed-for heir in his arms. The christening was held three days later and, wrapped in furs and velvet, Jane attended. Princess Mary acted as godmother to her half-brother and four-year-old Elizabeth was carried by Thomas Seymour.

Some 2,000 shots were fired from the Tower of London and bells were rung throughout the kingdom. On 18 October, Henry had his son Edward proclaimed Prince of Wales, Duke of Cornwall and Earl of Carnarvon. The Seymour brothers were given generous endowments but Jane was suffering from puerperal fever. She took to her bed again on 19 October, became delirious and died near midnight on 24 October. Henry, now increasingly obese, bald and middle-aged, displayed real grief and wore black for a year. Princess Mary was chief mourner at her stepmother's funeral but Henry did not attend. He wished to be alone with his grief. Jane Seymour was buried as a queen – unlike Catherine of Aragon, who had died as princess dowager, and Anne Boleyn, who had died divorced and disgraced. Her hearse was taken to Windsor and interred in a vault in St George's Chapel. Henry was planning a great monument there for the grave he would eventually share with Jane, but it was never built.

4. Anne of Cleves of the House of la Marck (1515–57), reigned 1537
Parents: John III, Duke of Cleves, and Maria, Duchess of Jülich-Berg
Born: 22 September 1515 in Düsseldorf, Duchy of Berg, Holy Roman Empire
Nationality: German
Married: *c.* 6 January 1540, Palace of Placentia, Greenwich
Marriage Annulled: 9 July 1540
Children: None
Died: 16 July 1557, Chelsea Old Palace or Manor, London
Buried: 4 August 1537, Westminster Abbey

Anne was born in the small north German state of Cleves, close to the border of the Netherlands. The events of the split from Rome left England isolated, and probably vulnerable. It was these circumstances that led Henry and his ministers to look at the possibility of a bride to secure an alliance. Henry also wanted to be sure he was getting a desirable bride, so he had agents in foreign courts report to him on the appearance and other qualities of various candidates. In 1539 it became politically necessary for Henry to form an alliance with the princes of Protestant Germany and what is now the Netherlands. Thomas Cromwell, shortly after Jane Seymour's death, had begun looking for a foreign bride for Henry. It was suggested that Henry marry one of the daughters of the Duke of Cleves. Cleves was seen as an important potential ally in the event that France and the Holy Roman Empire decided to move against the countries who had thrown off papal authority. Henry needed to judge whether to proceed with the marriage treaty and Holbein was dispatched to paint Anne and her sister Amelia. The tradition that Holbein's portrait flattered Anne derives from the testimony of Sir Anthony Browne, who said that Henry was so dismayed by her appearance at Rochester, having seen her pictures and heard advertisements of her beauty, that his face fell.

When Anne arrived in England, Henry thought her 'nothing so fair as had been reported'. All his life, Henry had a boyish enthusiasm for 'disguisings'. On 1 January 1540, when he went to meet Anne of Cleves for the first time in the Old Hall behind Rochester Castle, he and five of his gentlemen dressed alike in coats and hoods, disguising his identity. After a while he revealed his true identity, then abruptly left. He had taken an instant dislike to his fiancée, saying that she smelled, and he did not even bother offering her the furs he had brought as a gift to 'nourish love'. However, no one other than Henry ever described Anne as repugnant. Sir Anthony Denny, groom of the stool and one of Henry's closest companions, was told by Henry that he doubted Anne's virginity, on account of 'her brests so slacke'.

Henry tried to wriggle out of wedding Anne, but was duty bound to proceed on 6 January 1540. Anne's upbringing in Cleves had concentrated on domestic skills and not the music and literature so popular at Henry's court. Henry did not find his new bride at all attractive and is said to have called her his 'Flanders Mare'. Tension between the Duke of Cleves and the Holy Roman Empire was increasing towards war and Henry, who had dissipated his incomes, had no wish to become involved. Henry had also become attracted to the young Catherine Howard. Anne knew of Henry's past record. She testified that the marriage had never been consummated and that her previous engagement to the son of the Duke of Lorraine had not been properly broken. With the annulment, Henry designated Anne the 'king's beloved sister' and she settled down to life in England, being given properties including Hever Castle, formerly the home of Anne Boleyn. No longer married to Anne, Henry even discovered a fondness for her and they became friends. Anne attended the coronation of her former stepdaughter, Mary I, but lived away from court until her death in 1557.

5. **Catherine Howard** (1521/25–42), reigned 1540–42
Born: *c.* 1521–25 in Lambeth, London, or Horsham, Sussex

Parents: Lord Edmund Howard, third son of the Duke of Norfolk, and Jocasta 'Joyce' Culpeper
Nationality: English
Married Henry: 28 July 1540 at Oatlands Palace, Surrey
Children: None
Died: 13 February 1542, executed for high treason at Tower Green
Buried: 13 February 1542, chapel of St Peter ad Vincula, Tower of London

Catherine was Anne Boleyn's first cousin and the third of Henry's consorts to have been a member of the English gentry instead of European nobility. Catherine's father, Lord Edmund Howard, was a younger son. With ten children and no right to inheritance under primogeniture, he depended on the generosity of wealthier and more powerful relatives. In 1531, through the influence of his niece Anne Boleyn, Edmund Howard obtained a position as comptroller for Henry VIII in Calais. When her father went to Calais, Catherine Howard was sent to the home of Agnes Tilney, Dowager Duchess of Norfolk, her father's stepmother. About 1536, while living with Agnes Tilney, Catherine Howard had an unconsummated sexual relationship with a music tutor, Henry Manox. The duchess reportedly struck Catherine when she caught her with Manox. Henry Manox was replaced in young Catherine's affections by Frances Dereham, a secretary. Catherine and Dereham apparently did consummate their relationship, reportedly calling each other 'husband' and 'wife' and promising marriage, which to the Church amounted to a contract of marriage. Henry Manox heard gossip of the relationship, and reported it to the duchess, who ended the relationship.

Catherine was then sent to court to serve as a lady-in-waiting to Anne of Cleves, soon to arrive in England. This assignment was probably arranged by her uncle, Thomas Howard, Duke of Norfolk. Anne of Cleves arrived in England in December of 1539, and Henry may have first seen Catherine Howard then. At court, Catherine drew the king's attention, as he was quite quickly unhappy in his new marriage. Henry started courting Catherine, and by May was publicly giving her gifts. Anne complained of this attraction to the ambassador from her homeland. Catherine was just twenty years old. Henry was nearly fifty, expanding in girth and had an ulcerated leg which caused him difficulty in walking. After his marriage to Anne was annulled on 9 July, Henry and Catherine were married on 28 July 1540. On their wedding day, Thomas Cromwell, who had arranged the marriage of Henry to Anne of Cleves, was executed. Catherine was publicly announced as queen on 8 August.

The vivacious young girl brought back some of Henry's zest for life. The king lavished gifts on his young wife and called her his 'rose without a thorn' and the 'very jewel of womanhood'. However, Catherine soon became repulsed by her elderly, 20-stone husband and the foul-smelling ulcers on his legs, and she embarked on a liaison with Thomas Culpeper, one of Henry's favourites. Their meetings, which became known in the court but were kept from Henry, were arranged by her lady-in-waiting Lady Rochford. This was

Jane Boleyn, widow of the executed George Boleyn. She had given evidence against George at Anne Boleyn's trial. Catherine was barely literate, and wrote the following incriminating letter to Culpeper when married to the king:

> Master Culpeper, I heartily recommend me unto you, praying you to send me word how that you do. It was showed me that you was sick, the which thing troubled me very much till such time that I hear from you, praying you to send me word how that you do, for I never longed so much for a thing as I do to see you and to speak with you, the which I trust shall be shortly now ... I pray you to give me a horse for my man for I had much ado to get one and therefore I pray send me one by him and in so doing I am as I said before, and thus I take my leave of you, trusting to see you shortly again and I would you was with me now that you might see what pain I take in writing to you. Yours as long as life endures, Katheryn.

Catherine Howard became even more reckless, bringing her old lovers Henry Manox and Frances Dereham to court as her musician and secretary. Dereham bragged about their relationship, and she may have made the appointments in an attempt to silence them about their past. Catherine Howard represented a more Catholic-leaning conservative faction, and her Protestant enemy Archbishop Thomas Cranmer heard of her affairs and of her pre-contract with Dereham.

On 2 November 1541, Cranmer confronted Henry with the allegations about Catherine's past and present indiscretions. Dereham and Culpeper confessed to their part in these relationships after being tortured, and Henry abandoned Catherine, not seeing her again after 6 November. Catherine was charged by Cranmer with 'unchastity' before her marriage, and with concealing her pre-contract and her indiscretions from the king before their marriage, thereby committing treason. She was also accused of adultery, which for a queen consort was also treason. Upon 22 November 1541, it was proclaimed at Hampton Court that Catherine had 'forfeited the honour and title of queen', and was from then on to be known only as the Lady Catherine Howard. Under this title she was executed for high treason three months later. The marriage was never annulled. Culpeper and Dereham were executed on 10 December and their heads displayed on London Bridge. Culpeper was beheaded, possibly because of his former closeness to the king, but Dereham was hanged, drawn and quartered.

On 21 January 1542, Parliament passed an Act of attainder making Catherine's actions an executable offence. She was taken to the Tower on 10 February, Henry signed the Act of attainder, and she was executed on the morning of 13 February.

She was buried without any marker in the chapel of St Peter ad Vincula. Jane Boleyn, Lady Rochford, was also beheaded and buried with Catherine Howard.

6. **Catherine Parr** (*c.* 1512–48), reigned 1543–47
Born: *c.* 1512 at Kendal Castle, Cumbria, or Blackfriars, London

Parents: Sir Thomas Parr of Kendal, Westmorland, and Maud Green
Nationality: English
Married:(1): Edward Borough, son of Baron Borough of Gainsborough, 1529
Married (2): John Nevill, Baron Latimer of Snape Castle, 1534
Married Henry: Henry VIII, Queen's Closet, Hampton Court Palace, 1543
Married (4): Thomas Seymour, 1547
Children: Mary Seymour (1548)
Died: 5 September 1548
Buried: 5 September 1548, St Mary's Chapel, Sudeley Castle, Gloucestershire

Her name has been alternately spelled Catharine, Catherine, Katharine or Kateryn, but throughout this book I have used Catherine. She was the eldest daughter of Sir Thomas Parr and his wife Maud Green, both of whom were at the court of Henry VIII, Maud having been a lady-in-waiting to Catherine of Aragon and having named her daughter after her. Catherine Parr was fluent in French, Latin and Italian and began learning Spanish when she became queen. Catherine's first husband died around 1533 and her second, Lord Latimer, died in March 1543, leaving her a widow for the second time, now at the age of thirty-one.

Using her late mother's friendship with Catherine of Aragon, she took the opportunity to renew her friendship with the former queen's daughter, Lady Mary Tudor. By 16 February 1543, Catherine had established herself as part of Mary's household, and it was there that Catherine caught the attention of the king. Although she had begun a romantic friendship with Sir Thomas Seymour, the brother of the late queen, she saw it as her duty to accept Henry's proposal over Seymour's. Seymour was given a posting in Brussels to remove him from the king's court. Just twenty people attended the wedding to Henry.

Catherine enjoyed a close relationship with Henry's three children and was personally involved in the education of Elizabeth and Edward. She was influential in Henry's passing of the Third Succession Act of 1543, which restored his daughters, Mary and Elizabeth, to the line of succession. Because of her strong Protestant faith, Catherine provoked the enmity of powerful Catholic officials, who sought to turn the king against her. Catherine and her ladies were known to have possessed banned books, which was grounds for arrest and execution on charges of heresy. To gain evidence against the queen, Anne Askew, a well-known Protestant, was questioned and tortured, but refused to recant her faith or give evidence against Catherine and her ladies. However, there was enough other evidence against the queen to issue a warrant for her arrest in 1546. The warrant was accidentally dropped, and someone loyal to the queen saw it and then quickly told her about it. After learning of the arrest warrant Catherine became ill, either as delaying tactic or from a genuine panic attack. Henry went to see her and chastised her for her outspokenness about the reformed religion. He told her that she was forgetting her place by instructing him on such matters. Catherine's response in her defence was that she was only arguing with him on these issues so she could be instructed by him, and to take his mind off other troubles. She and the king were reconciled, although there were rumours that Henry was looking for another wife.

Charles Brandon, the son of William Brandon, Henry VII's standard bearer who was killed at Bosworth, had married Henry VII's daughter Mary against Henry VIII's wishes, but had been rehabilitated to become the king's friend and Duke of Suffolk. After Mary's death, Suffolk married the beautiful Catherine Willoughby. Suffolk died on 22 August 1545, and it was rumoured that King Henry had considered marrying Catherine Willoughby as his seventh wife while he was still married to Catherine Parr, her close friend. The Duchess of Suffolk was still only in her mid-twenties. In February 1546, Van der Delft wrote, 'I hesitate to report there are rumours of a new queen. Some attribute it to the sterility of the present queen, while others say that there will be no change during the present war. Madame Suffolk is much talked about and is in great favour; but the king shows no alteration in his behaviour to the queen, although she is said to be annoyed by the rumour.' The friendship of the two Catherines remained strong, and after Henry VIII's death in January 1547 the duchess helped fund the publication of one of Catherine Parr's books.

Catherine probably expected to play some role in the regency for the new nine-year-old king, Edward VI, but this was not to be. Only a few months after Henry's death Catherine secretly married Thomas Seymour, and the quickness and secret nature of the union caused a scandal. However, Catherine was still able to take guardianship of Princess Elizabeth, and Seymour purchased the wardship of the king's cousin Lady Jane Grey. During this time, rumours of a relationship between Elizabeth and Seymour arose and Elizabeth was sent to another household in the spring of 1548.

After three previous marriages and at the age of thirty-six, Catherine was pregnant for the first time. In June 1548, she moved to Sudeley Castle in Gloucestershire to await the birth of her child. She gave birth to Mary on 30 August but fell ill with puerperal fever, dying on 5 September. Catherine was buried, with Lady Jane Grey as the chief mourner, in the chapel at Sudeley Castle, where the tomb can still be visited today. Her only daughter, Mary Seymour, died in childhood.

7

King Edward VI: Edward the Pious, 1547–1553

Parents: Henry VIII and Jane Seymour
Born: 12 October 1537 at Hampton Court
Ascended to the throne: 28 January 1547, aged 9 years 3 months
Crowned: 19 February 1547 at Westminster Abbey
Married: Never married
Siblings: Mary I, Elizabeth I, Henry Fitzroy (illegitimate, but recognised)
Died: 6 July 1553 at the Palace of Placentia, Greenwich, aged 15 years, 8 months and 23 days
Death proclaimed: 10 July 1553
Reigned: 6 years and 5 months
Buried: Henry VII's Chapel, Westminster Abbey

The motherless prince was the only male Tudor heir of his generation. He had two sisters, and Henry VIII's sisters Mary and Margaret themselves had several daughters. If Edward died without a male heir, the throne would pass to a woman and the Tudor dynasty would end. After Jane Seymour's death following childbirth on 24 October 1537, Henry had married Anne of Cleves and Catherine Howard before wedding Catherine Parr on 12 July 1543. Edward Tudor had lived in secure seclusion for almost six years until his father married the widowed Catherine Parr. Henry VIII had done all he could to protect his son's health, knowing that his own brother Arthur had died as a teenager. Henry demanded exacting standards of security and cleanliness in his son's household, stressing that Edward was 'this whole realm's most precious jewel'. Visitors described the prince as a contented child.

Edward began his formal education at the age of six, learning languages, philosophy, geometry and how to play the lute and virginal. His religious education was probably devised by Cranmer to favour the reforming agenda, which was reinforced by the fiercely Protestant Catherine Parr. He was provided with toys and comforts, including his own troupe of minstrels. Henry took a keen interest in his son's education and Catherine Parr became like a mother to Edward and his sister Elizabeth, who had also never known a mother. Edward indeed called Catherine his 'most dear mother', and in September 1546 wrote, 'I received so many benefits from you that my mind can hardly grasp them.'

Edward was said to be normally strong, healthy, studious and intelligent, and fond of hunting and hawking. Other children were brought to play with Edward and he shared his formal education with the sons of nobles, 'appointed to attend upon him'. Edward grew close to his half-sister Elizabeth, just four years older than him, with whom he shared a household for some years. However, his much older half-sister, Mary, was an equally fervent Catholic. Mary believed that Edward was a pawn of Protestant heretics. Throughout his childhood and youth, Edward was said to have read twelve chapters of scripture daily and enjoyed sermons, and was called a 'godly imp' by John Foxe. He came to be depicted during his life and afterwards as a new Josiah, the biblical king who destroyed the idols of Baal. Edward once asked Catherine Parr to persuade Lady Mary Tudor 'to attend no longer to foreign dances and merriments which do not become a most Christian princess'. Thus Edward became known as 'the Pious'.

King Henry's death had been expected for at least a year, and 1546 saw the various court factions intriguing for power. The religious conservatives lacked leaders, while the Protestant radicals were younger and more energetic, being led by Edward Seymour, Earl of Hertford, and John Dudley, Viscount Lisle, the son of Henry VII's former minister Edmund, who had been executed by Henry VIII. The king's main administrator, William Paget, also aligned with them, and the young Edward VI was himself a deeply committed Protestant with a strong personality.

Upon Henry VIII's death, Edward Seymour and William Paget agreed to delay the announcement until arrangements had been made for a smooth succession. Seymour rode to collect Edward from Hertford and brought him to Enfield, where Elizabeth Tudor was living. He and Elizabeth were told of the death of their father and heard a reading of the will. The Lord Chancellor, Thomas Wriothesley, announced Henry's death to Parliament on 31 January 1547, and general proclamations of Edward's succession were ordered. Soon after, the nobles of the realm made their obeisance to Edward at the Tower and Edward Seymour was announced as Protector, subsequently being appointed Duke of Somerset. Henry VIII was buried at Windsor on 16 February, in the same tomb as Jane Seymour, as he had wished. Edward VI was crowned at Westminster Abbey on 20 February. The ceremonies were shortened in consideration of his young age, and also because the Reformation had rendered some of them inappropriate.

Somerset's faction tampered with Henry's will, which an Act of Parliament had given the force of statute. Originally, the will had stipulated that if Edward, Mary and Elizabeth died childless, the English crown would have reverted to the Stuart descendants of Margaret Tudor, Queen of Scotland and Henry VII's eldest surviving child with issue. However, the new will provided that the succession followed Edward. If he died without heirs it would then pass to Mary, then to Elizabeth, and then to the Greys, thus cutting the Stuarts out of the succession. The exclusion of the Stuarts was probably authentically Henry's wish. Since childhood he had hated his sister, who died in 1541.

This smooth takeover was largely the work of William Paget, but it primarily benefited Seymour. Following his appointment as Duke of Somerset and Lord Protector, he forced out his main enemy, Thomas Wriothesley. After handing out large rewards from the Crown's wealth to friendly councillors, Somerset thereupon ignored the regency council and ruled as an autocrat.

Since he was a minor, Edward was placed ostensibly under the control of this regency council. Neither the dowager queen, Catherine, nor Edward VI's sisters were permitted to see the new king. Edward was Duke of Cornwall from his birth, but he was never proclaimed Prince of Wales, and was only nine when he succeeded his father as King of England and Ireland and Supreme Head of the English Church. When Edward came to the throne, his half-sisters Mary and Elizabeth were thirty-one and fourteen years old respectively. Edward was king for only six years, and, by the time of his death at the age of fifteen, England had witnessed the full-scale introduction of Protestantism.

Somerset held power from 1547 to 1549. His main rival was his brother, Thomas Seymour, who began visiting his nephew Edward VI, attempting to gain his affections by giving him presents and money. Since Somerset was strict with his nephew and kept him constantly short of money, the king was grateful for the gifts. Thomas Seymour urged Edward to throw off the Protector within two years and 'bear rule as other kings do', but Edward, schooled to defer to the council, failed to cooperate. In the spring of 1547, using Edward's support to prevent Somerset's opposition, Thomas Seymour secretly married Henry VIII's widow Catherine Parr, whose Protestant household included the eleven-year-old Lady Jane Grey and the thirteen-year-old Lady Elizabeth Tudor. Thomas secured the guardianship of Lady Jane Grey, telling her parents he would arrange her marriage to the young king. Thus, he came into control of two of Henry VIII's heirs.

Somerset viewed Scotland as an easy target which he could use to increase his popularity, as the death of James V had left the infant Mary, Queen of Scots, on the throne. Somerset was an efficient soldier, and led a punitive expedition against the Scots for their failure to fulfil their promise to betroth Mary, Queen of Scots, to Edward. He destroyed the Scots army at the Battle of Pinkie Cleugh on 10 September 1547. It was part of the conflict initiated by Henry VIII, known as the 'Rough Wooing', to try and unite England and Scotland by marriage between Edward VI and Queen Mary. It was seen as the first 'modern' battle in the British Isles.

It was a catastrophic defeat for Scotland, and became known there as 'Black Saturday'. When the Scottish army was halted, it came under heavy fire on three sides from ships' cannon, Somerset's artillery, arquebusiers and archers, to which they could not reply. It was the first British battle decided by firearms and cannon. However, Somerset failed to follow this up with satisfactory peace terms, instead forcing the Scots into the arms of the French. The infant Queen Mary was smuggled out of Scotland, and under the terms of the Treaty of Haddington, July 1548, Mary married the Dauphin, Francis. The French sent a large army to Scotland, cutting off the isolated English garrisons, and also besieged English-held Boulogne. The war was prohibitively expensive and forced further debasement of the coinage.

In summer 1548, a pregnant Catherine Parr discovered Thomas Seymour embracing Lady Elizabeth Tudor, so transferred Elizabeth from her household. Catherine Parr died in childbirth in September, and Thomas Seymour resumed his attentions to Elizabeth by letter, planning to marry her. Elizabeth may have been receptive, but, like Edward, was unready to agree to anything unless permitted by the council. By 1548, the regency council was becoming aware of Thomas Seymour's bid for power. Somerset tried to save his brother from ruin, calling a council meeting so that Thomas might explain himself, but Thomas did not appear. On the night of 16 January 1549, perhaps to take the young king away in his own custody, Thomas was caught trying to break into the king's apartments at Hampton Court Palace.

Thomas Seymour had forged keys to Edward's apartment at Hampton Court and, in the middle of the night, decided to risk all on kidnapping the king. He entered through the privy garden, but in the room outside Edward's bedroom he woke up the king's pet spaniel. The dog began barking, and Seymour shot it. A yeoman of the guard appeared, demanding an explanation, as Edward stood in his bedroom doorway. Not yet twelve, the boy was in his nightshirt and clearly terrified. Seymour told them he had come to test the effectiveness of the king's guards, but the dog had attacked him so he was forced to shoot. The guard allowed him leave but, upon learning of the incident, the council decided to confine Seymour to the Tower while they investigated. Seymour's being caught outside the king's bedroom at night with a loaded pistol also cast suspicion on Elizabeth's involvement with Thomas. The official charge was attempting to murder Edward. On 18 January, the council officially sent agents to question everyone Seymour had conspired with, including Princess Elizabeth and all her household. Edward, whom Seymour was accused of planning to marry to Lady Jane Grey, testified about the secret pocket money from the earl. Elizabeth showed great courage in her answers, managing to convince the council that she was not part of any plot to kill the king and herself marry Seymour to take the throne.

Seymour refused to appear privately before the council, haughtily saying that he would settle for nothing less than an open trial. However, the council had him arrested on various charges, including embezzlement at the Bristol mint. On 22 February, the council officially indicted him of thirty-three charges of treason. Seymour had no open trial in which to make his case and a Act of attainder was passed on 4 March, approved by Parliament and King Edward. Somerset delayed signing the death warrant of his brother, so the council, led by Dudley, went to the young king for his signature. Thus on 20 March, the king's uncle Thomas Seymour, Baron Sudeley, was beheaded at the Tower of London. Somerset's delay in condemning his brother resulted in growing tensions in the council. His family had been disgraced, and he was angry at the councillors for proceeding so rapidly with the matter. His own position as the king's main adviser now was in danger.

The 1540s was a time of acute price inflation, and the purchasing power of silver was falling at the same time as the actual silver content of English coins was decreasing. Population increase was outpacing agricultural production, so by 1547 the cost of food was 45 per cent higher than in 1540. Wages could not keep pace, and their real value fell by about 50 per cent over the decade, so anyone living on a fixed income suffered and only large farmers profited. Debasement of the currency led to a fall in value of the pound abroad. This should have helped English exports, but cloth exports did not grow, probably because of war across Europe. Protestant bishops such as Hugh Latimer preached that these economic problems resulted from moral failings. The 1547 Poor Law was passed to try to stop the rural poor leaving their parishes. For a first offence, able-bodied vagrants were branded with a 'V' and sentenced to two years of servitude, in other words slavery. For a second offence, the punishment was death. There is no evidence that the law was enforced, however. In 1548, Somerset tried ineffectively to prevent the enclosure of land, but there were agricultural riots in the spring and summer.

Somerset was careful not to officially declare the country Protestant. With the Franco-Scottish alliance a constant problem, the Protector did not wish to alienate the neutral Holy Roman Emperor, Charles V. Somerset wanted to avoid the alliance between France, Spain and Scotland that Henry VIII's ministers had feared. He therefore allowed Princess Mary Tudor, Charles's cousin, to celebrate Catholic services despite Edward VI's opposition. However, his government gradually introduced a stronger degree of Protestantism. Unlicensed preaching was banned on 24 April 1548, and all preaching was banned just five months later. Instead, clergy had to recite twelve government-approved homilies from the pulpit. They declaimed against good works and purgatory, while advocating salvation through faith alone. Images were later outlawed, altars were removed, relics, statues, effigies and stained glass were destroyed and private Masses proscribed.

Somerset and Cranmer became the architects of the conversion from Catholicism, and the Church of England became more explicitly Protestant, assisted by Edward's strong feelings. The Book of Common Prayer was imposed by the Act of Uniformity in 1549, introducing Protestant doctrine while retaining traditional ceremonies. Marriage of the clergy was allowed, and Somerset abolished the medieval laws against heresy and allowed the printing of the Scriptures in English. He also abolished the chantries, endowments that paid stipends to priests to pray for the dead. Expressing Protestant opposition to belief in Purgatory and prayers for the dead, the Crown now seized the proceeds from these endowments.

The imposition of the Book of Common Prayer, replacing Latin services with English, led to rebellions in the West Country. Rebels were supported by conservative clergy and joined by some local gentry. Its date of introduction was 9 June, and the rebellion began on 10 June. The rebels intended to march on London, but the need to besiege government forces in Exeter delayed their advance. Exactly one month later rebellion also broke out in Norfolk, where agricultural enclosures had created serious ill feelings between gentlemen and peasants. The rebels were led by Robert Kett, a tanner and yeoman farmer who wanted the government to introduce agrarian reform. He believed that the central government would support them against the local nobles, as they were Protestant in sympathy. Kett, an able military commander, captured Norwich and easily repulsed the first government attacks. However, once the rebellion in the south-west had been suppressed, the government turned its full attention to Norfolk. John Dudley, Earl of Warwick, bloodily defeated the rebels on 17 August 1549 – about 3,000 died in battle and about fifty were hanged afterwards.

The other members of the Privy Council now increasingly doubted Somerset's competence, and these 1549 rebellions, along with his unsuccessful war with France, confirmed their view. They disliked his arrogance and his attempts to restrict their access to Edward VI. Somerset took Edward to Windsor as the Privy Council controlled London, resigning as Protector on 11 October 1549 when he saw how isolated he was in council. John Dudley, now Duke of Northumberland, overthrew him in 1551. Somerset had been in absolute control over the council and was popular with the poor through his promoting reform of agricultural laws, creating fixed rents and trying to abolish enclosures. He had also attempted to reform the judicial system in favour of equality for all. Both these factors made him unpopular with his fellow nobles on the council, along with the problem that he was too moderate to satisfy any faction. For instance, he would not allow anyone to be tortured or burned over religious matters. His tolerance of the poor and Catholics was unwelcome among his peers.

However, while Somerset was criticising the rents charged by his fellow nobles, he was spending massive amounts of public money. His London residence, Somerset House, cost an incredible £10,000, and other homes were built to enhance his reputation as Lord Protector. After five years in power, Somerset had effectively cemented the new religion in England while avoiding foreign war or invasion, but also offended virtually every noble in the country. John Dudley, Earl of Warwick and soon to become Duke of Northumberland, had manoeuvred Somerset out of power, taking his place but not the title of Lord Protector. Northumberland treated the fifteen-year-old Edward as an adult, unlike Somerset who had treated the king like a child. He encouraged Edward VI to proclaim his majority and formally become king.

Northumberland was effectively in power between 1550 and 1553, and used the Privy Council to govern. He even invited Somerset back to the council, but then grew suspicious that Somerset and Sir William Paget were plotting against him. Northumberland fabricated charges against the unfortunate Somerset, who was executed on 22 January 1552, an event dispassionately mentioned by Edward VI in his diary thus: 'The Duke of Somerset had his head cut off on Tower Hill between eight and nine o'clock in the morning.' Edward had seen both of his mother's brothers now executed in the last four years. William Paget kept his life but was forced to retire. Protestant reform increased, with the new Prayer Book of 1552 being definitively Protestant. Altars were turned into tables, most remaining religious imagery destroyed, and religious orthodoxy was enforced by a more stringent Act of Uniformity.

One of Northumberland's first actions was to end the wars with France and Scotland initiated by Somerset. He surrendered the besieged town of Boulogne and withdrew the English garrisons from Scotland. Edward VI also surrendered all claim to marriage with Mary, Queen of Scots. Northumberland's intention was now focussed upon preventing the Catholic Mary Tudor from succeeding Edward VI. He knew that Henry VIII's will and the normal laws of inheritance provided that Mary should succeed to the throne if Edward VI died childless, and the king was not known for his vigorous health. The nobility had profited immensely from the Dissolution of the Monasteries and none of them wished for the reinstatement of papal taxation under a Catholic queen. They were determined to keep their land grants, gold plate, silver chalices and other treasures. As Lord President of the Council, Northumberland worked hard to influence Edward as the young king was ailing from 1552. Northumberland hurriedly married his son Lord Guilford Dudley to Lady Jane Grey, one of Henry VIII's great-nieces and a claimant to the throne. In May 1553, it was known that Edward was dying. Under Northumberland's influence, Edward removed his two sisters, Mary and Elizabeth, from the succession and instead made his cousin Lady Jane Grey his successor.

Edward died an agonising death at just fifteen, possibly from a combination of tuberculosis and measles. He died at Placentia Palace on the Thames in Greenwich, and his last words were said to have been, 'Oh my Lord God, defend this realm from papistry and maintain Thy true religion.' By Edward's new order of succession, Mary Tudor was again made illegitimate and the throne was passed to Northumberland's daughter-in-law Lady Jane Grey. Edward died on 6 July 1553. His death was kept secret for four days, not publicly proclaimed until 10 July 1553. However, Jane Grey was only queen for a few days until, with overwhelming popular support, Mary Tudor took the throne.

8

Lady Jane Grey: The Nine Days' Queen Who Never Was, 1553

Parents: Henry Grey, Duke of Suffolk, and Lady Frances Brandon
Born: 1536 or 1537 in Bradgate Park, Leicester, or London
Deposed: 19 July 1553
Ascended to the throne: De facto 6 July 1533, proclaimed 10 July 1553, aged 16 or 17
Married: 25 May 1553 at Durham Place, the Duke of Northumberland's town mansion in London
Spouse: Lord Guilford (Guildford) Dudley (*c.* 1535–54)
Siblings: Lady Catherine Grey (1540–68), Lady Mary Grey (1545–78)
Children: None
Executed: 12 February 1554 at the Tower of London, aged 16 or 17
Buried: 12 February 1554, chapel of St Peter ad Vincula

Jane Grey was an heiress to the English throne because her maternal grandmother was Princess Mary Tudor, the daughter of Henry VII. After the death of her first husband, King Louis XII of France, in 1515, Mary had secretly wed her true love, Charles Brandon. Brandon was Henry VIII's best friend, having been created Duke of Suffolk in 1514. Under the terms of the Third Act of Succession (1544) and Henry VIII's last will and testament (1547), the Suffolk line would inherit the throne if Henry VIII's children died childless. In other words, the throne would pass to Edward VI, but if he died childless, and then Mary and Elizabeth died childless, the throne passed to Lady Frances Brandon, Suffolk's wife. Her daughter Jane Grey was the next in line.

In 1552, with Edward VI's health rapidly failing, there was a succession crisis. According to Parliament and Henry VIII's will, Mary Tudor was next in line. However, she was Catholic, in her late thirties. Edward was a devout Protestant and did not want Catholicism restored in England. Urged on by self-interested advisers led by Northumberland, Edward removed Mary from the succession on the grounds of her illegitimacy, as she had been declared so by Parliament in 1532. However, if Edward removed Mary, he also had to remove Elizabeth even though she was a Protestant. Elizabeth had also been declared a bastard by Parliament, in 1536. In his Device for the Succession, written in his own hand, Edward wrote that they were both 'illegitimate and not lawfully begotten'.

Edward thereby removed the succession from the heirs of Henry VIII and gave it to the heirs of Henry's younger sister Mary. The elder sister of Henry VIII was Margaret Tudor, and her ten-year-old granddaughter Mary, Queen of Scots, had a better claim by all the accepted laws of primogeniture but was a Catholic. The situation was unprecedented, as all of the possible candidates for the throne were women. Because of the secret marriage of Mary Tudor and Charles Brandon, the first woman to rule England in her own right would be Jane Grey.

Jane was raised, with her two sisters, at Bradgate on the edge of Leicester's Charnwood Forest. Jane's nurse was a woman called Mrs Ellen and would remain with her until Jane's execution. In March 1547 Lady Jane Grey entered the household of the dowager queen, Catherine Parr. Catherine Parr had retired from court upon Edward VI's accession, living in her dower manor, Chelsea. She had planned to live with Thomas Seymour, Edward VI's uncle, the man she had longed to marry before Henry laid claim to her. She also brought with her the thirteen-year-old Princess Elizabeth Tudor.

At Catherine Parr's house, Jane Grey became devoutly committed to Protestantism. Thomas Seymour began flirting with the young Elizabeth, and received £2,000 from Jane Grey's father in return for a guarantee that Jane would marry King Edward. Elizabeth was sent away from Seymour's attentions, and Catherine died after childbirth in 1548. The red-haired Jane Grey, small for her age, acted as chief mourner. Her parents wrote to Thomas Seymour, consoling him on the loss of his wife and saying that Jane should now be sent home, as Catherine had died. Seymour delayed any action. He had been boasting about his intent to destroy his overbearing brother Edward, Lord Somerset, and he had encouraged gossip that he would marry Princess Elizabeth. On 17 January 1549, Thomas Seymour was arrested at Seymour Place in London. Jane Grey was immediately brought home by her alarmed parents. On 20 March 1549, Thomas Seymour was executed on Tower Hill. His brother, the Lord Protector Edward Seymour, was later also executed, being replaced as the main power in the realm by John Dudley, Duke of Northumberland.

European Protestants were hopeful that Edward VI would marry Jane Grey, who was now fourteen, but Edward was in serious discussions regarding the French princess Elisabeth. In spring 1552, Edward fell ill. Northumberland and Edward's other advisers could not allow the Catholic Mary Tudor to succeed him. Jane's parents agreed to her marrying Northumberland's eldest son, Lord Guildford Dudley, and in late April or early May their betrothal was announced. Jane had protested against the marriage, but was persuaded by 'the urgency of her mother and the violence of her father'. On 25 May 1553, Jane married Guildford at the Dudleys' London residence, Durham House, one of the great homes of Tudor England.

Edward realised he was dying, and in late 1552 or early 1553 he began his Device for the Succession. At first he left the throne to Lady Frances Grey and her male heirs, then to Jane Grey and her male heirs. However it was evident that Frances Grey would have no more children, and that none of her daughters would bear children in time. Thus the dying king simply left the throne to 'L. Jane and her heires masles'. To gain government support, Northumberland spent June 1553 persuading the Privy Council, judiciary and various churchmen to endorse Edward's device. The Lord Chief Justice, Sir Edward Montague, and the Archbishop of Canterbury, Thomas Cranmer, were unhappy, but Northumberland accused them of being traitors, and the king ordered them to obey. Thus the letters patent for the Limitation of the Crown were endorsed with the Great Seal on 21 June. They were recognised by the Lord Chancellor, the Privy Councillors, twenty-two peers of the realm, the Lord Mayor of London, various aldermen and sheriffs, the secretaries of state (including William Cecil, Elizabeth I's great statesman) and various judges and churchmen. Edward VI did not live long after this, dying on 6 July 1553 after months of pain.

Dudley, in his capacity as President of the Council, announced Edward's death to Jane, who was stunned when named his successor. The Lords of the Council took a solemn oath to shed their blood in defence of her claim. Jane said a prayer, and stated that if it was God's will that she be queen, then she would trust in God to help her govern England for His glory. Edward's death was kept secret until 10 July 1553, when the new queen was taken in full state along the Thames from Syon House to Westminster and the Tower of London. It was custom that all new sovereigns must come to the Tower and take possession of it at the beginning of their reign.

Jane was visited by the Lord Treasurer, the Marquess of Winchester, who brought a selection of the royal jewels for her to try on. Among them was the crown, and Winchester asked her to check if it fitted properly. Jane refused, as she seemed to have realised the extent of Northumberland's plotting to manipulate Edward. He knew that the devout Protestant king wanted the throne to go to his equally devout cousin Jane. However, Northumberland wanted his own son crowned king, with Jane's royal blood being used to maintain his control of England, transforming his family into royalty. The angry Jane Grey told those assembled that she would gladly make her husband Guildford a duke, but that he would never be king. Later that evening, the Sheriff of London and various heralds and trumpeters marched to the Eleanor cross in Cheapside to proclaim Jane queen, but the announcement was supposedly met with silence. The people were expecting a different queen.

However, Northumberland controlled London, the Tower (with its royal apartments and armoury), the Treasury and the Navy. No councillors had offered any resistance to Jane's proclamation as queen. Her only rival was Mary Tudor, thirty-seven, often ill and with no organised support or wealth.

Mary's situation was so desperate that her champion, the Emperor Charles V, urged his ambassador to be friendly with Northumberland. He wanted Northumberland's promise to protect Mary. It seemed as if Jane Grey was to be secure as queen. In early July, Northumberland had sent a summons for Mary to come to her brother Edward's deathbed. She set out from Hunsdon Palace in Hertfordshire, but had not travelled far before a message reached her that the summons was a trap. Whoever sent the message altered British history. Mary immediately turned back and, with half a dozen attendants, went to Kenninghall in East Anglia. She had allies there and was near ports to sail for safety in the Spanish Netherlands. Northumberland sent his son Robert Dudley after her, but Mary evaded capture. Upon 9 July, three days after Edward's death, Northumberland was forced to act without her in his captivity. The Bishop of London, Nicholas Ridley, preached at St Paul's Cross, calling Mary and Elizabeth bastards, singling out Mary as a papist who would destroy the true religion and make England the pawn of foreign powers. The next day, Jane was proclaimed queen.

However, on that day the council received a letter from Mary. It expressed her surprise that they had not announced her brother's death to her, his heir. They were commanded to proclaim her queen in London. The councillor responded by reminding her of her illegitimacy and inability to inherit 'the Crown Imperial of this realm'. They wrote that she must demonstrate her obedience to the 'Sovereign Lady Queen Jane' and turn herself over to the authorities. The Spanish envoys did not respond to Mary's desperate pleas for help; she was helpless. It looked as if flight was her only option.

Northumberland did not realise how weak Mary's position was, and tried urgently to convert her potential supporters to his side. Mary was not the only one affected. Princess Elizabeth Tudor knew that her own claim to the crown would be null if Jane Grey was recognised as queen, and kept a deliberately diplomatic low profile, neither supporting nor rejecting Queen Jane. Dudley marched to seek support, while somehow the country turned against him. Whereas Somerset had tried to be fair to the people, Northumberland was seen as siding with the nobles. He was not popular, and there was a groundswell of opinion that it was not fair that the rightful queen was in danger from him and his army. While the nobles had backed the powerful Northumberland, Norwich, one of the wealthiest towns in England, declared Mary queen, as did Colchester, Devon and Oxfordshire. Mary was in Framlingham Castle in Suffolk, and Northumberland sent six royal ships to its port to cut off Mary's possible escape. All the ships deserted and proclaimed Mary queen. Men were ordered by their lords to join Northumberland's army but refused.

When the news had reached London that the ships had deserted Northumberland, most of the councillors decided to change sides. On 18 July, most of Lady Jane's councillors left the Tower, pretending to visit the French ambassador, but instead went to the Imperial embassy, and assured Charles V's envoys that they had always been loyal to Mary. They said that they had been physically kept prisoner by Northumberland, and had been forced to declare Jane queen. However, they had freed themselves and wanted to proclaim Mary Queen of England. They did this around five o'clock in the evening, on 19 July, and Londoners celebrated wildly. All foreign ambassadors were astounded, and the French envoy wrote, 'The atmosphere of this country and the nature of its people are so changeable that I am compelled to make my despatches correspondingly wavering and contradictory.'

Jane's father went to her as she ate supper that night and told her that she was deposed. They took down the cloth of estate from above her head. He ordered his men to leave their weapons and then went to Tower Hill, proclaiming Mary queen. He then left for his London residence, leaving Jane Grey alone in the Tower as a prisoner. Mary was riding to London, now accepted as queen. Northumberland was arrested and his entire family was taken to the Tower. As they were being marched through the streets, the crowd pelted them with filth and insults. On 3 August, Mary made her state entry into London. As she rode past cheering crowds, clad in purple velvet and rich jewels, Jane Grey was in prison, along with her husband and her father-in-law. Mary began arranging her marriage to Philip of Spain, the son and heir of Charles V. Renard wrote, 'As to Jane of Suffolk, whom they tried to make Queen, she [Mary] could not be induced to consent that she should die.' Mary believed her cousin was innocent of any intrigue, never having intended to be queen, and was unwilling to punish her.

Northumberland was condemned to death, but Mary gave in to immense pressure and ordered Jane and Northumberland's four sons to stand trial. They all pleaded guilty to the charge of high treason. Sentence was passed against them; the men would be hanged, drawn and quartered and Jane would be burnt or beheaded at the queen's pleasure. However, Renard reported in his subsequent dispatches that 'it is believed that Jane will not die,' and, a week later, 'As for Jane, I am told her life is safe.' Meanwhile, her parents had left the Protestant Church. Henry Grey was forced to pay a £20,000 fine but was given a general pardon and returned to court. His wife Frances was Queen Mary's favourite and their two daughters, Catherine and Mary Grey, were her ladies-in-waiting. In fact, Frances Grey was shown great favour at court, even gaining precedence over Princess Elizabeth. Most observers believed Jane would soon be pardoned and released, free to join her family at court. The Greys seemed to be recovering their status, but Mary's desperate desire to wed Philip of Spain was soon to have tragic consequences. Thomas Wyatt's rebellion of January and February 1554 against Queen Mary I's plans to marry Philip led directly to the execution of both Jane and her husband.

The date of the execution was set for Friday 9 February 1554, but Mary, who hated executing her cousin, tried one last time to save her soul. She sent John Feckenham, Dean of St Paul's, to sway Jane to the Catholic faith. She rebutted his arguments, and the executions were delayed until 12 February. The sixteen-year-old Jane chose her dress, composed her speech, and appointed the two members of her household who would accompany her and dispose of her body. She watched her husband's execution from her window; Guildford died with great courage and she saw his blood-splattered body driven to St Peter ad Vincula, his head wrapped in a cloth beside the body. Since she was a princess of royal blood, her execution was private. The executioner swung his axe and severed her head. Blood splattered across the scaffold and many of the attendants. The executioner then lifted her head and said, 'So perish all the Queen's enemies. Behold, the head of a traitor.' Permission had to be granted for her burial at St Peter ad Vincula since the church had recently become Catholic again. Feckenham had to go to court for the permission, so Jane's body lay exposed for almost four hours, spread across blood-soaked straw. The French ambassador reported seeing it there hours after the execution. Her attendants kept watch, though they were not allowed to cover the corpse. Finally, Jane's body was laid to rest between the bodies of Anne Boleyn and Catherine Howard – two other beheaded queens.

9

Queen Mary I, or 'Unbloody Mary': Queen Consort of Spain, 1553–1558

Parents: Henry VIII and Catherine of Aragon
Born: 18 February 1516 at Palace of Placentia, Greenwich
Ascended to the throne: 19 July 1553, aged 37 years 5 months
Crowned: 1 October at Westminster Abbey
Married: Prince Philip of Spain (1527–98), 25 July 1554 at Winchester Cathedral
Queen Consort of Spain: 16 January 1556 – 17 November 1558
Siblings: Edward VI, Elizabeth I, Henry Fitzroy (illegitimate, but recognised)
Children: None
Died: 17 November 1558 at St James's Palace, aged 42 years 9 months
Reigned: 5 years and 4 months
Buried: Westminster Abbey

Mary was England's first female ruler in her own right, without a male consort or acting as regent for an infant son. The only previous candidate, Empress Matilda (1102–67), Henry I's heir, was expelled by the English barons and her cousin Stephen of Blois was made king. (Indeed, Matilda was never formally declared Queen of England, but instead was titled 'Lady of the English'.) Henry VIII was pleased with Mary's birth in 1516, proudly displaying the infant Mary to visiting ambassadors and noblemen, while expecting that a male heir would soon follow. She was considered one of the most important European princesses and Henry used her as a pawn in political negotiations. Mary's mother, Catherine of Aragon, was deeply devoted to her as she was Catherine's only child to reach maturity. Catherine was the youngest daughter of Ferdinand of Aragon and Isabella of Castile, the 'Catholic Kings' who united Spain geographically and spiritually. Through her mother, Catherine could trace her lineage to John of Gaunt, and grew up as an *Infanta* of Spain. Unlike Henry, her claim to royalty was not a mere few decades old. As such, she was naturally proud and dignified. Mary inherited Catherine's pride and sense of destiny, as well as her mother's enduring love for Spain. When Mary became queen, this affection was to have terrible consequences.

Educated by her mother and a ducal governess, Mary was as a child betrothed to her cousin, the Holy Roman Emperor Charles V, Charles I of Spain. Charles made the demand that she come to Spain immediately, accompanied by a huge cash dowry, but Henry VIII ignored the request and Charles then refused the marriage. Meanwhile, Henry invested the nine-year-old Mary as Princess of Wales in 1525, and she held court at Ludlow Castle. Only a few weeks before the investiture, Mary had attended a ceremony in which her father ennobled his illegitimate son, Henry Fitzroy, as Duke of Richmond. Henry meant to soothe Catherine's fears that Mary's position as the only legitimate Tudor heir was being undermined. Henry sharply rebuked Catherine for criticising his open affections for Fitzroy and the accompanying titles and wealth.

When Catherine fell from favour, Mary also suffered. Henry sent Catherine to one decaying residence after another, dismissing several of her devoted servants. Although deprived of her title, home, jewels and companionship, Catherine never recognised the divorce. She refused the title of princess dowager, offered by Henry as recognition of her marriage to Arthur, Prince of Wales. In 1533, when Anne Boleyn bore Elizabeth, Mary was asked to accept that her mother's marriage was not valid and that she was thus illegitimate. She refused, and so she was sent to be lady-in-waiting, aged seventeen, to her recently born half-sister Elizabeth. From 1531, aged fifteen, she had been kept separate from her mother and thus developed a lasting hatred of Anne Boleyn. Mary persuaded herself that Henry VIII had been Anne Boleyn's pawn. Anne took an equal dislike to Mary. After all, Elizabeth was legitimate only if Mary was not, and vice versa. Mary's antipathy extended to Anne's daughter, Elizabeth.

Unlike Mary, Elizabeth was recognised as a princess of the realm, and the teenaged Mary began to suffer from a variety of illnesses, probably stress-related. These lasted all her lifetime, causing such symptoms as severe headaches, nausea, insomnia and infrequent menstruation. After Anne Boleyn's fall from grace, Henry offered to pardon Mary and restore her to favour in 1536, but only if Mary acknowledged him as head of the Church of England and admitted the 'incestuous illegality' of his marriage to Catherine. Mary refused to do so until her cousin, Charles V, persuaded her otherwise, an action she was to always regret. Meanwhile, Catherine of Aragon had died at Kimbolton Castle. She had not seen Mary for years, although they had written to one another, against Henry's orders, in great secrecy.

Anne Boleyn's execution on charges of incest and treason had made Elizabeth illegitimate, but Mary was named godmother to Henry and Jane Seymour's son, Prince Edward, born in October 1537. When Jane died shortly after her son's birth, Mary was the chief mourner. Jane had desperately tried to reconcile Mary with her father, but Mary's refusal to acknowledge Henry as head of the Church had made it impossible. Indeed, the Duke of Norfolk told Mary that if she had been his daughter he would have knocked her head 'against the wall until it was as soft as baked apple'. In 1544, a statute restored Mary as heir to the throne after her half-brother Edward.

Like her mother, she was a devout Catholic and she detested the religious changes of her father and her half-brother. When Edward became king in 1553, Mary continued to attend Catholic Mass in her own private chapel. When Edward ordered her to desist she appealed to her cousin, Emperor Charles V. He threatened war with England if she was not left alone. The unlikely circumstances of her becoming queen are related in the previous chapter on Lady Jane Grey, whom Mary did not want executed. When she became queen, Mary had no real idea of how the nation had changed. She had spent the last few years in the countryside, surrounded by a Catholic household and sympathetic nobles. She never realised the extent of Protestantism in the vital areas of London and its surrounding countryside. Mary assumed that all of England wished to return to the early 1520s, the years before the break with the Roman Church. Unfortunately, she assumed that the popular support which had given her the throne indicated support for Catholic rule as well as her rightful queenship. Mary attended Mass with her Privy Councillors but, on 12 August 1553, told her council that she would not 'compel or constrain other men's consciences'. She hoped her subjects would open their hearts to the truth and soon return to the true faith. On Mary's succession, about 800 Protestants fled to the Continent.

Mary believed that she must marry, as no woman had ruled England in her own right. She was advised that Philip of Spain, heir to the Hapsburg Empire, was the most sought-after prince in Europe. She was deeply religious and had spent the past twenty years essentially alone. Thirty-seven years old and chaste, she wondered whether the twenty-six-year-old widower Philip would want her. Her adviser Renard assured her that Philip would be delighted to wed Mary, saying that they would have children together and ensure England had a Catholic succession. Mary replied that she had never considered marriage until God had raised her to the throne. However, now that she was queen, she would lead her subjects down the path of righteousness. She agreed to marry Philip in late October 1553, but had no idea that there would be a hostile reaction, both from her subjects and the King of France. Englishmen believed that Philip's father Charles V wanted to drag England into another costly and ineffectual war against France. Charles wanted control of the vital sea route between Spain and the Netherlands. With Protestant propagandists and the French ambassador spreading rumours about Spanish invasion, there was discontent across the land. Philip was heir to the throne of Spain, and Mary's choice was opposed both in the Privy Council and in Parliament. Wives were expected to obey their husbands, and Spain was far more powerful and wealthy than England at this time, so nobles and commoners alike feared Spanish Catholic domination of England.

Thus Mary's officials worked to limit Philip's powers in England. Under the terms of her marriage act, Philip was to be styled 'King of England' and Parliament was to be called under the joint authority of the couple, but for Mary's lifetime only. England would not be obliged to provide military support to Philip's father in any war, and Philip could not act without his wife's consent or appoint foreigners to office in England. Philip did not like these imposed conditions, but agreed for the sake of strategic gains from the marriage. Indeed, his aide wrote to a correspondent in Brussels, 'The marriage was concluded for no fleshly consideration, but in order to remedy the disorders of this kingdom and to preserve the Low Countries.' To elevate his son to Mary's rank, Emperor Charles V ceded the crown of Naples, as well as his claim to the Kingdom of Jerusalem, to Philip. Thus Mary became Queen of Naples and titular Queen of Jerusalem upon marriage. Their marriage took place just two days after their first meeting. After the wedding, they were proclaimed 'Philip and Mary, by the grace of God, King and Queen of England, France and Naples, Jerusalem and Ireland, defenders of the faith, Princes of Spain and Sicily, Archdukes of Austria, Dukes of Milan, Burgundy and Brabant, Counts of Hapsburg, Flanders and the Tyrol'. In January 1556, Mary's father-in-law abdicated and Philip became King of Spain, with Mary as his queen consort. Philip was declared king in Brussels, but Mary stayed in England.

There were riots across the country after the marriage, and when Sir Thomas Wyatt's rebels reached London he found the bridges closed to him. Wyatt surrendered, and was tried and executed along with approximately ninety rebels, many of whom were hanged, drawn and quartered. Wyatt himself, after being severely tortured in the hope of extracting a confession implicating Elizabeth, was beheaded at Tower Hill and his body quartered. Mary had refused to let the Tower guns be turned on the traitors. Mary was now advised by others, including Renard, to be harsher, to show a stern example; this sealed the feat of Lady Jane Grey.

Mary became determined to undo the religious changes of Henry and Edward. Catholic Mass was restored in December 1553, and in 1554 married clergy were ordered to leave their wives or lose their posts. In November 1554 the Act of Supremacy was repealed. The first Protestant martyr was John Rogers, burned on 4 February 1555, followed by the burning of the bishops Hugh Latimer of Worcester and Nicholas Ridley of London. When Ridley was asked if he believed the Pope was heir to the authority of Peter as the foundation of the Church, he replied that the Church was not built on any man but on the truth Peter confessed, that Christ was the Son of God. Ridley said he could not honour the Pope in Rome since the papacy was seeking its own glory, not the glory of God. Neither Ridley nor Latimer could accept the Roman Catholic Mass as a sacrifice of Christ. Latimer told the commissioners, 'Christ made one oblation and sacrifice for the sins of the whole world, and that a perfect sacrifice; neither needeth there to be, nor can there be, any other propitiatory sacrifice.' These opinions were offensive to Roman Catholic theologians.

Both Ridley and Latimer were burned at the stake in Oxford on 16 October 1555. As he was being tied to the stake, Ridley prayed, 'Oh, heavenly Father, I give unto thee most hearty thanks that thou hast called me to be a professor of thee, even unto death. I beseech thee, Lord God, have mercy on this realm of England, and deliver it from all her enemies.' Ridley's brother had brought some gunpowder for the men to place around their necks so death could come more quickly, but Ridley still suffered greatly. With a loud voice, Ridley cried, 'Into thy hands, O Lord, I commend my spirit ...', but the wood was green and burned only Ridley's lower parts, not touching his upper body. He was heard to repeatedly call out, 'Lord have mercy upon me! I cannot burn. Let the fire come unto me, I cannot burn.' One of the bystanders finally brought the flames to the top of the pyre to hasten Ridley's death. Latimer died much more quickly; as the flames quickly rose, Latimer encouraged Ridley, 'Be of good comfort, Mr. Ridley, and play the man! We shall this day light such a candle by God's grace, in England, as I trust never shall be put out.' The martyrdoms of Ridley, Latimer and Thomas Cranmer are today commemorated by a monument in Oxford. Mary believed that she was carrying out the will of God, and her constant saying was, 'In thee, O lord, is my trust, let me never be confounded: if God be for us, who can be against us?'

Mary's first parliament of 1553 had abolished all Edward VI's religious legislation, turning the clock back to 1547. During 1554–55, Parliament undid most of the religious legislation of Henry VIII's reign and restored the papal supremacy. However, MPs refused to restore monastic lands (they had profited immensely from buying them), and only with great difficulty were persuaded to restore the payment of annates (the whole of the first year's profits of a benefice) to the Church. Late in 1554, Reginald Pole, with his attainder reversed, arrived in England as papal legate and formally restored England to obedience to Rome. In 1555 he was appointed cardinal, and in 1556 became Archbishop of Canterbury. Despite her age of thirty-seven, Mary announced in 1555 that she was pregnant. When it became clear that she was not, and indeed would never have a child, Mary became all the more determined to extirpate 'heresy' from England before she died. She seemed to think that the failure of her marriage was owing to God's divine vengeance for not uprooting the heresies still practised in England.

In all about 275 Protestants were executed between 1555 and 1558, later being included in John Foxe's *Acts and Monuments of the English Martyrs*. Most of them were artisans from south-east England, where Protestantism had spread most widely under the energetic administration of Edmund Bonner, Bishop of London. To history, mainly because of Foxe's book, the queen became known as 'Bloody Mary'. It was the godliness of many of her victims that made them stand out, but these deaths were not numerous in comparison with the violence that characterised the Reformation on the Continent, nor indeed with the 10,000 or so killed in her father's reign. The people in general were hostile to the executions, and over the course of Mary's reign sheriffs and justices of the peace grew increasingly unwilling to participate. Many more Protestants fled abroad. In 1556, Thomas Cranmer, the former Archbishop of Canterbury, was burnt. The burnings gained sympathy for the Protestants, alienating nobles and commons alike.

The years 1555 and 1556 saw extremely poor harvests and were followed by a serious influenza epidemic, which killed perhaps 6 per cent of the population. From 1556, Philip tried to overcome the resistance of the Privy Council and involve England in war with France. Philip's cause was helped by the abortive invasion by Thomas Stafford, a Protestant exile in France. In April 1557 he landed at Scarborough, where he was defeated almost immediately and subsequently executed. Although Henry II of France denied initiating the raid, England declared war on France. The English Navy lent Spain important support at sea. Nevertheless, the war was regarded as disastrous because, in January 1558, England lost Calais. It cost more to maintain than it was worth economically or militarily, but England regarded its loss as a massive humiliation. English prestige abroad also suffered because it was evident that English resources were not adequate to mount a serious attempt to regain the lost territory. Calais had stayed in English hands for over two centuries, since 1347.

With this loss came good news for the beleaguered Mary, who was sure she was pregnant again, at the age of forty-two. She entered seclusion in late February 1558, and on 30 March drafted her will, worded in such a way to indicate that she thought she was pregnant. After the symptoms began to fade, Mary was left quite ill and became progressively worse, possibly suffering from stomach cancer. She was lucid enough to agree to pass the crown to her half-sister, adding that she hoped Elizabeth would maintain the Catholic faith in England. On 16 November 1558, Mary's will was read aloud in keeping with custom. The queen was lucid during the Mass held in her chamber the next morning, after which her priest performed the last rites and she died. Elizabeth gave her a royal funeral, and her body was interred in Westminster Abbey in the chapel built by her grandfather Henry VII. Her heart and bowels were placed in the Chapel Royal at St James's Palace. Half-Spanish, married to a Spaniard and desperate for a child, Mary never understood her people properly. She went unmourned by most of the nation because of the burnings and the loss of Calais. Her last words were said to have been, 'When I am dead and opened, you shall find Calais lying in my heart.'

10

Queen Elizabeth I: 'The Virgin Queen', 1558–1603

Parents: Henry VIII and Anne Boleyn
Born: 7 September 1533 at Palace of Placentia, Greenwich
Ascended to the throne: 17 November 1558, aged 25 years 2 months
Crowned: 15 January 1559 at Westminster Abbey
Married: Never married
Siblings: Edward VI, Mary I, Henry Fitzroy (illegitimate, but recognised)
Children: Several alleged, none confirmed
Died: 24 March 1603 at Richmond Palace, aged 69 years 6 months
Reigned: 44 years and 4 months
Buried: 28 April 1603, Westminster Abbey

The last of the line of Tudors was the granddaughter of Henry VII, the Earl of Richmond who had led the last successful invasion of British soil, and overcame the greater force of Richard III at Bosworth Field. Britain became a power on the world stage under Elizabeth, and her reign saw the greatest flowering of culture – the Elizabethan Age – in the history of the islands. Elizabeth I came to the throne on the death of her half-sister, Mary I, on 17 November 1558. She had to work hard to survive until the time of her accession, learning many important lessons along the way about politics, economics and diplomacy. The England that Elizabeth inherited was on the verge of bankruptcy, was riven religiously, at war, and had little international standing. When she died forty-four years later, England was a comparatively stable country, with an expanding economy, power on the international stage and on the verge of acquiring an empire.

Around the time that Henry decapitated Catherine Howard for adultery, Elizabeth told her childhood companion Robert Dudley that she would never marry. She was eight years old and had lost her mother and had known three stepmothers, two of whom were dead. Henry's sixth wife, Catherine Parr, then brought Elizabeth into the family home. She protected Elizabeth from Henry when he fell into a great rage at a question that Elizabeth had asked him. Elizabeth was thirteen when, with her nine-year-old brother Edward at the royal palace of Enfield, she was told of Henry's death. Elizabeth went to live with the queen dowager and her new husband, Lord Thomas Seymour, Lord Admiral. Catherine had hoped to marry Seymour before Henry decided that she was to be his new queen. He was the brother of Edward Seymour, Lord Protector of England, who was running the land for Edward VI. Thomas Seymour took an extremely unhealthy interest in the young princess. It is recorded that both Catherine and Thomas used to rise early to 'tickle' Elizabeth in bed. It was thought best that Elizabeth left the household after several scandals involving her and Seymour. Soon after this, Catherine died giving birth to a daughter. Thomas Seymour now planned to marry King Edward to Lady Jane Grey and to marry Elizabeth himself, and formally asked for Elizabeth's hand in marriage. Elizabeth later called Thomas Seymour 'a man of much wit and little judgement'. Seymour was later executed, and Elizabeth placed in the Tower of London. Edward VI henceforth saw Elizabeth as a threat, and she responded by wearing plain black or white gowns, and building up such an attitude that he later called her 'sweet sister temperance'.

Northumberland took over from Edward Seymour as Protector, and was the father of Robert Dudley, Elizabeth's childhood friend. The ailing Edward VI agreed with Northumberland to 'bastardise' Elizabeth and Mary, as the claim to the crown fell on his family if they were excluded. His daughter-in-law Lady Jane Grey was proclaimed queen, but Mary succeeded on 19 July 1553. After Mary acceded she was always suspicious of the Protestant Elizabeth, and set about restoring the Catholic faith in England. A plot in 1554 for Edward Courtenay to marry Elizabeth and depose Mary was revealed. Elizabeth was taken by boat to the Tower of London. Late at night, the boat stopped at the Traitor's Gate. Elizabeth, cold and wet, just sat in the boat for hours, refusing to get out, and there was an impasse. No-one could lay hands on the royal princess. She feared that she would never come out, but her governess eventually convinced her that she was safe, and she was confined in the Bell Tower.

Elizabeth was fortunate. The new queen refused to sign her death warrant, believing that there could be a popular rising. Elizabeth was released from the Tower but kept a virtual prisoner in the dilapidated Palace of Woodstock for a year. Elizabeth's early life had been full of uncertainties, and her chances of succeeding to the throne seemed very slight once her half-brother Edward had been born in 1537. She was then third in line behind her Roman Catholic half-sister, Princess Mary, who was seventeen years her senior. Roman Catholics, indeed, always considered Elizabeth illegitimate. Mary could not have children, and her husband, Philip of Spain, recommended that she installed Elizabeth as her heiress to the crown. Next in line was Mary, Queen of Scots, and it was in the Spanish interest that England did not pass into the hands of a monarchy with close links with France.

Elizabeth succeeded to the throne on her half-sister's death on 17 November 1558. In the first week of her reign, the unmarried Elizabeth, aged just twenty-five, sought to allay the fears of her subjects by promising them her devotion, insisting there would be no marriage or children to distract her from duty. Holding her coronation ring aloft, she declared, 'Behold the pledge of this, my wedlock and marriage with my kingdom. And do not upbraid me with miserable lack of children: for every one of you, and as many as are Englishmen, are children and kinsmen to me.' When the queen died forty-four years later, the coronation ring was so embedded in her skin that it had to be filed from her finger.

The new queen was fluent in six languages and was intelligent, determined and shrewd. During her reign, a secure Church of England was established. Its doctrines were laid down in the Thirty-Nine Articles of 1563, a compromise between Roman Catholicism and Protestantism. Elizabeth herself diplomatically refused to 'make windows into men's souls ... there is only one Jesus Christ and all the rest is a dispute over trifles'. She asked only for outward uniformity. Most of her subjects accepted the compromise as the basis of their faith, and her Church settlement probably saved England from religious wars like those suffered by France in these times. She was a Protestant, but she was not a dogmatic woman.

Elizabeth had excellent political judgement and chose her ministers well. Her administration consisted of around 600 officials administering the great offices of state and a similar number dealing with the Crown lands that funded the administrative costs. Social and economic regulation and law and order remained in the hands of the sheriffs at local level, supported by unpaid justices of the peace. Elizabeth's reign also saw many voyages of discovery, including those of Francis Drake, Walter Raleigh and Humphrey Gilbert, particularly to the Americas. These expeditions prepared England for an age of colonisation and trade expansion, which Elizabeth herself recognised by establishing the East India Company in 1600.

Elizabeth fell in love with Lord Robert Dudley, later to become Earl of Leicester, and made him her master of horse, but her advisers were against a marriage. The sudden death of his wife, Amy Robsart, in 1560 destroyed any chance of a wedding. She was found with a broken neck at the bottom of a staircase, and Dudley was believed to have been responsible. However, the two were very close for the next ten years, and some believe they may have had children. Historians believe that Leicester died of stomach cancer, malaria or a heart condition. He had been unwell for some time, and a week before his death he dined with Queen Elizabeth and said his last farewell. On hearing of his death, she locked herself in her apartment until Lord Burghley had the door broken down a few days later. Elizabeth kept his last letter, sent six days before his death in 1588, in her bedside treasure box. She wrote on it 'his last letter' and it was still there when she died fifteen years later.

Elizabeth almost died from smallpox in 1562; had she done so, civil war between the Protestant supporters of Catherine Grey and the Catholic supporters of Mary, Queen of Scots, might have followed. Elizabeth's early years saw other problems, in particular the wars in Scotland and France inherited from Mary. English support for the John Knox's successful Scottish Protestant rebellion of 1560, combined with the outbreak in 1562 of the

French Wars of Religion, lessened both threats. Unlike her father, Elizabeth made peace as soon as possible and tried to stay out of expensive wars. The queen attempted to maintain peaceful relations with Spain, although she refused to marry Philip when he proposed. Philip had been married to her sister Mary.

When Elizabeth was not working with the great William Cecil, Lord Burghley, on political matters, she enjoyed her court entertainment, having a troupe of actors called the Queen's Men (or Players). She particularly liked Shakespeare's work, and great English musicians such as Purcell, Tallis and Byrd flourished under her. She loved to ride horses, worrying her advisers, and hunted deer and stags with her courtiers. She also enjoyed cockfighting, bear-baiting and tennis. A skilled musician and dancer, the young Elizabeth also enjoyed classical literature and wrote poetry. Country houses such as Longleat and Hardwick Hall were built, miniature painting reached its high point and theatres thrived – the queen attended the first performance of Shakespeare's *A Midsummer Night's Dream*. The image of Elizabeth's reign is one of triumph and success. The queen herself was often called 'Gloriana', 'Good Queen Bess' and 'the Virgin Queen'. Investing in expensive clothes and jewellery to look the part, like all contemporary sovereigns she cultivated her image by touring the country in regional visits known as 'progresses', often riding on horseback rather than by carriage. Elizabeth made at least twenty-five progresses during her reign, but never ventured as far north as York or left England. At home she wore simple gowns, but fashion indicated social status so Elizabeth had to set the standards in her favourite colours of black and white, which represented virginity and purity. The elaborate neck ruff was the biggest of the fashions set by her, as starch had been discovered. Dudley gave her a watch placed in a bracelet, possibly the first wristwatch in the world. She wore little make-up until an attack of smallpox in 1562, after which it was needed to cover her facial scars. The bewigged monarch painted her face with white lead and vinegar, rouged her lips, and covered her cheeks with red dye and egg white. The lead had long-term effects on her health.

However, Elizabeth's reign was one of considerable danger and difficulty, with threats of invasion from Spain through Ireland, and from France through Scotland. Much of northern England was in rebellion in 1569–70. A papal bull of 1570 specifically released Elizabeth's subjects from their allegiance, and she passed harsh laws against Roman Catholics after plots against her life were discovered. One plot involved Mary, Queen of Scots, who had fled to England in 1568 after her second husband's murder and had subsequently married a man believed to have been involved in his murder. As a possible successor to Elizabeth, Mary spent nineteen years as Elizabeth's prisoner because she was the focus for rebellion and possible assassination plots, such as the Babington Plot of 1586. In a letter of 1586 to Mary, Elizabeth wrote, 'You have planned ... to take my life and ruin my kingdom ... I never proceeded so harshly against you.' Despite Elizabeth's reluctance to take drastic action, on the insistence of Parliament and her advisers Mary was tried, found guilty of treason and executed on 8 February 1587 at Fotheringhay Castle. One of the first acts of her son, James I, on his accession to the English throne was to raze the castle to the ground.

Elizabeth's principal suitors – those given serious consideration by her advisers – were the Duke of Angoulême (third son of Francis I) in 1534; a prince of Portugal in 1542; a son of the Earl of Arran in 1543; Prince Philip (Philip II of Spain) in 1544; Sir Thomas Seymour in 1547; the Prince of Denmark in 1552; Edward Courtenay, Earl of Devonshire, in 1553–4; Philibert Emanuel, Duke of Savoy, in 1554; the Prince of Denmark (again) in 1554; Prince Eric of Sweden in 1556; Don Carlos (the son of Philip II, mentioned just twelve years earlier!) in 1556; Philip II (again) in 1559; Prince Eric of Sweden (again) in 1559; the son of John Frederic, Duke of Saxony, in 1559; Sir William Pickering in 1559; the Earl of Arran in 1559; Henry Fitzalan, Earl of Arundel, in 1559; Robert Dudley in 1559; King Eric of Sweden (a third attempt) in 1560; Adolphus, Duke of Holstein, in 1560; King Charles IX in 1560; Henri, Duke of Anjou, in 1560; Robert Dudley (again) in 1566; Henri, Duke of Anjou (again) in 1570; and, finally, from 1572 to 1585 Francis, Duke of Alençon, later Duke of Anjou. We can see the virtual 'feeding frenzy' of 1559–60, when Elizabeth and her advisers realised that she was coming to the end of her childbearing years and wished for an heir and stability. The possible answer is that Elizabeth could never marry without destabilising the realm – as long as she was uncommitted, there would be no disorder between powerful courtiers. These nobles would fight against each other and possibly disrupt the Tudor dynasty, but equally would not brook a foreign king over them.

Meanwhile, in 1570 the Pope issued a bull of excommunication and deposition. This papal document decreed that Elizabeth I was excommunicated (excluded from the Church) and deposed. Her Catholic subjects no longer had to obey her:

> Elizabeth, the pretended queen of England and the servant of crime ... with whom as in a sanctuary the most pernicious of all have found refuge ... She has followed and embraced the errors of the heretics ... We declare her to be deprived of her pretended title to the crown ... We charge and command all and singular the nobles, subjects, peoples ... that they do not dare obey her orders, mandates and laws ...

In 1581, the fines for non-attendance at Church of England services (aimed at Catholics) were increased, although in some areas they were not imposed. In 1585, all Catholic priests were ordered to leave England within forty days or face a charge of treason. Despite these measures, most English Catholics remained loyal to the queen when the Spanish Armada sailed in 1588. The ships that fought the Armada were commanded by a Catholic, Lord Howard of Effingham. Philip II ruled the Spanish Netherlands, but the Dutch turned Protestant and in 1568 they rebelled against the Catholic king's rule. Elizabeth was reluctant to become involved, but from 1578 onward the Spaniards were winning and in 1585 Elizabeth was forced to send an army to the Netherlands. Philip II believed he had a claim to the English throne through his marriage to

Mary. He had long wished to invade the small, weaker England and recover the nation for the Catholic faith. Elizabeth had encouraged English privateers such as Francis Drake to attack Spanish ships, and some of this treasure had been used to bolster the Dutch revolt against Spanish rule.

In April 1587, Francis Drake had sailed into Cadiz harbour and destroyed part of the fleet that was preparing to invade. Drake boasted that he had 'singed the king of Spain's beard'. Even so, the next year the invasion fleet was ready and it sailed in July 1588. The Spanish Armada consisted of 130 ships and about 27,000 men. The plan was to send the Armada to Calais to meet a Spanish army grouped there. The Armada would then transport them to England. The queen made her famous speech to her army at Tilbury Fort in 1588 when expecting the invasion:

> I know I have but the body of a weak and feeble woman; but I have the heart of a king, and of a king of England, too; and think foul scorn that Parma or Spain, or any prince of Europe, should dare to invade the borders of my realms: to which, rather than any dishonour should grow by me, I myself will take up arms; I myself will be your general, judge, and rewarder of every one of your virtues in the field.

The English fleet was gathered at Plymouth. When the Spanish arrived, they sailed in a crescent formation. The English harassed the Spanish ships from behind. In Drake's words, they 'plucked the feathers'. However the English were unable to do serious damage to the Armada until they reached Calais.

When the Armada arrived, the Spanish troops in Calais were not ready to embark and there was nothing the fleet could do except wait at anchor in the harbour. However the English prepared fireships. They filled ships with pitch and loaded guns – the guns would fire when flames touched the gunpowder – and set them on fire before steering them towards the Spanish ships. In panic, the Armada broke formation. Spanish ships scattered. The Spanish ships were now vulnerable and the English attacked, doing considerable damage. Finally, the Armada sailed north around Scotland and west of Ireland. However, they sailed into terrible storms and many of their remaining ships were wrecked.

Charles Howard, a close friend and adviser to Elizabeth, rose to be Lord Admiral of the fleet defending England against the Armada. He happily admitted his inexperience in naval warfare, and thus surrounded himself with the best captains of the age – Drake, Hawkins and Frobisher. Lord Howard said after the battle,

> The sailors cry out for money and they know not when they will be paid. Sickness and death begin to grow among us. It is a most pitiful sight to see how the men, with no place to go, die in the streets. It would grieve any man's heart to see those that have served so bravely, die so miserably.

After the English victory, the ordinary sailors were put ashore and left to starve, with no help from their queen. However, Howard, later Earl of

Nottingham, sold his own silver plate to pay for clothing, food and ale for the men.

It was in Elizabeth's reign that England turned from being a peripheral player in world affairs to a major one. On the other hand, the nation also suffered from high prices and severe economic depression, especially in the countryside, during the 1590s. The war against Spain was not very successful after the Armada had been beaten and, together with other campaigns, it was very costly. Though she kept a tight rein on government expenditure, Elizabeth left large debts to her successor. Wars during Elizabeth's reign are estimated to have cost over £5 million (at the prices of the time) which Crown revenues could not match – in 1588, for example, Elizabeth's total annual revenue amounted to some £392,000. Despite the combination of financial strains and prolonged war after 1588, Parliament was not summoned more often. There were only sixteen sittings of the Commons during Elizabeth's reign, five of which were in the period 1588–1601. Although Elizabeth freely used her power to veto legislation, she avoided confrontation and did not attempt to define Parliament's constitutional position and rights.

Parliament sat for less than three years of her forty-four-year reign. The official summons to Parliament called on the Members to advise the monarch, but in practice Elizabeth was rarely interested in the opinions of her Members of Parliament. One exception was in 1586, when Elizabeth summoned Parliament to ask its view of whether she should execute Mary, Queen of Scots. The main purpose of Parliament, so far as Elizabeth I was concerned, was to vote on taxation; of thirteen sessions of Parliament, she asked all but one for money. The monarch generally paid for the day-to-day administration of government from 'ordinary revenues' such as customs duties, feudal dues and the income from royal land. Parliamentary taxation was meant to cover 'extraordinary expenditure', especially war. However, Parliamentary taxation never supplied enough to cover Elizabeth's military expenditures, and so she was forced to sell land and resort to semi-legal schemes. Crown revenue did increase during Elizabeth's reign, but not as much as inflation. The queen failed to increase feudal dues or customs and was forced to make sales of royal land, becoming increasingly dependent on parliamentary subsidies and forced loans. Elizabeth, aided by Cecil, was firmly in control of major policies and often ignored the Privy Council's advice.

Throughout her reign she balanced the various political factions at court and in council, but her final years saw increasingly bitter conflict between the Cecils and Robert Devereux, 2nd Earl of Essex. Essex was appointed Lord Lieutenant of Ireland in 1599 and placed in charge of a large English army to suppress Irish rebels. Instead, he signed an unauthorised truce with the Earl of Tyrone, the greatest rebel, and returned to England without permission. Elizabeth deprived Essex of his titles and ordered his arrest. He responded by attempting a coup against Elizabeth in January 1601. On the eve of his rebellion, Essex's followers arranged a special performance of Shakespeare's *Richard II*, hoping that the play, dealing with the deposition of a monarch often associated with Elizabeth, would arouse support for their own scheme.

The coup was a complete failure, and he was executed for treason in February. The Cecil faction remained dominant not only until Elizabeth's death in 1603, but even after, as Sir Robert Cecil made a smooth transition to being the main adviser of James I. James's succession was helped by Elizabeth's execution of England's last duke, Norfolk, after the Ridolfi plot of 1572. Like her grandfather Henry VII, Elizabeth was careful to limit the power of the nobles. She followed a policy of not creating any new marquesses or viscounts, and created very few barons and even fewer earls.

Elizabeth chose never to marry. If she had chosen a foreign prince, he would have drawn England into foreign policies for his own advantage (as in her sister Mary's marriage to Philip of Spain); marrying a fellow countryman could have drawn the queen into factional infighting. Elizabeth used her marriage prospects as a political tool in foreign and domestic policies. The 'Virgin Queen' was presented as a selfless woman who sacrificed personal happiness for the good of the nation, to which she was, in essence, 'married'. Late in her reign, she addressed Parliament in the so-called 'Golden Speech' of 1601 when she told MPs that this would be her final parliament: 'There is no jewel, be it of never so high a price, which I set before this jewel; I mean your love.' She seems to have been very popular with the vast majority of her subjects. The Elizabethan era (1558–1603) was one of prosperity for England. Living standards for the rich and the middle class rose substantially. However, the prosperity was not shared equally. Conditions for the poor did not improve, and there were many beggars. Elizabeth's frugality did mean that, despite long and expensive wars with Spain and in Ireland, she left a debt of only about £300,000 to James I. This can be contrasted with Philip II of Spain, who repudiated his huge debts four times during his reign despite his massive incomes from the New World.

Elizabeth's expenses included over £110,000 spent on food for the royal household and court and over £73,000 on wages and salaries to royal officials. Maintenance of royal castles, houses, palaces and ships cost over £51,000. Her jewels, clothes, coaches and barges cost around £20,000 a year, to which we must add £6,000 or so in alms and gifts to dignitaries, and £5,000 for processions, triumphs, shows and pageants. To this £265,000 we must add incidental expenses. The cost of the war in Ireland between 1599 and 1603 ran to over £1 million, but with the advice of William and his son Robert Cecil, Elizabeth managed to be financially astute.

Overall, Elizabeth's always shrewd and often decisive leadership brought successes during a period of great danger both at home and abroad. She died at Richmond Palace on 24 March 1603, having become a legend in forty-five years on the English throne. Desperately ill during her last days, Robert Cecil said that she should take to her bed, and her anger flared: 'Must! Is must a word to be addressed to princes? Little man, little man! Thy father, if he had been alive, durst not have used that word.' She never named her successor, for she knew that Robert Cecil was carefully laying plans for James VI of Scotland, the son of Mary Stuart and Darnley, to follow her. Her death day was the same as that of her father, Henry VIII. Her magnificent funeral on

28 April saw national mourning, and the date of her accession was a national holiday for two hundred years.

Robert Cecil, 1563–1612

As noted above, Elizabeth called Cecil 'little man'. She also called him 'my pygmy' and 'my elf', and his enemies noted his 'wry neck', 'crooked back' and 'splay foot'. A son of the great William Cecil, he was small and deformed, which was said to be the result of being dropped by his nursemaid. Weak in health, Cecil was extremely sensitive about his looks. In 1588 he was described in Motley's *History of the Netherlands*:

> A slight, crooked, hump-backed young gentleman, dwarfish in stature, but with a face not irregular in feature, and thoughtful and subtle in expression, with reddish hair, a thin tawny beard, and large, pathetic, greenish-coloured eyes, with a mind and manners already trained to courts and cabinets, and with a disposition almost ingenuous, as compared to the massive dissimulation with which it was to be contrasted, and with what was, in aftertimes, to constitute a portion of his own character.

He was raised with Robert Devereux, Earl of Essex, as his father was the guardian of Essex. He worked for the spymaster Walsingham and also as a diplomat, and in 1589 Cecil began to perform the duties of Secretary of State, being knighted two years later. In 1597 Cecil became chancellor of the Duchy of Lancaster, and in 1598 succeeded his father as principal secretary. Cecil and Essex continuously clashed at the court of the queen and in the Privy Council, and with Essex's downfall in 1601 Cecil entered into secret negotiations with James VI of Scotland to arrange his succession on the death of Elizabeth. In 1605 Cecil was created Earl of Salisbury, but in that year was implicated in the Gunpowder Plot. In 1608 he was made Lord Treasurer. For his political cunning, he was known as 'the fox'. Cecil died on 24 May 1612 in Marlborough, while returning to London from taking the waters at Bath. During his long career he had amassed a large fortune, besides inheriting a considerable portion of Lord Burghley's landed estate. At Hatfield he built the magnificent house of which he himself conceived the plans and the design, but which he did not live to inhabit, its completion almost coinciding with his death. He was disliked by Londoners, and a ditty current after his death was 'But now at Hatfield lies the Fox, who drank while he lived and died of the pox.'

11

Unknown Tudors

Henry VII's Son? Sir Roland De Velville, 1471/74–1535

gwr o lin brenhinoedd	*a man of kingly line*
ag o waed ieirll i gyd oedd	*and of earl's blood*

Elegy to Sir Roland de Velville by Daffyd Alaw, 1535

Sir Roland de Velville (also spelt Vielleville, Veleville and Vieilleville) was Constable of Beaumaris Castle from 1509 to 1535. He was reputed to have been a natural son of Henry VII, born to a Breton lady while Henry was in exile in Brittany between 1471 and 1485. He accompanied Henry and Jasper Tudor from their exile in Brittany and France to the Battle of Bosworth Field, probably aged only around fourteen. Henry was then aged twenty-eight. Although perhaps just of 'military age' at that time, he was too young to be Henry's 'friend' or a mercenary in his own right. He was brought up at court, where he spent the next twenty-five years of his life. A favourite of the king, he was treated as an equal by the highest-ranking members of the aristocracy. De Velville was given no official 'position' but lived as a member of the royal household. He was not a young page, but someone who participated in court activities such as jousting and hunting with Henry VII and the Duke of Buckingham.

He was given 10 marks in 1488 'by way of reward', and figured honourably among the esquires who took part in the prolonged tournaments held at the creation of Henry VII's son, Henry, as Duke of York in 1494. As 'king's servant' De Velville was given a grant for life of an annuity of 40 marks out of the issues of the county of Wiltshire, and after the Battle of Blackheath he was knighted on 17 June 1497. After helping to disperse the rebels gathered on Blackheath de Velville married Agnes Griffith, a member of the most powerful family in north Wales at the time, the Griffiths of Penrhyn, a branch of the Tudor family. As Sir Roland he was summoned to attend upon the king during the reception of the Archduke Philip in 1500.

Under his possible half-brother Henry VIII, Sir Roland was appointed

Constable of Beaumaris Castle on 3 July 1509. He was also given during pleasure an annuity of £20 and a livery of clothes. The appointment made him one of the richest men in north Wales. Even after his allowance of nearly £300 a year for soldiers' wages was discontinued in 1516, his income from his annuities and constable's fee was over £240 a year. Altogether, during Henry VIII's reign he received over £6,100 from the Chamberlain of North Wales, and a further £1,200 from Exchequer revenues. The wages of household servants and of soldiers or guards for the safe keeping of Beaumaris Castle would have represented a substantial item of expenditure, but it seems unlikely that he maintained a regular garrison throughout his years as constable. Unlike many men of his rank, he did not spend money on building; Beaumaris Castle remained his only residence until his death, and repairs to it were met from royal revenues.

Some of de Velville's income was apparently devoted to purchases of land, and six acquisitions by him are recorded in documents surviving in the Lleweni papers. Four of these are grants by Owen ap John ab Owen ap Tudor Fychan, a member of the senior branch of the Tudor family, of parcels of land in the ancestral Tudor estate of Penmynydd. In 1512, as 'a native of Brittany', he was granted letters of denization for himself and the heir of his body. De Velville was summoned to attend on the king during his meeting with Charles V at Gravelines in 1520. In his will, Velville directed that he should be buried in the monastery of the Friars Minor of Llanfaes, the Franciscan house about a mile to the north of Beaumaris. Llanfaes was the burial place of Goronwy ap Tudor (d. 1382), the direct paternal ancestor of the Tudors.

Katheryn of Berain (in Welsh Catrin o Ferain) was a Welsh noblewoman who lived from 1540 or 1541 until 1591. She was known as 'Mam Cymru', the mother of Wales, and made four rich marriages, with her descendants accruing power across Wales. She is sometimes referred to as Katheryn Tudor, her father being Tudor ap Robert Vychan, and her mother Jane Velville. Her maternal grandfather was Sir Roland de Velville. Katheryn was said to have been a ward of Queen Elizabeth, and was the heiress to the Berain and Penmynydd estates in Denbighshire and Anglesey. It was believed by her descendants that de Velville was Henry VII's son.

The Bastards of Henry VIII by Bessie Blount

Henry Fitzroy (1519–36): Almost Henry IX and King of Ireland

The product of Henry and his long-term mistress Elizabeth ('Bessie') Blount, Henry Fitzroy was the only bastard that the king acknowledged. When he was born, Henry VIII was almost twenty-eight and was delighted as his ability to father a male heir was no longer in doubt. For proving that King Henry was capable of fathering healthy sons, Elizabeth Blount prompted a popular saying, 'Bless 'ee, Bessie Blount', often heard during and after this period. Thomas Wolsey was Fitzroy's godfather, and he was given his own household of princely status and housed at Durham Place in the Strand.

King Henry was fond of his son, and created him Knight of the Garter at the age of six in 1525. Later that year he was created Earl of Nottingham, and on the same day he was made Duke of Richmond. A month later, in July and aged just seven, Fitzroy was made Admiral of England, Ireland and Normandy. The boy also became Warden of the Cinque Ports and Lord Lieutenant of Ireland. With other titles and incomes, he became the richest person in the kingdom after his father. When Fitzroy was made Lord Lieutenant of Ireland there was a plan to crown him King of Ireland, but it was opposed by the king's councillors. Fitzroy was also made Lieutenant General north of the Trent and warden of all marches towards Scotland. He was sent to live in the north of England to help control the area, living in the castle at Sheriff Hutton just north of York. In 1527, Henry VIII sent Richard Croke to the Vatican to research the possibilities of making Fitzroy his legitimate heir. However, while there Croke was given new instructions – to look into the possibility of Henry VIII divorcing Catherine of Aragon and remarrying to provide himself with a legitimate son. On 9 August 1529 Fitzroy, always referred to as 'the Prince', was made a temporal lord in Parliament and was asked by his father to bring charges against Wolsey. He was now aged ten.

On his return to court in Windsor he was joined by his mother, Bessie Blount, now widowed. Henry Howard, Earl of Surrey, the eldest son of the Duke of Norfolk, also joined them. Of a similar age, Surrey was to become Fitzroy's closest friend. At Christmas 1529, Fitzroy was given a suite of rooms at Windsor that were usually used by the Prince of Wales. Princess Mary, as Princess of Wales, was given a less important suite, demonstrating that Henry regarded Fitzroy as more important than his legitimate daughter.

Various European marriages were proposed for Fitzroy, but he married Lady Mary Howard, Surrey's sister, in 1533. However, the marriage was never consummated.

Fitzroy was to travel to Ireland with an army to be made king, but was recalled when he arrived in Wales to make the crossing. By November 1535 Fitzroy was back in the court at Windsor Castle, seeing his father daily. On one occasion, after Anne Boleyn had again miscarried, the king told Fitzroy that he, along with his sister Mary, were lucky to have escaped death from poisoning by Anne Boleyn. Fitzroy attended Anne Boleyn's mock trial and execution. On 30 June 1536, the new Act of Succession was put before Parliament. It was to enable Henry to nominate the seventeen-year-old Fitzroy as his heir to the throne. Fitzroy should have attended Parliament but was ill, with pains in his chest and a cough. Henry Fitzroy, Duke of Richmond, died of consumption at St James's Palace, so England never had a Henry IX and Ireland never had a Tudor king.

Elizabeth Tailboys (1520–63): The Real Queen Elizabeth I?

Born a year after Henry Fitzroy, Bessie Blount's daughter Elizabeth could have taken the throne on the death of Queen Mary in 1558. Both children were conceived during a period when Henry VIII lived a few miles away from Bessie's home and when he was known to visit her regularly. This was also two years before Bessie married Gilbert Tailboys, who later gave Elizabeth his surname. The date of Elizabeth's birth made her younger than Mary I but older than Elizabeth, both of whom were also declared illegitimate by the king when he deemed his marriages to their mothers invalid. Bessie also had a third child, George Tailboys, born two years after Elizabeth and indisputably fathered by her husband Gilbert. Elizabeth Norton's *Bessie Blount: Mistress to Henry VIII* (2012) is the best account of the woman who could have been queen.

Sir John Perrot (1528–92)

Sir John Perrot was given massive estates in Pembrokeshire by his father, Henry VIII. His mother was Mary Berkeley, a lady of the royal court and wife of Sir Thomas Perrot. Edward VI, Mary and Elizabeth I all seem to have acknowledged John Perrot as a half-brother. A giant of a man, Perrot strongly resembled his father. Sir John was one of the four knights who carried Elizabeth I's canopy at her coronation. In 1554, at a tournament for his half-sister Queen Mary Tudor and her husband, Philip of Spain, he 'fought best of all' of the Spanish and English grandees. Mary herself gave out the prizes, including 'a diamond ring of great value'. Perrot made vast wealth from his time as Vice-Admiral for West Wales, much from collusion with pirates, and built a great manor at Haroldston outside Haverfordwest, also rebuilding Laugharne and Carew castles as manor houses.

Queen Elizabeth appointed him Lord President of Munster to suppress a rebellion there, which he did within a year. He was then appointed Lord Deputy of Ireland from 1584 to 1588 by Elizabeth, but was arrested on a false charge of treason in 1591 and sentenced to death. She had sent him to Ireland in command of a fleet to intercept a possible invasion of Ireland by the Spanish, but he had acted in a high-handed manner there, just as the Earl of Essex did when he followed him. Perrot's comments about his half-sister were reckless. She had appointed a Mr Errington to be clerk of the Exchequer in Ireland, and Sir John exclaimed, 'This fiddling woman troubles me out of measure. God's dear Lady, he shall not have the office! I will give it to Sir Thomas Williams!'

Similarly, at the time of the Spanish invasion of 1588, he was reported to have said, 'Ah, silly woman, now she will not curb me! Now she shall not rule me! Now, God's dear Lady, I shall be her white boy again!' He added, when Sir John Garland brought him a letter from the queen, 'This it is, to serve a base-born woman! Had I served any prince in Christendom, I had not been thus dealt with!' When told he must die, he exclaimed, 'God's death! Will my sister sacrifice her brother to his frisking adversaries?' Queen Elizabeth refused to sign the death warrant of her half-brother and planned to pardon him, but he died in 1592 in the Tower of London, aged sixty-five.

The Boleyn Children

Mary Boleyn (1499/1500–1543) was the elder sister of Anne Boleyn, and one of his mistresses in the period from 1521 to 1526. Mary was also rumoured to have been a mistress of Francis I of France for some period between 1515 and

1519. She had two children believed to be fathered by Henry VIII. Mary Boleyn was married first in 1520 to William Carey, a favourite of Henry, a gentleman of the Privy Chamber and Esquire of the Body. He died in 1528 of the sweating sickness. Mary married William Stafford in secret in 1534, the year after sister Anne married the king. Stafford was a soldier of good family but few prospects, and the marriage to a man considered beneath her station angered both Henry VIII and her sister, Queen Anne, resulting in Mary's banishment from the royal court. She spent the remainder of her life in obscurity.

Her daughter Catherine Carey (*c.* 1524–69) was believed to be the child of Henry VIII, and her later life seems to indicate the truth of the matter. After her marriage in 1540 she became Lady Knollys. Although never acknowledged by the king, Catherine was given deference by the court as she aged and came to resemble Henry. Catherine went on to become maid of honour to both Anne of Cleves and Catherine Howard, Henry's fourth and fifth wives. As Protestants, she and her husband fled to Germany under the reign of Mary I.

Princess Elizabeth wrote to her 'cousin' there and Catherine was appointed Chief Lady of the Bedchamber after Elizabeth took the crown. For the first ten years of the reign, Lady Catherine combined the most senior post among the ladies-in-waiting with motherhood to more than a dozen children. At court, Catherine was acknowledged as the queen's favourite among her first cousins, and Elizabeth's lack of other female relatives to whom she felt close may be adequate to explain this favoured position. Catherine died in 1569 at Hampton Court Palace, and was buried in Westminster Abbey. She was an ancestress of Diana, Princess of Wales.

Catherine's brother Henry Carey (1526–96) was also thought to be Henry's son. From the age of two, Carey and his elder sister Catherine came under the wardship of their maternal aunt Anne Boleyn, who was engaged to Henry VIII. Anne Boleyn acted as her nephew's patron and had him provided with an excellent education. Carey served twice as an MP, being knighted in 1558, and being created Baron Hunsdon by his first cousin Elizabeth I. The manor and estates of Hunsdon had previously belonged to Mary I. Carey was also granted an annual pension of £400. In 1560, Henry was appointed Master of the Queen's Hawks and in 1561 became a Knight of the Garter. In 1564, Carey was appointed Captain of the Gentlemen Pensioners, in effect Elizabeth's personal bodyguard. He was a patron of the Lord Chamberlain's Men, Shakespeare's playing company.

In the Catholic Rising of the North of 1569–70, Carey was lieutenant-general of Elizabeth's forces and beat off a rebel attack, effectively ending the rising. Elizabeth congratulated him as his 'loving kinswoman'. Many more appointments followed before he died at Somerset House and was buried in Westminster Abbey. On his deathbed, Elizabeth offered to create him Earl of Wiltshire. He refused, saying, 'Madam, as you did not count me worthy of this honour in life, then I shall account myself not worthy of it in death.' His wife Anne Morgan was a lady of the Privy Chamber to the queen, and was left in debt on Carey's death. Elizabeth paid for his funeral expenses and gave Anne a gift of £400, as well as an annual pension of £200 from the Exchequer.

Other Claimants to Bastardy

Henry VIII had many mistresses, so there may be unknown or stillborn or miscarried children. Apart from Bessie Blount, Mary Boleyn, Mary Berkeley and the Shelton sisters, he had relationships with Anne Boleyn, Jane Seymour and possibly Catherine Howard prior to marriage. Other alleged mistresses include Jane Popincourt, Anne Bassett, Elizabeth Carew, Etiennette de la Baume, Lady Anne Hastings, Jane Pollard, Agnes Blewitt Edwardes, Joan Dingley and Elizabeth Amadas. He was also said to be interested in Mary Fitzroy, Elizabeth Hervey, Mary Skipwith, Elizabeth Brooke (Lady Wyatt), Anne Bassett and Catherine Willoughby. Interestingly, Henry was always afraid of assassination. The result of this was that whenever he went on progress or visited others' houses he took his royal locksmith, Henry Romains, and portable royal locks to make his bedchamber secure from attack. It is a real pity that Romains never committed to writing his memoirs.

Thomas Stucley (*c.* 1520–78) was the son of Sir Hugh Stukeley (Stucley) and Jane Pollard. A mercenary, he fought in France, Ireland and at the Battle of Lepanto before his death at the Battle of Alácacer Quibir. It was alleged in his lifetime that he was a son of Henry VIII. A Catholic, his life is too detailed for this publication but a play was made of his life, *The Famous History of the Life and Death of Captain Thomas Stukeley* (1605).

Richard Edwardes (*c.* 1523–66) was born to Mrs Agnes Beaupenny Blewitt Edwardes. It is said his mother left the court of Henry VIII and Catherine of Aragon pregnant with the king's son. She lived at Greenham Manor, near the King's Hunting Lodge, where she conceived the boy. Richard was referred to as the bastard son of Agnes and Henry, and Henry was noted as being very fond of the boy. Henry provided a stipend for Richard's childhood support, and guaranteed and paid for his education at Oxford. Richard's mother, Agnes Blewitt, was allowed to add the Tudor roses to her personal crest. Though educated at Oxford to be a lawyer, Richard Edwardes never practised law, instead becoming a cleric in the Anglican Church. He was a poet and playwright of some renown, writing plays such as *Palamon and Arcite* for Queen Elizabeth. At his passing he was noted by a contemporary as being a writer in the same class as Shakespeare.

Ethelreda (Etheldreda) Malte (*c.* 1527/35 – *c.*1559) was born to Joan Digneley or Dingley, alias Dobson. Sometimes referred to as Audrey, she was well known at court and reputed in contemporary reports to be Henry's daughter. She was the wife of poet and writer John Harrington, Treasurer to the King's Camps and Buildings, before Isabella Markham. It has been suggested that her mother was a laundress to the court. Although he never openly acknowledged Etheldreda, Henry VIII gave his tailor, John Malte, land and properties when Malte recognised Etheldreda as his illegitimate daughter. On 18 March 1554, Etheldreda Malte was among the six ladies who accompanied Elizabeth to the Tower, where the future queen was imprisoned under suspicion of causing rebellion. Etheldreda was one of Elizabeth's ladies-in-waiting, a notable honour for one who was not a noble, and was present at the coronation of Elizabeth I on 15 January 1559, and she died that same month.

Antonia Fraser, in *The Six Wives of Henry VIII*, noted, 'By the end of January [1542], the king was said to have cheered up a little, although his health remained poor and his weight in consequence increased. But he did at least enjoy "a great supper" with twenty-six ladies at his table and another thirty-five at a table nearby. Among those singled out by his attentions were Sir Anthony Browne's niece, Lord Cobham's sister and Mistress Anne Bassett. Of the latter Marillac commented sourly that she was "a pretty young creature with wit enough to do as badly as the other if she were to try".'

Some of us may unknowingly be descended from this monarch. In *A Dark History: The Kings and Queens of England*, Brenda Ralph Lewis writes that, 'in the late 1530s, a man called William Webbe complained that, while he was riding in broad daylight with his mistress near Eltham Place, they encountered the king, who took an immediate fancy to the "pretty wench", pulled her up onto his horse, and rode off to the palace where he ravished her and kept her for some time'. Alison Weir reports that Webbe was a courtier, and presumably there was nothing he could do about it. This would not, presumably, be a solitary event.

12

Tudor Court and Royal Household

The court was the seat of the government in England. It was a concept as well as an entity, symbolising the magnificence and pre-eminence of the prince. The court was used by Henry VIII to show how rich and powerful he was, to deter people and nations from plotting against him. In August 1546 he entertained the French ambassador and 200 companions, plus 1,300 of the English court, for six days. All the activities at court were planned to show Henry's talents and interests. The court was a centre for art, music, dance, poetry and tournaments, the most fashionable place in the land. In the sixteenth century, the king was considered the anointed of God, and was required to maintain his position at the top of the 'Great Chain of Being'. As a woman and therefore naturally inferior to a man according to the Great Chain of Being, Elizabeth felt the need to exemplify her magnificence at court even more than her father. Not only did she have to preserve her position as the Queen of England, but she also had to maintain her position as a religious leader. In order to create an appropriate level of magnificence, Elizabeth had everyday tasks turned into ceremonial functions; even something as simple as setting the table for the queen's dinner required the setters to kneel before the empty table and place the utensils on the table with due reverence.

Generous hospitality was probably the most useful and common form of conspicuous consumption for nobles. The efficiency and gentility offered by the household in the provision of such hospitality, as well as the hospitality itself, would affect those whom the lord was attempting to influence. Elizabeth, in the early part of her reign, needed to impress a number of people that she could rule England well. Many of the people Elizabeth wished to impress were the ambassadors present from foreign courts, especially those of France and Spain, and had permanent lodgings at the court. Because of these permanent observers, even the menial tasks needed to be performed in such a way as to promote an aura of respect and awe. These rituals could be so elaborate that they evolved into 'quasi-religious observances'. This need for an element of religion in her household was only to be expected in a monarch who was the temporal head of the Anglican Church. These displays had a practical purpose. They suggested an inherent sinfulness in rebellion, which was critical in an age that was prone to sedition.

The royal household was organized into two major sections, classified as the chamber and the household, and which Edward IV defined in the *Liber Niger* as the *Domus Regie Magnificencie* and the *Domus Providencie*. The first section was responsible for maintaining the splendour of the court and the second was responsible for the practical running of the court. The control of the household was divided between the Lord Steward and the Lord Chamberlain. The Lord Steward was responsible for the *Domus Providencie*, as well as accounting and household management. He was aided by the Board of Greencloth, which consisted of the Treasurer of the Household, the Comptroller and various clerks in addition to the Lord Steward. The Treasurer, Lord Steward, and Comptroller were collectively known as the whitestaves because of the white rods they carried as a badge of their office. The Lord Chamberlain was responsible for 'public ceremony and ... the king's private service', in other words the *Domus Regie Magnificencie*. He was assisted by the vice-chamberlain and often by some of the gentlemen ushers within his department.

Sovereigns 'held court', where people were theoretically free to approach them, usually with petitions of some kind or other. Courtiers wanted to be near the king because it was a chance to be noticed and to make a good impression. In return, they might get jobs and titles for their family and friends. Courtiers had their own rooms in Henry's palaces. They brought their own servants with them who often had to make do with sleeping in the corridors. When Henry stayed at Hampton Court up to a thousand people would accompany him, so Hampton Court had three enormous kitchens.

The king's chamber was divided into the Privy Chamber (distinguished from bedchamber in 1559), an outer chamber (often styled the presence chamber) and the great hall. The Privy Chamber was the most influential department in the royal household. It housed the king's 'privy lodging', consisting of bedroom, library, study and of course the toilet. Originating under Henry VII, the privy chamber developed through a process of reform and reorganisation between 1518 and 1536. By the time of Henry VIII it had become an institution with a regular staff of its own, including gentlemen, ushers, grooms and pages. Prior to the evolution of the Privy Chamber the chamber had been divided into three sub-departments – the jewel house, under a master, and both the wardrobe of robes (distinct from the Great Wardrobe situated outside of the court) and the wardrobe of beds, each under a yeoman. These three departments took care of the sovereign's jewels, clothing and mattresses. Still other specialised officers of the chamber were the monarch's secretary, chaplain, physician, surgeon, apothecary, barber, henchmen or young gentlemen in attendance under their master, and finally there were the Esquires of the Household.

The most important innovation in the administration of the royal chamber in the sixteenth century was the creation of the post of gentleman in the Privy Chamber, created around 1518 by amalgamating the posts of the two earlier officers – Esquires of the Household and the Knights of the Body. The Privy Chamber became a separate household department under the command of one of the two chief gentlemen who also assumed the title of Groom of the Stole. The primary duty of the Groom of the Stole (or Stool) was to see that 'the house of easement be sweet and clear'. He emerged eventually as the manager of the Privy Chamber as well as the privy purse. The gentlemen were assisted by the grooms of the privy chamber who, under the supervision of the gentlemen ushers, attended to the cleanliness of the rooms.

During 1549–53, there were six principal gentlemen and twenty-six 'ordinary' gentlemen in Edward VI's Privy Chamber. As salary, a gentleman received £50 a year, a gentleman usher £30 and a groom £20. The gentlemen were regular officers of the court and thus belonged to what was called 'the ordinary of the king's honourable house'. The post of the gentleman was therefore lucrative. However, the most important attraction of the post was not its profits. Indeed, in the sixteenth century parents were prepared to send their children to serve at the courts without any salary or fee. The most important thing was proximity to the monarch.

Progresses

Once a year the queen would go on a progress to the southern counties, but most of the time she resided in one of her great royal palaces, be it Whitehall, Hampton Court, Greenwich, Richmond, Westminster, St James, Windsor Castle or, later in her reign, Nonsuch Palace. All these palaces were, in their different ways, magnificent to behold, with high, elabonate towers and a mass of spiralling chimneys. Whitehall was reputedly the largest palace in Europe, spanning an incredible twenty-three acres, and it was in this palace Elizabeth lived more than any other. It was important that the court moved after a few weeks as the palaces needed to be 'aired and sweetened'. Sewerage facilities were primitive, so if the palaces were not cleaned frequently they became unhygienic and unpleasant places. When the court was not in residence, the palace would be cared for by a keeper and resident staff and they were expected to have things ready so that the queen and her court could arrive at a moment's notice. Windsor Castle, for example, was the strongest castle and was best placed to offer defence should enemy forces invade the country, so it was imperative that the queen and court could escape there in the event of an invasion.

At her accession, the queen inherited over sixty royal residences. Some Elizabeth occasionally frequented, but many were dilapidated. Others fell into ruin over the course of the reign as the cost of maintaining them was enormous. One solution was to bestow these residences on favoured courtiers. Robert Dudley, Earl of Leicester, did particularly well in this regard, receiving Kenilworth Castle in Warwickshire among others. The most expensive honour of all was that of housing Queen Elizabeth and her household. Elizabeth went on constant progresses about the country in the summer, when travelling was easier and plague was likely to be in London. Along with bringing her into closer contact with her subjects, this was beneficial as she saved a great deal of money by making the nobles with whom she stayed foot the bill for her visit. Many nobles begged off the honour of her stay for fear of bankruptcy.

The chaos that followed Elizabeth's summer progress prompted one historian to write, 'Nothing save war was more disruptive to the orderly well-being of court life than a royal progress.' When the queen went on progress 'she was not content to be accompanied by a mere handful of courtiers and ladies-in-waiting; she took along a great multitude and a large train of luggage, furnishings, food, and other supplies'. Burghley tried to get the queen to limit the number of people she took on progress, but she was unwilling to compromise. To maintain the level of magnificence expected of her, she expected both her courtiers and her household to behave as though they were in residence at one of her palaces. Among those from whom she expected undiminished service were the members of the household. They succeeded, but only by having 'every department ... trundling round the countryside on an assortment of wagons'. The baggage alone could require between 300 and 500 carts.

Robert Dudley used much of his new-found wealth to extend and improve Kenilworth Castle, soon one of the country's most splendid estates. In 1575, he put on a nineteen-day summer extravaganza for Elizabeth that was one of the most splendid ever to take place on English soil. The gunfire and fireworks that greeted her arrival were seen and heard over twenty miles away. There were jousts, bear-baiting and a stupendous hunt at which Elizabeth killed six deer. The hunting party was interrupted by figures dressed as gods of the woods, appearing from the trees to address her. She then watched a pageant on the lake, where a 'mermaid' swam, drawing her tail through the water, and an actor sat astride a splendidly constructed dolphin, from whose belly a melodious six-part song emanated. Shakespeare immortalised this event in *A Midsummer Night's Dream*. In the play, the contentious and sexually frustrated relationship between Oberon and Titania, the king and queen of the fairies, mirrored that of Leicester and Elizabeth. He may have been making one last effort to woo her, but they were both now forty-two. He had put on weight, gone bald, had swellings in his legs and his complexion was flushed.

A Courtier and a Fart

In an admittedly familiar tale, Edward de Vere, 17th Earl of Oxford, is alleged to have let off a loud fart when making a deep bow to Queen Elizabeth I. He was so ashamed that he left the country, in self-exile for seven years. Upon his return to court, Elizabeth greeted Oxford with the double-edged assurance, 'My lord, I had forgot the fart.'

A Courtier and a Pimp

Sir William Compton (*c.* 1482–1528) was one of the most prominent courtiers of Henry VIII. He was about nine years older than the king, but the two became close friends. An attendant on Prince Henry, upon the accession he became Henry's Groom of the Stool, the man in closest contact to the young king. Compton was also the steward of several royal manors.

In 1510, shortly after her second marriage, Anne Stafford was the subject of scandal when her brother Edward, the 3rd Duke of Buckingham, after hearing rumours concerning Anne and Compton, found the two together in Anne's room. Compton was forced to take the sacrament to prove that he and Anne had not committed adultery, and Anne's husband, the Earl of Huntingdon, sent Anne away to a convent sixty miles distant from the court. There is no evidence establishing that Anne and Compton were guilty of adultery. In 1521 Henry sent Compton to arrest the Duke of Buckingham, who was later executed for treason. In 1523, Compton took the unusual step of bequeathing land to Anne in his will and directing his executors to include her in the prayers for his kin.

One of his duties, according to the courtier Elizabeth Amadas, was to procure women for Henry and arrange trysts with them at his home in Thames Street, London. Amadas may have been the mistress of Henry between his relationships with Mary and Anne Boleyn, as she was arrested for treason in 1532, claiming to be the king's mistress and describing Anne Boleyn as a harlot who should be burnt. She also said that Henry, by setting aside Catherine of Aragon for a younger woman, was encouraging the men of England to do the same. She alleged that Compton, along with Sir John Dauncy, Privy Councillor and Knight of the Body to Henry, had brought messages from the king to her. Compton acquired significant influence over Henry when it came to granting land and favours to the aristocracy, and made a fortune himself before succumbing to the sweating sickness.

12

The Great Ministers of State

Cardinal John Morton, Archbishop of Canterbury, *c*. 1420–1500

Practically nothing is known of the Dorset-born Morton's life before the late 1440s, when he was enrolled at Balliol College, Oxford. After an early career in the Church, by 1456 Morton had gone into Lancastrian royal service, being made chancellor of Edward, Prince of Wales. An experienced lawyer by this point, Morton was responsible for drafting the bills of attainder against the Yorkist lords in 1459. However, in 1461 the Yorkist Earl of March was crowned Edward IV, and Morton was captured after the Battle of Towton while trying to escape to Scotland. He was thrown in the Tower and attainted. Luckily, he was able to escape and join the exiled Lancastrian court, consisting of Queen Margaret of Anjou and Prince Edward, in France, where he would remain until the brief Lancastrian readeption of Henry VI in 1470–71.

Morton escorted Queen Margaret and Prince Edward on their return from exile. Edward was killed following the Battle of Tewkesbury, his mother captured and Henry VI murdered shortly after, ending the House of Lancaster and forcing Morton to declare allegiance to Edward IV and the Yorkists. His surrender was accepted and he received a full pardon. Because of his undoubted expertise and capabilities, Morton became Master of the Rolls from 1472 to 1479, also serving as an ambassador to the French and Burgundian courts. In 1478 or 1479 he was made Bishop of Ely by the Pope. When Edward IV died in 1483 and the throne was usurped by his brother Richard, Duke of Gloucester, Morton was suddenly arrested, imprisoned and attainted by the new king. He was placed in the custody of the Duke of Buckingham, Richard III's most staunch supporter, at Brecon Castle. He intrigued with Margaret Beaufort, Queen Elizabeth Woodville and Buckingham to help Henry Tudor's invasion, but a series of rebellions, including that of Buckingham, were soon put down and the duke was executed. Morton managed to escape to Flanders, and then travelled to Rome where he informed the Pope of Henry's intent to take the throne from Richard III. Morton was able to warn Henry Tudor that he was about to be handed over to Richard, enabling Henry to escape just in time from Brittany to France.

As a reward for his loyalty Morton became the first Tudor's most trusted adviser, helping to establish the Tudor dynasty by advocating the marriage of Henry to Elizabeth of York. Henry VII made Morton Archbishop of Canterbury in 1486 and appointed him Lord Chancellor of England in 1487. In 1493, Pope Alexander VI appointed Morton a cardinal. Morton built the 'old palace' of Hatfield House, where Elizabeth Tudor grew up. Morton was tasked with restoring the royal estate, depleted by Edward IV and the Wars of the Roses. By the end of the reign, the king's frugality, and Morton's tax policy, carried out by Edmund Dudley and Richard Empson, had replenished the treasury. Morton gave the famous statement, later known as 'Morton's Fork', that no one was to be exempted from taxes: 'If the subject is seen to live frugally, tell him because he is clearly a money saver of great ability, he can afford to give generously to the king. If, however, the subject lives a life of great extravagance, tell him he, too, can afford to give largely, the proof of his opulence being evident in his expenditure.' Morton was a great advocate of rights for the Church and believed that it could work together with the government without being completely destroyed. However, by the end of his life Canterbury was unpopular among the common people, being blamed for a number of taxes. He was personally named by the Cornish rebels when they revolted in 1497. As a young man, the statesman Sir Thomas More served in the Morton household. He later wrote that Morton was 'a man not more venerated for his high rank than for his wisdom and virtue'. Cardinal Morton died at Knole, Sevenoaks, in Kent in 1500 in his eightieth year and was buried in the crypt of Canterbury Cathedral.

Cardinal Thomas Wolsey, Archbishop of York (*c.* 1473–1530)

Like many men of non-noble origins in this period, Ipswich-born Wolsey chose the Church as the best route to personal advancement. He graduated from Oxford, became chaplain to Sir Richard Nanfan and caught the eye of Henry VII, becoming a court chaplain. He was now mentored by the influential Richard Fox, Bishop of Winchester, and in 1509 Wolsey became a member of the King's Council, having been used in the diplomatic service. He made a journey to Flanders and back as special envoy to Emperor Maximilian with such rapidity that when he returned on the third day the king, believing he had not yet started, rebuked him for remissness. Soon appointed Master of the Rolls, Wolsey's grasp of practical affairs enabled him to initiate reforms which greatly accelerated the business of the court. On 2 February 1509 he was made Dean of Lincoln, and on the subsequent accession of Henry VIII he received an assurance of the continuance of royal favour in his appointment as almoner.

By 1512 he was exercising marked influence in political affairs and his share in the royal favour was already attracting the dislike of the old nobility. In foreign and domestic business alike, the king followed Wolsey's counsel and daily entrusted more power to his hands. Fresh preferments continued to pour in on him. He began to keep some state, and when he accompanied the king to France in June 1513 he was followed by a train of 200 gentlemen. In

1514 the Pope appointed Wolsey Bishop of Lincoln. Later that year he became Archbishop of York, and he had thus obtained, at around forty years of age, the highest spiritual and temporal dignities that a subject could hope for. His power with the king was so great that the Venetian ambassador said Wolsey now might be called *ipse rex*, the king himself.

In foreign policy, he tried to lead Henry back to his father's policy of an alliance with France in opposition to Ferdinand of Spain and the Emperor Maximilian. But the French conquest of Milan in 1515 checked this scheme, and led Wolsey to make new treaties with Maximilian and Ferdinand. After Ferdinand's death his policy was calculated to meet the entirely new situation. Ferdinand's successor, Charles V, now held Spain, the Indies, Sicily, Naples and the Netherlands, with reversion of the Duchy of Austria. Rivalry became inevitable between the two young kings of France and Spain, Francis and Charles, and Wolsey saw the advantage England had from the benefits each perceived in an English alliance. At this time the Pope was endeavouring to raise a crusade against the Turks, and Wolsey cleverly succeeded in effecting a universal peace to which the Pope and emperor as well as Francis and Charles were parties. Under cover of this peace, Wolsey pushed forward his favoured policy of alliance with France.

However, in January 1519, the situation was changed by the death of Emperor Maximilian and the consequent contest for the imperial crown. When Charles was duly elected emperor, the rivalry between the houses of Hapsburg and Valois was accentuated. Instead of three powers – Maximilian, Francis and Charles – Wolsey now had only two to reckon with and to play off against one another. He determined on a policy of neutrality with the view of giving England the decisive power in guiding the destinies of Europe. Meetings between Henry and both the rival monarchs took place; he met Charles at Canterbury and Francis at the celebrated Field of the Cloth of Gold. But a second meeting with the emperor followed immediately and Henry's personal predilections were in favour of an alliance with him rather than with France. War broke out, and both parties were soon willing to accept England's mediation, Wolsey conducting a long conference during which his behaviour was more diplomatic than honest. Before the conference was over he signed a secret treaty with the emperor which provided for an offensive and defensive alliance against France. This was a new policy for him to adopt, and it is clear that in this treaty his own wishes were overruled by Henry's desire for a new war with France, and it was not till two abortive campaigns had disillusioned the king that Wolsey was again able to resort to diplomatic measures. This treaty with the emperor was, however, of importance in Wolsey's own life as it opened up the way for his possible election to the papacy. He was twice unsuccessful, however.

In 1525, the defeat and capture of Francis at the Battle of Pavia made the dominant power of Charles a danger to all of Europe. In the face of this peril, Henry reluctantly made a new treaty with France. It was a difficult policy for Wolsey, for, having incurred the jealousy of the nobility by his power, he had aroused the hostility of the people by financial exactions and provoked the enmity of all by the extravagant pomp with which he surrounded himself on all his public appearances. He could rely only on the king's favour, and he knew that to lose this was complete ruin. Just at this critical juncture, the king raised the question of divorce in order that he might marry Anne Boleyn. Wolsey did not wish Henry to marry Anne, but he was not averse to ridding himself of Catherine of Aragon's adverse political influence, for her sympathy with her nephew the emperor caused her to dislike Wolsey's French policy. Anne Boleyn, regarding Wolsey as responsible for the long delay before her marriage to Henry, had set herself to bring about his fall. He was kept at a distance from the court and was known to be in disgrace. An indictment was moved against him in November, and on the 19th he had to surrender the great seal of England. On 22 November he was forced to sign a deed confessing that he had incurred a praemunire and surrendered all his vast possessions to the king, including Hampton Court. On 30 November judgment was given that he should be out of the king's possession and should forfeit all his lands and goods. He remained at Esher through the winter, disgraced, though not without occasional messages of kindness from the king. His health, which had been bad for many years, now failed seriously.

In February he received a general pardon, and the possessions of his archbishopric were restored to him except for York House, which he had to convey to the king. He was then allowed to retire to York, where he spent the last six months of his life in devotion. His last days were embittered by the news that the king intended to suppress the two colleges, at Ipswich and Oxford, which he had founded with such care. The former perished, but Christ's College survived, though not in the completeness he had intended. He was in residence near York, preparatory to being enthroned in York Minster, when, on 4 November, commissioners from the king came to arrest him on a charge of high treason. He slowly travelled towards London as an invalid, knowing well what to expect. 'Master Kingston,' he said, 'I see the matter against me now it is framed; but if I had served God as diligently as I have done the king He would not have given me over in my grey hairs.' The end came at Leicester Abbey, where, on arrival, he told the abbot, 'I am come to leave my bones among you.'

Wolsey's foreign policy was practical, being aimed to help English trade and to maintain peace, to secure union with Scotland and to effect ecclesiastical reforms. His failure was owing to the selfishness of Henry. The question of the divorce not only led to the fall of Wolsey, but withdrew England for generations from European politics and made the country a pariah.

The Prince of Darkness – Thomas Cromwell, Earl of Essex (*c.* 1484–1540)

Thomas Cromwell's father, Walter, was a blacksmith, cloth merchant, brewer and fuller, and a known drunkard of vicious disposition. At the age of eighteen, in 1503, Thomas fled from his violence to Italy to serve as a mercenary in the French army. He spent much of his early adulthood as a soldier on the Continent, later becoming an accountant, moneylender and merchant in Italy. He returned to England around 1512, studied law and married a wealthy widow.

In 1520, in a pivotal career move, he became legal secretary for Cardinal Wolsey. Wolsey became Cromwell's mentor and rapidly advanced his career. In 1523 Cromwell became a Member of Parliament, where he greatly extended the power of the House. During this time he also started to dissolve failing monasteries, at this stage to help build a college and school for Wolsey. However, Wolsey fell out of favour with Henry for failing to secure him a divorce from Catherine of Aragon. Cromwell was distraught, not just for the death of his friend and mentor but for the looming end of his own career.

After this huge setback, Cromwell had to earn the king's confidences directly. He rose swiftly after devising a clever strategy to enable Henry to divorce Catherine. The Pope had refused to annul Henry VIII's marriage to Catherine of Aragon. To bypass this, Cromwell suggested Henry make a break with Rome and place himself as head of an English Church. By 1532 he was the king's chief minister, a man of extreme competence. The resulting break with Rome also led to the closing of hundreds of religious houses, known as the Dissolution of the Monasteries. Between 1536 and 1540 Cromwell presided over the dissolution of 800 monasteries, with their great wealth passing to the Crown.

His policies provoked the most dangerous rebellion of the century, the Pilgrimage of Grace, but Cromwell skilfully weathered the storm and was able to survive politically. Meanwhile, he continued to accumulate offices and great wealth with amazing speed. Nothing was done without gifts of gold and silver changing hands first. His income in 1537 was over £12,000, which is equivalent to more than £4.5 million today. A particular rhyme of the times remembers Thomas Cromwell: 'Hark, hark, the dogs do bark, / The beggars are coming to town. / Some in rags and some in jags / And one in a velvet gown.' 'Jags' was a garment with slashes or slits exposing material of a different colour, especially popular among rich nobles. It refers to the Dissolution of the Monasteries, with monks and abbots begging in the streets. He was certainly corrupt, as were most courtiers of Henry VIII; Cromwell was just more successfully rapacious than others. Henry personally appointed him to the Order of the Garter, the highest order of chivalry, and then created him Earl of Essex in 1540.

No one in the sixteenth century did more than Cromwell to shape the course of English history. Thomas Cromwell never became as personally wealthy and powerful as Cardinal Wolsey, but he had much more influence on government because of the administrative changes that he instituted during the 1530s. Thomas Cromwell aimed at creating a bureaucracy that could administer the whole of England in both secular and religious matters. He aimed at uniform standards, the suppression of privileged jurisdictions, and increased central control.

Among his accomplishments, he implemented the establishment of royal supremacy. His Dissolution of the Monasteries represents the greatest single act of privatisation in the history of Britain. He founded the Ministries of

Augmentations and First Fruits to handle income from the Dissolution. He founded the Courts of Wards and Surveyors, which allowed more efficient taxation and leasing. He integrated the kingdom politically by extending sovereign authority into northern England, Wales and Ireland, actions which angered the great feudal lords. Importantly, Cromwell used the power of that relatively new invention the printing press, thus spearheading the first propaganda campaign in English history.

However, in 1540 Cromwell persuaded Henry to agree to marry Anne of Cleves, a German princess who was a member of a Protestant defensive alliance. Henry's third wife, Jane Seymour, had died following childbirth in 1537. Cromwell hoped that the marriage to the German princess would secure support against the Catholic Holy Roman Emperor and strengthen the international ties of Protestantism. It was Cromwell's undoing. A diplomatic masterstroke was undone by Henry's dislike of his plain new wife and his new love for Catherine Howard. To annul the marriage Henry had to give humiliating evidence of its failings in a Church court, and he subsequently withdrew his support from Cromwell. Cromwell was disliked by many at Henry's court because of his arrogant manner and working-class origins. After a great clash with Thomas Howard, Duke of Norfolk, Cromwell was charged with heresy, treason and corruption and, despite his pleas for mercy, was executed at the Tower of London on 28 July 1540. On that very day, King Henry VIII married his fifth wife, Catherine Howard, the niece of the Duke of Norfolk.

Thomas Cromwell had been denied a trial as an Act of attainder had been used against him. He was accused of releasing men convicted or suspected of treason, misusing and expropriating funds, taking bribes, making appointments without royal approval, being a 'detestable heretic' who had spread heretical literature throughout the kingdom, being a 'maintainer and supporter of heretics', speaking treasonable words and being a sacramentary, a supporter of Zwingli and someone who denied the real presence of Christ in the sacrament. Although sentenced to hanging, drawing and quartering, Henry commuted the sentence to a beheading despite Cromwell not being a nobleman by birth. It is said that Henry VIII intentionally chose an inexperienced teenaged executioner. He made three attempts at chopping off Cromwell's head before he succeeded. After execution, Cromwell's head was boiled and then set upon a spike on London Bridge, facing away from the City of London.

Henry VIII used to hit Cromwell about the head when he was angry, but came to appreciate his true value after the execution. In March 1541, the French ambassador in England wrote that Henry bemoaned that his councillors 'by false accusations … made him put to death the most faithful servant he ever had'. In the following year, the king was blaming others for Cromwell's death, realising the loss of one of the most trusted and efficient ministers he had ever had. He never appointed another chief minister, but for the first time ran policy himself. Seven years later the king died, having wasted the entire amount gained from the monasteries in a huge and totally unsuccessful war against France, leaving England penniless and isolated. In a strange case of history repeating itself, that great church destroyer Oliver Cromwell was directly descended from Thomas Cromwell's sister Katherine, who had married Oliver's great-grandfather Morgan Williams. The family then began adopting the more influential Cromwell surname. Oliver Cromwell was one of ten children and initially signed his name as 'Cromwell, alias Williams'.

Elizabeth's Men

Sir Nicholas Bacon (1510–79) became Keeper of the Privy Seal in 1558 and a member of the Privy Council. In 1559 he was authorised to act as Lord Chancellor and retained the post until his death in 1579.

Sir Francis Knollys (1514–96) had strong Protestant convictions, which helped him to rise at court under Edward VI. He moved to Frankfurt and Strasbourg while Mary ruled. He returned on Elizabeth's accession and she appointed him to her Privy Council in December 1558. Knollys married Catherine Carey (Mary Boleyn's daughter) and was thus Elizabeth's first cousin. For much of Elizabeth's reign he sat in Parliament and acted as government spokesman there. In 1568–69 he was jailor to Mary, Queen of Scots, and tried to convert her to the Genevan brand of Protestantism.

Sir Walter Mildmay (1523–89) married Sir Francis Walsingham's sister, Mary, in 1546. Elizabeth appointed him to her Privy Council and in 1566 made him Chancellor of the Exchequer. Like Knollys, he had strong puritan sympathies. In 1584 he founded Emmanuel College, Cambridge, with the specific aim of training learned ministers.

Sir Francis Walsingham (1532–90) was appointed Secretary of State in 1572 on Burghley's promotion to Lord Treasurer. He held the post until his death in 1590. Walsingham had chosen exile when Mary I became queen and he always remained a fervent Protestant. He showed a talent for uncovering Catholic plots against Elizabeth. He played a key role in the exposure of Mary Stuart's part in the Babington conspiracy and in her subsequent execution.

Sir Robert Cecil (1563–1612) was the second son of William Cecil. In the 1580s, he sat in Parliament and acted as Elizabeth's envoy in unsuccessful attempts to negotiate peace with Spain. During the 1590s he took over the responsibilities of Secretary of State and was formally appointed to the post in 1596. He clashed with Essex and after that earl's fall became dominant in government and helped organise James I's unchallenged succession.

Sir Francis Bacon (1561–1626) was Sir Nicholas Bacon's son and also became Lord Chancellor. A man of immense ability, Sir Francis Bacon was a lawyer, politician, the author of some of the finest essays in the English language and wrote the first systematic exposition of the inductive method in science.

William Cecil, the Architect of Elizabethan England (1520–98)

Cecil came from a Welsh family whose name was anglicised from Seisyllt, in the service of the Tudors after Henry VII toppled Richard III in 1485.

William's father Richard of Burghley married a local heiress in Northampton, and thus gained the manor of Bourne. Richard was a Groom of the Wardrobe at court, and William served as a page there before he entered St John's College, Cambridge, in 1535. He married in 1541 when he went to Gray's Inn to practise law, but his wife died in 1543, leaving him a son, Thomas. William Cecil was rewarded by Henry VIII in 1542 for defending royal policy, and given a place in the Court of Common Pleas. In 1543 he entered Parliament aged just twenty-three. He rose to prominence under Somerset and became Secretary of State under Northumberland. His discrete silence about his Protestant sympathies enabled him to serve Mary I on several diplomatic missions.

It appears that the Cecils were responsible for keeping the young Elizabeth at Hatfield House, safely away from the intrigues of Mary I's court. Elizabeth seemed to know William Cecil very well, for upon his appointment as her sole secretary she told him, 'This judgement I have of you, that you will not be corrupted by any manner of gift and that you will be faithful to the state and that, without respect of my private will, you will give me that counsel which you think best.' He remained her chief councillor to his death, when Elizabeth was at his bedside. 'No prince in Europe hath such a counsellor as I have in mine,' she once said. She knew that he always gave his best advice, and would not be swayed by pressure. In turn, he knew how to put up with her extremes of temper by tactically retreating – he advised a younger man, 'Good my Lord, overcome her with yielding.'

After a second marriage in 1545, he joined an influential Protestant circle at court. When Edward VI succeeded to the throne, Cecil joined the household of the Protector, the Duke of Somerset, becoming his secretary in 1548. However, when Somerset fell from power Cecil was caught up in his disgrace and despatched to the Tower of London for two months in 1549. Nevertheless, the abilities of Cecil were so highly regarded that he gained royal favour and became one of two secretaries to the young king, who gave him a knighthood in 1551. Cecil had acted as a go-between between the two main rivals for power over the young Edward, Edward Seymour, Duke of Somerset, and John Dudley, Earl of Warwick. When Somerset fell from power the second time, in 1551, it was Warwick who proposed Cecil's knighthood, and Cecil committed himself to Warwick, who now became Duke of Northumberland. However, when Northumberland proposed altering the succession, Cecil sided with the judges on the Tudor side, although fearing arrest and contemplating flight. Only on the royal command of Edward did Cecil capitulate to Northumberland's demands. He deserted Northumberland on Edward's death to side with the Tudors.

He met Mary Tudor as representative of Edward's council, and she called him 'a very honest man'. Cecil was now offered a post in Queen Mary's court, but unlike most of his colleagues preferred to withdraw from the Catholic milieu until Elizabeth's expected Protestant accession. His backing for Elizabeth, when it looked as if she was more likely to be executed than succeed to the throne, was something that kept the two very close throughout the next forty years. He immediately became her principal secretary and chief adviser on her accession in 1558. His first act was to persuade the reluctant Elizabeth to intervene in Scotland and sign the Treaty of Edinburgh, to remove French troops from there.

Cecil was a superb statesman and first helped Elizabeth to get the state on a sound economic footing, including adopting a new coinage in 1561. Elizabeth operated a rotating court, spending her time at the stately homes of various subjects. Given her vast army of retainers, this saved enormous sums of money and ensured that no one individual became too rich. Her subjects vied with each other to offer the most splendid sojourn at their estates, which helped add to the pomp and panoply of the Elizabethan period, while costing her nothing. To heal the terrible religious divisions (her half-sister predecessor Mary had executed 500 Protestants), Cecil and Elizabeth worked together on a compromise settlement to establish the Anglican Church in 1559. Cecil also ended the expensive war with France, organised an efficient secret service to snuff out Catholic attempts on Elizabeth's life and dramatically strengthened the army and navy.

He was chancellor of the University of Cambridge from 1559, and survived an attempt to sack him as Elizabeth's secretary by the jealous lords Leicester and Norfolk in 1568. He had introduced Norfolk into the council to balance Leicester's power. John Dudley's son Robert, Earl of Leicester, became emotionally close to Elizabeth, weakening Cecil's position. Despite threats of resignation, Elizabeth came round to siding with Cecil and rewarded him with the lucrative mastership of the Court of Wards in 1572. She had created him 1st Baron Burghley in 1571. In 1572 he also became Lord Treasurer and a Knight of the Garter. His loyalty, industry and judgement were indispensable to the queen – he was her mainstay throughout most of her reign. While opposing Dudley, Cecil was sympathetic to Protestant desires for Elizabeth to marry and produce an heir, resisting Mary Stuart's claims to succeed. He recommended the Hapsburg suitor, the Archduke Charles. In the early 1570s Cecil was in diplomatic overdrive, aiding the Dutch while soothing Spanish feelings and trying to achieve a French alliance. He knew that war would overstretch England's finances and thereby endanger the Tudor monarchy. Cecil said that 'a reign gaineth more by one year's peace than ten years' war'.

In 1568, Mary Stuart, Queen of Scots, fled to England. The Ridolfi plot to put Mary on the English throne with a Spanish invasion led to Norfolk's execution. The close attention paid to Mary, Queen of Scots, by Cecil later led to the discovery of the Babington plot, and her trial for treason and execution in 1587. Equally, Cecil's insight into Spanish intentions led to preparations for naval resistance that helped beat the Armada in 1588. Cecil's elder son, Thomas, commanded a ship in the English fleet. Cecil had previously put out peace feelers to the Duke of Parma, the Spanish commander in the Netherlands, in 1585, again earning Leicester's enmity. Nonetheless, Cecil tried for peace with Spain again in 1587. The former Spanish ambassador to Elizabeth's court summed up his feelings about Britain's chief economist and diplomat: he was 'the man that does everything'.

Elizabeth's principal councillor now presided over the coaching of his son Robert, born in 1563, towards the post of Elizabeth's secretary, which he took in 1596. Thus the 'reign of the Cecils' continued. William Cecil retired with ill health but still remained active, urging peace with Spain for fear of a costly war against a Franco-Spanish alliance. He died in 1598 before negotiations were concluded, and is buried at St Martin's church, Burghley. The consummate master of Renaissance statecraft, famed over Europe, his talents as a diplomat, statesman and administrator were unparalleled. Of himself he said, 'I have gained more by my temperance and forebearing than ever I did with my wit.' A contemporary observation of Cecil showed that he kept his thoughts and feelings under control: 'He had no close friends, no inward companion as great men commonly have ... nor did any other know his secrets; some noting it for a fault, but most thinking it a praise and an instance of his wisdom. By trusting none with his secrets, none could reveal them.'

Burghley House is probably the most magnificent Elizabethan building in Britain, built between 1565 and 1587 and still lived in by his descendants. At one point he had been offered an earldom by Elizabeth, but refused on the grounds of its great expense. Overworked and in ill health, Cecil was an expert in finances, religion and socio-economic policy. He also coordinated the Privy Council, which met almost every day, and was the queen's chief councillor and secretary; he managed Parliament and presided over the Exchequer as well as being a JP in five counties. Britain's de facto Foreign Secretary and chief diplomat, he made Britain respected as a European power and he was ruthless with any opposition to his beloved queen. He served Elizabeth as Secretary of State from 1558 to 1572, and as Lord Treasurer from 1572 until his death in 1598. He was Elizabeth's chief adviser and supervised the whole of English administration. Without Cecil, it is difficult to envisage an Elizabethan Age.

The Courtier Survivor – William Paulet, 1st Marquis Of Winchester (1483/85–1572)

Paulet was a Privy Councillor for thirty years, so adept at altering his views that both Mary and Elizabeth reappointed him as Lord Treasurer, the latter when he was seventy-four. His presence gave continuity to a government which experienced four monarchs (Henry VIII, Edward VI, Mary and Elizabeth) and four changes of religion in just twelve years between 1547 and 1559. He was almost fifty years old before he became a courtier, after being a lawyer living in Hampshire, serving as sheriff and justice of the peace. During the 1520s he came to the attention of Henry VIII and was appointed first as Surveyor of the Woods, followed soon after by an appointment as Master of the Wards, both administrative roles. Paulet's success in enlarging and improving the system of wardship, increasing the income to the king, led to him being appointed as Comptroller of the Royal Household in 1532. This role put him at the centre of the court, close to the king, and for the rest of his life Paulet played the role of courtier.

During the next eighteen years, Paulet held each of the four household officer appointments. As Comptroller and later Treasurer of the Household, he was responsible for the 'below-stairs' departments of all the houses in which the king lived, ensuring the supply of everything necessary to feed and lodge a court of several hundred people and overseeing the supplies and running of kitchens which each day prepared up to 600 meals for both dinner and supper. A further appointment as Lord Chamberlain gave him responsibility for the organisation of the 'above-stairs' department, the state apartments, where the ceremony observed by the courtiers and the decoration of the chambers were used to create the image of Henry VIII as a magnificent king. Paulet's last household appointment was as Lord Great Master, with overall control of every aspect of life in the royal palaces. By the time he was sixty-six he had more experience than any other courtier of how the palaces operated. He might have been expected to retire to Hampshire, but his next appointment, as Lord High Treasurer, set him on a new career.

If Henry VIII had lived it is unlikely that he would have given Paulet such an exalted position. Edward VI was nine years old when he came to the throne so England was governed by the sixteen executors whom Henry VIII had named to be his son's Privy Council. Paulet was one of these men, and for two years he supported Edward Seymour, Duke of Somerset, as Lord Protector, but in 1549 he sided with John Dudley, Earl of Warwick, in a bid to reduce Somerset's power, a bid which ultimately led to Somerset's overthrow. Warwick took Somerset's place as leader, but he realised that he needed to cultivate supporters. During the next four years, Paulet and the other leading members of the council rewarded themselves with titles and appointments – rewards from Warwick for past support and inducements for future loyalty.

Within two years Paulet was created Earl of Wiltshire and Marquis of Winchester, and he soon took up his post as Lord High Treasurer – the second-highest post in England. However, these rewards were insufficient to guarantee Paulet's unwavering support – his first loyalty was to the Crown – and he soon opposed Warwick, now Duke of Northumberland, in his plans to put Lady Jane Grey upon the throne. Having taken part in the downfall of Somerset, Paulet now played his part in the downfall of Northumberland. However, in both instances he stayed loyal to the Crown and followed the path he believed was best for England.

Paulet served four monarchs as an administrator and politician. On one occasion Elizabeth I announced that, of all her councillors, only Paulet was on her side, and she once joked, after a visit to Basing House, 'For, by my troth, if my lord treasurer were but a young man, I could find it in my heart to have him for a husband before any man in England.' Sadly for Paulet, at the age of seventy-six he must have seemed truly ancient to the twenty-six-year-old queen. Paulet was still working when he died aged eighty-seven in 1572.

As Marquis of Winchester he had become the senior peer in England. He had been a participant in many of the famous events in Tudor history, played a central role at royal weddings, coronations and funerals and, as a councillor and member of the House of Lords, he influenced major changes to the religion, economy and social fabric of England. Paulet believed that he survived because he tried to treat people gently so as not to alienate men and make enemies. Once, when asked how he managed to survive so many storms not only unhurt but rising all the while, Paulet answered, 'By being a willow, not an oak.'

PART 2

Interesting Facts Regarding Tudor Life

14

Law, Order, Crime and Punishment

Law and Order

Since the fourteenth century there had been laws against vagabonds, but from 1530 new laws started being passed in response to growing problems. Over a third of the population lived in poverty. Poor women and men who lost their spouses and had young children were desperate to remarry, as two incomes were needed to survive. Many were forced into crime or begging to survive. From 1530, the old and disabled poor were given licences to beg. However, anyone roaming without a job was tied to a cart in the nearest market town and whipped until they were bloody. A law of 1547 said vagabonds, i.e. the homeless, could be made slaves for two years, and if they ran away during that time could be branded with a 'V' and made slaves for life. This terrible law was abolished in 1550. Once again, flogging was made the major punishment for vagrancy. Throughout the Tudor period the number of beggars and robbers increased, especially in London, which attracted vagrants from all over Britain. *A Manifest Detection of Diceplay*, published in 1552, gives the first detailed description of the criminal networks of Tudor London. Because most people did not travel far, anyone who did was often treated with suspicion, especially if not well dressed, and could be arrested by local JPs. Travelling actors had to have a licence, otherwise they would be breaking the law for operating outside their home areas. A poor person in a wealthy area was often thought to be a criminal.

For begging one could be whipped until bleeding, and more. For stealing a small item one could be placed in stocks and pelted with objects. For stealing a shilling, hanging was likely. Supporting the destitute became a major problem, not helped by the Dissolution of the Monasteries in 1536, as these had been a significant source of charitable relief and had also provided a great deal of direct and indirect employment. In 1572, because of the twin problems of increasing poverty and displaced agricultural labourers looking for work in cities, it was decided to tax the richer classes to help pay for the poor. The Poor Relief Act of 1576 established the principle that if the able-bodied poor needed financial support they had to work for it.

The Elizabethan 'Poor Laws' distinguished two types of people who needed support: the able-bodied, who could work but did not; and the 'impotent poor' or 'deserving poor', those who were too old or sick to provide for themselves. The first group was classed as 'vagrants' or 'sturdy beggars', and could be whipped all the way back to their home parishes. The problem was that the only place anyone could get help was in the village of their birth, or where they had lived for the last three years. If you asked for help elsewhere you would be sent back home, but still had nowhere to live and no job. The second group, impoverished by misfortune and sickness, were to be given support and materials for a productive activity, usually spinning or weaving. Overseers of the poor in each parish were authorised to levy a 'poor rate' on all the householders to cover the costs of these benefits. Many people capable of work feigned illness to become one of the 'deserving poor', a parallel seen today.

The 1601 Act for the Relief of the Poor made parishes legally responsible for the care of those within their boundaries who, through age or infirmity, were unable to work. The able-bodied were offered work in a 'House of Correction', the precursor of the workhouse, where the 'persistent idler' could be punished. It proposed the building of housing for the 'impotent poor', the old and the infirm, but most assistance was granted through a form of poor relief known as 'outdoor relief', with money, food or other necessities given to those living in their own homes, funded by a local tax on the property of the wealthiest in the parish. Laws were harsh and wrongdoing was severely punished, but there was no police force to enforce law and order. Crime was endemic because of poverty, and perhaps over 70,000 people were executed during the reign of Henry VIII alone, most for very minor crimes such as stealing.

Trials for the upper classes were designed in the favour of the prosecutors and conducted at the Star Chamber at the Palace of Westminster, made up of Privy Councillors and judges. Defendants were not allowed legal counsel. The Star Chamber witnessed the trials of royalty and nobility between 1487 and 1641, its primary function being to hear cases involving political libel, high treason, alchemy, blasphemy, sedition, spying, rebellion, murder, witchcraft and heresy. The punishment for most of the crimes was death. Minor punishments would include taking lands, titles and wealth from those who had been found guilty. It was set up to ensure the fair enforcement of laws against powerful people, who might not be convicted by ordinary courts. Its sessions were held in secret and became greatly feared. There was no jury, no right of appeal and no witnesses. Evidence was only given in writing. The court evolved into a political weapon to use against any opponents of the policies of the monarch.

Punishments

Prison was rarely used as a punishment, and gaols were basically holding areas until trial, after which the prisoner was given a physical punishment like flogging. More serious crimes were punished by death. Beheading was reserved for the wealthy; ordinary people were usually hanged. It was believed that if a criminal's punishment was severe and painful enough then the act would not be repeated, and others would be deterred as well. This author remembers a story, possibly apocryphal, that burglary was endemic in the Weimar Republic but vanished when Hitler introduced the death penalty for the crime. Public executions were regarded by many as entertainment in the sixteenth century. People would queue through the night to get the best places, and taverns, ale merchants, pie sellers and producers of execution memorabilia prospered. The 'private' execution of Anne Boleyn within the Tower was restricted to the members of the Tudor court and the nobles of the land, including close members of her family, but her death was still witnessed by several hundred spectators.

The dreadful punishment of being hanged, drawn and quartered was described by William Harrison as follows:

> The greatest and most grievous punishment used in England for such as offend against the State is drawing from the prison to the place of execution upon an hurdle or sled, where they are hanged till they be half dead, and then taken down, and quartered alive; after that, their members and bowels are cut from their bodies, and thrown into a fire, provided near hand and within their own sight, even for the same purpose.

Hanging from the gallows was the normal method of execution. Relatives would often pull on the legs to shorten the suffering. Women found guilty of treason or 'petty treason' were sentenced to be burned alive at the stake, and some were 'pressed', i.e. crushed to death. Execution by burning, favoured by the Catholic Inquisition and Mary I, was a terrible death. Tudor executioners sometimes showed mercy to their victims by placing gunpowder at the base of the stake, which helped the victims to a swifter and less painful death. The only other respite from the excruciating pain of being burnt to death was if the victims died of suffocation through smoke inhalation and lack of oxygen. Being boiled alive was a rare punishment.

Lesser punishments included whipping. Many towns had a whipping post. The victim was chained to the post, stripped to the waist, whether male or female, and flogged. One could be whipped for stealing a loaf of bread. The pillory was commonly called 'the nutcrackers', because it looked like the victim's 'nut' or head was to be cracked open in a wooden vice. It was later known as a 'Norway neckcloth', as it was often constructed of Norway fir. Timber became a rare commodity and had to be imported in Henry VIII's reign because of the extensive building of ships and houses. The pillory was a T-shaped block of wood with holes for the hands in the crossbar of the T. The person being punished would have to stand in the device in the middle of the market to be ridiculed by passers-by, or perhaps have things thrown at them, or be kicked, punched and the like.

With stocks, the culprit sat on a wooden bench with his ankles, and sometimes his wrists or even neck, thrust through holes in movable boards. Punishment in the stocks generally lasted for at least several hours. For lesser crimes such as stealing a bird's egg the missiles thrown at the culprit might include stinking eggs, sewage or rotten food, but it was not unknown for people to lose eyes or their lives when attacked with stones. The Statute of Labourers 1351 ordered the punishment of the stocks for unruly artisans, and ruled that stocks should be made in every town and village in England. Although never abolished, the punishment of the stocks began to die out in England in the nineteenth century. The ducking stool was a punishment for women. Accused witches were dunked into a river to see if they were innocent or guilty. If they floated, they were considered guilty and burnt at the stake. If they sank, they were innocent but died anyway by drowning. Either way, they perished. Hot irons were used to burn letters onto the skin of an offender's hand, arm or cheek. A murderer would be branded with the letter M, vagrants with the letter V, and thieves with the letter T. Some people who stole things from shops had their hands cut off.

The 'brank', also known as the gossip's or scold's bridle, was a punishment for women who gossiped or spoke too freely. It was a large iron framework placed on the head of the offender, forming a type of cage. There was sometimes a metal strip on the brank that fit into the mouth and was either sharpened to a point or covered with spikes so that any movement of the tongue was certain to cause severe injuries to the mouth. It was used to humiliate women who 'by brawling and wrangling amongst her neighbours breaks the public peace, increases discord and becomes a public nuisance to the neighbourhood'. It often had ridiculous adornments designed to humiliate its victim. In some towns, the brank had a bell attached to its rear to announce the presence of the victim, who was instantly mocked by the people she 'endangered' through gossip. The duration of this torture could range from a few hours to months. In some cases, the victim was left to die with the brank attached to her face. The 'Drunkard's Cloak' was a punishment for public drunkenness. The drunk was forced to don a barrel and wander through town while the villagers jeered at him. Holes were cut in the barrel for the person's hands and head, causing it to become like a heavy, awkward shirt.

Cooking the Cook

The growing influence of the Boleyns at court was deeply resented. Richard Roose, or Rice, was the cook of John Fisher, Bishop of Rochester, at whose palace several servants died of 'poisoning' after eating porridge or soup. The bishop survived. Rumours circled at court that it was not the cook who had poisoned the soup but someone else far closer to the king, namely Anne Boleyn and her faction. It was said that the Boleyns wanted to assassinate Bishop Fisher due to his refusal to acknowledge Anne as queen, and that Anne had 'bewitched' the king. There is absolutely no evidence that Anne was involved, despite the fact that a massively popular romantic novelist has claimed that Anne was a murderer. Henry himself did not believe such nonsense. Under torture the cook was found guilty and Henry changed the law to make it legal to boil people alive as a capital punishment. On 15 April 1532 Richard Roose was taken to Smithfield, where he was boiled alive in a large cauldron in front of a large crowd. His execution is estimated to have lasted for two entire hours. The *Chronicle of the Grey Friars of London* gives a date of 1531 (spelling modernised): 'This year was a cook boiled in a caldron in Smithfield for he would have poisoned the bishop of Rochester

Fisher with divers of his servants, and he was locked in a chain and pulled up and down with a gibbet at divers times till he was dead.' Henry is said to have cruelly exclaimed, 'I cooked the cook!' as a joke to his courtiers. Bishop Fisher was himself beheaded in 1535.

The Talking Heads

Beheading with an axe was the most common form of execution for the nobility and victims often took several blows before the head was finally severed. Following the execution, the severed head was held up by the hair by the executioner. This tradition was not just to show the crowd the head, but also to show the head of the victim to its own dead body. Consciousness remains for at least eight seconds after beheading, until the lack of oxygen causes unconsciousness and mercifully death. When the head had witnessed its own body, it was then turned to face the crowd. The heads of Tudor traitors were placed on stakes and displayed in public places such as on the ramparts of castles or such prominent spots as London Bridge. Henry VIII was thoughtful enough to pay for an expert French swordsman to carry out a clean execution of Anne Boleyn, instead of the more brutal (and more likely to miss) axe. On 19 May 1536 it is reported that as the swordsman held up Anne's head to show the crowd, her eyes were still moving and her lips were framing her dying prayer. After Mary, Queen of Scots, was executed upon 8 February 1587 at Fotheringhay Castle, a contemporary account tells us that 'her lips stirred up and down a quarter of an hour after her head was cut off'. During this time, her little dog, which was found nestling between her skirts, was pulled out, and insisted upon lying between the severed head and Mary's shoulders.

Cromwell's Botched Job

Upon 28 July 1540, Henry VIII had his former chief minister, Thomas Cromwell, beheaded. The vindictive king ordered that the execution was to be carried out by an inexperienced youth, who only succeeded at the third attempt. Like Thomas More's, Cromwell's head was boiled and placed on London Bridge.

The Mad Axeman

On 27 May 1541, Margaret de la Pole, the sixty-seven-year-old Countess of Salisbury, was dragged unwillingly to her execution at the Tower. As she struggled, the first blow of the axe smashed into her shoulder. She leapt up from the block, and the headsman pursued her. He struck her eleven more times before she fell dead.

More's Pickled Head

Thomas More was executed in 1535 for disagreeing with Henry VIII's divorce of Catherine of Aragon. A month later, his daughter Margaret Roper passed in a boat under London Bridge, where More's head was spiked on a long pole. According to John Aubrey, she cried, 'That head has lain many a time in my lap. Would to God it would fall into my lap as I pass under!' Her prayer was answered. This was her story when arrested for being in possession of her father's head. It seems a little more likely that she bribed the bridge keeper rather than let him throw it into the river. She was brought before council and asserted that her father's head 'should not be food for fishes'. Margaret was imprisoned. When released she pickled More's head in spices, and when she died in 1544 it was placed in her coffin.

How to Impress a Woman

The Rising of the North in 1586 was the last open attempt made by the Catholics to re-establish the faith. Instead of helping their cause it brought untold sufferings upon innumerable families, and the publication of a bull from the Pope, in which Elizabeth I was declared guilty of heresy and her English subjects absolved from their allegiance, only served to increase the persecutions of Catholics. Upwards of 800 Catholics perished on the gallows after the rising, and fifty-seven noblemen and gentlemen were attainted by Parliament, and their estates confiscated. Severe penal enactments were passed by which anyone refusing to attend the reformed service was liable to fine and imprisonment. To become a priest, or to harbour one, or be present at Mass, were crimes punishable with death. At York alone, twenty-eight priests were hanged, disembowelled and quartered for exercising their sacerdotal functions; eleven laymen were executed for harbouring priests; and Margaret Clitherow of York was barbarously pressed to death for the same crime upon 25 March 1586. On hearing at her trial that she would die by 'peine forte at dure' (long and hard pain, by being pressed to death), Margaret allegedly said, 'God be thanked. I am not worthy of so good a death as this.' She was placed on the ground with her arms stretched out on either side, her hands tied to posts. A sharp stone was placed under her spine and a door across her torso, upon which more and more weights were added. Canonised in 1970, her right hand is kept in St Mary's Convent, York. We remember Mary I as 'Bloody Mary' as she was later despised as a Catholic, but if the nation had returned to Catholicism, we would be remembering 'Bloody Elizabeth' rather than 'Gloriana'.

Henry's Sense of Humour

The Pilgrimage of Grace involved an army of some 20,000–30,000 outraged peasants and gentry, and outnumbered Howard's royalist army. Henry, with the advice of Cromwell, surprised the 'Pilgrims' by agreeing to all their demands, and they went peacefully home. Then he raised an army. Finding their demands not satisfied, they revolted again and were brutally put down. Robert Aske, the leader of the original protest, begged when sentenced to be hanged, drawn and quartered, to be fully dead before being dismembered. Henry promised and then, with cruel humour, instead had Aske hung in chains from the walls of Clifford's Tower at York Castle, a lingering death from starvation and thirst. Instead of taking about six minutes to die, it would have taken about six agonising days.

The Tyburn Tree

During Queen Elizabeth's reign, London's notorious Tyburn Tree attracted thousands of spectators every week. It was a huge wooden triangle with up to twenty-four bodies swinging from its beams by nooses, gasping their last breaths. Executions took place at Tyburn for almost 600 years, with the first recorded as William Longbeard in 1196 and the last being John Austen in 1783. In between, tens of thousands of highwaymen, robbers, forgers, murderers, traitors and other convicted men and women met their end at Tyburn. From the Reformation period onwards, this included many Catholics who would not abandon their faith. The original Tyburn trees used for hangings were a row of elms alongside an underground stream called Tyburn Brook. However, it was the huge, triangular 'Tyburn Tree', erected in 1571 and made of thick wooden crossbeams nine feet long on eighteen-foot legs, that is associated with the mass executions during the Tudor era and afterwards. The site of the Tyburn Tree is said to be at what is now Marble Arch, or slightly to the north-west at Connaught Square. Many bodies were found when Connaught Square was being built in the 1820s, so it is possible that some Tyburn victims were buried where they died.

Mass executions took place on Mondays, when prisoners were transported from Newgate Prison to Tyburn in an open wagon, often in their finest clothes. The procession was watched by a large and enthusiastic crowd. Once at Tyburn, those due to die were put onto a specially built horse-drawn carriage that was moved under the Tyburn Tree. Nooses were placed around their necks and then the carriage driven away, leaving the condemned suspended until they died. Hangings were witnessed by thousands of spectators who would pay to sit in open galleries erected especially for the occasion, as well as in rented upper-storey rooms in houses and pubs. After the corpses were cut down from the gallows there was a rush to grab the bodies, as some believed their hair and body parts were effective in healing diseases. Close to the site, at 8 Hyde Park Place, is the Tyburn Convent. Founded at the beginning of the twentieth century, it contains a Shrine of the Martyrs in remembrance of more than 350 Catholics who died at Tyburn during the Reformation.

A Law Against Welshmen and Buggery

In 1536, Henry VIII signed an all-purpose law against Welshmen and buggery with the title 'An Act for the Continue of the Statutes for Beggars and Vagabonds; and against Conveyance of Horses and Mares out of this Realm; against Welshmen making Affrays in the Counties of Hereford, Gloucester and Salop; and against the vice of Buggery'.

Henry VIII's Special Treatment for the Insane

In the downfall of her husband George Boleyn and her sister-in-law Anne Boleyn, Jane Rochford found herself dragged into a maelstrom of intrigue. When Thomas Cromwell sent for Rochford, he already had much of what he needed not only to bring down Anne Boleyn and her circle but to make possible the king's marriage to Jane Seymour. Jane Rochford was questioned relentlessly and at length, and had to answer every accusation – there were no defending lawyers or intermediaries to help her. She buckled under the pressure of interrogation and gave Cromwell what he wanted, a statement implicating her husband in acts of incest with his sister Anne. Another charge against Anne at her trial, though it was not spoken in court, was that Anne had told Jane that the king was impotent, a piece of information Cromwell had obtained from Jane. Cromwell was happy to find a scapegoat to exonerate the king from the charge of callously killing his innocent wife. After the deaths of George and Anne, Jane Rochford was absent from court owing to the loss of her lands and income. Cromwell gave her some funds, grateful for her assistance.

She was eventually able to return to court and served Henry's later wives as a lady-in-waiting, and quickly became a favourite of the young Catherine Howard. Jane was lady of the bedchamber to Anne Boleyn, Jane Seymour, Anne of Cleves and Catherine Howard. Jane was selected to bear the train of the Princess Mary at Jane Seymour's funeral. When Henry VIII wanted a quick divorce from his fourth wife, Anne of Cleves, Rochford provided evidence, saying that Anne had confided that the marriage had not actually been consummated. This report was included in the divorce proceedings. Once Catherine Howard's affair with Thomas Culpeper was discovered through a letter she wrote him, she and Lady Rochford were detained. When Catherine was accused of the affair, which amounted to treason against the king, Jane Rochford first denied knowledge of it. The interrogation of Jane over this matter caused her to lose her sanity, raising questions whether she would be well enough to be executed.

The letter to Culpeper, in Catherine's handwriting, contained the sentence, 'Come when my Lady Rochford is here, for then I shall be at leisure to be at your commandment.' Jane had a nervous breakdown after months of interrogation and was declared insane, but Henry VIII had a special law passed which allowed him to execute an insane person. Jane Boleyn was charged and tried. The Act of attainder against 'Lady Jane Rocheford' called her 'that bawd'. She was found guilty, and her execution took place on Tower Green on 3 February 1542, after Jane made a prayer for the king and said she had falsely testified against her husband. She was buried at St Peter ad Vincula church.

The Trial of the Dead Cock

On 28 October 1562, the Battle of Corrichie was fought. It was prophesied before the fight that George Gordon, the rebel Earl of Huntley, would lie that night in the Tolbooth in Aberdeen, without a mark upon him. Known as the 'Cock of the North', Gordon took this as a good omen but just after the battle suffered a fatal attack of apoplexy. His body was laid out in the Tolbooth. Subsequently, his embalmed body was obliged to stand trial for treason.

Bad News for Nagging Wives until 1967

In 1585 scolding was criminalised, remaining illegal until 1967, along with offences such as barratry (the vexatious incitement of quarrels or lawsuits), eavesdropping, challenging someone to a fight and being a 'common night walker'.

The School for Pickpockets

A cut-purse: so called by one Wotton, who in the year 1585 kept an academy for the education and perfection of pickpockets and cut-purses: his school was near Billingsgate, London. As in the dress of ancient times many people wore their purses at their girdles, cutting them was a branch of the light-fingered art, which is now lost, though the name remains. Maitland, from Stow, gives the following account of this Wotton: This man was a gentleman born, and sometime a merchant of good credit, but fallen by time into decay: he kept an alehouse near Smart's Key, near Billingsgate, afterwards for some misdemeanour put down. He reared up a new trade of life, and in the same house he procured all the cut-purses about the city, to repair to his house; there was a school-house set up to learn young boys to cut purses: two devices were hung up; one was a pocket, and another was a purse; the pocket had in it certain counters, and was hung about with hawks bells, and over the top did hang a little sacring bell. The purse had silver in it; and he that could take out a counter, without noise of any of the bells, was adjudged a judicial NYPPER: according to their terms of art, a FOYSTER was a pick-pocket; a NYPPER was a pick purse, or cut-purse. The origin of Fagin seems to have been one Wotton, who had fallen upon hard times. He therefore opened an academy for pickpockets at an alehouse near Billingsgate. Training involved being able to empty a practice purse without ringing any of the little hawk's bells hanging on it.

The 1811 Dictionary of the Vulgar Tongue, originally by Francis Grose

Moll Cutpurse, 'The Roaring Girl' Cross-Dresser (*c.* 1584–1659)

This young lady cuts across the Tudor and Stuart eras, but is worthy of a short account. Born Mary Frith, she was a notorious pickpocket and fence in London, first noted riding *Marocco* as a teenager in 1600. She began dressing in male clothes but never tried to hide her biological sex. At one stage she claimed she was a hermaphrodite and wore clothes that could be described as androgynous, such as a skirt, sword and jerkin. She was forced to do penance by the Church for persisting with her manly behaviour, which included petty thievery and pickpocketing – hence her nickname, as a thief would cut purses to steal their contents. There were no pockets at this time; purses were worn by both sexes, attached to a loop or belt. 'Moll', apart from being a nickname for Mary, was also common name for a young woman of disreputable character. Her adventures so caught the public imagination that two plays were written about her in her lifetime in 1611 and 1618, one called *The Roaring Girl*. This other name by which she was known, 'the Roaring Girl' is taken from 'roaring boys', young gentlemen who caroused in taverns and then picked fights on the street – the 'bovver boys' and 'skinheads' of yesteryear. Moll was often seen in public in a doublet and baggy breeches, smoking a pipe and swearing if she felt like it.

Moll was recorded as having been burned on her hand four times, a common punishment for thieves, and was at one time sentenced to do penance standing in a white sheet at St Paul's Cross during the Sunday morning sermon. It did little good, since she still wore men's clothing, and she set mirrors up all around her house to stoke her vanity. Her house was actually rather feminine, thanks to the efforts of her three full-time maids. Moll kept parrots and bred mastiffs, her dogs being particularly special. Each had its own bed with sheets and blankets, and she prepared their food herself.

She was first convicted in 1600 for stealing 2*s* 11*d*. She later performed in theatres wearing men's clothing, singing songs and playing the lute. Moll was arrested for being dressed indecently on 25 December 1611 and accused of being involved in prostitution. On 9 February 1612, she was required to do a penance for her 'evil living' at St Paul's Cross. She then put on a performance, according to a letter by John Chamberlan: 'She wept bitterly and seemed very penitent, but it is since doubted she was maudlin drunk, being discovered to have tippled of three-quarters of sack.' By the 1620s she was, according to her own account, working as a fence and a pimp. She not only procured young women for men, but also respectable male lovers for middle-class wives. In one case where a wife confessed on her deathbed infidelity with lovers that Moll provided, Moll supposedly convinced the woman's lovers to send money for the maintenance of the children that were probably theirs. It is important to note that, at the time, women who dressed in men's attire on a regular basis were generally considered to be 'sexually riotous and uncontrolled', but Moll herself claimed to be uninterested in sex.

The First Highwaymen

In 1572 Thomas Wilson, a Crown servant and diplomat, wrote *A Discourse upon Usury*, a dialogue in which one character commented that highway robbers were likely to be admired for their courage in England, while another suggested that a penchant for robbery was one of the Englishman's besetting sins. By the middle of Elizabeth's reign, the authorities were showing alarm at the increasing use of pistols by highway robbers.

William Harrison, in his *The Description of England* (1587), wrote about the large numbers of robberies that took place in Elizabethan England and said that these were usually committed by extravagant young gentlemen and underpaid serving men. He claimed that highway robbers had spies in every inn, watching to see who was worth holding up on the road:

> Unto this sort [labourers, small tenant farmers, small retailers, and craftsmen] also may our great swarms of idle serving men be referred, of whom there runneth a proverb; Young serving men, old beggars: because service is none heritage. These men are profitable to none, for if their condition be well perused, they are enemies to their masters, to their friends, and to themselves: for by them oftentimes their masters are encouraged unto unlawful exactions of their tenants, their friends brought unto poverty by their rents enhanced, and they themselves brought to confusion by their own prodigality and errors, as men that, having not wherewith of their own to maintain their excesses, doo search in highways, budgets [wallets or pouches], coffers, males [bags or packs], and stables, which way to supply their wants.

The dramatist Robert Greene (1558–92) popularised true crime accounts and underworld exposés with his series of 'conny-catching' pamphlets. The last of these, *The Blacke Bookes Messenger* of 1592, purports to be the autobiography of a highway robber named Ned Browne. Greene led a dissolute life and was said to have died from 'a surfeit of pickle herring and Rhenish wine'. Greene is most familiar to Shakespeare scholars for his pamphlet *Greene's Groats-Worth of Wit*, which alludes to a line, 'O tiger's heart wrapped in a woman's hide', found in Shakespeare's *Henry VI, Part 3* of 1591:

> ... for there is an upstart Crow, beautified with our feathers, that with his Tygers hart wrapt in a Players hyde, supposes he is as well able to bombast out a blanke verse as the best of you: and being an absolute Johannes factotum [Jack of all trades, master of none], is in his owne conceit the onely Shake-scene in a countrey.

Greene evidently complained of this 'upstart' actor who believed he could write as well as university-trained playwrights like himself.

Robert Parsons, a Jesuit, in 1596 wrote *The Jesuit's Memorial for the Intended Reformation of England, Under their First Popish Prince* as a policy recommendation for a hoped-for Catholic successor to Elizabeth I. He commented on social problems in England and noted that many of the men who committed robbery were gentlemen's sons. He thought that one reason robbery was so common was that it was not seen as a serious offence. He notes,

> One thing also in particular, for very honour of our Realm, and saving the Lives and Souls of infinite Men, is greatly wished might be recommended to his Majesty, [Philip of Spain] and effectually redressed, which is the multitude of Thieves that rob and steal upon the High-ways in England, more than likely in any other Country of the World; they being also sometimes of no base Condition, or Quality, that do it; but rather Gentlemen, or wealthy Men's Sons, moved thereunto not so much of poverty and necessity, as of light estimation of the fault, and hope of Pardon from the Prince; whereby it cometh to pass, that albeit the English Nation, as by experience is found, be not so inclined to steal in secret as some other Nations are, and that more are put to Death in England, for punishment of that Fact, than in many other Nations together; yet is this enormity of robbing upon the High-ways much more frequent and notorious in England, than any where else in Christendom; which is a great infamy to our Government, and hurt to the Commonwealth ... surely it is great pity to see so many consumed by Gallowses in England, more perhaps than in half Christendom besides.

In Shakespeare's *Henry IV, Part 1*, one of the main characters is the highway robber Sir John Falstaff. In his comedy *Every Man out of His Humour*, Ben Jonson satirised the admiration for highway robbers that was shown by certain young men.

The Counterfeit Crank

Caveat or Warning for Common Cursitors, Vulgarly Called Vagabonds was first published in 1566 by Thomas Harman. In his list of rogues is 'Nicholas Blunt (alias Nicholas Jennings, a counterfeit crank)'. Harman recounts Blunt's appearance at his lodgings in London on All Hallows Day 1566 seeking alms, spattered with dirt, naked from the waist upwards, in filthy rags, his face smeared with fresh blood from the 'falling sickness', epilepsy or palsy. Being suspicious, Harman questioned him, and Blunt claimed to have been suffering from the falling sickness for eight years, and to have been discharged from 'Bedlam' two weeks before, after being an inmate there for two years. Harman checked with the keeper of Bethlehem Hospital mental institution, who denied this. Harman then enlisted his printer to help track Blunt, and he charged two of his boys to follow him. They saw him beg all day, renewing the 'blood', that of an animal, from a bladder, and putting fresh mud on his clothes. They then followed him to Newington, south of the Thames, where the constable apprehended him. On being searched he was found to have collected 13*s* 3½*d*, whereas a labourer would have earned only 6*d* a day. Blunt was then stripped and found to be fit and well, but escaped naked across the fields in the dark.

Having then spent a few months begging in seaman's apparel, pretending to be a mariner whose ship had been lost at sea, he was again spotted by the printer. To avoid the printer's suspicion, Blunt vanished but reappeared a few days later in the guise of an out-of-work hat maker, Nicholas Jennings, dressed in 'a black frieze coat, a new pair of white hose, a fine felt hat on his head [and] a shirt of Flanders work esteemed to be worth sixteen shillings'. On New Year's Day 1567, the printer recognised him and, matching Blunt's lies with 'fair allusions', managed to trick him into custody. Blunt escaped yet again, but the printer was 'lighter of foot' and 'with a strong hand' apprehended him. After strenuous denials, Blunt made a confession and was found to have 'a pretty house' in Newington, 'well furnished, well-stuffed, with a fair joint-table, and a fair cupboard garnished with pewter, having an old ancient woman to be his wife'. Blunt was imprisoned in the new Bridewell, then whipped at a cart's tail through the streets of London and put in the pillory at Cheapside. He was pilloried twice, once in his rags and once in his expensive clothes, then released upon condition 'he truly labour to get his living'.

Tower of London Executions

These were reserved for the nobility, and number as follows: Henry VII (1485–1509) executed eleven; Henry VIII (1509–47) executed thirty-one; Edward VI (1547–53) executed five; Mary I (1553–58) executed nine; and Elizabeth I (1558–1603) executed eight, including five 'unruly youths'. All were executed on Tower Hill except Anne Boleyn, Margaret Pole, Catherine Howard, Jane Boleyn and Jane Grey on Tower Green, and Essex upon the Broad Walk in the Tower or on Tower Green. While the Tower Hill executions were seen by the general public, the six Tower Green beheadings were private affairs and all the bodies are buried in St Peter ad Vincula church in the Tower. The Earl of Essex, in 1601, was the last person executed inside the Tower.

15

Classes and Income

During the Tudor and early Stuart period there was a great increase in social mobility, with wealth and political influence shifting from the nobility and clergy towards a 'middling class' of gentry, yeomen and burghers. With hard work and good luck, a husbandman could rise to become a yeoman. In turn, a yeoman could buy a coat of arms and become a gentleman. Gentry and merchants, by marriage and wealth, could join the nobility. Ambitious upper- and middle-class men benefited from the growing wealth of the country. However, for the poor life hardly altered, with around a third to a half of the growing population living at subsistence level. In 1577, William Harrison, a church minister, wrote *The Description of England*:

> We in England divide our people commonly into four sorts. The first are gentlemen, which covers everyone from nobles to professionals; next come the citizens of the cities, who are free men with special privileges; next come the yeomen of the countryside; and finally the poor – farm workers, servants and vagrants, who have 'neither voice nor authority'.

Another division would be into five broad groups: nobility; gentry and rich merchants; yeomen, citizens and craftsmen; husbandmen and labourers; and vagrants and beggars.

Nobility

The nobility owned huge amounts of land and included the powerful archbishops and bishops, who were often more politicians and diplomats than clergymen. All were entitled to sit in the House of Lords. Under Henry VII onwards, the nobility generally lost influence, while the bishops after the Reformation only remained powerful if they supported the monarch. The nobility could not be imprisoned for debt, nor could they be flogged, tortured or pilloried. If they committed a capital crime they could not be hanged or otherwise abused, and could only be beheaded. If they were to be tried for an offence, they could only be tried by a body of other nobles, or by the Star

Chamber of the Privy Council. Most nobles inherited extensive lands and generous incomes, although there was a growing class of commoners in town and country who accrued more money than many of the nobility.

Many nobles ran up massive debts and needed to marry into fresh sources of income. In the later Tudor era, marriages between impoverished nobles and the wealthy middle class began to appear, enabling the nouveaux riche to achieve respectability in society and the nobles to retain their lifestyles and estates. However, many upper-class marriages had to be sanctioned by the monarch, or often by the Church when relations or former annulments were involved. There were quite distinct degrees of status in the nobility, which contained between each step numerous sub-steps to account for sons, daughters, etc. In descending order of precedence, the major degrees of nobility were: Duke/Duchess (of whom there were none by 1600); Marquess/Marchioness (there was one marquess and one dowager marchioness by 1600); Earl/Countess (only eighteen earls were left by 1600); Viscount/Viscountess (only two by 1600); and Baron/Baroness (thirty-seven in 1600).

The higher the rank, the higher was the status of the holder, with the rare office of duke usually only belonging to a close royal relative. Although real power was derived not from rank but from the amount of land one owned, much income and many offices would also come from the favour and preferments of the monarch, so nobles attended court to be close to the king or queen and not be sidelined from power and wealth. There were fewer and fewer great nobles because of Elizabeth's policy of limiting their power and numbers. Of the fifty-five peers of the realm at the end of Elizabeth's reign, only two or three lords had an income of over £10,000 a year. This compares to the queen's £300,000. The earls and the marquess received around £5,000 each, and the barons and viscounts about £3,000, but some lords earned as little as £300. Except when on progress, the monarch's court was always in residence in or near London, and if any nobleman wished to play any role in the management of the nation, wanted to improve his position or defend his position from enemies, he had to come to court and own a London town house. The most expensive, and necessary 'honour' of all was that of housing the monarch, especially Elizabeth and her household. Luckily for those in the North she never travelled as far as York, but her expensive 'progresses' about the country brought her into closer contact with her subjects, leaving London during the summer 'plague season'. She also saved a great deal of money, but many nobles begged off the honour of her stay for fear of bankruptcy.

Gentry and Merchants

It was said that 'gentlemen are made good cheap in England', as anyone with a Master's degree from Oxford and Cambridge counted as a gentleman, as did any member of the leading professions of physician and lawyer. In rural areas the means of gentlemen varied enormously, from small farmers to wealthy landowners. 'Gentlemen' held political power locally as justices of the peace and nationally as Members of Parliament. Gentry made up only around 2 per cent of the English population by 1600, but owned 50 per cent of land, compared to the nobles' 15 per cent. Church and Crown owned much of the remainder. Apart from owning large amounts of land, gentlemen were usually well educated and the more distinguished had a family coat of arms. The gentry were the elite of the countryside, either lords of a manor (in which case they held the land outright) or gentlemen freeholders (tenants of some greater lord). They lived off rents paid by their tenants, and did no manual labour to support themselves. This ability to live without manual labour was the measure of 'gentility', being a *gentil homme*, or gentleman. Nothing of importance in their neighbourhood went forward without their knowledge and consent or, if they were absent landlords, the consent of their steward or bailiff. Their economic power was supplemented by the government with legal power. The most substantial country gentlemen were appointed as justices of the peace, enforcing the law and meting out justice in their community. The gentry also filled all the other local offices, such as sheriff or surveyor of the roads. Often the offices carried with them no pay, but they did confer power, which brought added prestige and was often supplemented with gifts, what we would today term *baksheesh* or bribes.

From the gentry ranks were drawn the knights. Knighthood ceased to be a purely military appointment under the Tudors, with many knights gaining their positions through non-military service to the Crown. A knighthood was not hereditary, and though it gained the holder some status, it did not in any way increase his income or his actual power. Just below the knights were the esquires, distinguished from the rest of the gentry by the bearing of heraldic arms. A gentleman with a coat of arms had the privilege of suffixing his name 'esquire', just as a knight could prefix his name with 'sir'. All of the above degrees of the gentry could hold local and national governmental offices, as well as serve in the House of Commons.

The era saw the rise of modern commerce with the emergence of the wool, cloth and weaving trades and exports. A very prosperous merchant class emerged, leading to a surge in building in the active wool areas and ports. Great 'wool churches' can be seen in the Cotswolds, Lavenham, Leominster, Stamford and elsewhere. In the growing cities, the richest merchants were very wealthy; for example, the aldermen of London were richer than almost all landed gentlemen. Merchants became increasingly important in political attitudes, and their rise, along with that of the gentry, would eventually form a main cause of the English Civil War (1642–51).

Yeomen, Citizens and Craftsmen

Yeomen could be as wealthy as gentlemen but they worked alongside their men. Yeomen and craftsmen were often able to read and write. 'Wage labourers' worked for yeomen. Yeomen were fairly wealthy men, not born members of the gentry but rich enough to own their own houses and employ servants. Yeomen either owned the freeholds to their land or rented land from gentlemen, which they farmed. They were successful farmers and were rich enough to be able to afford labourers to do the heavier farming jobs for them. Their land was generally controlled through 'freeholds', perpetual leases that carried little or no rent, and possibly some leases as well. The yeoman did not own his own land by law, as the lord of the manor still held the title, but in practice, a freehold was indistinguishable from direct ownership. If the family of a yeoman worked hard to enlarge and consolidate their holdings, they could eventually be accepted into the gentry by income or marriage. Their incomes were in excess of £40 per annum in 1600. Citizens included rich merchants and craftsmen, who lived in the towns. Merchants made their living by trading goods with ship owners. Craftsmen were skilled men who could command a good price for the goods that they made, and were often members of trade guilds.

Husbandmen and Labourers

Husbandmen earned about £15 per annum in 1600, and were below the yeomen in rural society. They were free tenant farmers, and sometimes small landowners, but below yeomen in status. They rented land from another party, either a yeoman or one of the country gentry or aristocracy. The more fortunate husbandmen were 'copy holders', holding leases that guaranteed tenancy of the land at the same rent for the duration of the lease, with most leases lasting generations. A typical holding that might support a single family would be around twenty-five acres. In good times, the husbandman fared well by the standards of the day. He and his family usually had enough to eat, although work was hard.

A labourer lacked enough land to maintain himself and his family, although he often had a cottage, a small garden and grazing rights on the local common, and worked for wages of around £9 a year. Labourers worked for citizens, yeomen or shopkeepers. Many of these labourers were sons and daughters apprenticed to tradesmen. Boys stayed as apprentices with 'masters' until they were twenty-four years old, and girls until they were twenty-one years old. Labourers were employed to do heavy jobs on the farms or in the craft shops. In 1515, an Act was passed which fixed a labourer's minimum wage at 3*d* per day for winter months and 4*d* per day for summer months, with bonuses to be paid at harvest time. A labourer could expect to work from sunrise to sunset in the winter and from sunrise to early evening in the summer. Sundays and some saints' 'holy days' were free time, the origin of holidays. The going rate for day labour (i.e. those not permanently employed as wage labourers) in 1600 was about 1*s* per day when work was available, but agricultural work was seasonal and many labourers would only have been able to find work for six months in the year. Skilled workers were to be paid 5*d* per day during the winter and 6*d* for summer days.

Within the villages there were specialists at one trade or another, such as blacksmiths, carpenters, thatchers, potters, weavers and the like. Many of these people were also peasant farmers who held plots insufficient to support them, known as 'cottars', and supplemented their incomes with their trades. They were not members of a guild since the craft guilds only existed in the towns. Cottars possessed nothing, not even their rented cottage and perhaps an acre or two of land, also rented. If they were resourceful, with skills such as carpentry or weaving, they could supplement their minimal income. If not, they might follow the harvest, working for a pittance and enduring harsh conditions. There was also usually at least one alehouse in every village, with the ale usually being brewed by a woman who kept the premises.

Every gentleman's household, and many yeoman households, had servants. The status of servants varied, depending upon where in the household hierarchy the servant was, and the status of the servant's master. The servant wore the badge or livery of his master and represented his master wherever he went. Where a common wanderer without the proper papers would be treated as a vagrant, a servant could move freely, since it was assumed that he was on his master's business. A man in livery thus had the right of free travel. A gentleman, of course, could go wherever he wanted. The usual criterion for the local authorities was that if a traveller was a well-dressed man on a horse or a servant in livery, he could travel freely. However, if he was on foot and poorly dressed, he was a dangerous vagrant and was beaten, put in the stocks and generally made to feel unwelcome. Soldiers, tradesmen and pedlars who had valid reason to travel would be issued 'testimonials' by the justices of the peace or other substantial persons, in order to avoid such treatment. Pedlars and tinkers were welcome for the goods or services they provided, but they had an unsavoury reputation for thievery, deceit and seduction of the local females. The 1871 Pedlars Act defines them as

> any hawker, pedlar, petty chapman, tinker, caster of metals, mender of chairs, or other person who, without any horse or other beast bearing or drawing burden, travels and trades on foot and goes from town to town or to other men's houses, carrying to sell or exposing for sale any goods, wares, or merchandise, or procuring orders for goods, wares, or merchandise immediately to be delivered, or selling or offering for sale his skill in handicraft.

Soldiers were a group that did not fit neatly into the structure of society. The officers were gentlemen and were regarded as normal members of the gentry, but the rank and file were generally feared for their predatory reputation, despised for their poverty and envied for their freedom. They were generally treated cautiously, and all were generally glad to see them leave their area. Their women, the 'camp followers', were generally regarded as thieves and harlots.

Vagrants and Beggars

Vagrants and beggars made up the lowest classes. There was no welfare or unemployment system but poor people did receive some help from the government due to the constant possibility of some kind of peasants' revolt. They came to be paid out of the Poor Tax taken from lower-class landowners. In 1536, laws were introduced that punished those who could work but chose not to, called the 'undeserving poor'. In 1536, Thomas Cromwell also proposed an ambitious scheme for poor relief. It was based on the idea that the able-bodied should be employed on public projects, such as road and bridge building, while the infirm were supported from charitable contributions. Workhouses would be built for their accommodation. Unfortunately, he wanted to finance the scheme by an income tax, so Parliament rejected it. Cromwell's ambitious schemes for social reform collapsed because the Tudor state was dependent on the voluntary cooperation of local gentry, who were unconvinced by the benefits of his reforms and unwilling to pay. The Church also helped some of those who were unable to work due to ill health or disability. Apart from criminals, others at the bottom of the social classes were the scavengers, whose job it was to clean the filthy streets of the towns, clearing up the piles of refuse, litter and the occasional dead body.

Cromwell attempted to prevent rural depopulation, which was causing crime and begging in the towns. An Act of 1534 limited the number of sheep that anyone could own to 2,400, and a 1536 Act was aimed directly against land enclosures. He also tried to combat rising prices through laws setting an upper limit on the price of many goods including meat and wine, but they proved impossible to enforce.

Elizabethan Incomes

Around 1580, the annual income of Elizabeth I was around £60,000 while the great nobles earned around £15,000 to £25,000 per annum. (By the end of her reign, her income was about £300,000, which shows the heavy inflation, but also her gains from increased trade and duties.) The Archbishop of Canterbury made £30,000 per annum, while Lord Burghley was making about £4,000 a year. A country gentleman would be comfortable upon £50 to £150 per annum, and a successful merchant could make anything between £100 and £25,000. Skilled labourers were 8*d* to 12*d* (a shilling) per day, and unskilled 3*d* to 4*d*. A carpenter could earn 5*s* a week, and a coney-catcher (a rabbit catcher, the origin of conman) 14*s* in a very good day for the furs and meat. Servants' incomes do not include tips, but a manservant generally made around a mark a quarter, i.e. £2 12*s* 4*d* per annum. A groom would earn half that, a maid perhaps £2 to £4 a year, and a stable boy around £2 a year. A country parson was paid a pound a year, so either relied upon multiple offices or a local lord or gentleman for a living income. An agricultural labourer was only paid 2–3*d* a day, a ploughman 1*s* a week with board, a shepherd 6*d* a week with board and a thatcher around 2*s* for five days' work. Some poor cottars who paid their rents in kind might have an income around zero, while others might make as much as £20 or more per annum. Out of this would come rents, which might be anywhere from negligible to almost the entire cash income of a cottar. Since he grew most of his own food, his family would seldom starve even if he had almost no money. There was no standing army, but if enlisted for war or defence a captain was paid 6*s* a day; a lieutenant 3*s*; an ensign, drummer and a sergeant 1*s* 6*d* each and a common soldier 8*d* a day.

16

Tudor Clothes and Fashions

There were many changes in fashion, from hats to footwear, involving jewellery and even armour. We have a real heritage of paintings of the clothes and fashions of the nobility, as nearly all art was portraiture at this time and much has survived in museums. However, very few examples of clothes worn by working people have survived. Clothes would have been worn until they fell apart or were passed to offspring, generally worn to destruction and then used as rags. Children generally dressed like their parents, a habit that only changed in this writer's lifetime. All classes wore multiple layers to keep out the cold, as temperatures dropped worldwide with the advent of the Little Ice Age.

Clothes indicated one's position in society, with laws being passed to ensure that no one dressed above their station in life. In 1510 – and at various other times in the sixteenth century – Parliament passed a law defining the dress of each class from labourers to the aristocracy, telling everyone what they could and could not wear. These 'sumptuary laws' stated the colours as well as the type of clothing an individual was allowed to own. Complicated laws said that only people with a certain amount of wealth could wear certain expensive materials such as velvet and silk. Gentlemen would be fined and servants and labourers could be put in the stocks for three days, but the laws were often flouted.

These complex sumptuary laws, known as the Statutes of Apparel, were enforced by Elizabeth herself in Greenwich on 15 June 1574. Her ministers wanted to maintain social structure as well as to keep a firm restraint on the people's expenditure towards clothing, but the laws were almost impossible to enforce. They began,

> The excess of apparel and the superfluity of unnecessary foreign wares thereto belonging now of late years is grown by sufferance to such an extremity that the manifest decay of the whole realm generally is like to follow (by bringing into the realm such superfluities of silks, cloths of gold, silver, and other most vain devices of so great cost for the quantity thereof

as of necessity the moneys and treasure of the realm is and must be yearly conveyed out of the same to answer the said excess) but also particularly the wasting and undoing of a great number of young gentlemen, otherwise serviceable, and others seeking by show of apparel to be esteemed as gentlemen, allured by the vain show of those things ...

Only the members of the royal family were allowed to wear purple, or to own robes trimmed with ermine. Less noble folk wore clothing trimmed with either fox or otter. Furs included also cat, rabbit, beaver, bear, badger and polecat.

Both men and women wore knitted stockings (hose) held up with ties. The rich wore silk hose, and others wool. Hose were hand knitted, and thus had seams as people could not knit stockings in tubes. In general, underpants were rare among men and knickers were not worn by women. The rich spent a fortune, being greatly influenced by the monarch and the court. Fashions and fabrics were constantly changing, with a wide choice of materials including silks, velvets and linen. Fabrics were dyed or printed in a variety of colours and were often richly embroidered. The most expensive dyes were bright red, purple and indigo. Commoners used mostly vegetable dyes such as madder for red and woad for blue. Their plain and coarse clothes were homemade, usually using wool from their own sheep, spun and dyed at home with vegetable dyes, but generally woven by a professional weaver. Poor men would wear a shirt with breeches (short trousers) and a jerkin (waistcoat). Poorer people often wore brown, yellow or blue. Clothes were rarely washed, and the poorest often did not possess a single change of clothes.

The basic garment worn by all men, women and children was the smock or chemise, a long, T-shaped linen garment worn next to the skin. Women wore this with at least one petticoat, plus corsets if they were well off, while men wore 'braies', similar to our boxer shorts. Sleeves were separate and were tied onto the jerkin in colder weather. Most would have a knee length woollen cloak for cold weather. Poor women had a plain gown with a top and skirt, which was always shorter than those worn at court, to keep out of the mud. Working women needed to be able to move freely, and everyone in the lower classes worked to scrape a living.

The distinctive Tudor fashion we all recognise is the ruff, worn by richer men, women and children. It evolved from the small fabric ruffle, at the drawstring neck of the shirt or chemise. They served as changeable pieces of cloth that could themselves be laundered separately while keeping the wearer's doublet from becoming soiled at the neckline. They were also used on wrists, and a New Year's gift made by her ladies for Elizabeth in 1565 specifies 'ten yards is enough for the ruffs of the neck and hand'. The discovery of starch allowed ruffs to be made wider without losing their shape. Later ruffs were separate garments that could be washed, starched, and set into elaborate figure-of-eight folds by the use of heated cone-shaped goffering irons. Ruffs were often coloured during starching, vegetable dyes being used to give the ruff a yellow, pink or mauve tint. A pale blue colour could also be obtained by using smalt, but Elizabeth I banned its use 'since blue was the colour of the

Above: 1. Richard III with his queen, Anne Neville, from *Richard, Duke of Gloucester, and the Lady Anne* by the American artist Edwin Austin Abbey (1852–1911).

Below: 2. Margaret Beaufort, Countess of Richmond and Derby (1443–1509) was the mother of Henry VI and a key figure in the Wars of the Roses. She arranged her son's funeral and died five weeks later.

Left: 3. Elizabeth of York (1466–1503) was the eldest child of Edward IV. Her marriage to Henry Tudor united the warring houses of York and Lancaster. Queen Consort of Henry VII, she was the mother of Henry VIII.

4. The famous Hans Holbein cartoon of Henry VIII as he has been remembered ever since. Drawn in black ink on paper as a preliminary study for the mural painting in Whitehall Palace that was destroyed by fire in 1698. The other half of the cartoon, featuring Jane Seymour and Elizabeth of York, was lost.

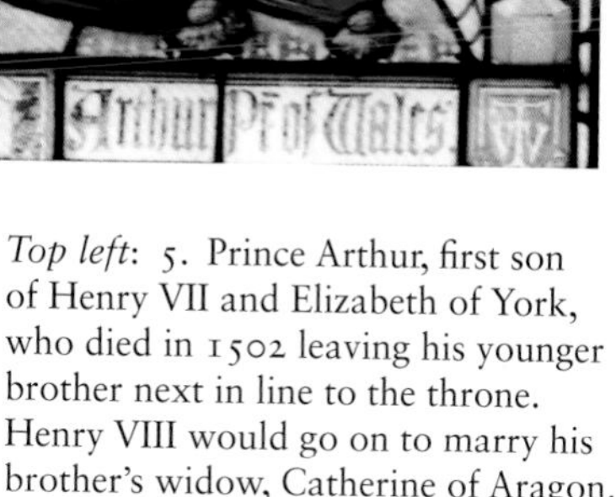

Top left: 5. Prince Arthur, first son of Henry VII and Elizabeth of York, who died in 1502 leaving his younger brother next in line to the throne. Henry VIII would go on to marry his brother's widow, Catherine of Aragon.

Top right: 6. Mary Rose Tudor, younger daughter of Henry VII and Queen of France by her marriage to Louis XII. She was the grandmother of the ill-fated Lady Jane Grey.

Right: 7. Margaret Tudor, elder daughter of Henry VII and wife of James IV of Scotland. Henry VIII excluded her from his will but her line inherited the throne in 1603.

Above left: 8. A statue of Catherine of Aragon, Henry VIII's first wife, in front of the Archbishop's Palace in Alcalá de Henares, Spain, where she was born on 16 December 1485.

Above right: 9. Preparatory drawing for *Portrait of Sir Thomas More* by Hans Holbein, commissioned in 1526. More (1478–1535) was sainted by the Catholic Church, and was a fierce persecutor of Protestants, executed for refusing to support Henry VIII's annulment from Catherine of Aragon.

Below: 10. Henry VIII's will, dated 30 December 1546. The will was signed with a stamp rather than the sign manual; this would cause problems in the future.

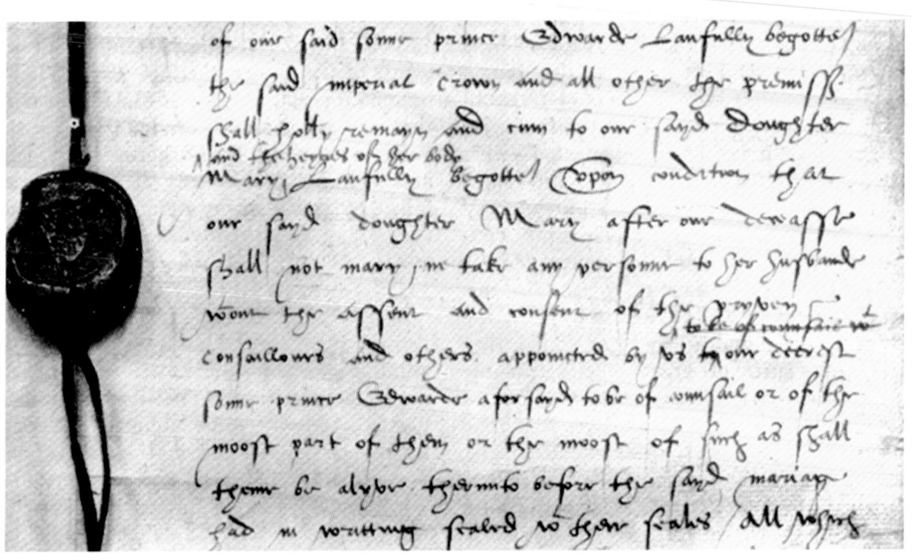

Above left: 11. Anne Boleyn (1501–36), Henry's second, ill-fated wife; pen-and-ink drawing by Holbein.

Above right: 12. Thomas Cranmer (1489–1586) who, as an obscure cleric, suggested that Henry should canvas the opinion of the universities in Britain and abroad as to the validity of Henry's marriage to Catherine of Aragon.

Below: 13. The Field of the Cloth of Gold, the scene of the great meeting between Henry VIII and Francis I, 7 June 1520.

Above left: 14. William Warham, Archbishop of Canterbury from 1503 to 1532, who had serious doubts about the validity of Catherine of Aragon's first marriage to Henry VIII's brother Arthur.

Above right: 15. The powerful Thomas Wolsey (1473–1530) from a drawing by Jacques le Boucq. Not the obese figure of the more familiar likenesses.

Below: 16. Tomb of Thomas Howard, 3rd Duke of Norfolk and uncle to both Anne Boleyn and Catherine Howard (Henry VIII's second and fifth wives respectively).

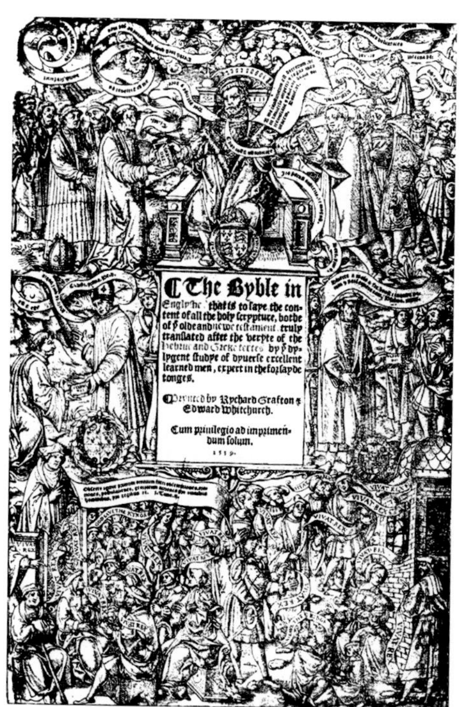

Above left: 17. The title page of the first edition of the 'Great Bible' from 1539. Depicted as God's vicar, Henry symbolically hands out the Word of God to the hierarchies of his realm, represented by Cranmer on his right and by Cromwell on his left. The preacher at the bottom left proclaims, 'Obey the prince...', and his subjects duly respond, 'Long live the king.'

Above right: 18. Henry VIII in council. The king sits enthroned beneath a 'cloth of estate' expressing his royal rank. Also known as the 'cloth of state', or 'canopy of state', it was usually placed above a throne or altar which had been raised upon a dais.

Below: 19. Henry VIII's palace of Nonsuch, built somewhat in imitation of Francis I's chateau of Chambord. Nonsuch was demolished in the late seventeenth century. It was supposedly constructed in part using materials looted from the dissolved monasteries.

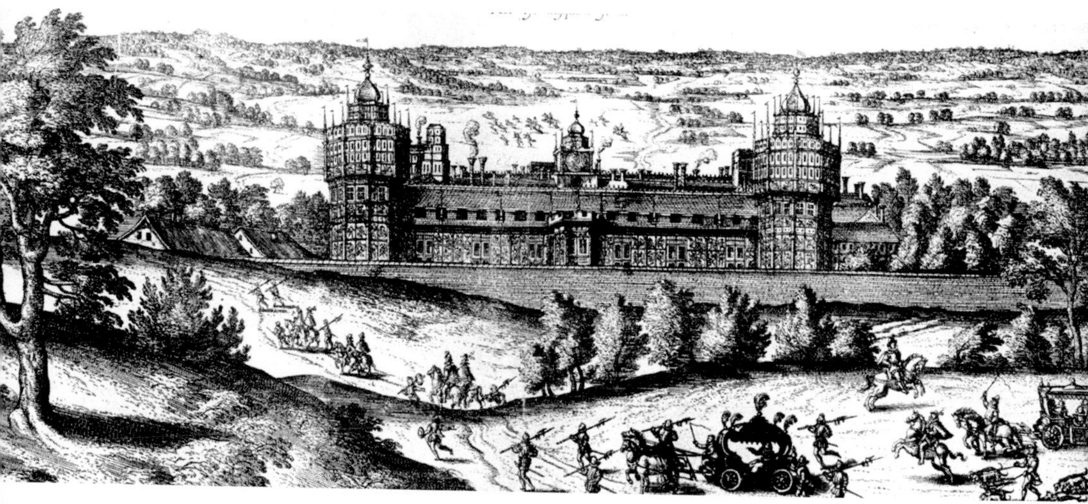

20. A plan of the Westminster and Whitehall palaces, from a later version of the 1578 map known as Ralph Agas's map (but not actually by him).

Above: 21. Whitehall Palace, which Henry VIII acquired on the fall of Thomas Wolsey in 1529. Whitehall would become a key royal residence for the rest of the Tudor period.

Below left: 22. Funeral effigy of Elizabeth Blount, Lady Tailboys, Henry VIII's mistress and the mother of his first son, Henry Fitzroy.

Below right: 23. The tomb of Henry Fitzroy, Duke of Richmond, Henry VIII's bastard son.

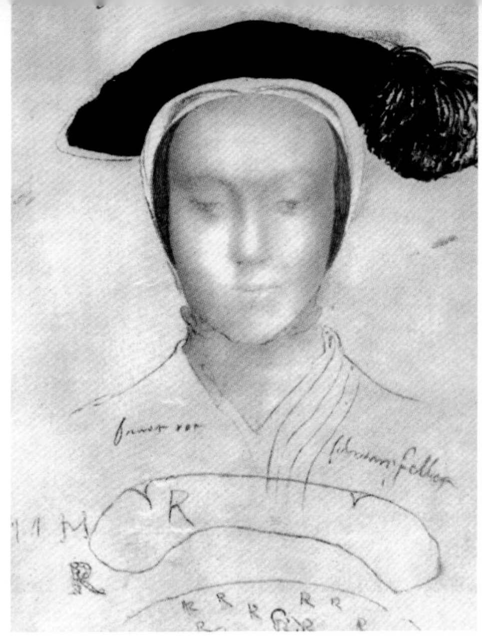

Above left: 24. Mary Howard, Duchess of Richmond and widow of Henry Fitzroy, Henry VIII's only illegitimate son.

Above right: 25. Margaret Shelton, later Lady Heveningham. Henry was rumoured to have at one time been interested in her.

Left: 26. Holbein's painting of Henry's third and favourite wife, Jane Seymour. Although no great beauty, Jane carried little political baggage and had no personal agenda. She was widely admired for her sweet disposition.

Below left: 27. Anne of Cleves, Henry VIII's fourth wife. His marriage to her after the death of Jane Seymour turned out to be a mistake, brought on by the need for a German ally. The marriage lasted six months.

Above left: 28. Henry VIII's fifth wife, Catherine Howard, is depicted as the Queen of Sheba, with Henry VIII as King Solomon, in this stained-glass window at King's College Chapel, Cambridge.

Above right: 29. Catherine Parr, Henry VIII's last queen, from a stained-glass window in Sudeley Castle.

Below right: 30. Edward VI by Hans Holbein. Edward was born on 12 October 1537, and this drawing was made at some point before Holbein's death in 1543.

Below left: 31. Edward VI's 'Device' for the succession, in which he names Lady Jane Grey as his heir. The amendments to the document are not written in the king's hand, which makes all the difference to its meaning.

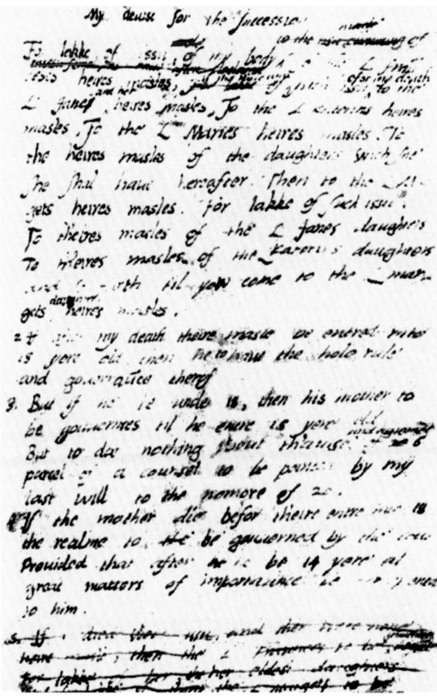

My deuise for the succession

For lakke of issu of my body

heires masles, ... befor my death to the

L' Janes heires masles, To the L Katerins heires

masles, To the L' Maries heires masles, To

the heires masles of the daughters wich she

she shal haue hereafter. Then to the L Mar-

gets heires masles. For lakke of such issu,

To theires masles of the L Janes daughters

To theires masles of the Katerins daughters

and so forth til yow come to the L Mar-

gets daughters heires masles.

2 If after my death theire masle be entred into

18 yere old, then he to have the hole rule

and gouernauce therof

3. But if he be under 18, then his mother to

be gouuernres til he entre 18 yere old

But to doe nothing w'out th'auise of 6

parcel of a counsel to be pointed by my

last will to the nombre of 20.

4 If the mother die befor theire entre into 18

the realme to be gouuerned by the counsel

Prouided that after he be 14 yere al

great matters of importaunce be opened

to him.

Left: 32. Lady Jane Grey. Recommended by Edward VI as an alternative to Mary for the succession, she was defeated in July 1553, and executed after the Wyatt rising in February 1554, at the age of seventeen.

Above: 33. Unsurprisingly, Henry's eldest daughter, Princess Mary, refused to accept her illegitimacy. Anne Boleyn attempted to win her friendship on a number of occasions, before admitting defeat and threatening, 'If I have a son, as I hope shortly, I know what will happen to her'.

Below: 34. The burning of Hugh Latimer and Nicholas Ridley at Oxford on 16 October 1555, depicted in John Foxe's *Book of Martyrs*.

Above: 35. Elizabeth I is seen here in *An Allegory of the Tudor Succession*, by Lucas de Heere, from around 1572. It celebrates the harmony established by Queen Elizabeth I. Elizabeth holds the hand of Peace, followed by Plenty. Her father Henry VIII, the founder of the Church of England, sits on his throne, and passes the sword of justice to his Protestant son Edward VI. On the left are Elizabeth's Catholic half-sister and predecessor Mary I and her husband Philip II of Spain, with Mars, the God of War. The picture, a gift from Queen Elizabeth to Sir Francis Walsingham, exemplifies the sixteenth century's fascination with allegory, the queen's vision of herself as the culmination of the Tudor dynasty and her concern with the legitimacy of her regime.

Right: 36. Robert Dudley, Earl of Leicester (1532/3–84), from his tomb in Warwick. Dudley was Elizabeth I's greatest favourite, with speculation that the pair would marry.

Left: 37. Francis, Duke of Alençon (1555–84), who may have come closer than anyone to securing the hand of Elizabeth I in marriage. In 1579, arrangements began to be made for marrying him to Elizabeth. Alençon, now Duke of Anjou, was the only one of Elizabeth's foreign suitors to court her in person. He was twenty-four and Elizabeth was forty-six. Despite the age gap, the two soon became very close, Elizabeth calling him her 'frog' on account of a frog-shaped earring he had given her. This may well be the origin of the derogatory term for Frenchmen.

Below: 38. The Great Seal of Elizabeth I.

Bottom: 39. Elizabeth I's signature.

Above left: 40. The Spanish Armada depicted just off the French coast in George Carleton's *Thankfull Remembrance.*

Above right: 41. The Babington Plot, pictured in George Carleton's *Thankfull Remembrance.* In 1586, Anthony Babington was the central figure in a plot to assassinate Elizabeth I and liberate Mary, Queen of Scots.

Below: 42. Elizabeth I in old age.

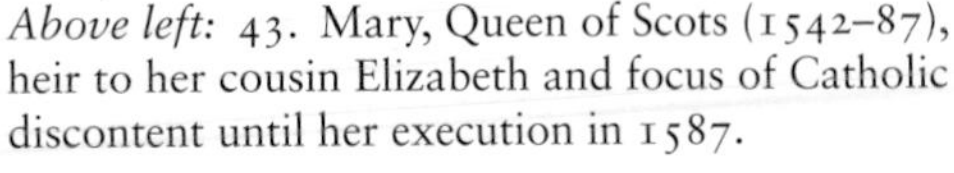

Above left: 43. Mary, Queen of Scots (1542–87), heir to her cousin Elizabeth and focus of Catholic discontent until her execution in 1587.

Above right: 44. Tudor woman and child.

Left: 45. Jasper Tudor (1431–95), uncle of Henry VII. A constant supporter of Henry Tudor during the Wars of the Roses, Jasper's role in establishing the Tudor dynasty cannot be overstated. He was the only noble present at both the first and last battles of the Wars of the Roses, the First Battle of St Albans in 1455 and the Battle of Stoke Field in 1487.

flag of Scotland'. At their most extreme, ruffs were a foot or more wide. These cartwheel ruffs required a wire frame called a *supportasse* or under-propper to hold them at the fashionable angle. By the end of the sixteenth century, ruffs were falling out of fashion in Western Europe, in favour of wing collars and 'falling bands', collars that lay flat on the shoulders.

Female Dress, 'Swete Bagges', 'Bum Rolles' and Bared Breasts

Ordinary people were forbidden by law to wear gold, jewels or rich fabrics, even if they could afford them. Women usually wore a thick woollen 'kirtl', a square-necked, ankle-length dress with a fitted, laced bodice and full skirts. Better-off women wore a long, open, wide-sleeved gown over the kirtl. Girdles, then a wide belt, were made from cord or chain and worn around the waist to carry personal possessions, as clothes had no pockets as we know them today. In European clothing, pockets began by being hung like purses from a belt which could be concealed beneath a coat or jerkin and reached through a slit in the outer garment. The purse or pouch was also called a hanging pocket. Wearers would also attach other valuables to their girdle, such as a rosary, a Book of Hours, pomanders (scented oranges), chatelaines (a clasp or chain to suspend keys, etc.) and even daggers. The drawstring purse would hang from the girdle on a long cord and would vary according to the fashion, status and lifestyle of the wearer. Ladies' handbags, like pockets, were not to appear for centuries.

During the Elizabethan era, women's skirts expanded to enormous proportions. Consequently, small medieval girdle purses were easily lost in the large amounts of fabric. Rather than wear girdle pouches outside on their belt, women began to wear their pouches under their skirts, and men would wear pockets, called *bagges*, made of leather inside their breeches. Peasants and travellers might wear large, satchel-like leather or cloth bags diagonally across the body. In addition, in a time when personal hygiene was lacking, many aristocrats in the sixteenth century would carry what were called 'swete bagges', bags that were filled with sweet-smelling material. Just as pomanders hung from the girdle in the fifteenth century, these swete bagges were filled with powder from sweet-smelling herbs and spices, such as lavender, or with perfumed balls of cotton. Swete bagges might also be stored with clothes and linens or set among sheets and pillowcases.

Sleeves were tied or pinned onto the bodice, showing the smock underneath and probably an apron over the top to keep the dress as clean as possible. Females wore a shift, an undershirt of linen or wool for the poor and cotton or silk for the rich. Over this was worn a farthingale, a hoop skirt stiffened with osiers (willow cuttings), rope and, from around 1580, whalebone. The fashion began with Joan of Portugal, who died in 1475, and spread through Spain. Catherine of Aragon brought the farthingale into England on her marriage to Prince Arthur in 1501. It was said that Joan had invented the device to disguise her pregnancies of two illegitimate children. These so-called 'Spanish farthingales' were an essential element of Tudor fashion in England, and there are references to them in Elizabeth I's Wardrobe Accounts in 1585 and 1586 for: 'making of thre rolles of hollande clothe with wyers bounde with reben' and 'making of a rolle of starched buckeram with whales bone'.

Most farthingale hoops were made of willow sticks softened in water then bent to shape, and they served to give structure to a skirt. Skirts eventually became so wide that the wearer would have to walk through doors sideways. This contrasted strongly with the narrow and tapering bodice to emphasise a small waist. With wider and wider skirts, a 'bum rolle', a roll of material like a thick sausage, was worn low on the back to make a pronounced shape. This was worn by both rich and poor. Women then usually put on another petticoat and underskirt. A poor woman's overdress would be made of a heavy durable material like worsted or wool. A rich woman's outer garments were made of velvets and silks. In the winter a pair of sleeves would be attached to the dress at the shoulders, with ties.

Henry II of France was married to Catherine de' Medici, who enforced a ban on thick waists at court attendance during the 1550s. For this reason, she was credited with the need for corsets. They appeared around this time in England, and for 400 years, became women's primary means of support, with laces and stays made from whalebone or metal. The corset was originally known as 'a pair of bodys' in the late sixteenth century, being a simple bodice, stiffened with boning of reed or whalebone. The centre front was further reinforced by a busk made of wood, horn, whalebone, metal or ivory. It was most often laced in the back, and was, at first, a garment reserved for the aristocracy. Women's clothing gave them a triangular shape. Their corsets were tight fitting making their waists very thin, while their petticoats and gowns were very wide.

To return to Joan of Portugal, she attracted great criticism for wearing dresses that displayed too much décolletage, but gowns which exposed a woman's neck and top of her chest were very common across Europe until the Victorian period. Ball or evening gowns especially featured low, square décolletage designed to display and emphasise cleavage. Low-cut dresses that exposed breasts were considered quite acceptable, and a woman's bared legs, ankles, or shoulders were considered to be more risqué than exposed breasts. Elizabeth I was said to have owned a thousand dresses, and is recorded as exposing her breasts to foreign ambassadors when quite aged. From 1440, Agnès Sorel is credited with starting the fashion when she wore deep, low, square décolleté gowns with fully bared breasts in the French court. Known as the *Dame de beauté*, she was the favourite mistress of Charles VII of France and is considered the first officially recognised royal mistress. During the sixteenth century, women's fashions with exposed breasts were common in society across Europe, from queens to common prostitutes, and emulated by all classes.

In Britain, even Mary II and Charles II's wife Henrietta Maria were depicted with fully bared breasts. The architect Inigo Jones designed a masque costume for Henrietta Maria that fully revealed both of her breasts. In upper-class circles the display of breasts was at times regarded as a status symbol, as a sign of beauty, wealth or social position. From the Renaissance onwards, the bared breast invoked associations with the nude sculptures of classical Greece that were exerting an influence on art, sculpture and architecture of the period. Dresses for the rich would have been laced at the back and boned with whalebone around the bodice to achieve the straight, upright shape that was fashionable. The lace would be loosened during pregnancy because there was no specially designed maternity wear. Fastenings for clothes were mainly ties or buttons, of highly decorated gold or silver for the rich. In the sixteenth century buttons were usually for decoration. The poor would cut buttons off worn-out clothes and sew them onto others to save having to buy new ones. Gloves would have been cut at the knuckles to show off rings underneath.

Male Dress and 'Family Jewels'

Males wore loose breeches, long hose and a thick belted 'jerkin', similar to a long waistcoat. A merchant or farmer might wear a leather 'doublet', which was a thick, quilted upper garment, over breeches. Over the jerkin rich men wore a gown, or later in the sixteenth century a cloak or cape. However, instead of a doublet, most working men wore a loose tunic, being cheaper and easier to work in. Some workmen wore a leather jerkin called a buff jerkin. Daggers and purses were hung on leather thongs from the belt. Hats and caps were also usually worn, both to keep warm and to avoid washing the hair. Men usually wore at least one undershirt, then an under-jacket or tunic.

During Henry VIII's reign, clothing, particularly for men, became far more elaborate, with men's clothing layered and padded to emulate the king's growing physique while each of his six queens brought new styles of women's clothes to court. In Elizabethan times, 'trunk-hose' replaced breeches in the upper classes, and became so enormous that sitting down was all but impossible. While women's clothes were designed to make them look triangular, men's clothes made them look square. They wore short jackets and the shoulders of their coats were cut wide.

The history of the 'codpiece' we see on suits of armour is closely related to its counterpart in civilian male costume. From the mid-fourteenth-century onward, male garments for the upper body had occasionally become so short as to almost reveal the crotch. Before the development of trousers, men wore leggings tied to their undergarment or a belt and the crotch was hidden with a flap secured to the upper inside edge of each legging. At the beginning of the sixteenth century, this flap began to be padded and thus visually emphasised. The codpiece was an inverted triangular piece of material sewn into the hose around a man's groin and held closed by string ties. Later it would become padded, boned and oversized, often being used to carry a small weapon or jewels. This may well be the origin of the term 'family jewels', referring to male genitals. The codpiece remained commonplace in European male costume until the end of the sixteenth century. On armour, the codpiece as a separate piece of plate defence for the genitals appeared during the second decade of the sixteenth century and remained in use and fashion until about 1570. Thickly padded on the inside, it is attached to the armour at the centre of the lower edge of the metal skirt. While its early form was rather cuplike, it remained under the direct influence of civilian costume, and later examples are somewhat more pointed upward. It was, however, not typically worn with armour for use on horseback. It got in the way, and the armoured front bow of the war saddle usually offered enough protection for the groin area. The codpiece is usually found on armour used for fighting on foot, both in war and tournament, and, although of some protective value, it was always as much an element of fashion as one of defence.

Hats and Shoes

Everyone wore some kind of headwear, and different trades had their own distinctive headgear. Women kept their heads covered at all times, often with a tight-fitting linen 'coif', which could be worn under a bonnet or veil. Fashionable headwear for women included the French hood and the gable headdress, while versions of the coif and the veil remained popular. Nightclothes were worn only by the wealthy. Ordinary people slept in their smocks, although everyone would have worn nightcaps to help keep them warm in bed in these years of icy winters. In 1488, the price of knitted woollen hats was fixed by law. Women working in the fields wore caps to keep the sun off their skin, and it was fashionable to have pale skin. In 1571 a law was passed which decreed that everyone over the age of six years old had to wear a woollen cap on Sundays and on holidays, in order to help England's wool trade. Royalty and the nobility were excused from obeying this law. The taller the hat the more important the man, so poor men wore woollen flat caps.

Tudor streets were compacted earth, with no pavements, and in rain churned to thick mud. Towns had no proper sewers, except in Bristol where sewers led to the Avon. Kitchen and toilet waste was usually thrown from pails into the streets where it lay in heaps at street corners. In the country the ditches running between properties were used as open sewers. It was very hard to keep feet clean and dry, and shoes were very rarely waterproof so walking was unpleasant. Several types of overshoe were devised to raise the foot above the ground, generally known as 'pattens'. They were types of wooden shoes, with blocks underneath that gave extra height to the wearer. They were designed to be slipped on over an ordinary shoe. Pattens first appeared in the fourteenth century and by Tudor times were worn by everybody.

17

Schools and Learning

By the mid-sixteenth century it is estimated that only 20 per cent of men and 5 per cent of women were literate, though this may mean that they could only sign their names. Only a very small percentage of Tudor children went to any school, and children were only taught those skills that their parents thought would be necessary for their adult life. Most parents saw little point in educating daughters to write or even read, and they were either kept at home by their parents to help with housework, or sent out to work to bring money in for the family. Poor children were not educated at all, as they were needed for their labour as soon as they were capable. Richer boys might begin school aged four, and move to grammar school when they were seven. The wealthiest families hired a tutor to teach boys at home. Richer boys were educated for work, and richer girls for marriage and running a household.

Schoolmasters received no training and the quality of teaching varied enormously. Many were clergymen trying to enhance their poor stipends. However, from 1559 no one was allowed to teach children unless he had a licence from the local bishop, an attempt to ensure that teachers were morally fit to instruct children. Only by the later sixteenth century were there a few female teachers. There was hardly any free education, with three types of schools: parish, petty and grammar. Parish schools were not free and were more numerous, with over half the parishes in England having one by the end of the Tudor period. They taught singing so that boys could be choristers, but also reading, writing and simple arithmetic, and were attended by both boys and a few girls. The church or the schoolmaster's home often served as the schoolhouse.

The most elementary level of education for middle-class boys was conducted at a petty school. This was conducted not in a school but in the house of a teacher, the word 'petty' deriving from the French *petit*, meaning small. These schools were often run by a well-educated local housewife, so were also called dame schools. The education consisted of being taught to read and write English, learning the catechism and taking lessons in behaviour.

Of the two types of grammar schools, the private ones were attended only by fee-paying children. Others were funded by people who left money in their wills, often stipulating that all or a set number of places should be free so that poor children could go. Grammar school was usually seen as preparation for university, with girls only rarely attending as they were not allowed a university education for centuries. The school day started at about 6 a.m. and ended at about 5.30 p.m., five days a week. Children of the gentry were usually taught at home by private tutors but some did go to grammar schools, especially later in the period. Other than the parish schools there was very little provision for girls, although upper class girls were always taught at home. On the whole they learned reading, writing, needlework, French, singing, dancing, music, manners and morals. Archery and hunting were sometimes included. Even by the end of the Tudor period, girls were not invariably taught to write. It was important for Tudor girls to learn how to govern a household and become skilled in all housewifely duties in preparation for the only real career option for a middle- or upper-class girl, which was marriage. They would be taught obedience to the male members of the family, which makes the positions of Mary I and Elizabeth I anomalous for the period across the Western world.

From the age of seven to fourteen, middle-class boys were educated at grammar schools that may have been founded with endowments but were often financed by the local trade guilds. The rudiments of Latin were taught, using the textbook known as *Lily's Latin Grammar*. A horn book and the Tudor alphabet were the tools used to provide this basic level of Tudor education. The book was authorised by Henry VIII as the sole Latin grammar textbook to be used in education and schools. In 1558 a child's speller was written in England as spelling consistency gradually emerged. The curriculum for seven-year-olds consisted of learning parts of speech, verbs and nouns. Aged eight, boys would be taught the rules of grammar and sentence construction. When nine, education concentrated on English–Latin and Latin–English translations. Between the ages of ten and fourteen, education focussed on the following lessons: Latin–English translations; literature, including the works of great classical authors and dramatists such as Ovid, Plautus, Horace, Virgil and Cicero; religious education; arithmetic; and occasionally the study of history, astrology and Greek.

A similar range of lessons were taught by the tutors of wealthy Tudors as part of a standard curriculum. These studies included various languages, grammar, theology, history, rhetoric, logic, philosophy, arithmetic, literature, geometry, religion and music. At fourteen, Tudor education continued at university. Oxford and Cambridge were the only two English universities and the most popular choices for completing the Tudor education. A classical Tudor education would have been provided at both universities, giving the following choices. Education in the arts would have included philosophy, rhetoric, poetics, natural history, etc. The liberal arts would have included grammar, logic, music, astronomy, arithmetic and geometry. Theology concentrated upon a religious education. Medicine included the study of Hippocrates and Galen, and Arabic and Jewish medical texts. There were also law degrees, the best opportunity for an administrative career.

The first academic houses were monastic halls. Of the dozens that were established in Oxford during the twelfth to fifteenth centuries, none survived the Reformation. Henry VIII closed both the monasteries and their schools, and the overall level of schooling initially declined. He refounded many former monastic schools, known as 'king's schools'. During the reign of Edward VI, many free grammar schools were set up to take in non-fee-paying students.

Oxford and Cambridge Colleges Founded under the Tudors

Oxford University

The only two universities in England were Oxford, founded before 1171, and Cambridge, founded in 1209. Scotland had no less than four universities: St Andrews (between 1410 and 1413); Glasgow (1451); Aberdeen (1495) and Edinburgh (1583). The oldest of Oxford's existing colleges are University, Balliol and Merton, established between 1249 and 1264, although there is some dispute over the exact order and precisely when each began teaching. The fourth-oldest college is Exeter, founded in 1314, and the fifth is Oriel, dating from 1326. Six colleges were founded at both Oxford and Cambridge under the Tudors.

At Oxford, Brasenose College was founded in 1509 and was for centuries associated with Lancashire and Cheshire, the county origins of its two founders. Corpus Christi College was founded in 1517 by Richard Foxe, Bishop of Winchester. The library, founded at the same time as the college, was perhaps the largest and best furnished library then in Europe. Erasmus noted in a letter of 1519 that it was a library *inter praecipua decora Britanniae* ('among the chief beauties of Britain'), and praised the fact that it was a *biblioteca trilinguis* (trilingual library), containing as it did books in Latin, Greek and Hebrew. The year 1546 saw the foundation of Christ Church. Like its sister college, Trinity College, Cambridge, it was traditionally considered the most aristocratic college of its university. Christ Church has produced thirteen British prime ministers, which is equal to the number produced by all forty-five other Oxford colleges put together. It had been planned by Wolsey before his fall. Trinity College was founded in 1554 by Sir Thomas Pope and its full name is 'The College of the Holy and Undivided Trinity in the University of Oxford'. St John's College was founded in 1555 by the merchant Sir Thomas White, Lord Mayor of London, following Pope's example. It was intended to provide a source of educated Roman Catholic clerics to support the Queen Mary's Counter-Reformation. St John's is the wealthiest college in Oxford, with a financial endowment of £340 million as of 2012. Jesus College, founded in 1571, was known for centuries as 'the Welsh College'. It was founded by Elizabeth I for the education of clergy, and a major driving force behind its establishment was Hugh ap Rhys, a Brecon clergyman.

Cambridge University

Jesus College, Cambridge, was established between 1496 and 1516, and its full name is 'The College of the Blessed Virgin Mary, Saint John the Evangelist and the glorious Virgin Saint Radegund'. Its common name comes from the name of its twelfth-century chapel, Jesus Chapel, and it is on the site of a Benedictine nunnery. Christ's College was founded by Henry VII's mother, Lady Margaret Beaufort, in 1505, being the twelfth of the Cambridge colleges to be founded in its current form. It was originally established as God's House in 1437. St John's College was established in 1511, and its full name is 'The Master, Fellows and Scholars of the College of St John the Evangelist in the University of Cambridge'. Trinity College has a full name of 'College of the Holy and Undivided Trinity' and was founded by Henry VIII in 1546 from the merger of two existing colleges: Michaelhouse of 1324 and King's Hall of 1337. Henry had been seizing Church lands from abbeys and monasteries at the time, and Oxford and Cambridge, being both religious institutions and rich, expected to be dissolved. The king passed an Act of Parliament allowing him to suppress, and confiscate the property of, any college he wished. The universities used their contacts to plead with his wife, Catherine Parr. She persuaded her husband not to close them down, but to create a new college. The king did not want to use royal funds, so he instead combined two colleges and seven hostels to form Trinity. Emmanuel College was founded in 1584 by Elizabeth's chancellor, Sir Walter Mildmay, in existing Dominican friary buildings. He intended Emmanuel to be a college of training for Protestant preachers to rival the successful Catholic theological schools that had trained Dominican friars for years. Sidney Sussex College dates from 1596 under the terms of the will of Frances Sidney, Countess of Sussex. She left the sum of £5,000 together with some plate to found a new college at Cambridge University 'to be called the Lady Frances Sidney Sussex College'. Oliver Cromwell attended but never graduated, and his head is now buried beneath the college's ante-chapel.

Tudor Schools Founded

Some academics have complained of a decline in teaching standards after the Dissolution, but the Tudor era saw an explosion in schools across Britain, with the rise of the middle classes driving demand for education to replace that formerly given by monks. For instance, Henry VII as a child had been educated by monks from Monkton Priory next to Pembroke Castle, and then by private tutors. The drive was also fuelled by printing and the new learning from the Renaissance and scientific discoveries. The loosening of the grip of restrictive Church teachings allowed progress in ideas and thought and an increased emphasis upon new learning. There were few known schools prior to 1485. Here follows a list of schools known to have been established at this time. The Minster School, York (627); St Peter's School, York (627); Beverley Grammar School (*c.* 700); the Pilgrims' School (*c.* 900); Wells Cathedral School (909); the King's School, Ely (970); Lincoln Christ's Hospital School (1090); Salisbury Cathedral School (1091); Ludlow College/Palmer's Guild (1200); St Paul's Cathedral School (1129); Hull Grammar School (*c.* 1330); Hereford Grammar School (poss. 676, mentioned in 1384); Cirencester Grammar School (1461); Lancaster Royal Grammar School (1235); Northallerton

College (1323); Bourne Grammar School (1330); Bablake School (1344); Doncaster Grammar (1350); Prince Henry's High School (1376); New College School (1379); Winchester College (1382); Katherine Lady Berkeley's School (1384); Penistone Grammar (1392); Sponne School (1430); Seven Oaks School (1432); Chipping Camden School (1440); Eton College (1440); Adams' Grammar (1442); City of London School (1442); St Dunstan's College (before 1446); Hartsmere School (1451); St Bartholomew's School, Newbury (1466); Oswestry School (1407); Chorister School (1416); Magdalen College School, Oxford (1480); and Thomas Rotherham College (1483).

Apart from these thirty-five schools, six other pre-Tudor schools were given royal charters under the Tudors, namely the King's School, Canterbury (abbey founded 597), granted a royal charter in 1541; King's School, Rochester, of 604, given a charter in 1541; Derby School of 1160, given a charter in 1554; Westminster School of 1179, given a charter in 1540; Colchester Royal Grammar School of 1206 had a charter in 1585; and Hanley Castle High School of 1326 received a charter in 1544.

Twenty schools were refounded under the Tudors, such as the Royal Grammar School, (poss. 685, refounded 1566); St Alban's School (*c.* 948, refounded 1549); Warwick School (tenth century, refounded 1545); Bedford School (1086, refounded 1552); Norwich School (1096, refounded 1547); the King's School, Pontefract (1139, refounded 1548); Derby School (1160, refounded 1554); Abingdon School (pre-1256, refounded 1563); King Edward VI Grammar School, Louth, (1276, refounded 1551); Southwell Minster School (pre-1313, refounded 1547); Reading School (refounded 1486, royal charter 1541); Bristol Cathedral School (refounded 1542); the King's School, Grantham (1329, refounded 1528); the King's School, Ottery St Mary (1335, refounded 1545); Wisbech Grammar School (1379, royal charter 1549); Ipswich School (1399, royal charter 1566); Royal Latin School (1423, royal charter 1548); Durham School (1414, refounded 1541); Bromsgrove School (1476, refounded 1553); and Stamford School (1309, re-endowed 1532).

There were thus only sixty-one pre-Tudor schools, many attached to abbeys and churches, of which twenty were refounded or re-endowed under the Tudors and another six given royal charters. We can compare this to the 118 years of Tudor rule, when around another 153 schools opened in England and Wales, beginning with Stockport Grammar (1487) and ending with Beaumaris Grammar School in 1603.

18

Science and Scientists

Apart from increased international trade helping spread ideas across the known world, two major innovations helped the West overtake China in technological advancement. Although the Romans had been greatly skilled glassblowers, the skill had been lost in Europe, only returning through the Arabic nations. Chemistry experiments are more easily carried out under and within glass, with reactions being more visible. Also, the use of the ceramics of the time tended to interfere with any reactions. The second innovation was a by-product of the Renaissance. As well as the more well-known artistic revolution, there was an upsurge in the popularity of science because of the new desire for learning. Men now tended to fear the teachings of the Roman Church less, especially across the newly Protestant regions of northern Europe. For the first time the writings of Islamic scholars, including mathematicians, astronomers and physicians, were sought after, translated and studied by many Christians. The new printing presses massively assisted this process of information sharing. However, pioneering scientists were still persecuted as evil magicians and witches by the Church.

Additionally, the new physical sciences were gaining favour with the noble classes across Europe. These sciences were based upon the original theories of alchemy, but increasingly discarded the concepts of magic in favour of reason and logic, and eventually led to what we now know as physics and chemistry. During the Tudor period alchemy reached its highest importance, whereas astrology was slowly being replaced by empirical astronomy. Such was the importance of alchemy that Shakespeare dedicated *The Tempest* to it, with the main character being a powerful sorcerer, probably based upon Dr John Dee, an alchemist and Elizabeth I's personal consultant.

As understanding of the natural world quickly developed, more and more alchemists and physicians began to be seen as 'magicians' by an illiterate and uneducated population, who burnt John Dee's fabulous library at Mortlake. Many 'doctors' made no attempt to correct this mistake and some advocated being able to control unseen natural forces. Astrology, numerology and talismans commonly outlined many treatments and experiments, but this was regarded as separate from 'black magic', which was associated with diabolical interventions. To escape from accusations of witchcraft, alchemists devised a system of classification which divided magic into two categories, black and white. Naturally, their system of 'natural magic' was the white magic, working solely with the magic that existed in all natural things. The other, black magic, was sorcery, whose practitioners were accused of gaining power from the devil to aid their own ends. Alchemists considered themselves experts in many fields, from astrology to primitive chemistry, and enjoyed a great deal of power under the Tudors. Elizabeth I consulted John Dee in his role as an astrologer to find the most suitable date for her coronation, and later in life sponsored his project to find the 'Elixir of Life'.

Even at this point, when magic and science were starting to be regarded as separate entities, most Tudor alchemists still dreamed of finding the 'Elixir of Life' or the 'Philosopher's Stone', which would be a source of eternal youth and health. It would also give them the power to transmute base metals such as iron and lead into valuable gold and silver. They believed that all elements were composed of the same matter, and just differed in terms of purity. Thus, what we would call an impossible 'transformation' from iron into gold they would see as a simple process of 'purification'. Attracted by the prospects of youth and money, nobles and kings across Europe rushed to sponsor alchemists and their experiments, spurring chemical invention. Unfortunately, the field was full of charlatans such as John Dee's co-worker Edward Kelley. While alchemists and their counterparts in astrology and 'natural magic' gained a great deal of power in the Tudor period, James I came to the throne in 1603 as a man who hated 'magicians'. Many who had lived in luxury under the reign of Elizabeth were forced into hiding and poverty.

Against this 'magical' background, we can say that the scientific revolution began in the Tudor era, following Continental developments and Arab influences. William Caxton had brought printing technology from Flanders in 1476 and book publishing blossomed, allowing easier access to information. It was possibly the most fertile time in European history, as the shackles of religious dogma were thrown off by those who dared. We must briefly examine European developments in Tudor times because they quickly came to England, leading us from the medieval period into the modern world. Men such as Leonardo da Vinci (1452–1519) and Nicolaus Copernicus (Mikolai Kopernik 1473–1543) changed history and influenced mankind.

In da Vinci's notebooks we read, 'Iron rusts from disuse; stagnant water loses its purity and in cold weather becomes frozen; even so does inaction sap the vigour of the mind.' This restless polymath was always conscious of the value of using his time wisely, writing that 'learning never exhausts the mind' and 'as a well-spent day brings happy sleep, so a life well spent brings happy death'. However, he was acutely aware that he could not achieve all that he wanted to achieve in his lifetime, writing, 'I have wasted my hours.' Thus hours were important to him, not days or months, in his constant struggle for self-improvement. Da Vinci was possibly the greatest genius in known history, moving easily between painting, architecture, anatomy, sculpture, music, geometry, science and engineering. He was in Florence at age seventeen, apprenticed to Verrochio, whose artistry he soon surpassed. In 1481 he moved to Milan, where he painted the *Virgin of the Rocks* and *The Last Supper*. He consulted on architecture in Venice from 1495 to 1499, became a military engineer for Cesare Borgia and returned to Florence, where he painted the *Mona Lisa*. On his return to Milan he concentrated on scientific studies, and in Rome he came into contact with Michelangelo and Raphael. Leonardo wrote the first systematic explanations of how machines work and how the elements of machines can be combined. Some 500 years later, many of the sketches in his surviving notebooks can be used as blueprints to create perfect working models. Among his ideas were tanks, helicopters, solar power, calculators, engines and double hulls. He even developed a rudimentary theory of plate tectonics, and as a scientist this amazing polymath advanced knowledge in the fields of hydrodynamics, optics, civil engineering and anatomy.

In *On the Revolutions of the Heavenly Spheres* (*De revolutionibus orbium coelestium*) of 1543, Copernicus wrote, 'Finally we shall place the Sun himself at the centre of the Universe. All this is suggested by the systematic procession of events and the harmony of the whole Universe, if only we face the facts, as they say, "with both eyes open".' Copernicus was the Polish proponent of the theory that the Sun, and not the Earth, is in the centre of our universe, first proposed by Aristarchus. He studied in Italy and then practised medicine in Poland, but was officially employed as a canon in Olstzyn Cathedral. Patient study and calculation led him to the conclusion that the earth turns upon its own axis, and, together with the planets, revolves around the Sun, whereas religious teaching was that the Earth was the centre of God's universe. Around 1513, he wrote a short account of his sun-centred cosmology for friends he had met in Rome. A full account of the theory, *De revolutionibus*, was not published until he was near the end of his life. He is said to have received a copy of the printed book on his deathbed. Copernicus' heliocentric system was thought implausible by the vast majority of his contemporaries, and by most other astronomers and natural philosophers, until the middle of the seventeenth century. Its main defenders included Johannes Kepler and Galileo Galilei, but there was strong opposition from the Church.

Galileo Galilei (1564–1642), an Italian scientist, made one of the first telescopes. It was about as powerful as an opera glass, and found the Sun moving unmistakably on its axis, Venus showing phases according to her position in relation to the Sun, Jupiter accompanied by revolving moons, or satellites, and the Milky Way composed of a multitude of separate stars. Galileo rightly believed that these discoveries confirmed the theory of Copernicus. Galileo was also the first Westerner to discover sunspots, in 1613, and discovered that the Milky Way was made up of many individual stars. Another man of genius, the German Johannes Kepler (1571–1630), worked out the mathematical laws which govern the movements of the planets. He made it clear that the planets revolve around the Sun in elliptical instead of circular orbits. A key figure in the scientific revolution, Kepler's laws provided a foundation for Newton's 'theory of universal gravitation'. Although Kepler's university astronomy teacher, Michael Maestlin, was forced to teach him the Ptolemaic world system, in private Maestlin had told his graduate students of Copernicus' heliocentric theory. Because of his talent as a mathematician, in 1600 Kepler was invited by Tycho Brahe to Prague to become his assistant and to calculate new orbits for the planets from Brahe's observations. Brahe died in 1601 and Kepler was appointed his successor as Imperial Mathematician, the most prestigious appointment in mathematics in Europe. In 1604 Kepler published *Astronomia pars optica* (*The Optical Part of Astronomy*), in which he discussed atmospheric refraction, lenses and gave the modern explanation of the workings of the eye. In 1606 he published *De stella nova* (*Concerning the New Star*) on the new star that had appeared in 1604. In 1613, Kepler demonstrated that the Christian calendar was in error by five years, and that Jesus had been born in 4 BCE, a conclusion now universally accepted.

Gerhardus Mercator (originally Gerard de Kremer of Flanders, 1512–94) was appointed Court Cosmographer to the Duke of Jülich-Cleves-Berg in 1564. He knew that mariners had no dependable nautical charts. Compass bearings were contrary to chart indications, so on a long voyage ships had to approach land and use coastal features to estimate exactly where they were, and then proceed to their destination. No one could truly represent the globe on a flat level to be of navigational use on ships. In 1569 Mercator found the solution, projecting the world onto a cylinder. His 'Mercator Projection' world map had the parallel lines of latitudes and meridians of longitude intersect each other perpendicularly, and stretched the distances on the parallels with the same factor as the distances on the meridians. Apart from being the first man to show a round earth on a flat map, Mercator was the first person to use the terms of North and South America, and the first to depict the New World as stretching from the northern to the southern hemisphere. The Mercator projection revolutionised world trade and exploration. When the problem of measuring longitude at sea was solved, oceangoing navigation and world trade grew exponentially. Mercator was the first to use the term 'atlas' for a collection of maps, 'to honour the Titan, Atlas, King of Mauritania, a learned philosopher, mathematician, and astronomer'.

Abraham Ortelius (Abraham Ortels of Antwerp, 1527–98) was the first to propose how continents are formed by 'Continental Drift'. Ortelius had been influenced by Mercator to become a scientific geographer. At Mercator's prompting, in 1564 he produced the first modern atlas, an eight-leaved map of the world. It was reproduced in fifty-three maps in *Theatrum orbis terrarum* (*Theatre of the World*) in 1570. In 1575 Ortelius was appointed geographer to Philip II of Spain, and produced a work on ancient geography, *Synonymia geographica*, in 1578. It was expanded as *Thesaurus geographicus* in 1587, and in another expanded edition of 1596 he proposed 'Continental Drift', writing that the Americas were 'torn away from Europe and Africa ... by earthquakes and floods ... The vestiges of the rupture reveal themselves, if someone brings forward a map of the world and considers carefully the coasts of the three [continents].'

Modern medicine was kick-started by the Swiss-German Philippus Aureolus

Theophrastus Bombastus von Hohenheim ('Paracelsus', 1493–1541) and his belief that minerals and chemicals could be used to treat diseases. Paracelsus was a physician, botanist, alchemist and astrologer, founding the discipline of toxicology. He is known as a revolutionary for insisting upon using observations of nature rather than looking to ancient texts, in open and radical defiance of medical practice of his day. Modern psychology often also credits him for being the first to note that some diseases are rooted in psychological illness. Andreas Vesalius (1514–64), a Fleming who studied in Italian medical schools, gave to the world the first careful description of the human body based on actual dissection. He was thus the founder of the study of human anatomy. His dissections of the human body helped to correct misconceptions dating from ancient times. Surgery and anatomy were then considered of little importance in comparison to the other branches of medicine. However, Vesalius believed that surgery had to be grounded in anatomy. Unusually, he always performed dissections himself and produced anatomical charts of the blood and nervous systems as a reference aid for his students, which were widely copied. Henry VIII legalised human dissection to enable research, as he was always worried about his health.

In Vesalius' footsteps, and growing up in Tudor times, stepped William Harvey (1578–1657). He wrote in 1628 that the heart 'is the household divinity which, discharging its function, nourishes, cherishes, quickens the whole body, and is indeed the foundation of life, the source of all action'. This English physician was the first man to describe accurately how blood was pumped around the body by the heart. Educated at Cambridge University, he then studied medicine at the University of Padua under the surgeon Hieronymus Fabricius. Fabricius knew that veins had one-way valves, but did not know their function. Harvey discovered what part the valves played in the circulation of blood through the body, announced the discovery of the circulation of the blood and thereby founded the study of human physiology.

Copernicus, Galileo, Kepler, Vesalius, Harvey, and their fellow workers built up the 'scientific method'. In the Middle Ages students had mostly been satisfied to accept what Aristotle and other philosophers had said, without trying to prove their statements. Kepler, for instance, was the first to disprove the Aristotelian idea that, as all perfect motion is circular, therefore the heavenly bodies must move in circular orbits. Similarly, the world had to wait many centuries before Harvey showed Aristotle's error in supposing that the blood arose in the liver, went thence to the heart, and by the veins was conducted over the body. The new scientific method rested on observation and experiment. Students learned at length to take nothing for granted, to set aside all authority, and to go straight to nature for their facts. As Lord Bacon declared, 'All depends on keeping the eye steadily fixed upon the facts of nature, and so receiving their images simply as they are, for God forbid that we should give out a dream of our own imagination for a pattern of the world.' Modern science, to which we owe so much, is a product of the Renaissance.

The Elizabethan era saw significant scientific progress. Thomas Gresham made arrangements for the proceeds of the Royal Exchange to fund Gresham College in London, where the professors had to provide public lectures. Established in 1597, this college filled the need for public education in the new sciences, there being no university in London at the time. The physician William Gilbert (1544–1603) is credited by many as the father of electricity and magnetism, and helped to prove that the Earth was not the centre of the universe. To aid navigation, Gilbert tried to clarify his understanding of the compass and the phenomenon of magnetism. To prove his hypothesis regarding the magnetism of the planet, Gilbert conducted seventeen years of experiments, this being one of the first examples of what we now call the experimental scientific method. The revolutionary new concept of using experimentation to support one's hypothesis radically changed the course of science, ushering in an entirely new age of scientific theory, exploration, and discovery. Gilbert collaborated with ships' captains, navigators and compass makers, performing elaborate experiments using a spherical magnetic lodestone and a freely moving needle. He discovered that it was possible to create magnets from ordinary metals by rubbing them with a magnet. Gilbert also learned how to strengthen magnets, and he noticed that magnets lost their power when exposed to extremely high temperatures. When he observed that magnetic forces often produced circular motions, he began to connect the phenomenon of magnetism with the rotation of the earth. This led to his discovery of the earth's own magnetism, and provided the theoretical foundation for the science of geomagnetism. In 1600 he became president of the Royal College of Physicians, and served as physician to Elizabeth I and to her successor James I. Also in 1600, his *De magnete* (*On the Magnet and Magnetic Bodies, and on the Great Magnet the Earth*) was quickly accepted throughout Europe as the standard work on electrical and magnetic phenomena.

As well as augmenting Robert Recorde's writings, John Dee wrote the seminal 'Mathematical Preface' to Billingsley's translation of Euclid in 1570. His preface has been called a 'landmark in mathematical thought'. Dee published *General and Rare Memorials pertayning to the Perfect Arte of Navigation* in 1577. He was born Ieuan Ddu (Black John), who became known as John Dee and the original 'Black Jack', who became Elizabeth I's tutor, a man respected at court who was also a noted mathematician, antiquary, astronomer, philosopher, geographer, propagandist, astrologer and spy. How many people these days can put that on their business card? He was known as 'the last royal wizard' and 'the magus of his age'. John Dee went to St John's College, Cambridge, in 1543, and was nominated as a foundation fellow of Trinity College, Cambridge, in 1546, before in 1546 moving to Louvain (Leuven) in modern-day Belgium because science and mathematics were better established there. He believed that English humanism was not scientific enough, and made contact with some of the finest minds in mathematics and geography, such as Mercator, Ortelius and Gemma Phrysius. Dee advised Drake upon his circumnavigation, and schemed a Northwest Passage with Gilbert. Substantial advancements were made in the fields of cartography and surveying from Dee's work.

Robert Recorde (1510–89) was born in Tenby, Wales. Recorde's invention of the 'equals' sign (=) revolutionised algebra, and his mathematical works were translated and read all over Europe. Although a doctor of medicine at the royal court, he was more noted for his astronomy and mathematics. In 1551 Recorde wrote *Pathway to Knowledge*, which is considered to an abridgement of Euclid's *Elements* and has been called a 'landmark in mathematical thought'. It is certainly the first English translation, in which Recorde rearranged Euclid's writings to make better sense. This was his only book that is not written in the form of a dialogue between a master and student. The year 1552 saw the publication of his *The Grounde of Artes*, a book for learning arithmetic, dedicated to King Edward VI, his patron. The textbook went into twenty-six editions by 1662, 'teaching the perfect work and practice of Arithmeticke etc.', in Recorde's own words. It discusses Arabic numeral operations, counter-computation, proportion, fractions and the 'rule of three'. His arithmetic book was notable in being innovative in two respects. Firstly, it was written as a dialogue between a master and pupil to keep it interesting, and secondly it used the device of pointing fingers at important points in the text (a precursor to Windows icons!). In 1557 appeared *The Whetstone of Witte*, his textbook of elementary algebra. In this he invented the = sign using two parallel line segments, 'because no 2 things can be more equal', and to 'avoid the tedious repetition of equals to'. Recorde's *The Urinal of Physick* of 1548 was used by uroscopy practitioners and remained in print into the seventeenth century. The textbooks of this mathematician, merchant, doctor of medicine, navigator, teacher, metallurgist, cartographer, inventor and astronomer were studied across the Western world.

The first book of Leonard Digges (1520–59) was *The General Prognostication* of 1553, and this and other versions were extremely popular, partly because they were written in English when standard scientific publications were normally in Latin. The books were early almanacs, with data for astronomy and astrology, calendars of Church events and moon motions for several years, information on timekeeping and weather phenomena and even instructions for bloodletting. This mathematician and surveyor was a great populariser of science, and apparently invented both the refracting and reflecting telescopes. Around 1551 Leonard Digges invented the theodolite, as well as inventing and improving a number of other items for use by surveyors, carpenters and masons. A theodolite is a precision instrument for measuring angles in the horizontal and vertical planes, mainly used for surveying. The first occurrence of the word theodolite is found in his posthumous *Pantometria* of 1571. He took part in the ill-fated Protestant rebellion in 1554, led by Sir Thomas Wyatt against England's new Catholic queen, Mary I. Digges was condemned to death but had his sentence commuted, instead forfeiting all his property and estates. Penniless, he spent the rest of his life trying to regain his properties and reputation, dying in 1559, which probably explains why his telescope was not popularised. One night in 1572, his son, the Elizabethan astronomer Thomas Digges, saw a bright new 'star' in the sky. It should not have been there. The Tudors believed that heaven, where

God lived, was perfect and unchanging, and the appearance of this bright new star completely undermined their whole system of belief. However, Digges' observation was not just quietly recorded and lost; observational science came of age when Digges recorded the first observed supernova. It rapidly became common knowledge thanks to a really dangerous piece of high technology: the printing press.

Thomas Harriot (1560–1621) has been called 'the greatest English scientist of the age', and became a loyal friend to Sir Walter Raleigh and a permanent part of his household. He was paid to lecture Raleigh's sea captains on navigation and astronomy. In 1585 he went to Roanoke in Virginia, having learned the Algonquian language from American Indians. On his return to England, Harriot wrote his famous *A Brief and True Report of the New Found Land of Virginia*. He courted controversy and spent some time in jail by speaking out for Raleigh. In 1605, he voluntarily took up residence in the Tower to be close to Raleigh and his other great patron, the Earl of Northumberland. Hariot made important advances in optics, mathematics and astronomy.

Sir John Harington (1561–1612) of Bath invented the flush toilet. Before the flush toilet, and the consequent need for sewage disposal systems, human waste was simply emptied into the streets, causing epidemics. Harington was a courtier at Queen Elizabeth I's court, known as her 'saucy godson'. However, because of his salubrious poetry, translations and other writings, he fell in and out of favour with the queen, as well as with her successor, James I. The work for which he remains known today, *A New Discourse of a Stale Subject, called the Metamorphosis of Ajax* (1596) is a political allegory, a coded attack on the 'stercus' or excrement that was poisoning society with torture and state-sponsored libels against his relatives. Because of its allusions against the queen's favourite, the Earl of Leicester, Harington was banished from court and later was imprisoned. Harington composed this author's favourite political epigram as a result: 'Treason doth never prosper: what's the reason? / Why, if it prosper, none dare call it treason.'

Harington called his toilet the Ajax, a pun on 'jakes', the contemporary word for toilet. The slang term 'jacksy' is sometimes still heard today. It was installed at his manor in Kelston near Bath, which he built between 1584 and 1591. Queen Elizabeth temporarily forgave him for his slanders, and visited his house at Kelston in 1592. There are conflicting reports regarding whether the queen used his new invention, or ordered one for her palace at Richmond. Harington's water closet had a pan with an opening at the bottom, sealed with a leather-faced valve. A system of handles, levers and weights poured in water from a cistern, and opened the valve while cleaning the bowl. However, the public carried on using chamber pots, which were usually emptied from an upstairs window into the street below. Alternatively, in cities 'night soil' collectors gathered buckets of human waste at night from toilets and cesspits. This was then thrown into streams or used as fertiliser, causing illness and sometimes epidemics. In 1738, a valve-type flush toilet was invented by J. F. Brondel. In 1775, Alexander Cummings of London first patented a flushing water closet, a device similar to Harrington's Ajax. His S-trap is still in use today, using standing water to seal the outlet of the bowl, preventing the escape of foul air from the sewer.

Space does not permit the inventions and innovations of the age to be covered comprehensively, but some more must be briefly mentioned. In 1564, Guilliam Boonen came from the Netherlands to be Elizabeth's first coachbuilder, introducing the new European invention of the spring-suspension coach to England as a replacement for litters and carts. Coaches quickly became fashionable, and disapproving Puritan writers noted the 'divers great ladies' riding 'up and down the countryside' in their new coaches. They caused the first traffic jams upon London's crowded streets. The first blast furnace appeared in 1491 at Buxted, and the Weald became a centre for iron trade, peaking in 1590. The iron was especially useful for making cannons for the rapidly growing English fleet. Cannon had been first used in Europe by the Islamic Turks to knock down the impregnable walls of Christian Constantinople in the thirteenth century and they were rapidly developed. By the time of Henry VII, castles had outlived their usefulness for the great nobles as Henry owned most of the gunpowder in the kingdom. Henry VII also equipped his Yeomen of the Guard with the new arquebus (harquebus, harkbus or hackbut), meaning 'hook gun', an early muzzle-loaded firearm, the forerunner of the rifle. The printing press is mentioned elsewhere, and was quickly used in England to print copies of the Bible in English and to distribute government notices. Tyndale's English Bible led to the first standardisation of the English language. 'Wad', or graphite, was discovered by shepherds in the Lake District in the mid-sixteenth century and was used as the first 'lead' pencil, leading to life drawing and portraiture for all classes.

19

Music, Dance, Songs and Rhymes

Tudor Music

Musicians were supported in royal courts and houses of the nobility, and the rising merchant class led to even more musical patrons. With growing wealth, opportunities grew for new professions like choirmaster, singer, teacher, composer and instrument builder. Almost compulsory church attendance led to the popularity of hymns and singing, and the invention of music printing made music books more affordable, assisting the growth of performance and composition. Songs and ballads were sung in the villages and fields by workers to ease their monotonous tasks, much as sea shanties developed among seafarers. Local songs were sung at festivals, and cheap, home-made folk instruments were popular, such as in Wales the *pibgorn* (a type of hornpipe), *pibe cyrn* (a type of bagpipe) and *crwth* (a type of lyre, dating at least from the eleventh century). The ability to play a musical instrument was an essential skill both at court and in the great houses, and Elizabeth I was noted to be 'particularly good at the virginals'. There is also a miniature by Nicholas Hilliard of Elizabeth playing the lute. Henry VIII composed several ballads and church music, much of which has been lost. A keen musician and dancer, Henry VIII had a large collection of musical instruments which he played. When he died he left a collection of instruments that included a mechanical virginal, seventy-eight flutes, seventy-eight recorders and five bagpipes.

The Tudor harp was smaller than the modern harp, with fewer strings. It was only about thirty inches in length, consisting of an upright triangular frame containing a series of graduated vertical strings. The *citole* was an ancestor of the guitar, with a fretted neck and four wire strings which were plucked. The gittern was similar, with a more rounded body, but both were overtaken in popularity by the four-, five- or even sixteen-string lute, plucked using a quill as a plectrum. The chittarone lute measured six feet tall, with an elongated neck to which long bass strings were attached to an additional peg box. The viol or viol da gamba was a fretted instrument, similar to the modern violin but played sitting down, resting between the legs of the player. In three sizes, they came to be used in chamber music. The rebec was another bowed, stringed instrument, usually with a narrow, boat-shaped body and between one and five strings. Played with a bow on the arm or under the chin, it is an ancestor of the violin.

The fiddle was one of the most popular street instruments as it was easily carried. The dulcimer is a sound box with strings stretched across it and is played by striking the strings with two wooden hammers. The hurdy-gurdy was a very popular instrument, along with the bagpipe, and the characteristic form had a short neck and a boxy body with a curved tail end. It was played by turning a small wheel with one hand while the other hand pressed down on a set of keys to adjust their pitch. As the wheel turns, it rubs against the strings (like the bow on a violin), and this makes the strings vibrate. The spinet is a small and compactly built upright piano which generates sound by plucking a string rather than striking one. The clavicytherium is a harpsichord that is vertically strung. The virginal is a small type of primitive harpsichord, with the strings plucked rather than struck, and Henry VIII bought five in 1530. The harpsichord family is thought to have originated when a keyboard was fixed to the end of a psaltery, providing a mechanical means to pluck the strings. Psalteries were wire-strung instruments mounted on a hollow wooden box. They were played sitting down with the instrument placed on the performer's lap.

The above list of string and keyboard instruments is not exhaustive, and the same applies to wind instruments. The shawm was a reed instrument with vent holes, a predecessor to the hautboy. The hautboy sounded through a reed, similar to the modern oboe. The bagpipe was an ancient instrument used by the poorest people and was made using a goat or sheep skin and a reed pipe. The crumhorn (curved horn) was introduced in the fifteenth century as a double reed musical instrument. The gemshorn was made of an ox horn and used as a flute-like musical instrument. The lizard was an s-shaped horn and the sackbutt was an ancestor of the modern trombone.

Tudor Dance

Dancing was extremely popular with all classes, being considered 'a wholesome recreation of the mind and also an exercise of the body'. New styles of music and musical instruments, along with the combination of different instruments, led to new dances. Court dances enjoyed by the upper classes were often imported from Italy, Spain or France. These new dances had to be learnt and 'dancing masters' were employed. Many of the court dances were performed as couples and the suggestive Tudor court dance called the Volt was the only dance which allowed the dancers to embrace closely. The most important Tudor dances were the refined Pavane, energetic Galliard and the Almain.

The poorer classes enjoyed traditional country dances such as the jig, Morris dancing, sword-dancing, the brand and the brawle. Morris dance is usually accompanied by music, based on rhythmic stepping and the execution of choreographed figures by a group of dancers, usually wearing bell pads on their shins. Implements such as sticks, swords and handkerchiefs may also be wielded by the dancers. Philip Stubbes, a sixteenth-century pamphleteer, wrote, 'They strike up the devil's dance withal: then march this heathen company towards the church and churchyards, their pypers pyping, the drummers thundering, their stumpes dancing, their bellies jyngling, their handkercheefes fluttering about their heads like madde men'. It was later banned by the Puritans. (Speaking of 'madde men', the BBC's popular *Countryfile* TV programme featured the Thaxted Morris Men of Essex in 2013. Before the filming was allowed, there was an extensive health and safety check and a risk assessment exercise. The world has indeed gone 'madde'.) The comic actor Will Kempe (d. 1603) gave the name 'Nine Days' Wonder' to his dancing a Morris dance in 1600 the hundred miles between London and Norwich. However, he spread it out over several weeks. Kempe was as famous for his stage jigs as for his acting in regular drama. The jig featured as many as five performers in a partially improvised song-and-dance routine. Jigs had plots, often bawdy, but the emphasis was on dancing and physical comedy.

Country dance was performed by couples in round, square, or rectangular sets in much simpler and repetitive forms than those of the royal court dance. Dancing for the poor would have been passed down through the generations, and was performed at fairs and festivals. Many of the dances were steeped in old customs and rituals, such as dancing around the Maypole. The Christmas festival included the carole, which was the most popular dance song that could be danced in a circle, or in a chain, or as a processional. Modern Christmas carols are derived from this practice.

Old pagan rituals had been combined with Christian festivals in order to ensure their acceptance by the common people. The following is a list of Tudor festivals and rituals, some of which, like the Maypole dance, were pagan in origin.

January	Twelfth Night, festival and feasts featuring Tudor dance
February	St Valentine's Day, the Tudor festival celebrating love with singing, dancing and pairing games
April	All Fool's Day, where the jesters, or 'Lords of Misrule', of the Tudor court took charge for the day; their activities included different forms of dancing and odd suggestions for couples
May	May Day – The traditional festival where villagers danced around the maypole
June	Midsummer Eve and the summer solstice of 23 June was celebrated with bonfires and dancing
July	Swithin's Day, celebrated with music and dancing
August	Lammas Day, on 2 August, celebrating the first wheat harvest of the year; candle-lit processions, dance and apple bobbing featured
September	Michaelmas, 29 September, included dancing
October	St Crispin's Day on 25 October, with revels, dance and bonfires
November	The Day of the Dead, All Souls Day or All Hallow's Day (Halloween) was celebrated with revels, dance and bonfires
December	The feasts and Christmas celebrations, including caroles and dancing

Tudor Songs and Nursery Rhymes

'The Twelve Days of Christmas' originated under Elizabeth I, as a way for Catholic Tudors to share their beliefs secretly with other Catholics: 'On the first day of Christmas my true love gave to me a partridge in a pear tree' ('true love' represents God, and the partridge represents Christ). 'On the second day of Christmas my true love gave to me two turtle doves' (the two turtle doves represent the Old and New Testament), and so on: 'three French hens' represent the Trinity; 'four calling birds' represent the Four Gospels; 'five golden rings' represent the five Catholic obligatory sacraments (baptism, communion, confirmation, penance and last rites; 'six geese a laying' represent the six days of creation; 'seven swans a swimming' represent the seven sacraments; 'eight maids a milking' represent the eight beatitudes (days required for Catholics to receive communion); 'nine ladies dancing' represent the nine fruits of the Holy Spirit; 'ten lords a leaping' represent the Ten Commandments; 'eleven pipers piping' represent the Eleven Apostles, excluding Judas; and 'twelve drummers drumming' represent the twelve points of the Apostles' Creed.

Humpty Dumpty may be related to Cardinal Wolsey, who was charged with resolving the 'great matter' of the king's divorce from his wife of some twenty years, Catherine of Aragon. Wolsey was in great difficulties as the servant of two masters – Henry and the Pope, whose office had been responsible for granting the king permission to wed his dead brother's widow in the first place. He sat 'on the wall' desperately seeking for a solution that would keep everyone happy: an impossible task. The egg comparison is a harsh but fair comment on the large figure of the cardinal that we can see in paintings. That he had a great fall is true; he was stripped of his office and had to ask the king's permission to retire to his remaining property, a broken man who had surrendered his great and beautiful palace at Hampton Court to no effect. The king, hearing that he had been taken gravely ill and was likely to die of his depression, sent a troop of horse riding after him with a token gift of a ring and the promise that his life was safe. It was too late, though, and Wolsey died, like Humpty, a broken man that couldn't be put together again.

'Mary, Mary, quite contrary, / How does your garden grow? / With silver bells, and cockle shells, / And pretty maids all in a row' seems to date from the second half of the fifteenth century. Mary came to the throne soon after the death of her brother Edward VI and immediately reversed all the changes he had introduced, trying to make the country Roman Catholic again. Thus she was thought 'quite contrary'. The 'pretty maids all in a row' were the nuns that returned to England during Mary's reign, lined up praying in church. Silver bells were rung during the celebration of the Mass and cockle shells were Catholic symbols, souvenirs worn by pilgrims to the shrine of Saint James of Compostela in northern Spain. By the sixteenth century they had become a generic pilgrim symbol and some say they were incorporated decoratively into the exteriors of houses sympathetic to the Catholic cause during the reign of Queen Elizabeth so that fugitives would know when they were safe. Mary appointed Stephen Gardiner as Archbishop of Canterbury and he helped to persecute Protestants, becoming hated. Thus we read, 'How does your garden (Gardiner) grow?'

In this interpretation, both the things mentioned in the garden, neither of which are flowers, are the common names given to instruments of torture used to convince Protestants to renege on their beliefs. The 'silver bells' were thumbscrews, which crushed the thumb between two hard surfaces by the tightening of a screw. The 'cockle shells' were instruments of torture which were attached to the genitals. The garden could also refer to Mary's inability to produce an heir, dying of stomach cancer which mimicked the bloating effects of pregnancy. Some variations on the rhyme say 'How does your graveyard grow?' – a reference to the reign, which saw many martyrs dying for their beliefs. Others say the Mary in this rhyme is Mary, Queen of Scots.

'Pussy cat, pussy cat, where have you been? / I've been to London to look at the Queen. / Pussy cat, pussy cat, what did you do there? / I frightened a little mouse, under the chair' is said to be based on a story that one of the ladies-in-waiting to Elizabeth had a cat which once accidentally brushed against the queen's foot. Fortunately the queen had a sense of humour and allowed the cat to wander where it liked as long as it kept the room free of mice. 'Old Mother Hubbard' and 'Little Boy Blue' both reputedly refer to Henry VIII's friend Cardinal Wolsey, who was hated by Anne Boleyn despite the fact that he had arranged Henry's divorce from his first wife, Catherine of Aragon. 'Old Mother Hubbard / Went to the cupboard / To get her poor doggie a bone, / When she got there / The cupboard was bare / So the poor little doggie had none.' King Henry VIII was the 'doggie' and the 'bone' of contention refers to the divorce with Catherine of Aragon. The 'cupboard' relates to the Catholic Church, which refused the divorce and led to the demise of Old Mother Hubbard – Cardinal Wolsey.

Another rhyme possibly about Wolsey runs, 'Little Boy Blue, Come blow your horn, / The sheep's in the meadow, The cow's in the corn; / But where is the boy / who looks after the sheep? / He's under a haystack, Fast asleep. / Will you wake him? / No, not I, / For if I do, He's sure to cry.' It is suggested that the title 'Little Boy Blue' was derived from Wolsey's blazon of arms, which featured the blue faces of four leopards as opposed to traditional scarlet cardinal robes. He was called the 'Boy Bachelor' after obtaining his degree from Oxford at the unusually early age of fifteen.

The expression 'blowing one's own horn', meaning to brag, was certainly practised by Wolsey. Between 1514 and 1525 he transformed a medieval manor into the magnificent Hampton Court Palace. It was an ostentatious display of his wealth and his power, giving rise to the rhyme uttered by his enemies: 'Come ye to court? Which Court? The King's Court or Hampton Court?' The anti-Wolsey propaganda worked and in 1529 Henry declared all of Wolsey's lands and possessions forfeit and they became the property of the Crown. At this time England was a prosperous nation, largely through the wool trade and the export taxes on wool, which had augmented both Henry's treasury and Wolsey's assets. The words 'where's the boy who looks after the sheep?' could refer to Wolsey's concern with lining his own pockets with wool revenues, as opposed to those of the country. Wolsey may have acted as a 'hayward' for his father's livestock. The hayward impounded stray livestock and led the sowing and harvesting, and supervised hedging and temporary fencing around livestock and hay meadows. The hayward's symbol of office was a horn, which he blew to give warning that cattle were invading the crops. Perhaps the waking up refers to Wolsey's last illness, when he was heading to London for probable execution. Upon waking he would realise his imminent death from illness or beheading.

'Rain, rain, go away, / Come again another day. / Little Johnny wants to play; / Rain, rain, go to Spain, / Never show your face again!' The origins of the lyrics to this nursery rhyme date back to the Spanish Armada. The attempt failed, not only because of the swift nature of the smaller English ships but mainly due the terrible storms and adverse winds that scattered the Armada fleet. John Hawkins was the chief architect of the Elizabethan navy, making its ships fast and highly manoeuvrable. Hawkins was determined that his navy, as well as having the best fleet of ships in the world, would also have the best-quality seamen. He petitioned and won a pay increase for sailors, arguing that a smaller number of well-motivated and better-paid men would be more effective than a larger group of uninterested men. He made important improvements in ship construction and rigging, but is less well known for his inventiveness as a shipwright than for his financial management.

His innovations included sheathing the underside of his ships with a skin of nailed elm planks sealed with a combination of pitch and hair smeared over the bottom timbers as a protection against the worms that attacked the wooden hulls in tropical seas. Hawkins also introduced detachable topmasts; they could be hoisted and used in good weather and stowed in heavy seas. Masts were stepped further forward, and sails were cut flatter. His ships were 'race-built', being longer and with forecastle and poop greatly reduced in size. The Spanish galleons lumbered in seaworthiness compared to John Hawkins' fleet. Along with Drake and Frobisher, Hawkins was a vice-admiral of the English fleet which harried the Spanish ships. The fleet admiral, Lord Howard, had little knowledge of naval warfare and delegated the battle tactics to Hawkins.

'Little Jack Horner' was reputed to be steward to the bishop of the last Abbot of Glastonbury, Richard Whiting. He was sent to Henry VIII with a Christmas gift of twelve title deeds to manorial estates in an attempt to secure the king's good will. While on his way, Horner stole the deed to the manor of Mells, this being the 'plum' property of the twelve manors. The remaining eleven manors were given to the Crown but the manor of Mells became the property of the Horner family: 'Little Jack Horner sat in the corner, / Eating a Christmas pie; / He put in his thumb, / And pulled out a plum / And said, What a good boy am I!' In 1539, Whiting was arrested and placed in the Tower. He was then taken to Glastonbury with two of his monks, John Thorne and Roger James, where all three were fastened upon hurdles and dragged by horses to the top of Glastonbury Tor, overlooking the town. Here they were hanged, drawn and quartered, with Whiting's head being fastened over the west gate of his now deserted abbey and his limbs exposed at Wells, Bath, Ilchester and Bridgwater. Even if the Horner tale is untrue, it is worth recounting the story of Whiting.

As a member of the House of Lords, he should first have been attainted by Parliament and then beheaded, but Henry's viciousness against men who had principles is always worth repeating. As with Richard III, many people have an image of some monarchs which encompassed far more nobility than their worth.

'Goosie goosie gander where shall I wander, / Upstairs, downstairs and in my lady's chamber / There I met an old man who wouldn't say his prayers, / I took him by the left leg and threw him down the stairs.' The 'lady's chamber' refers to a highborn lady having her own chamber, which was once referred to as a solar. The origins of the rhyme are said to date to the sixteenth century and refers to Catholic priests hiding in 'priest holes', very small, secret rooms constructed in houses to hide Catholics. The moral of the rhyme is that something unpleasant would occur to anyone found not saying their prayers. However, this author has found a more believable origin. Southwark, on the Thames in London, was where sailors spent their money in taverns and brothels. These and others across English ports were created by Henry II (1154–89) to raise revenues for the Crown. By the sixteenth century, Southwark's biggest brothels were owned by the Bishop of Winchester, who gave discounts to priests. In the Reformation of the 1530s, Henry VIII took over the wealth of the cathedrals and abbeys and Church lands, and also these brothels. Prostitutes were known as 'geese' as they could give you a nasty 'goosebite'. 'Goosebite' was the term used for any venereal disease. Henry closed down the brothels, so the 'geese' had to ply their trade elsewhere, often in their clients' homes or wandering around the streets.

'Ride a cock horse to Banbury Cross / To see a fine lady upon a white horse / With rings on her fingers and bells on her toes / She shall have music wherever she goes.' This is thought to relate to Elizabeth I, who travelled to see a huge stone cross while on progress to Banbury. At this time Banbury had many crosses – the High Cross, the Bread Cross and the White Cross – but these were destroyed by Puritans in 1600. Elizabeth was always resplendent with jewellery, and any 'rings on her fingers' could be seen even if she was wearing gloves, as holes were cut to display them. 'And bells on her toes' refers to the fashion of attaching bells to the end of the pointed toes of shoes. Banbury was situated at the top of a steep hill, and in order to help carriages up the steep incline a white cock horse (a large stallion) was made available to help with this task. When the queen's carriage attempted to go up the hill a wheel broke and she chose to mount the cock horse to reach the cross. Her visit was so important that the people of the town had the cock horse decorated with ribbons and bells and provided minstrels to accompany her – 'she shall have music wherever she goes'.

The characters in the nursery rhyme 'I Had a Little Nut Tree' are believed to refer to the visit of Juana, Queen regnant of Castile, who visited Henry VII's court in 1506: 'I had a little nut tree, / Nothing would it bear / But a silver nutmeg, / And a golden pear; / The King of Spain's daughter / Came to visit me, / And all for the sake / Of my little nut tree. / Her dress was made of crimson, / Golden was her hair, / She asked me for my nut tree / And my golden pear. / I said, "So fair a princess / Never did I see, / I'll give you all the fruit / From my little nut tree".' Juana was the daughter of King Ferdinand and Queen Isabella of Spain, the elder sister of Catherine of Aragon. She had married Philip the Handsome of Burgundy in 1496, and in late 1505 the pair decided to travel to Castile. Leaving Flanders, their ships were wrecked on the English coast and the couple were guests of Henry, Prince of Wales (later Henry VIII), and Joanna's sister Catherine of Aragon at Windsor Castle. Juana, later to be known as 'Joanna the Mad', had a fair complexion, blue eyes and her hair colour was between reddish-blonde and auburn, like her mother and sister Catherine. In September 1506, Philip died suddenly of typhoid fever in Castile. Some suspected that he had been poisoned by his father-in-law, Ferdinand II, who had always disliked his foreign Hapsburg origins and with whom he never wanted to share power.

Prince Arthur had died in 1502, so Catherine was widowed and Henry VII faced the challenge of avoiding the obligation to return her dower, half of which he had not yet received, to her father. To settle the matter, it was agreed that Catherine would marry Henry VII's second son, Henry, Duke of York, who was five years younger than she was. The death of Catherine's mother, however, meant that her 'value' in the marriage market decreased. Castile was a much larger kingdom than Aragon, and it had been inherited by Catherine's mentally unstable elder sister, Joanna. The marriage was delayed until Henry was old enough, but Henry VII procrastinated so much over payment of the remainder of Catherine's dowry that it became doubtful that the marriage would take place. She lived as a virtual prisoner at Durham House in London until her wedding to Henry, at his dying father's insistence, on 11 June 1509, seven years after Prince Arthur's death.

There is an extensive nursery rhyme, the first verse of which is 'London bridge is broken down, dance over my Lady Lee, / London bridge is broken down, with a gay ladye'. 'Lady Lee' is Lady Margaret Wyatt, the sister of the poet Thomas Wyatt. When Margaret married Sir Anthony Lee, she became Lady Lee. As the Wyatts and Boleyns were neighbours, Anne and Margaret were childhood friends. Later, Margaret became a lady-in-waiting to Anne and attended her until her execution on the scaffold. It is believed that this rhyme describes the rise and fall of Anne Boleyn, 'the gay ladye'.

20

Composers and Artists

Composers

The Tudor 'Golden Age' saw the flowering of England's first composers and the rapid emergence and development of the music forms of the anthem, madrigal, masque and opera. There were many new songs and hymns, and composers for the voice generally made use of two styles, the traditional air (*ayre*), and the madrigal. The air was a solo song with lute accompaniment. The madrigal was a short love poem, easily set to music. The most popular instrument was the lute, and it led to a variety of different musical instruments being developed, noted in the last chapter. English church music before the Reformation was strictly linked to the liturgical needs of the service, limiting the choice of texts and genres available to the composer.

Combinations of Tudor musical instruments were still in the experimental stage but provided the opportunity to create unusual and creative music. Tudor musicians now experimented with various combinations, the most popular being called an 'English consort' of violin, flute, lute and viol, in effect the first English string quartet. It proved so popular that in 1599 Thomas Morley published *Consort Lessons*. Tudor monarchs were patrons of all the arts and encouraged composers and musicians. Music and song lyrics were printed during the Tudor era but these were sold as separate documents. The Tudor composer John Dowland (1563–1626) published his *First Booke of Songes or Ayres* in 1597 which became a highly profitable bestseller.

Many readers will recognise the names of Thomas Tallis (1505–85) and William Byrd (1543–1623), but the emergence of new English music gave us other Tudor composers such as: John Taverner (1490–1545); Robert Johnson (1500–60); Christopher Tye (1500–73); John Marbeck (1510–85); John Sheppard (1515–58); William Mundy (1529–91); Robert Parsons (1535–71); Robert White (1538–74); John Dowland (1563–1626); Thomas Morley (1557–1602); Thomas Campion (1567–1620); John Farmer (1570–1601); Thomas Tomkins (1572–1656); Thomas Weelkes (1576–1623); and Orlando Gibbons (1583–1625), the latter of whom carried on the traditions under the Stuarts.

Most of John Taverner's music is vocal, and includes Masses, magnificats (canticles sung for Mary) and motets. His best-known motet is '*Dum transisset sabbatum*', and his best-known Mass was based on a popular song, 'The Western Wynde'. The composer Sir John Taverner is his direct descendant, and Peter Maxwell-Davies has composed an opera, *Taverner*, about the remarkable life of this Tudor organist and composer. Thomas Tallis is regarded as 'the father of English cathedral music', but very many of his works were destroyed by Puritans in the despoliation of cathedral libraries in the seventeenth century. He is known to have become organist at Waltham Abbey, where, on its dissolution in 1540, he received, in compensation for the loss of his preferment, 20*s* for wages and 20*s* for reward. Not long after his dismissal from Waltham, Tallis was appointed a gentleman of the Chapel Royal in Henry VIII's court, and the English school of music owes more to him than to any other composer of the sixteenth century.

William Byrd wrote in many of the forms current in England at the time, including different types of sacred and secular polyphony, keyboard and consort music. He produced sacred music for use in Anglican services, although he converted in later life and wrote Catholic sacred music as well. In 1575, Byrd and Tallis were jointly granted a patent for the printing of music and ruled music paper for twenty-one years, one of a number of patents issued by the Crown for the printing of books on various subjects. In 1588 and 1589 Byrd also published two collections of English songs, and his output of about 470 compositions demonstrates his reputation as a master of European Renaissance music. Byrd was able to transform many of the main musical forms of his day and stamp them with his own identity. Baldwin, in a long poem, placed Byrd at the head of the musicians of his day:

> Yet let not straingers bragg, nor they these soe commende,
> For they may now geve place and sett themselves behynde,
> An Englishman, by name, William BIRDE for his skill
> Which I shoulde heve sett first, for soe it was my will,
> Whose greater skill and knowledge dothe excelle all at this time
> And far to strange countries abrode his skill dothe shyne ...

Like Tallis and Byrd, William Mundy's career spanned the Reformation, the Edwardian entrenchment of reform, the Marian reaction and the Elizabethan re-entrenchment. Of the other great sacred music composers of his age, Taverner, Tye, Tallis and Sheppard were older and their compositional ways largely set by the time of the religious upheaval, while Byrd, Morley and later Weelkes, Gibbons and Tomkins had never been schooled in pre-Reformation styles. Among Mundy's near-contemporaries, Robert Parsons and Robert White wrote wonderful music but both died young in the 1570s, and never fulfilled in the English language what they had promised in the Latin.

Artists

Jewellery and metalwork were regarded as extremely important, with far more being spent on them than on painting. Holbein produced many spectacular designs for now-vanished table ornaments in precious metals, and the miniaturist Hilliard was also a practising goldsmith. The main artistic interests of Henry VIII were music, building palaces and tapestry, of which he had over 2,000 pieces, costing far more than he ever spent on artists. Elizabeth spent even less, but took a personal interest in painting, keeping her own collection of miniatures locked away, wrapped in paper upon which she wrote the names of the sitter. She is reputed to have had paintings of her burnt that did not match the iconic image she wished to be shown. In both Tudor and Stuart times foreign artists led schools in England, bringing with them Renaissance influences. The demand for religious images had declined and artists sought alternative work across Europe. However, a native school of painting developed, and Nicholas Hilliard was Elizabeth's 'limner and goldsmith', famed for his delicate miniature masterpieces. With the near extinction of religious painting during the Reformation, and little interest in landscapes or classical mythology at this time, the portrait became the most important form of painting for all the artists of the Tudor court, and the only one to have survived in any numbers. The court painters most will know are Holbein and Hilliard.

Hans Holbein the Younger (*c.* 1497–1543) was a German artist and printmaker, and one of the greatest portraitists of the sixteenth century. He first came to England from 1426 to 1428 and was welcomed into the humanist circle of Thomas More, where he quickly built a good reputation. After returning to Basel for four years, he resumed his career in England from 1532 until his death from plague in 1543. This time he worked under the patronage of Anne Boleyn and Thomas Cromwell. By 1535 he was a King's Painter to Henry VIII, producing not only portraits and festive decorations but designs for jewellery, plate and other precious objects. His portraits of the royal family and nobles are a record of the court in the years when Henry was asserting his supremacy over the Church and it is Holbein who has given us the iconic images of More, Cromwell and Henry VIII. He embedded layers of symbolism, allusion and paradox in his art, for instance in what is perhaps his greatest painting, *The Ambassadors*. The work incorporates a grossly distorted skull, and it is believed that there are references to learning, religion and mortality, where 'sciences and arts, objects of luxury and glory, are measured against the grandeur of Death'. No certain portraits of Anne Boleyn by Holbein survive, perhaps because her memory was purged in 1536. Holbein was employed as a King's Painter on an annual salary of £30, but was never the highest-paid artist on the royal payroll; the royal 'pictor maker', Lucas Horenbout, and other Continental artists working for the king earned more. In 1537, Holbein painted what has become perhaps his most famous image – that of Henry VIII standing in a heroic pose, with his feet planted apart. Holbein may have painted as many as 150 portraits of the king, his wives and family and courtiers. He painted a large mural for the Palace of Whitehall. It showed Henry and his third wife, Jane Seymour, and his parents, the first Tudors. Holbein also designed furniture, jewellery, buttons, buckles and the king's state robes.

Lucas Horenbout, pioneer of the English tradition of the portrait miniature, was a King's Painter from 1531 until his death in 1544. He was a Flemish artist who moved to England in the mid-1520s and worked as King's Painter and court miniaturist to Henry VIII. His miniatures include two of Catherine of Aragon and one of Mary I.

Levina Teerlinc of Bruges (1510/20–76) was a painter to the courts of Henry VIII, Edward VI, Mary I and Elizabeth I. Known as a miniaturist, her annuity for this position was £40, more than Holbein had been paid. She also served as a gentlewoman in the royal households of Mary and Elizabeth. She might have trained Nicholas Hilliard in the methods of miniature portraiture. Hilliard would go on to be the supreme miniature portraitist of the era.

Marcus Gheeraerts the Younger (1561/62–1636) was a Flemish Protestant refugee portraitist who arrived in England as a child with his father, the painter Marcus Gheeraerts the Elder. He has been described as 'the most important artist of quality to work in England in large-scale between [Hans] Eworth [1510–78] and Van Dyck'. He became a fashionable portraitist in the last decade of the reign of Elizabeth under the patronage of her champion and pageant-master Sir Henry Lee. Lee commissioned Gheeraerts to paint the famous *Ditchley Portrait* of the queen.

George Gower (1540–96) was Elizabeth's Serjeant Painter from 1581 until his death, and also a 'gentleman', being the grandson of Sir John Gower of Stettenham, Yorkshire. This was unusual for the time, as artists were effectively ranked as servants, but reveals the increasing status of portraiture in sixteenth-century England. There is a painting of Elizabeth I attributed to Gower. His fully documented portraits, such as those of Sir Thomas and Lady Kytson, show that he commanded the patronage of the important and wealthy from an early age, while his self-portrait of 1579, the first known example by an English artist on such a scale, gives an indication of the bold characterisation with which he depicted his subjects. Gower seems to have been the leading English portraitist of his day.

Nicholas Hilliard (1547–1619) was the most celebrated of all practitioners of his art, and a central figure in establishing the portrait miniature as a distinctive genre in Britain. He was the son of an Exeter goldsmith and trained in this craft, completing a seven-year apprenticeship in London in 1569. It is not known how he learnt miniature painting, but by 1572 he was working for Elizabeth I, with his first surviving portrait of her dating from that year. Later Hilliard also worked for James I, but after the turn of the century his position as the leading miniaturist in the country was challenged by his former pupil Isaac Oliver.

21

Theatre, Literature and Poetry

Printer's Progress and the *Book of Riddles*

We must again mention the importance of the printing press in the spread of literacy and literature. Sir Thomas Malory (*c.* 1405–71) wrote the Arthurian epic *Le Morte d'Arthur* from around 1451 to 1469, though it was not published until 1485. Malory had entitled it *The hoole booke of kyng Arthur & of his noble knyghtes of the rounde table*, but Caxton retitled it. It is generally regarded as the most significant accomplishment in English literature between the works of Chaucer and those of Shakespeare. In 1495, following Caxton's death in 1492 and after three years in litigation, the Alsatian Wynkyn de Worde (d. 1534) took over Caxton's print shop. He greatly improved the quality of the product, thereby being called 'England's first typographer'. De Worde is generally credited for moving English printing away from its late medieval beginnings and towards a modern model. Caxton had depended on noble patrons to sustain his enterprise. De Worde also enjoyed the support of patrons, principally Henry VII's mother Margaret Beaufort, but changed emphasis to the creation of relatively inexpensive books for a commercial audience and the beginnings of a mass market. Where Caxton had used paper imported from the Low Countries, de Worde used the product of John Tate, the first English papermaker.

De Worde published more than 400 books in over 800 editions. Religious works dominated his output, in keeping with the times, but de Worde also printed romantic novels, poetry, children's books and volumes on household practice and animal husbandry. He also innovated in the use of woodcuts as illustrations. De Worde moved his firm from Caxton's location in Westminster to London, becoming the first printer to set up a site on Fleet Street, in 1500. This stayed the centre of press printing in England until the late twentieth century. De Worde was the first to use Hebrew and Arabic characters (1524) and italic type (1528) in English books. His 1495 version of *Polychronicon* by Higdon was the first English work to use movable type to print music. Wynkyn de Worde published his collection of riddles, called *Demands Joyous*, meaning 'amusing questions', in 1511. The greater part are 'too strongly impregnated with indecency and profanity to be presentable here', but examples from the first book of English jokes include:

Demand: What bare the best burden that ever was borne?
Response: The ass that carried our Lady, when she fled with our Lord into Egypt.
Dem: What became of that ass?
Res: Adam's mother ate her.
Dem. Who was Adam's mother?
Res: The Earth.

Dem: How many calves' tails would it take to reach from the earth to the sky?
Res: No more than one, if it be long enough.

Dem: What is the distance from the surface of the sea to the deepest part thereof?
Res: Only a stone's throw.

Dem: What is it that never was and never will be?
Res: A mouse's nest in a cat's ear.

Dem: Why do men make an oven in a town?
Res: Because they cannot make a town in an oven.

Dem: How may a man discern a cow in a flock of sheep?
Res: By his eyesight.

Dem: Why doth a cow lie down?
Res: Because it cannot sit.

Dem: What is it that never freezeth?
Res: Boiling water.

Dem: Which was first, the hen or the egg?
Res: The hen, at the creation.

Dem: How many straws go to a goose's nest?
Res: Not one, for straws not having feet cannot go anywhere.

Dem: Which are the most profitable saints of the church?
Res: Those painted on the glass windows, for they keep the wind from wasting the candles.

Dem: Why doth a dog turn round three times before he lieth down?
Res: Because he knoweth not his bed's head from the foot thereof.

Dem: What is the worst bestowed charity that one can give?
Res: Alms to a blind man: for he would be glad to see the person hanged that gave it to him.

Dem: What is the age of a field-mouse?
Res: A year. And the age of a hedgehog is three times that of a mouse, and the life of a dog is three times that of a hedge-hog, and the life of a horse is three times that of a dog, and the life of a man is three times that of a horse, and the life of a goose is three times that of a man, and the life of a swan is three times that of a goose, and the life of a swallow three times that of a swan, and the life of an eagle three times that of a swallow, and the life of a serpent three times that of an eagle, and the life of a raven is three times that of a serpent, and the life of a hart is three times that of a raven, and an oak groweth five hundred years, and fadeth five hundred years.

Dem: What beast is it that hath her tail between her eyes?
Res: It is a cat when she licketh her arse.

Theatre

England in the Tudor era transformed from being a collection of regional economies, largely isolated from one another, into a far more integrated national economy. The growth of London played a crucial economic role in this development, and at the same time helped unify English culture. By 1600 it had become fashionable for the upper classes to spend part of each year in London, so the city developed entertainment for these rich clients. All cities had a favoured centre of entertainment, and in Tudor times it was Southwark. Southwark, including Bankside, was outside London's city boundaries, beyond the control of the city elders, making it a haven for prohibited activities such as bear-baiting, bull-baiting, prostitution ('Winchester geese') and unlicensed acting.

London Bridge was the only permanent Thames crossing, and if one wished to travel south from London, the south side of the bridge was in Southwark. Pilgrims used London Bridge to head to Canterbury. In the early medieval period, taverns to serve the pilgrim trade abounded and these, in turn, spawned London's first red-light district, with much of the rentals and incomes going into the coffers of the Bishop of Winchester. As well as carnal delights, Southwark developed as the focus for theatregoers. Royalty had mixed views on Southwark's offerings. In 1503 Henry VII closed Southwark's brothels, and in 1519 Henry VIII ordered Cardinal Wolsey to purge London and Southwark of brothels and gaming houses. In 1546 Henry VIII again commanded that the brothels be closed, although this was overturned by his son Edward VI a few years later.

In Henry VII's time, medieval 'mystery plays' and 'miracle plays' were standard fare, with the same plays being performed by the same troupes of actors across the country every year. However, as Catholicism lost favour, the Privy Council ordered that they should no longer be performed, and new works featuring history, love stories and morality were staged, giving opportunities to a new breed of actor-writers and actor-managers. Companies of actors came to be attached to noblemen, such as Lord Strange's Men, Lord Leicester's Men, the Lord Chamberlain's Men and the Lord Admiral's Men. London, with its growing population, became a magnet for performances in galleried inns and public spaces. It was during Elizabeth's reign that the first real theatres were built in England. Before theatres were built, troupes of actors travelled from town to town and performed in the streets, market squares or outside taverns. Some plays were originally performed in the courtyard of coaching inns, whose galleried design influenced the later design of playhouses such as The Globe. The first purpose-built playhouse in London, 'The Theatre', was built by James Burbage in 1576, north of the river in Shoreditch. Ten more theatres opened outside the City during the remainder of the reign of Elizabeth I, including four in Southwark. The Globe was built from the dismantled parts of The Theatre. It was surreptitiously taken apart while the landowner was away and shipped across the Thames to Southwark. The Globe opened in 1599, cementing Southwark's reputation as the place for theatrical entertainment. Although often considered William Shakespeare's theatre, the Globe was built by the Lord Chamberlain's Company of players, later known as the King's Men under James I. As a member of the company, Shakespeare was simply a shareholder in the new Globe.

These theatres were open to the air in the centre, or pit. Performances were given in daylight, due to the difficulty of lighting the stage and the unsafe nature of travel after dark. Groups of professional actors became common, but Tudor governments were suspicious of actors. They were regarded as layabouts who did no useful work, and from 1572 actors had to hold a licence from a noble. Without protection from a powerful person, actors could be arrested as vagrants. There were no female actors in the sixteenth century, with boys playing women's parts. Watching plays became very popular, helped by the rise of great playwrights such as Jonson, Marlowe and Shakespeare. By 1595, 15,000 people a week were watching plays in London. Those who could afford the best seats around the walls were sheltered from the weather, but poor customers, the 'groundlings', stood in the open air. The cheapest places were in the 'pit', the area in front of the stage, where people would pay about a penny to stand for the duration of the play. Rich people sometimes sat on the stage. The Lord Mayor of London issued an edict complaining about the capital's theatres, 'that in divers places, the players do use to recite their plays to the great hurt and destruction of the game of bear-baiting, and such-like pastimes, which are maintained for her majesty's pleasure'.

Literature and Poetry

Latin was still the language of literacy, despite the success of Geoffrey Chaucer. However, in 1589 Spenser's *The Faerie Queene* was a revelation of the possibilities of the English language in prose. Until the age of Chaucer, at the close of the fourteenth century, England had produced nothing which could enable her to rank among the literary peoples of Europe. Before the accession of Henry VII, Wyclif's Bible, Langland's *Piers Plowman* and the works of Chaucer himself were the only works in the English tongue that could in any sense be held to rank as classics. In Henry's first year as king appeared Thomas Malory's *Le Morte d'Arthur*, in Middle English, and it was a great success. Apart from Malory's work, the only great original work of the early Tudor period was Thomas More's *Utopia*, but it was written in Latin, not in English. More had been Speaker in the House of Commons, which declined to be browbeaten by Cardinal Wolsey, whom he succeeded as Lord Chancellor. More resigned the chancellorship on a point of conscience when he refused to admit that a secular authority could be supreme in spiritual matters. His ideal 'Commonwealth', his *Utopia*, anticipates modern Christian socialist ideals based not upon economic but upon moral foundations, reaching back to the communistic doctrines of Plato's *Republic*.

The vast majority of literary output was almost pamphleteering and theological controversy, and poetry did not become a classical genre until the latter years of Henry VIII. Surrey and Wyatt now produced verse, learnt mainly from Italian models, as a prelude to the Elizabethan outpourings of writing and poetry. Sir Thomas Wyatt (1503–42) was an English ambassador and lyrical poet, credited with introducing the sonnet into English literature. Twenty years of Elizabeth's reign had passed before any sign appeared that there was to be a revolution in literature. It was sparked, more than anything, by the competition to develop moneymaking plays. The exception was probably Edmund Spenser. In *The Shepheardes Calender*, he produced a poetic standard to prove the effectiveness of the English tongue in that field. However, not until ten years later did the first book of his *The Faerie Queene* enrich world literature.

William Shakespeare (1564–1616) is the most famous literary figure in the world, born in the same year as Christopher Marlowe. His father, John, was a glover, most notable for leaving a dunghill in Henley Street, Stratford-upon-Avon, in 1552. Stratford was a small town with a population of between 1,500 and 2,000. In 1557 John Shakespeare married a woman from nearby Wilmcote called Mary Arden, and they had eight children, one of whom was William. When he was eighteen, William Shakespeare married Anne Hathaway. They married in November 1582 and their daughter Susanna was baptised in May 1583. In 1585 their next children, a twin boy and girl, Hamnet and Judith, were baptised, but Hamnet died when he was eleven. In about 1587 Shakespeare left his wife and children in Stratford to become an actor and a playwright in London, and by 1592 he was making a name for himself. The theatres in London were closed from 1592 to 1594 because of plague but Shakespeare wrote two narrative poems during that time, *Venus and Adonis* (1593) and *The Rape of Lucrece* (1594). Shakespeare prospered via his plays, and in 1597 he bought a house and gardens in Stratford for £60.

A poet and actor, he is considered by many to be the greatest dramatist of all time. Some of Shakespeare's plays, such as *Hamlet*, *Macbeth* and *Romeo and Juliet*, are among the most famous literary works of the world. Shakespeare possessed a huge vocabulary for his day, having used over 29,000 different words in his plays. Today the average English-speaking person uses something like 2,000 words in everyday speech. Indeed, his apparent erudition is such that there are many other, more learned claimants to the authorship of his works, such as Christopher Marlowe, Edward de Vere, Francis Bacon, Ben Jonson, Sir Walter Raleigh, the Earl of Southampton or even Queen Elizabeth I.

The following are probably the best-known lines in English literature – Prince Hamlet's soliloquy on the nature of action and being, the meaning of life and death. Hamlet, the young Prince of Denmark, is musing on his way to a meeting with Ophelia after discovering that his beloved father has been poisoned by his new stepfather. His thoughts seem to give us Shakespeare's own ideas on the meaning of life and death, in one of the greatest speeches in literature:

> To be, or not to be: that is the question:
> Whether 'tis nobler in the mind to suffer
> The slings and arrows of outrageous fortune,
> Or to take arms against a sea of troubles,
> And by opposing end them? To die: to sleep;
> No more; and by a sleep to say we end
> The heart-ache and the thousand natural shocks
> That flesh is heir to, 'tis a consummation
> Devoutly to be wish'd. To die, to sleep;
> To sleep: perchance to dream: ay, there's the rub;
> For in that sleep of death what dreams may come
> When we have shuffled off this mortal coil,
> Must give us pause.

It is only possible to note the leading writers of Elizabeth's time. Edmund Spenser (1552–99) was a profound moral poet and a master of metre and language. He fought and held lands in Ireland, and in 1589 Sir Walter Raleigh encouraged him to return to London to seek court preferment and a Crown pension, and to publish the first three books of *The Faerie Queene* in 1596. He was only partly successful in his pension claims, writing in *Lines on His Promised Pension*, 'I was promised on a time / To have reason for my rhyme; / From that time unto this season, / I received nor rhyme nor reason.' Spenser had first published twelve pastoral eclogues of *The Shepheardes Calender* (1579), treating the shepherd as rustic priest and poet. After more publications, *Amoretti*, his sonnet sequence on his courtship of Elizabeth Boyle, and *Epithalamion*, a beautiful wedding poem in honour of his marriage in 1594, were printed. In 1596 the first six books of *The Faerie Queene*, Spenser's unfinished masterpiece, appeared. For this he invented the Spenserian stanza: nine lines, eight of iambic pentameter followed by one of iambic hexameter, rhyming ABABBCBCC. It is an allegory in praise of Elizabeth I: 'Her angel's face, / As the great eye of heaven, shined bright, / And made a sunshine in the shady place.' The work symbolically follows several knights in an examination of different virtues: 'Who will not mercy unto others show, / How can he mercy ever hope to have?' and 'Ill can he rule the great that cannot reach the small.' From his masterpiece, we also have the following phrase: 'Through thick and thin, both over bank and bush, / In hope her to attain by hook or crook.' Spenser seems to have died in poverty, and is buried in Westminster Abbey next to Chaucer. Spenser was known by his contemporaries as 'the prince of poets', as great in English as Virgil in Latin, and Milton claimed that Spenser was 'a better teacher than Aquinas'.

The first use of the phrase '*Ipsa scientia potestas est*' – 'knowledge is power' – seems to appear in *Sacred Meditations – The 11th Meditation of Heresies* in 1597. Sir Francis Bacon (1561–1626) wrote his *Sacred Meditations* in a single volume alongside his *Essays* and *The Couleurs of Good and Evil*, and dealt with the weighty issues of death, marriage, religion and so forth. This English author, statesman, courtier and philosopher was later Viscount of St Albans. Bacon joined Gray's Inn to study law in 1576 and was called to the Bar in 1582, at which point he began writing philosophical tracts in Latin. From 1584 he was an MP and later was attorney-general, solicitor-general and a queen's counsellor. Bacon was knighted on the accession of James in 1603, becoming Lord Chancellor in 1621, but because of debts had succumbed to political and judicial corruption. Bacon could not defend himself against twenty-three counts of corruption in 1621 as the case was so conclusive. He begged mercy and was forced to pay a huge fine of £40,000 to the king (later commuted), and banned from holding any office. Despite his huge intellect, proven by his many publications and lasting influence, he died £22,000 in debt. Among his words of wisdom are 'a wise man will make more opportunities than he finds'; 'by far the best proof is experience'; 'discretion in speech is more than eloquence'; 'he of whom many are afraid ought to fear many'; and 'silence is the virtue of fools'. Bacon was also the originator of the phrase about Mahomet and the mountain:

> Mahomet made the people believe that he would call a hill to him, and from the top of it offer up his prayers for the observers of his law. The people assembled. Mahomet called the hill to come to him, again and again; and when the hill stood still he was never a whit abashed, but said, 'If the hill will not come to Mahomet, Mahomet will go to the hill.'

Christopher Marlowe (1564–93) in *Dr Faustus*, published posthumously in 1604, wrote,

> Was this the face that launch'd a thousand ships
> And burnt the topless towers of Ilium?
> Sweet Helen, make me immortal with a kiss!
> Her lips suck forth my soul: see, where it flies!
> Come Helen, come give me my soul again.
> Here I will dwell, for heaven be in these lips,
> And all is dross that is not Helena.

The above quote is uttered by Faustus before surrendering himself to the possessor of 'this face', Helen of Troy. Marlowe, the precursor of Shakespeare, was stabbed in a mysterious tavern brawl at only twenty-nine. His killer was pardoned by Queen Elizabeth I. Marlowe had been a government spy and possibly an agent provocateur. However, he was named as a Catholic by his fellow playwright Thomas Kyd when Kyd was tortured. A warrant was put out for Marlowe's arrest, but days later Marlowe was killed. Only four years previously Marlowe had been charged with murder and imprisoned, but released after two weeks. In 1582 he was reported for being involved in another death, and also was deported from the Netherlands for counterfeiting. Nothing is definitive but it is thought that he wrote the plays *Tamburlaine the Great*, *The Jew of Malta*, *The Tragical History of Dr Faustus*, *Edward II* and the poetry *Hero and Leander* and *The Passionate Shepherd*. Another line from *Dr Faustus* is, 'O thou art fairer than the evening air clad in the beauty of a thousand stars.' Many people believe that Marlowe did not die, but took another identity and is the 'real' author of Shakespeare's works.

Thomas Kyd (1559–94) was educated at the Merchant Taylors School in London, and later shared a room with Christopher Marlowe. Ben Jonson called him the 'sporting Kyd', and it is believed that by 1589 he had written a lost *Hamlet*, probably the model for Shakespeare's play. Kyd's best-known play, *The Spanish Tragedy* (1589), was the most popular and influential tragedy of Elizabethan times, even more popular than Shakespeare's plays, and it continued to be performed throughout the Elizabethan period. The only other play which can be attributed to Kyd with certainty is *Cornelia* (1594), but *Soliman and Perseda* is usually attributed to him, and *Arden of Feversham* may be his. If so, Kyd is the founder of middle-class tragedy as well as the revenge play. Unfortunately, in 1593, after falling under suspicion of heresy due to the discovery of a heretical tract in his possession, he was arrested on the charge of atheism and tortured into giving evidence against his roommate Marlowe. Kyd denied the charge and attributed the offending tract to Marlowe, who had 'shuffled with some of mine (unknown to me) by some occasion or writing in one chamber two years since'. It is thought that Marlowe may have blamed Kyd, with Kyd returning the favour, and that Marlowe's death soon after was covertly arranged as a result. Evidence suggests that Marlowe may actually have been an agent provocateur employed by the Privy Council in its anti-Catholic activities. Kyd was eventually released from prison, but seems to have been broken by the imprisonment, torture, and disgrace. He died in poverty, not yet thirty-six years old, an awesome loss to literature.

Ben Jonson (*c.* 1573–1637) was the posthumous son of a clergyman, and worked as a bricklayer before serving in Flanders in the army. By 1597 he was an actor and playwright, and in that year he killed another actor in a duel. Convicted of murder, he was spared execution on pleading 'benefit of the clergy' as he was literate. Johnson was branded as a felon on his thumb and had all his possessions confiscated. His play *Every Man in His Humour* was performed in 1598 at the Globe with Shakespeare in the cast. His satirical comedies made him a celebrity, but he was imprisoned on charges for 'popery and treason' for *Sejanus* and later for anti-Scots sentiments in *Eastward Ho* (King James I was Scottish). He was also suspected of involvement in the Gunpowder Plot. *Volpone* (published in 1607) is his masterpiece, and he was made Poet Laureate in 1616. In Johnson's day he was idolised, and he is buried in Westminster Abbey. Some lines we remember from his works are, 'Drink to me, only, with thine eyes, / And I will pledge with mine; / Or leave a kiss but in the cup, / And I'll not look for wine'; 'I have it here in black and white'; 'Alas, all the castles I have are built on air'; and 'Boldly nominate a spade a spade'.

John Donne (1572–1631) also spanned Tudor and Stuart reigns, and in his meditations wrote,

> No man is an island, entire of itself; every man is a piece of the continent, a part of the main. If a clod be washed away by the sea, Europe is the less, as well as if a promontory were, as well as if a manor of thy friend's or of thine own were. Any man's death diminishes me, because I am involved in mankind; and therefore never send to know for whom the bell tolls; it tolls for thee ...

Donne was born into a Catholic family at a time of difficulties for that religion in England. First taught by Jesuits, he entered Oxford but did not take a degree for that would mean swearing the Oath of Supremacy to the king and Protestantism. His brother was imprisoned for sheltering a Catholic priest, dying in gaol. Donne began to question his faith, leading him to become perhaps the greatest of the metaphysical poets. A friend of Ben Jonson, he served on expeditions under the Earl of Essex. His career was ruined by a secret marriage, for which he was thrown into the Fleet Prison and dismissed from his post. Later, King James insisted that Donne took Anglican orders, being appointed a royal chaplain in 1607 and later becoming Dean of St Paul's. Donne was grief-stricken when his wife died, leading to his finest poetry, his 'meditations' on illness and death. In his series of elegies he wrote, 'Love built on beauty, soon as beauty, dies' and 'She and comparisons are odious', and, in his meditations, 'One short sleep past, we wake eternally, And Death shall be no more; Death, thou shalt die.'

22
Games, Leisure and Sports

> One of the differences between the socially cohesive society of the Tudors and fragmented modern society is that all classes used to go to the bear-baiting as well as the theatre, to a court ceremony as well as a public execution.
>
> Philip Howard, *London's River* (1977)

In Tudor times, people were expected to take part in sports suitable for their position in society. Noblemen and gentlemen took part in activities such as hunting and jousting, which trained them in horsemanship and the art of war. Labourers and craftsmen had hardly any time for games or sport. They were required by law to be fit for work six days a week, from 5 a.m. until 7 p.m. Sport and pastimes tended to mirror the likes and dislikes of the king or queen who reigned at the time. Henry VIII had a great love for hunting and jousting while Elizabeth I liked bear-baiting and bear gardens. However, not everyone was allowed to participate in sport, as it was heavily controlled by the government.

Under Henry VIII, a law was passed in 1512 banning the ordinary person from a whole range of games such as real tennis, cards, dice, bowls and skittles. The government wanted people to work more and play less. Such was the attempt to control the lives of the working classes that, in 1540, football was banned as men were getting injured and unfit for war service. In 1542 even shove-groat was banned, the game which we now call 'shove half-penny'. The view was that the working classes should spend their time at home or at work. Some forms of games might get out of hand and the authorities might lose control of the population. For this reason dice, cards and similar games were banned. However, there were no rules or regulations stopping the rich from taking part in what they saw as sport. It was only at Christmas that rules were slightly relaxed for the working classes, in celebration of the main religious holiday.

Sports

Practice with a longbow was still encouraged despite the advent of gunpowder and cannon. Accuracy was expected, and a law of Henry VIII decreed that no one twenty-four years of age or older should shoot at a target less than 220 yards away. Early guns were incredibly slow and proved useless in wet weather, so longbows were incredibly important in battle, providing a great leveller with armour-piercing capabilities. In 1485 Henry VII instituted his personal bodyguard, the Yeomen of the Guard, who were all trained archers, and in 1504 the use of the crossbow was forbidden by Act of Parliament because the longbow had been of so much greater benefit to the nation. Archery occupied an important position in the fashionable pastimes of the kingdom, and on the occasion of the marriage of Henry VII with Elizabeth of York it formed a great feature among the festivities, the king himself joining in the shooting at targets. Several Acts were passed under Henry VIII for the promotion of archery. One ordered that butts should be erected in all townships, and that the inhabitants should practise shooting at them on holidays. The same Act directed that every able-bodied man, if not an ecclesiastic or a judge, should practise with the longbow, and the guardians and employers of youth were ordered to bring up the boys in the practice of archery, negligence of this being punishable by fine. The practice of archery was strongly advocated from the pulpit, and so jealous were the English of rival nations competing with them that foreigners living in England were forbidden to use the longbow. As well as both Henrys, Edward VI devoted much of his time to the practice of archery, and it continued to be an object of attention during the reign of Elizabeth, with the price of bows again being regulated by statute. Bowyers were also commanded to keep in hand always a sufficient stock of bows. However, watching sport could be dangerous. In 1552, an eight-year-old spectator was killed during archery practice in Louth, Lincolnshire, and a ten-year-old died at a hammer-throwing contest in Corfe, Dorset.

Popular games included bowls, *jeu de paume* ('palm game', the ancestor of tennis and played without rackets), bull- and bear-baiting, dog fighting and cockfighting. Medieval tournaments were replaced by masques, a sort of play or spectacle full of allegory. Sometimes fireworks, which had just been invented, were a part of the masque. Alongside the theatre, bear-baiting was a wildly popular Tudor pastime. Huge English Mastiff dogs would be let loose to attack a large bear that had had its teeth filed down and was chained to a stake in the centre of an open arena. Several dogs would be allowed to attack at once, until the bear tired.

A ring was built in the grounds of Whitehall Palace so that Tudor kings and queens could watch in comfort from a window. In 1585, Members of Parliament banned bear-baiting but Elizabeth overruled them. Other 'sports' of Tudor England included blinded bears being whipped by a group of men and donkeys being attacked by a pack of dogs. Elizabeth is said to have enjoyed both. A German visitor to Tudor England wrote, 'The bear cannot escape from them [the men] because of the chain; he defends himself with all his force and skill, throwing down all who come within reach … and tearing the whips out of their hands and breaking them.'

A bear garden was where all manner of 'sports' involving animals took place, surrounded by an arena from where the public watched – the poor standing and the rich sitting. It may be that the design of the Globe was based upon a bear garden rather than a coaching inn's courtyard. Bankside was the most famous place in England for bear-baiting, which was only finally made illegal in 1835. Even then, one Member of Parliament argued that 'the British constitution must stand or fall with the British bear garden'. Some may know the famous Shakespearean stage direction in *The Winter's Tale*: 'exit pursued by a bear'. It is not known whether Shakespeare used a real bear from the London bear pits, or an actor in bear costume. A Dr Gunn, researching Tudor accidents, revealed, 'At least three people were killed by performing bears. One bear's value is listed as a princely twenty-six shillings and four pence.' Baiting bulls, badgers and boars with dogs was also common. Dog fighting and cockfighting were tremendously popular.

In 1487 we see first recorded the use of the word football to describe a game in which the ball is kicked. 'Mob football' was just as popular then as now, but the pitch was the distance from one end of a village to the other or from one village to another, and everybody joined in. Players could kick, throw or pick up the ball in an attempt to put it between the opponent's goalposts. There were no rules and the 'pitch' was often a large area including woods and even streams. Players were allowed to tackle, punch and trip the opposition. Injuries like broken limbs were common. The ball was made from a blown-up pig's bladder. There was no limit to the number of people on each side and the goalposts were set about one mile apart. A writer at the time described football thus: 'Football is more a fight than a game ... sometimes their necks are broken, sometimes their backs, sometimes their legs ... football encourages envy and hatred ... sometimes fighting, murder and a great loss of blood.' It seems that the practice of constant expectoration is a modern addition to the game. Football was banned in 1540 due to the fear that, because of the many injuries, men would not be fit for armed service. John Tyler and Thomas Wylson, aged fifteen and sixteen, died playing football, one falling heavily after tripping on a molehill and the other being accidentally stabbed in the thigh by the knife in the belt of the player he tackled. A similar football game is played every year on Shrove Tuesday at Ashbourne, Derbyshire, forming the world's oldest, largest and longest football game. The game is played over two days and involves thousands of players. The goals are three miles apart and there are only a few rules. The ball is hand-painted and filled with cork. It is thought that this game has been played for a thousand years.

Henry VIII had a stable of 200 horses, and was the first patron of horse racing, despite the Pope's demands for cessation of all racing in England. His favourite breeds were the Barbary from Spain and Italy and Neapolitan coursers, which cost about £20,000 in today's money. He encouraged the breeding of the Irish Hobby, an ancestor of the Connemara, and founded the Royal Paddocks at Hampton Court. He had stud farms at Hampton Court and in Nottinghamshire. For the nobility, tilting included a number of lance games, often used as training for jousting, where the competitor would attempt to strike an object with his lance, sword or other weapon.

The common object was a shield or board on a pole usually referred to as the quintain, although a mannequin was sometimes used. It was not unknown for a seated, armoured knight to act as the target. This game was open to all, popular with young men of all classes. In Offham in Kent, a quintain can still be seen. Hasted's 1782 *History of Kent* tells us,

> On Offham green there stands a Quintain, a thing now rarely to be met with, being a machine much used in former times by youth, as well to try their own activity as the swiftness of their horses in running at it. The cross piece of it is broad at one end, and pierced full of holes; and a bag of sand is hung at the other and swings round, on being moved with any blow. The pastime was for the youth on horseback to run at it as fast as possible, and hit the broad part in his career with much force. He that by chance hit it not at all, was treated with loud peals of derision; and he who did hit it, made the best use of his swiftness, least he should have a sound blow on his neck from the bag of sand, which instantly swang round from the other end of the quintain. The great design of this sport was, to try the agility both of horse and man, and to break the board, which whoever did, he was accounted chief of the day's sport.

Although the days of armoured mounted knights were largely over, rich people still enjoyed tournaments. The contestants dressed in heavier, more defensive armour than that used in battle and fought with shields, wooden lances and swords. On horseback, knights raced towards one another, trying to use their lance to knock the other off his horse. The armour and shield showed their colours and symbols. The 'individual joust' began after 1420 and involved an encounter with lances between two knights. The rules were definitive. If a combatant struck either rider or horse, he was disqualified. A clean hit to the centre or boss of the shield, shattering the lance or unseating the opponent scored points. Henry was a keen jouster. Twice he nearly died. On the first occasion he fought his friend, Charles Brandon, without covering his face. Brandon's lance landed just half an inch away from making a hole in the king's head. In the second instance, when Henry was forty-four years old, he was crushed by his horse and lay unconscious for two hours. Many thousands of people watched; not just nobles, although the entrance fee of about twelve pence ensured that the crowds were fairly wealthy.

There might also be plays and other entertainments put on at the same time. Many knights dressed up as heroes from history. When Henry married Catherine of Aragon in 1509, she played the role of a Greek goddess and the knights fought a joust for her favour. Armour had to be made to fit one person exactly. A suit of armour could cost more than £300, at a time when an ordinary family lived on around £10 a year. If one kept one's body in shape, one could wear the same suit for many years. Extra pieces could be added, depending on the type of fight. Different face and hand guards were used for the fight on horseback and the fight on foot. The horses also wore armour, with pieces to protect the horse's neck and forehead. There was also steel on the saddle to protect the rider. Henry VIII set up a workshop of German and Continental artisans to make armour at Greenwich Palace.

The nobility also enjoyed falconry and hunting deer with bows and arrows or hounds. Yeoman farmers could hunt foxes but the poor were only allowed to hunt hares and rabbits. Rich people also liked wrestling, quarterstaff contests and 'casting the bar', which was similar to shot-putting but with an iron bar. They also played forms of billiards, bowls, quoits and skittles, and board games like chess and backgammon. *Trucco*, also called trucks (or lawn billiards), was an Italian and then English lawn game played with heavy balls, large-headed cues called tacks, rings (the *argolis* or port), and sometimes an upright pin (the *sprigg* or king). Gaining popularity at the very end of the Tudor era, it probably evolved from ground billiards, and predated croquet.

Playing cards were also popular among the upper classes. Cards appeared in Spain and Italy about 1370, but they probably came from Egypt. They began to spread throughout Europe and came into England around 1460. By the time of Elizabeth's reign, gambling was a common sport. Cards were not played only by the upper class, as many of the lower classes had access to playing cards, although the majority gambled with homemade dice. The card suits tended to change over time, but most of the decks that have survived use the 'French Suit': spades, hearts, clubs and diamonds. Even before Elizabeth had begun to reign, the number of cards had been standardised to fifty-two cards per deck. They also played games like shove ha'penny or shove-groat, Nine Men's Morris, draughts and 'fox and geese'. Men also enjoyed cudgel play, where two people would try to hit each other over the head first with a heavy stick.

Royal tennis, 'the sport of kings' is now known as real tennis. The term 'tennis' is thought to derive from the French word *tenez*, which means 'take heed', a warning from the server to the receiver. Real tennis evolved, over three centuries, from an earlier ball game played around the twelfth century in France. By the sixteenth century the glove had become a racket, the game had moved to an enclosed playing area and the rules had stabilised. Royal interest in England began with Henry V but it was Henry VIII who made the biggest impact as a young monarch, playing the game at Hampton Court on a court he had built in 1530, when he was in his late thirties, and on several other courts in his palaces. It is believed that Anne Boleyn was watching a game of real tennis when she was arrested and that Henry may have been playing tennis when news was brought to him of her execution. It was played indoors in a large room with a net. Like tennis today, players had to hit the ball over the net. However, in the Tudor times, the ball could also be bounced off the walls and points were also scored by hitting the ball into one of three goals high in the walls. Tudor tennis rackets were made of wood and strung with sheep gut. The leather tennis balls were filled with hair. In 1580, Montaigne's *Essay xvii, That to Study Philosophy is to Learn to Die* describes how his brother Captain St Martin was killed by a tennis ball. He 'received a blow of a ball a little above his right ear, which, as it gave no manner or sign of wound or contusion, he took no notice of it, nor so much as he sat down to repose himself, but, nevertheless, died within five or six hours after, of an apoplexy occasions by that blow'.

Upon 11 January 1569, the first national lottery was drawn in England. Profits were intended for the repair of harbours and other public works, and state lotteries continued until 1826 when religious feelings caused their abandonment. In the 1860s, the publisher Robert Chambers wrote, 'It seems strange that so glaringly immoral a project should have been kept up with such sanction so long.'

The first handbook on how to swim was the brainchild of an eccentric 'crypto-Catholic' with a liking for controversy. Everard Digby aimed to turn swimming from a disregarded skill of bargees and boatmen into an accomplishment for gentlemen, to make them more like the Romans. To do this he wrote in Latin, the civilised language of Europe, the language used if one wished to be taken seriously. However, he also realised that pictures were needed to show how the strokes should be done. Thus Digby not only produced the earliest book of how to swim, in 1587, but one of the first visual guides to any sport. Digby's *De arte natandi* (*The Art of Swimming*) was not quite the first book on the subject. Nicholas Wynman, a Swiss, had written one in 1538, but that was a short work in praise of swimming, not a handbook of how to do it. Digby's is larger and more methodical. It starts with a survey of swimming, going back to classical times to explain why the skill is valuable and civilised. Lesson two is learning to swim. This should preferably be done with someone supporting you under the chin, or by using water wings made of two inflated pigs' bladders. The basic stroke to learn is like our breaststroke, although it has no name. After this you are taught how to turn in the water, and then to do other strokes. There is a backstroke with legs alone, a backstroke with arms and legs, a sidestroke, a breaststroke with legs alone and 'doggy paddle' – 'to swim like a dog'. Digby did not know the front or back crawl or the butterfly; these are modern inventions.

The Sporting Kings

A contemporary wrote of Henry VII's love of archery, 'See where he shoteth at the butts, / And with him are lords three; / He weareth a gowne of velvette blacke, / And it is coted above the knee.' Among the king's expenses are such items as 'lost to my lord Morging at buttes, 6*s* 8*d*' and 'payed to Sir Edward Boroughe, 13*s* 4*d*, which the king lost at buttes with his crosse-bowe'. Both Henry's sons were also expert archers, especially Arthur, the elder son. It came to be customary to call the champion archer 'Prince Arthur', and other good bowmen were called his knights. On the death of Prince Arthur his brother Henry became patron of the art, and Hall recorded that when he came to the throne 'he shotte as strong and as greate a lengthe as any of his Garde'.

Standing around six feet two inches, Henry VIII was very athletic in his first twenty years as king. He spent much of his time jousting, hunting, wrestling, shooting, dancing and playing tennis. He was considered a skilled hunter and frequently spent as many as five hours a day in the saddle out hunting for deer. However, events curtailed his activities. Henry suffered an attack of smallpox in February 1514 and an attack of malaria in 1521 and occasionally thereafter, especially in 1541. He was prone to headaches, sore throats and catarrh. He hurt his left foot playing tennis in 1527 and again in 1529. His greatest accident was in January 1536 when he fell from his horse while jousting. He was unconscious for two hours, and Anne Boleyn blamed her subsequent miscarriage of a male child on the shock at Henry's fall.

Hedgehog-Hunting Bounty

Millions of animals were hunted down and killed under Tudor rule because of a law passed by Henry VIII in 1532 and then added to by Elizabeth I in 1566. The law declared that every man, woman and child in the country had to kill as many animals as possible from a list of vermin. Each creature had a 'bounty' on its head because it was blamed for stealing food and spreading disease. Harvests had been poor, so food was scarce, and with a rapidly growing population sickness spread easily. Some birds, for instance kites, ravens, shags, kingfishers, woodpeckers and choughs, were worth a penny each, while foxes were worth twelve pence. Other creatures on the wanted list included hedgehogs, badgers, polecats and pine martens. Hedgehogs were hunted down was because it was thought that they used to suck the milk from cows at night, and a hedgehog was worth more than a wild cat, stoat or weasel. A farm worker could receive four pence for producing a dead one, more than his daily wage. The law was not abolished until the mid-eighteenth century.

23

Health and Medicine

Like the rest of the early modern world, England lacked adequate healthcare and sanitation. As a result, disease was common and included such killers as typhoid and smallpox. The Great Sickness, or plague, was endemic and hit towns particularly severely, with a high mortality in London in 1498, 1535, 1543, 1563, 1589 and 1603. Sufferers first complained of chills. This was followed by a high temperature, and the victim began to vomit. Soon the skin turned black as large boils appeared, and death followed soon afterwards.

The population of London increased from 100,000 to 200,000 between the death of Mary Tudor in 1558 and the death of Elizabeth I in 1603. Inflation was rapid and the wealth gap was wide. Men, women and children begged in the cities, the children earning sixpence a week. Life expectancy in towns was always much lower than in the countryside, but despite disease and high mortality the national population expanded greatly in the sixteenth century, from around 2.2 million in 1485 to 4 million by 1600. Smallpox was a serious killer, almost killing Elizabeth I and leaving her with pockmarks. Syphilis was also rampant. Dysentery was also a killer and many women died in childbirth. Child mortality was improved in comparison with earlier and later periods, at about 150 or fewer deaths per 1,000 babies. Many people also died in epidemics of sweating sickness, which first appeared in 1485. Sweating sickness was also known as *Sudor anglicus* (English sweat) and men suffered more than women did. It first occurred in 1485 and there were six major epidemics during the fifteenth and sixteenth centuries.

There were no sewers or drains, and common diseases arising from lack of sanitation included measles, smallpox, malaria, typhus, diphtheria, scarlet fever and chickenpox. Scrofula was a very common type of tuberculosis that affected lymph nodes in the neck and caused ulceration of the skin and was known as the king's evil. The symptoms of scurvy, caused by lack of vitamin C, which is found in fresh fruit and vegetables, could take several months to appear. Patients suffered from bruises or a rash, followed by sore and swollen gums. Then the teeth fell out. Internal bleeding caused pain in the joints and the disease could be fatal. In Tudor times the rich were more likely to suffer because they did not eat vegetables. Scurvy was quite a common disease in Britain until about 1800.

The average lifespan at birth was only thirty-five, that is only half of all people born lived to be that age. However, many died while they were still children. Out of all people born, between one-third and one-half died before the age of sixteen. If one could survive to the mid-teens, life expectancy reaches the fifties or early sixties, and some people lived to their eighties. Tudor doctors were very expensive and they could do little about illness partly because they did not know what caused disease. Doctors thought the body was made up of the four fluids or 'humours': blood; phlegm; choler or yellow bile; and melancholy or black bile. Anger-causing bile was believed to be produced in the spleen, thus shouting at someone is still referred to as 'venting your spleen'. In a healthy person all four humours were balanced, but too much of any one led to illness. For an excess of blood, one would be bled either with leeches or by cutting a vein. Excesses of other humours would be treated either by eating the right diet or by purging, i.e. taking medicines to cause vomiting. Infectious disease, like plague, was thought to be caused by poisonous 'vapours', which drifted through the air and were absorbed through the skin. The word influenza comes from 'influence' and malaria means 'bad air'. A major method of diagnosing sickness was uroscopy, using Robert Recorde's recommendations to examine urine by its appearance, its smell or even by its taste. There were dozens of urine indicators used by the physicians of Myddfai. Astrology also played a part in Tudor medicine, and nearly all doctors believed that different zodiacal signs ruled different parts of the body. Some went to the growing profession of herbalists, but poorer people went to see a local 'cunning' woman, a wise woman with great knowledge of herbal cures. Some actually worked. There were no anaesthetics, antibiotics or painkillers. If anyone needed to have an operation they would likely die from infection. Barbers trained as surgeons, as they had the sharpest tools.

William Turner (*c.* 1508–1568) is known as the 'Father of English Botany'. Turner left Morpeth aged about eighteen and studied to be a physician at Cambridge. As plants were then the main ingredients of all medicine, Turner wanted to be sure that the correct ingredients were being used for the prescriptions, so he began to document the first scientific descriptions of plants and the systematic process of giving plants common names. He named and described over 300 species, and his life's work, *A New Herball*, became the cornerstone for British botany. Turner was the first person to record, in English, the names and medicinal uses of plants. Before Turner, the names and uses of plants were only published in Latin, denying most people access and preserving the knowledge for educated doctors and priests. Turner also started to give plants a standard 'common' name, to avoid confusion when describing different species. We still use many of Turner's plant names today, including daffodil, daisy, monkshood, spindle and loosestrife. Because of Turner, practical botanical and medical knowledge would be widely available to medical practitioners and apothecaries.

Curious Cures and 'Proven' Baldness Remedies

Some thousand or so folk 'cures', used from before and throughout Tudor times, have been translated by this author in *Physicians of Myddfai: Cures and Remedies of the Mediaeval World.* They include an interesting remedy 'to reduce fatness', today's curse, using fennel as a digestive aid: 'Whoever is overly fat, let him drink the juice of fennel, and it will reduce him.' One of the (previously expurgated) cures was for 'protection from what a man can receive from a woman': 'Take the dung of an uncastrated stallion, and add linseed. Blend them together and boil to make pottage. Place on a bandage upon the sore. Apply that poultice until it removes all the burning from the wound. There apply the appropriate ointment, and it will be healthy.' Another formerly expurgated remedy for 'inflammation from a woman' was to 'take linseed and the milk of white goats and stew together. Then bath the penis in it twice a day. It is very soothing.'

Weil's Disease, *Leptospirosis*, was spread by rats and then known as 'black jaundice'. The remedy was to 'seek the tail of salmon, dry slowly and reduce to a powder. Let it be taken on ale, and the patient will be cured.' There were three (formerly expurgated) remedies for a man's swollen penis, one of which was to 'roast eggs until hard, and take out the yolk and make into a powder. Then make into a lotion and press through a linen cloth and place upon the penis. It is also good for arthritis and a number of other ailments.'

For 'dimness of sight', 'take the juice of red fennel, celandine, a little vinegar or verjuice, an eel's blood and a cock's gall. Mix these ingredients together, and set aside in a clean vessel until fermentation takes place. Take some of the clear liquor and put in a blind man's eyes. Science tells us that by these means, sight lost may certainly be recovered.' To know whether a patient will die or live, 'anoint the patient's heel with some hog's fat, and give the remainder to a dog to eat. If the dog will eat it, the patient will live, if not he will die.' An early method of diagnosing pregnancy was to 'have her urinate in a brass or copper vessel. Place a nettle in the urine, and if she is pregnant it will be covered with bloody spots.' To cure the plague, one of the remedies was to 'take the faeces of a young child between ten and twelve years of age, and reduce into fine powder. Then put two spoonfuls at most of the powder in a cupful of white wine. Let it be administered to the patient six hours at the most after he has sickened. The sooner the better it is done. Many have proved this.' For a cancer which has not developed fully, 'take dog's dung which has become white, and glass. Powder the glass as fine as you can, mixing the two together with some oil of olives (rancid oil is the best). Heat them together on the fire, then apply to the disease, and the patient will be cured.'

There are cures for cancer, the king's evil, etc., etc., but the only ones that might make this author his fortune are those for causing the hair to grow. One is to 'take barberry [*Berberis vulgaris*], and fill an iron pot with it. Then fill the pot with as much water as it will contain, and boil on a slow fire until reduced to half. With this water, wash your head morning and evening. Take care that the wash does not touch any part where hair should not grow.' Another reads, 'Take two spoonfuls of olive oil, two spoonfuls of new honey, and an onion as large as a pigeon's egg. Pound them together in a stone mortar until it becomes an ointment, and anoint your head with it night and morning. Wear a leather cap until the hair is grown. It is best to pound the onion well before it is added to the ointment.' A third is to 'shave the head clean with a razor, and take honey with the juice of onions in equal parts. Anoint and scrub the head well with this every morning and night. The head should be washed with the distilled water of honey. It is proven.' A fourth remedy for hair growth is to 'shave the head carefully, anoint with honey, and sprinkle the powder of mollipuffs upon it'. Mollipuffs is the warted puffball fungus, *Bovista officinalis*.

Smoking Is Good for You

In 1574, Nicholas Monardes wrote a work translated into English in 1586 as *Joyfull Newes out of the New-found Worlde*. He praised the newfound medicinal herb tobacco, ensuring that it became a universal remedy for centuries. Even in the mid-twentieth century the virtues of smoking were explained rationally by doctors and scientists.

The Governor of All Idiots

Mental illness usually led to one being locked up in filthy institutions. In January 1531, Henry VIII appointed Sir William Paulet 'Surveyor of the King's Widows, and Governor of All Idiots and Naturals in the King's Lands'.

Sleeping Sickness

On 27 April 1546, William Foxley, pot-maker for the Royal Mint at the Tower of London, fell asleep for a fortnight. The antiquarian John Stow (d. 1605) noted that he 'could not be wakened with pinching, cramping, or otherwise burning whatsoever'. Foxley lived for another forty years after 'awakening'.

The First Flush

Tudor toilets were non-existent, as noted in the section upon buildings. In 1596, Sir John Harington published his satire *The Metamorphosis of Ajax*, which contains the first design for a flushing toilet. He may have already installed one for his godmother, Elizabeth I, at Richmond Palace. 'Ajax' is a pun on jakes, contemporary slang for a lavatory. Elizabeth did not enjoy his Rabelaisian satire and exiled him.

'The French Disease'

The first well-documented outbreak of what we know as syphilis occurred in 1494 in the French army. The disease then swept across Europe in 1495 – 'its pustules often covered the body from the head to the knees, caused flesh to fall from people's faces, and led to death within a few months'. By 1505 the disease had spread to Asia, and within a few decades had 'decimated large areas of China'. In *Breverton's Nautical Curiosities* we read that syphilis 'was known as "the Great Pox" in the fifteenth century, and the variola virus was called "the small pox" to differentiate it. It was called the "French disease" in England, Italy and Germany, and the "Italian disease" in France. The Dutch called it the "Spanish disease", and the Russians called it the "Polish disease". The Turks called it the "Christian disease" and the Tahitians the "British disease". The national names are due to the disease often being spread by foreign sailors during unprotected sexual contact with local prostitutes. In its early stages, the Great Pox produced a rash similar to smallpox but smallpox was a far more deadly disease.' Untreated, the death rate from syphilis was between 8 per cent and 58 per cent and that from smallpox 20 per cent to 60 per cent (with over 80 per cent in children). The routine 'cure' was to 'sweat it out' in an early form of sauna.

Smallpox

This was so called to distinguish it from the 'Great Pox' because of the smaller pus-filled blisters covering the body, which were accompanied by high temperatures, vomiting and diarrhoea. Elizabeth almost died from it in 1562, and one of her attendants, Lady Mary Sidney, stayed by her side nursing the queen and was herself badly disfigured for life.

The 'Bloody Pox'

This was dysentery, caused by poor sanitation and infected food, and sufferers routinely died because of lack of clean liquids. Typhus, carried by lice, and typhoid fever, were also killers.

The Sweating Sickness – 'It's the Rich Wot Gets the Pain'

In 1485 Henry VII had decided to be crowned before Parliament met, but the 'sweating sickness', previously unknown, appeared in London. This extremely contagious plague or fever had broken out between Henry's landing upon 7 August and Bosworth on 22 August. Shortly after Henry, Jasper and Oxford were welcomed in London on 28 August it broke out in the capital, and it was blamed upon Henry's French troops. However, the French were not to blame, as it had not affected Henry's army in the three to five weeks of mustering, sailing and marching to Bosworth. Indeed, Thomas Stanley had excused himself from Richard III's court before Bosworth on account of the 'sweating sickness', and he had not then come into contact with Henry's forces.

Several thousand people died, and, strangely, the upper classes seemed to suffer more, as it killed two lord mayors, three sheriffs and six aldermen of London. It did not attack small children. Symptoms of sweating sickness included 'a sense of apprehension', shivers, dizziness, headaches, pain in the arms, legs, shoulders and neck, and fatigue or exhaustion. The illness had a cold, shivery stage followed by a hot, sweaty stage and could kill in hours. It was distinct from other epidemics in its rapidity, lasting twenty-four hours; anyone who survived that period usually recovered. In 1528, the French ambassador noted that one of Anne Boleyn's ladies-in-waiting had been stricken by it. Henry at this time was 'courting', and he reported,

> The king left in great haste, and went a dozen miles off ... This disease is the easiest in the world to die of. You have a slight pain in the head and at the

> heart; all at once you begin to sweat. There is no need for a physician: for if you uncover yourself the least in the world, or cover yourself a little too much, you are taken off without languishing. It is true that if you merely put your hand out of bed during the first twenty-four hours ... you become stiff.

The illness then spread into Europe, where it was known as the 'English Sweate', with a series of epidemics between 1485 and 1551. Its cause is unknown and it disappeared entirely after 1578.

'The Ague'

In low-lying marshes, thousands died from 'the ague', thought to be caused by the 'bad air' that rose like a mist from the wet ground. This 'bad air' gave its name to malaria, caused by the prevalence of mosquitoes before better drainage and farming. Henry VIII had recurrent attacks of malaria from the age of thirty-three.

Cholera, Typhus and Typhoid Fever

All could be deadly and were common. Later writers sometimes confuse typhus and typhoid fever. Cholera usually came through infected water or food, infesting the small intestine, leading to violent sickness and diarrhoea, with the victim wasting away. The typhus germ is passed on by the bite of a body louse, and was also known as 'putrid fever', 'ship fever', 'jail fever' and 'camp fever'. It could drive people into delirium and death. The typhoid germ entered through bad food and water, giving a fever and rash, and the secondary effects of bronchitis and pneumonia could kill.

Henry the Hypochondriac

Henry had seen his brother Arthur waste away of consumption (TB), which affected him greatly. The king often concocted his own remedies, using ingredients that ranged from plants, wines and rosewater to crushed pearls, worms and even lead monoxide. If plague or the sweating sickness occurred in London, he quickly escaped into the countryside.

Tudor Toilet Habits

Probably fewer than 5 per cent of the population had any type of toilet, and the poor used the fields and woods. For toilet paper, great mullein and other leaves could be used. The great houses and palaces had 'pissing areas' allotted for members of the court. In their first weeks at the court of Henry VII, Catherine of Aragon and her ladies were probably shocked to witness courtiers attending to their bodily needs when and wherever necessary. The huge fireplaces of the times seemed a popular choice for men to urinate in but, towards the ascension of James I, changing attitudes meant such behaviour began to upset people. In 1573, Thomas Tusser wrote in his *Five hundreth Goode Pointes of Husbandrie*, 'Some make the chimnie chamber pot to smell like Filthie stink, / Yet who so bold, so soone to say, though, how These houses stink.' Only the better houses had a primitive inside toilet. It was based on the same principle found in castles: a small, cell-like room adjoining the outer wall, called a 'jakes' or *garderobe*. There was a seat placed over an internal shaft, angled so human waste went down to an outside cesspool, or sometimes to a stream, as in the Tudor Merchant's House in Tenby.

The monarch's Privy Chamber probably acquired its name because of its proximity to the royal 'privy', their personal little room, enclosing a 'close stool', which was a boxed seat containing a fitted chamber pot. On her progresses Elizabeth I took not only her portable bath but also her portable toilet, a close stool covered with red velvet. Henry VIII had a black velvet close stool, decorated by ribbons, fringes and 2,000 glint-headed nails, to enclose his 'jordan', or chamber pot. For toilet paper, rich Tudors used saltwater and sticks with sponges or mosses placed at their tops, as Roman legionnaires had done, while royals probably used the softest lamb wool and cloths.

To be attendant to this royal function was considered one of the important roles of the bedchamber. The maids who took care of the cloths Elizabeth used during menstruation were in the position of being bribed by not only foreign dignitaries, but also the men of the Privy Council. William Cecil was kept informed about this intimate part of Elizabeth's life, and the knowledge that she functioned like a normal woman made him confident she could provide the country with an heir. Elizabeth had an extreme code of personal cleanliness for the times, wishing to bathe at least once a week. She encouraged similar behaviour in her courtiers, and would tell them if they stank.

24
Tudor Food and Drink

Food

Trade and industry flourished in the sixteenth century, making England more prosperous and improving the standard of living of the upper and middle classes. However, the lower classes did not benefit much and did not always have enough food. England's food supply was plentiful throughout most of the era, there generally being no widespread famines. Bad harvests caused distress, but they were usually localised. The most widespread hardship came in 1555–57 and 1596–98. In towns the price of staples was fixed by law, and in hard times the size of the loaf of bread sold by the baker was smaller. A series of bad harvests in the 1590s caused more widespread starvation and poverty. The success of the wool industry had decreased attention on agriculture, resulting in further starvation of the lower classes. Cumbria, the poorest and most isolated part of England, suffered a six-year famine beginning in 1594. Diseases and natural disasters also sometimes contributed to the scarce food supply.

Peasants mostly ate coarse bread and 'pottage', a thick soup in which onions, cabbage and beans were boiled up with herbs and perhaps a little pork or bacon. Most food was too expensive for the poor. For them, bread made from wheat was a rarity; usually it was coarse and made from barley or rye, but in hard times they used a mixture of beans, oats or acorns. Their diet was occasionally supplemented with locally caught fish, rabbits or birds, but taking any larger game was poaching and punishable. The poor also ate a great many more greens than the rich, who insisted that their vegetables be elaborately prepared. All classes ate fish, because the law required that fish be consumed on Fridays and Saturdays and other meats laid aside. This was a government-mandated support for the fishing industry.

Meat and fish were generally luxuries reserved for the rich, who could choose among 'brown meats' such as beef, veal, pork, lamb, mutton and venison, as well as rabbit, fowl, salmon, trout, eel and shellfish. A boar's head, garnished with bay and rosemary, served as the centrepiece of Christmas feasts, known as the Yule Boar. The rich also ate bittern, duck, geese, owl, pheasant, blackbirds, swans and peacocks. Pigeons, robins, sparrows, heron, crane, pheasant, woodcock, partridge and blackbirds were also eaten. People also ate badgers, hedgehogs, otters, tortoises and seagulls. Whole roasted peacock was served dressed in its own iridescent blue feathers (which were plucked, then replaced after the bird had been cooked), with its beak gilded in gold leaf. Roasted swan was often presented to the table with a gold crown upon its head. English law still stipulates that all mute swans are owned by the Crown and may not be eaten without permission from the queen. The Tudors liked spicy sauces and pies. The rich occasionally ate vegetables such as turnips, carrots and radishes, and fruits such as apples, plums, gages and wild strawberries.

The menu for a nobleman's dinner of around 1550 included roast beef, powder (salted) beef, veal, leg of mutton with 'gallandine sauce', turkey, boiled capon, hen boiled with leeks, partridge, pheasant, larks, quails, snipe, woodcock, salmon, sole, turbot and whiting, lobster, crayfish, shrimps, eel, pike, young rabbit, leverets, marrow on toast, artichokes, turnips, green peas, cucumbers and olives, quince pie, tart of almonds, fruit tarts and cheese. A merchant's dinner of the same time would be slightly less adventurous, featuring sausage, cabbage, porridge, pike with a 'high Dutch sauce', stewed carp, roasted blackbirds, larks, woodcock and partridge.

Desserts such as pastries, tarts, cakes and crystallised fruit were popular. Puddings were made with sugar and honey, and 'marchpane' (marzipan), a sweet made from ground almonds and sugar, was popular. It was often made into fancy shapes. Many courtiers had rotten teeth because of the diet. Vegetables were thought as food for the poor – the rich considered food from the ground to be lowly – and only made up about 20 per cent of the rich man's diet. Both rich and the poor had imbalanced diets. The lack of vegetables and fruits in their diets caused a deficiency in vitamin C, sometimes resulting in scurvy.

Yeoman farmers' wives grew vegetables, herbs and flowers for eating in their gardens. The variety of vegetables grown included leeks, garlic, peas, parsnips, skirrets (like parsnips), collards and kale (types of cabbage), lentils, turnips, broad beans, onions, spinach, carrots, beets, artichokes, radishes and asparagus. Vegetables were not eaten to accompany meat as nowadays, but would be used by the farmer's wife to make pottage, consisting of peas, milk, egg yolks, breadcrumbs and parsley flavoured with saffron and ginger.

Herbs were often used to flavour Tudor meals. Rich people would have had a separate herb garden to grow all of the mint, rosemary, thyme, sage and parsley they needed. Cloves, cinnamon, mace and nutmeg would have come from the other side of the world, from the Maluku Islands, and were very expensive. It was the quest for spices that drove the early explorers to cross the Atlantic, and later the Pacific, in search of a direct sea route to the Maluku Islands, also known as the Spice Islands. During the reign of Elizabeth I, dishes used spices imported from all corners of the world. There was pepper from India, cinnamon from Sri Lanka and nutmeg, mace and cloves from the Maluku Islands. They were used to make spiced wines, to flavour foods such as fish, jam, soup and, particularly, meat dishes. The popularity of these spices saw European empires develop in India and Asia.

Most meats were prepared by 'seething' (boiling), and sugar and currants were used in prodigious quantities when available to the rich later in the period. Salting and pickling were also common practices, since there was no refrigeration. Meat and fish was generally eaten fairly soon after slaughtering for this reason, or was pickled to keep for the future. Baking was done in iron boxes laid on the fire or in a brick oven set into the side of the fireplace.

Bread was the staple of the Elizabethan diet, and people of different statuses ate bread of different qualities. Wealthy people enjoyed a fine white bread called manchet that was made from wheat flour with a little bran and wheatgerm added. It was creamy yellow in colour. *Raveled* bread or yeoman's bread was made from coarser wholewheat flour with the bran left in, a darker colour and less expensive than manchet. 'Carter's bread' was dark-brown or black bread, the bread that the poorest people ate. It was made from *maslin*, a mixture of rye and wheat, or from *drage*, a mixture of barley and wheat, or from rye alone. Horse-corn was bread made from peas, beans, lentils and oats and was eaten by poor people when the wheat harvest failed. The bread would have been kept in an 'ark', a wooden box, to protect it from mice and damp.

Diners would eat off plates suitable to the wealth of the hosts. Food was often eaten off large slices of bread called trenchers, which could then be eaten at the end of the meal or in large houses given to the dogs, servants or the poor. Richer people generally ate off wooden trenchers and bowls for everyday meals, but might have pewter plates for special occasions. The wealthier would have pewter for daily use and silver for special occasions. Middling classes generally drank out of crockery of wood or leather, with pewter cups being a valued luxury. The very wealthy had glass goblets for the best company. Chinaware was unknown.

Feasts were commonly used to commemorate the 'procession' or progress of the monarch in the summer months, when the king or queen would travel through a circuit of other nobles' lands both to avoid the plague season in London and aid the royal coffers, which were often drained through the winter to provide for the needs of the royal family and court. This would include a few days or even a week of feasting in each noble's home, who, depending on his or her production and display of fashion, generosity and entertainment, could have his way made in court and elevate his or her status for months or even years. On one occasion in 1519, the 3rd Duke of Buckingham entertained Henry VIII at Penshurst Place at a cost of over £1 million in today's money. Two years later, such largesse had been forgotten and Buckingham was executed on a charge of treason.

Tudor feasts were legendary for their extravagance and Henry's annual hospitality bill was enormous. During Henry's reign, vegetables, previously considered poor man's food, became increasingly popular with the nobility. The king was especially partial to artichokes, loved fruit and, together with Anne Boleyn, shared a passion for strawberries and cherries. Around half of the population lived at subsistence level, but Henry VIII enjoyed banquets so much that he extended the kitchen of Hampton Court Palace to fill fifty-five rooms. His 200 members of kitchen staff provided meals of up to fourteen courses for the 600 people at court. Typical dishes included spit-roasted meat, usually a pig or boar. Only the rich could afford fresh meat year-round, and only the very rich could afford to roast it, since this required much more fuel than boiling. The richest employed a 'spit boy' to turn the spit all day, although dogs were also used. In a typical year, Henry's kitchen served 8,200 sheep, 2,330 deer, 1,870 pigs, 1,240 oxen, 760 calves and 53 wild boar. Each member of the court consumed about twenty-three animals every year.

In the sixteenth century, food was used to 'illustrate splendour and largesse'. Since Elizabeth's servants were a manifestation of her glory, her care of them would indicate how generous she could be, not just to her servants but, symbolically, to all of England. The queen's servants were allowed specific amounts of 'bread, wine, beer, fuel and light' each day, along with the leftovers from the state meals; these privileges were known as 'bouge of court'. Despite specific limits on consumption, the household commonly disregarded their allotments. In all cases the amount Elizabeth actually spent on her servants exceeds the amount budgeted, but the 'below-stairs' positions appear to have come closer to the amount they were allotted than the higher positions. For example, the Master of the Horse was allowed £310 17*s* 0*d*, but he actually spent £585 14*s*, 9*d*, whereas the cellar was allotted £65 10*s* 1*d* and actually spent £78 17*s* 4*d*. David Loades writes in *The Tudor Court* that there was 'considerable manoeuvring and competition among the courtiers' to get their rations from the privy kitchen because the food was better and they shared in the queen's prestige if they ate food that was prepared for her. As if to encourage this, 'the kitchen never closed, and the wine and beer cellars, far from being properly regulated, were also open all night to all comers'.

In 1563, William Cecil introduced 'Cecil's Fast', which imposed punishments for eating meat during Lent and on certain other days of the week. This was imposed to ensure the population consumed enough fish that an adequate number of seamen could earn their living. Thus it would be possible to maintain sufficient ships and crews who could defend England in time of war. In the 1580s, Cecil attempted to restrict the consumption within the household: 'He … ordered that the cofferer, clerks comptroller, and clerks of the Greencloth be allowed only "six dishes" instead of seven at dinner and that on two days a week no supper be served in the household.' This was disregarded, as most of the regulations concerning food were, and consumption continued as before. The concerns of magnificence triumphed over practical considerations.

Drink

Water was extremely unsafe to drink, especially in cities, where supplies became contaminated with sewage and from people cleaning clothes or animal carcasses in the drinking-water supply. In the cities, water carriers delivered water to your door for a fee and were used only by the rich. All the salt in their food made them thirsty. Courtiers were allowed a certain amount of wine each day. Servants were allowed to drink beer.

Alcohol, mostly beer or ale, was drunk instead of water and in country areas homebrewed ale or beer was the usual drink at most meals, including breakfast. Even children drank beer, theirs being weaker than that drunk by adults and known as 'small beer'. This was sometimes made of fermented herbs or weak cider. Because of its lower alcohol content, there was more chance of contamination. Wine had to be imported from the Continent so was an expensive luxury and only for the rich. Other drinks in sixteenth-century England included sherry, which was known as 'sack', and brandy. The origins of brandy are obscure, but it was a popular drink by the sixteenth century. The origins of whiskey are lost in history too, but by the sixteenth century it was being distilled in Scotland, Wales and Ireland and was a popular drink. People thought whiskey was medicinal. Numerous healths would be pledged during a courtly meal, and this would continue long after the food had been carried away. Before Henry VIII closed the monasteries, they provided a place where people could stay for a night and have a meal. After their closure, inns took over this role and, with alehouses and taverns, became far more popular.

Manners

In a civilised household, at some point before the meal the hands would be washed, often in water sweetened with roses or rosemary. In nearly every home, the meal would begin with the saying of Grace, after which the company would begin to eat. If a man had servants, they would pass from guest to guest with each dish, and the guests would help themselves to as much from each plate as they liked. Even in gentry households, the fingers were generally used for plucking out the tasty morsels from the dishes, the sign of good manners being that you did not return to the dish anything you had touched. If no servants were available, the women and children of the house would serve the dishes, sitting down to eat after all the men and guests had taken what they wanted. All men at the table ate with their hats on (unless they went hatless out of deference to a high-ranking member of their dinner party), and every well-bred guest had a clean, white napkin on the left shoulder or wrist, upon which soiled fingers or knives could be wiped. The servants who attended the table were hatless, since they could not remove their hats (their hands being full) and they would not dream of attending upon their betters with their hats on. Conversation at the table was considered commendable, but noisy behaviour was frowned upon.

When a guest came to supper, he or she would bring utensils along. The host was not expected to supply them. The rich would have a beautifully made and adorned knife and spoon (carried in an ornamental case in Tudor times). Only a spoon and a knife were used at mealtimes; forks were not used for eating with until the late seventeenth century. Tudors would have used a spoon for serving and a knife for cutting the food. Fingers were often used for eating. The poor man often went about with his spoon in his hat or his pocket, and his knife on his belt.

The Boke of Keruying (*The Book of Carving*) by Wynkyn de Worde, printed in 1508, lists the rules and customs which should be followed by those preparing and by those serving the dishes: it includes everything from the hand washing ceremonies to the exact placement of the trenchers (bread plates) by the carver, who could only touch the food with his left hand, with a thumb and two fingers, etc. One instruction is to 'place the salt on the right side of your Lord's seat, and the trenchers to the left of the salt. Then take the knives and arrange the loaves of bread side by side, with the spoons and napkins neatly folded by the bread. Cover your bread and trenchers, spoons and knives, and set a salt cellar with two trencher loaves at each and of the table ... then serve your Lord faultlessly.'

Beavers are Fish

Until they were hunted to extinction, beavers were classified as fish. Grilled beavers' tails were thus popular on Fridays, when it was forbidden to eat meat. Whale meat was fairly common and cheap, due to the plentiful supply of whales in the North Sea, each whale feeding hundreds of people. It was typically served boiled or very well roasted.

Badger Meat

Badger was eaten from before Tudor times until the Second World War, but it seems to have been a food only for the poor. Arthur Boyt, a seventy-three-year-old former civil servant and scientist, does not kill animals. All his free meat comes from the roads around his home on Bodmin Moor. 'I'm against the cull,' he said, 'but it would be ridiculous not to use the dead badgers. I've eaten badger for fifty-five years and I certainly haven't got TB. As with all meat you just make sure you cook it long and hot enough to kill any bugs.' Boyt's favourite part of the animal is the head: 'There's five tastes and textures in there, including the tongue, the eyeballs, the muscle ... The salivary glands taste quite different. And of course, the brain. You get that by putting a teaspoon in the hole in the back and rooting around.' In France, *blaireau au sang* (badger with blood) is still remembered. The Prussians even bred a dog, the dachshund (badger hound), to hound badgers out of their setts. European recipes for badger often ask you to lay it in running water for several days to get rid of a rank flavour. However, Boyt says that is only necessary for fox. Badger, though it does not need to be hung, can be eaten when it's 'quite green'. (This information comes from a report in *The Guardian*, 25 September 2012).

Tudor Toothache

Sugar was very expensive in the sixteenth century, so most people used honey to sweeten their food. Sugar, grown in Europe's colonies, became very popular with the wealthy but was far too expensive for the poor. Both Henry VIII and Elizabeth I loved sugar, and the second half of the sixteenth century saw an enormous expansion in its use. As a result, black teeth and toothache, virtually unknown in the centuries before, began to be a problem.

American Eating Habits

In the sixteenth century, new foods were introduced from the Americas. Columbus landed in the 'Indies' on his first voyage and Haiti on his second, where he discovered the other type of pepper we know today. Many new foods came to Europe from the newly discovered lands in the west: maize, potatoes, chocolate, peanuts, vanilla, tomatoes, pineapples, lima beans, sweet and chili peppers, tapioca and the turkey. The turkey arrived in Europe in 1523 or 1524 and in England shortly after that. The potato reached England at some point in the late 1500s. Possibly, Sir Francis Drake brought both from Cartagena when he picked up supplies there. English sailors found vast supplies of cod off the coast of what we now call Newfoundland in the late 1490s and began catching and bringing them back to England. Turkeys were introduced into England around 1525. Although potatoes were brought to England in the 1580s, at first few English people ate them. Elizabethan colonists in America had no forks, which accounts for the fact that Americans even now cut up their meat into bite-size portions before starting their meals.

The Most Famous Medieval Feast

'The Feast of the Pheasant' was held at Lille in 1454. From the *Memoires d'Olivier de La Marche*:

> The dishes were such that they had to be served on trolleys, and seemed infinite in number ... The figure of a girl, quite naked, stood against the pillar. Hippocras [mulled wine] sprayed from her right breast and she was guarded by a live lion who sat near her on a table in front of my lord the duke ... My lord the duke was served at table by a two-headed horse ... next came a white stag ridden by a young boy who sang marvellously, while the stag accompanied him with the tenor part ... Then two knights of the Order of the Golden Fleece brought in two damsels, together with a pheasant, which had a golden collar around its neck decorated with rubies and fine large pearls ...

The Who-Can-Eat-What Laws

In 1517 the Sumptuary Laws on feasting were passed, setting out the number of courses different ranks were permitted to eat during one meal. Cardinals were allowed nine, dukes and bishops seven, and so on, while those without a title but with an annual income of between £40 and £100 could ask for no more than three.

The Pork Butcher

In 1517, a butcher was caught selling stinking bacon and was paraded through the City of London. Two sides of rotting bacon were tied to him, two flitches of bacon borne before him, a sign on his head proclaimed his crime, and pans were clattered to draw attention to his misdemeanour.

The Bird Who Was a Fish

Friday was a meat-free day, but for centuries the Church had allowed barnacle geese to be eaten on a Friday. No one had seen the nests of the migrating geese and it was believed that they emerged from barnacles, so they were thus regarded as fish. Not until 1597 were their nests found on Novaya Zemlya in the Arctic Ocean by William Barents' expedition.

Hampton Court Kitchens

Built to feed the court of Henry VIII, these kitchens were designed to feed at least 600 people twice a day. You can still see the largest kitchens of Tudor England at Hampton Court today, and they are often still used to prepare Tudor meals. Between their construction in 1530 and the royal family's last visit to the palace in 1737, the kitchens were a central part of palace life. For many people today Hampton Court Palace is Henry VIII, and Henry's abiding reputation remains a 'consumer of food and women'. But Henry's vast kitchens in the palace were not for him. They were built to feed the six hundred or so members of the court, entitled to eat at the palace twice a day. This was a vast operation, larger than any modern hotel, and one that had to cope without modern conveniences. The kitchens had a number of master cooks, each with a team of yeomen and sergeants working for them. The members of Henry VIII's court required an endless stream of dinners to be produced in the enormous kitchens. This was all washed down with 600,000 gallons of ale each year, enough to fill an Olympic-size swimming pool, and around 75,000 gallons of wine, enough to fill 1,500 bathtubs.

25

Farming and Animals

Farming

England was an overwhelmingly rural and agricultural country. At the beginning of the sixteenth century, very few English towns had more than a few thousand inhabitants. In 1520, other than London, the only cities with over 7,000 inhabitants were Exeter, Bristol, Salisbury, Norwich, York and Newcastle. Those with over 4,000 people were Oxford, Gloucester, Colchester, Worcester, Coventry, Lynn, Yarmouth and Shrewsbury. London was vastly larger than any other English city, with a population of over 50,000 in the early sixteenth century. Tudor England was an agricultural society where most of the population lived in small villages and made their living from farming. Although the population doubled in the sixteenth century to about 4 million people, the towns were still small.

One effect of the rise in population was a general increase in prices, especially of food. During the century food prices rose fivefold, whereas prices of industrial manufactures only doubled. Production of food was the main economic activity, and the most important event of the year was the harvest. Harvests were especially bad in the years 1554–56 and 1594–97. Rising food prices severely hurt those on fixed incomes and those without enough land to supply their own needs. However, those with large farms were able to take advantage of rising food prices, and by increasing efficiency could maximise profits. Agricultural innovation, for example the use of water meadows, increased productivity per acre. The reclamation of marginal land, for example the draining of the East Anglian fens, also brought more land into productive use. The introduction of new crops, and their periodic rotation, increased the land's long-term fertility. Each year farmers cultivated only two-thirds of the land, letting the other third lie 'fallow' so it could recover its fertility. Manor lands were therefore farmed using the three-field system of agriculture. One field was devoted to winter crops, another to summer crops, and a third lying fallow each year. Alternatively one field was used for grain, one for hay, and a third left fallow, which frequently meant it was sown with a legume which would be ploughed under to enrich the soil.

Of the arable land of the manor, the lord reserved as much as he needed for his own use. The lord's land was called his 'demesne', or domain. The rest of the land he allotted to tenant peasants who cultivated their holdings in common. A peasant, instead of having his land in one compact mass, had it split up into a number of small strips, usually about half an acre each, scattered over the manor and separated not by fences or hedges but by banks of unploughed turf. The reason for the intermixture of strips seems to have been to make sure that each peasant had a portion both of the good land and of the bad, and the arrangement compelled all the peasants to labour according to a common plan. A man had to sow the same kinds of crops as his neighbours, and to till and reap them at the same time. Grain was cut with a sickle, and grass was mown with a scythe. It took five men a day to reap and bind a harvest of two acres. Besides his holding of farm land, each peasant had certain rights over the non-arable land of the manor. He could cut a limited amount of hay from the meadow, and turn so many farm animals such as cattle, geese, and swine on the waste ground. He also enjoyed the privilege of taking so much wood from the forest for fuel and building purposes. A peasant's holding, which also included a house in the village, thus formed a self-sufficient unit.

Four grains were widely cultivated: wheat, barley, rye and oats. Of these, wheat was most valued because it had the gluten content necessary to make good bread. All four could be sown in autumn for harvest the following summer. This so-called winter crop could be easily lost to a cold winter or stormy spring, so to ensure a harvest farmers would plant a second crop in the spring. This crop would not produce quite as well since it had not had as much time to grow. It was planted just as early as the farmers could get their wooden plough into the ground, probably in March, and would be harvested in early autumn.

Threshing took place in an open area of the barn where a special wooden floor was set up. Flails were used to beat the stalks, thereby causing them to shed their grain. The straw was then removed, and the grain scooped up with a wide, shallow winnowing basket. By tossing the grain into the air and fanning it, the lighter chaff (inedible husks) blew away until only the heavier grain remained. The heaviest grain fell closest to the winnower and was saved to plant next season. Grain that was to be eaten was dried in a kiln and taken in sacks to the local windmill or water mill to be ground into flour. People also grew flax and hemp as fibre crops, planting in March or April and harvesting in July. Hedges only came into use as boundaries in the later Middle Ages, as strip cultivation gave way to larger enclosures. Hedges required yearly maintenance, pruning, training and clearing of the ditches that ran alongside them, and this happened in February. Orchards existed, but were generally associated with large estates or monasteries,

As much as 90 percent of the population lived in rural farming communities, earning the majority of their income from either livestock or arable farming. Most labourers either rented a cottage and got paid wages by the farmer, or received a cottage in return for working for the farmer. A farm labourer was paid 6*d* a day and a loaf cost 2*d*. Labourers rose when the sun came up and went to bed when the sun set. The only light in the cottage came from the fire or from rushlights (candles made from reeds dipped in animal fat), which gave off very little light and stank. The day started as early as 3 a.m. during the summer. Pottage was the usual breakfast. Labourers were on fields by 5 a.m. After the midday meal, a small break was provided for the workers. As per the Elizabethan Statute of Artificers, labourers worked between 5 a.m. and 7 or 8 p.m. between March to September and from dawn to dusk between September and March.

Cattle

All farm animals were far smaller than today, for scientific breeding did not really exist. A full-grown ox reached a size scarcely larger than today's calf. The average weight of a cow was around 350 pounds, compared to 1,200–1,300 pounds today. Cattle were working animals, and farmers did not keep big herds, either for their milk or beef, because neither was used on a regular basis in the diet of the masses. Working oxen, usually castrated males, were kept to pull ploughs, harrows and other farming tools. The oxen were very distinctive from today's cattle, built to pull a plough, with great shoulders and horns. A few breeding cows were kept. Any excess milk from these was made into butter and cheese, and a small amount for the very young, very old and sick to drink. Smaller farms may well have shared a team of oxen. A team of two oxen and their ploughman could probably plough an acre in a day, and many Tudor fields were roughly this size. Cattle need more space than sheep, and, unlike sheep, a certain amount of shelter and feed in winter. Cattle would give horn, heated and shaped to make spoons and drinking vessels, and spices were kept in hollow horns with linen, dipped in melted beeswax, as a cover. Today we have evolved two very distinct types of cattle: beef cattle, bred for their quality of meat; and dairy cattle, bred for their milk production.

Sheep

Like cattle, sheep were much smaller than today, but selective breeding had begun to give bigger sheep and thereby larger wool yields. The average weight rose from around 28 pounds in 1500 to 46 pounds in 1600, but today's ewes are 100–200 pounds and a champion ram can now weigh 400 pounds. Sheep need little care the year round, producing wool, milk, more sheep and meat. It was important that they were marked, with notches on the ear and/or a splotch of dye on the back, since grazing land for sheep was often used in common. They were very small, and the fleece of a sheep often weighed less than two ounces. Wool was the material that everyone wore, and the quality of English wool was famous all over the known world. It was exported to the Low Countries, where it was spun and weaved into very fine cloth and imported back to England. Sheep did not need the top-quality grazing of the cattle and they were hardy enough to stay out all year round, often being brought down to lower, more sheltered land in winter. A shepherd can tend a large flock, and a ewe will have one or two lambs each year, increasing the flock. The Tudors used more sheep's milk than cow's milk, and it was made into butter and cheese, a large part of the ordinary person's diet.

In Tudor times, it was said that 'half the wealth of England rides on the back of the sheep'. 'Sheep turned grass into wool' to provide the raw material for the wool and weaving industry, which was by far the most dominant component of the economy. For this reason, the growing of sheep for wool was not just a matter for farmers. Its management was an integral and important part of the governance of the nation. The sixteenth century saw fundamental changes in agricultural practice. The manorial system was declining, and with it the army of peasants tied to their villages or tending the huge medieval flocks, both lay and ecclesiastically owned. This was hastened by the Dissolution of the Monasteries, and the breakup of their huge estates.

Early enclosures of arable land into sheep walks may have turned cottagers into 'landless vagabonds', but the countryside also became 'thickly dotted with the solid, well-proportioned homes of the middle-class husbandmen'. Although it was said at the time that 'sheep have eaten up our meadows and our downs, our corn, our wood, whole villages and towns', sheep also brought a new era of prosperity to the countryside. The sturdy yeoman farmer was prospering, and by 1600, more than 20 per cent of them had actually become freeholders. Many of them were literate enough to take advantage of the advice expounded by a new breed of agricultural writers, such as Thomas Tusser (1520–84), with his instructional poem *Five hundred points of Good Husbandry* (1573).

Although most commercial production of wool now comes from descendants of Spanish merino sheep, England produced Europe's finest wools during the Middle Ages. Spanish wools were among the worst in Europe and were used in the production of the very cheapest fabrics. There were two principal types of sheep in England: a small sheep producing short wool and a larger sheep producing long wool. The short-wooled sheep was a native of poor pastures, hills, moors and downs and produced wool prepared by carding that was used to make cloth (that is textiles of heavy texture thickened by fulling). The long-wooled sheep was found in rich grasslands, marshes and fens and produced wool prepared by combing and used for lighter worsteds and serges (materials which were not usually fulled). Both were less than half the size of the sheep we see today. Three breeds accounted for most wool production in the Middle Ages: the Ryeland, Cotswold and Lincoln. Ryeland was the most famous of short-wooled breeds, inhabiting the country between the Severn and the Marches of Wales, and was largely responsible for the 'Lemster ore', centred upon Leominster, the golden fleece of England. The bulk of the fine wool exported came from two long-wooled breeds, however, the Cotswold and Lincoln.

Pigs

Pigs were the third major type of livestock, again far smaller than today's breeds. Sows were bred in December or January and would deliver their piglets in March or April. Piglets stayed in the farmyard with their mothers until about August, when they were considered strong enough to be driven out to forage. In the autumn, swineherds drove the pigs out to feed upon acorns and beech mast to fatten up. Even very poor families could usually afford to raise a pig themselves, since pigs forage so well and cost little to feed. The salted meat and offal from an early winter butchering would have to last the whole winter. The Tudor pig was nearer to the wild boar in looks, and the Tamworth, a long-bodied, ginger pig, is about the closest we have in looks today.

The Tudor Hogbog

Unlike other farm animals, the pig does not need a field and acres of grassland to survive. The peasant's pig would have been kept in a small enclosure behind the cottage known as a hogbog. It was used by farmers and peasants to house both pigs and poultry. The pigs would occupy the ground space while the poultry resided in a raised henhouse, and the design saved both space and danger to the hens at night. Pigs were considered to be an incredibly useful animal to keep, and it was not uncommon for a Tudor peasant to receive a young pig in the spring as part of his wages. Not only did the pig eat any food leftovers, but pigs enjoy human waste. On one side of the pigsty was 'the midden', or human toilet, with a gentle slope into the pig quarters. The pig cleared the human waste, took nutrition from it, and made more manure. This then went onto the compost heap, which, when well rotted, was put on the Tudor garden to help the vegetables grow, which humans ate. However, a pig needed more food than just leftovers, and peasants had rights to take their animals onto common land to graze or into the landowner's woodland. This practice, 'pannage' is an ancient one used to fatten pigs before slaughter and salting for the winter. It was additionally useful in that the pigs ate green acorns and beech mast, both of which are poisonous to cattle and horses. There is still a 'pannage season' of sixty days in the New Forest. The pigs grazed on the undergrowth of plants, keeping the land clear of unusable plants so all the goodness in the soil could be used by the trees, and they also added richness to the soil by manuring it. Autumn was the traditional time for killing pigs, as they were well grown so there was no point trying to feed them over winter, except for the breeding sows and a boar.

Geese, Doves, Chickens and Blackbird Pies

The landowner and gentry would keep geese, to be eaten at feasts. The gentry would have had dovecots in their courtyards, as a great delicacy was 'squab', or young dove. As with pigs, many people would have kept chickens, not to be eaten until the end of their natural lives. They were needed for eggs, and for pest control in gardens. Many wild birds also found their way into the cooking cauldrons. The wealthy ate pheasant and grouse, while the poor might trap blackbirds to make into a pie. It is known that a sixteenth-century amusement was to place live birds in a pie, as a form of entremets. An Italian cookbook from 1549, translated into English in 1598, contained such a recipe. The nursery rhyme 'Sing a Song of Sixpence' has the line of 'four and twenty blackbirds baked in a pie'. The way Tudors made pie crusts was a little different in that the thick crust could be baked first, and would rise to form a pot, hence the term 'pot pie'. The lid would be removed from the pie, and birds would then be set inside, the lid put back on, and then this entertaining dish placed before the host of the party. Thus the birds were not actually cooked in the pie.

It is said that not only birds were baked into pies, but rabbits, frogs, dogs, dwarfs (who would pop out and recite poetry) and at one time a whole little musical group. Today the rich have strippers popping out of cakes. The experimental celebrity chef Heston Blumenthal attempted to create the dish for an episode of his television series *Heston's Medieval Feast*. Discovering that blackbirds are a protected species, he altered the recipe to pigeon. The pie and pie lid were cooked separately and allowed to cool, and live pigeons inserted only moments before presentation. Initial attempts resulted in the pigeons refusing to fly out. This was solved by using trained homing pigeons to fly to their cages suspended in the ceiling. When the pie was opened, the pigeons flew to their cages.

Horses

In Britain all the native breeds are classified as ponies, which, despite being strong as riding animals, are not built to pull ploughs. These are the New Forest, Dartmoor, Exmoor, Welsh Mountain, Fell, Dales, Highlands, Shetland and Connemara. Thus oxen were preferred as farm animals. All the heavy horse breeds came from the Continent, with France and Belgium supplying knights with horses built to carry enormous weights. Only the very rich kept these great horses for work on their farms. A team could work faster than a team of oxen, but were far more expensive, needed better grazing to keep in good condition to work, needed shelters and feeding in the winter and could not work on steep slopes or heavy ground.

Marocco the Horse and Moll Cutpurse

In 1600, the performing horse Marocco was ridden by its master, a Scot named Banks, over the roof of the old St Paul's Cathedral. A servant wished his master to see the spectacle and found him inside the cathedral. When he asked him to come out, the master replied, 'Away you fool! What need I go so far to see a horse on the top, when I can see so many asses at the bottom?' A year later a showman named William Banks bet Moll 'Cutpurse' £20 that she would not ride from Charing Cross to Shoreditch dressed as a man. She rode the famous performing horse Marocco to win the bet, flaunting a banner and blowing a trumpet as well. For this she was sentenced to carry out penance in St Paul's Cathedral. Moll is said to be the first woman in England to smoke tobacco. She had acquired a taste for cross-dressing, and carried on the habit until her death (for more on the remarkable Moll, see Chapter 14).

Enclosure

The monasteries were closed, and the great landowners who bought their estates began to keep great flocks of sheep to make immense profits in Europe.

They needed to fence in (enclose) their land to stop the sheep wandering and consequently threw poor people out of their houses, even destroying villages. They needed fewer labourers with the switch from crops to sheep. The 'dispossessed' poor were forced to wander through the country and towns trying to find work in the countryside or in towns. Many of these wandering looking for work were termed vagrants, and were forced to live by robbery and violence to survive. Sir Thomas More, in his 1516 work *Utopia*, suggested that enclosure was responsible for some of the social problems affecting England at the time, specifically theft.

Enclosure was the fencing in and farming, as personal property, of fields that had previously been leased to tenants or which had been used as common grazing land. It began in earnest in the reign of Henry VII, as common rights over land were thrown out by landowners. The previously used open-field system did not give itself up for fencing off, and production could be seen as small-scale. The use of enclosure was the start of a more scientific move in agriculture. Only a small proportion of English land was enclosed, but the social effects were magnified because enclosure was concentrated in a few areas, especially the Midlands. Selective breeding of animals could be attempted after enclosure, and for others there was a more concerted effort at growing crops to be sold at market on a more professional basis.

Throughout the medieval and modern periods, piecemeal enclosure took place when adjacent strips were fenced off from the common field. This was sometimes undertaken by small landowners, but more often by large landowners and lords of the manor. English *champaign* – extensive, open land – had been commonly enclosed as pastureland for sheep from the fourteenth to the sixteenth century as populations declined. Foreign demand for English wool also helped encourage increased production, and the wool industry was often thought to be more profitable for landowners who had large, decaying farmlands. The process sped up during the late fifteenth and sixteenth centuries as sheep farming grew more profitable. The loss of agricultural labour also hurt others, like millers, whose livelihood relied on agricultural produce.

Tudor authorities were extremely nervous about how the villagers who had lost their homes would react. In the sixteenth century, lack of income made one a pauper. If one lost one's home as well, one became a vagrant and was treated as a criminal. From the time of Henry VII onwards, Parliament began passing Acts to stop enclosure, to limit its effects or at least to fine those responsible. The first such law was in 1489. Over the next 150 years, there were eleven more Acts of Parliament and eight commissions of enquiry on the subject. There were popular efforts to remove old enclosures, and much legislation of the 1530s and 1540s concerns this shift. Angry tenants, impatient to reclaim pastures for tillage, were illegally destroying enclosures. Beginning with Kett's Rebellion in 1549, agrarian revolts swept across the nation, and other revolts occurred periodically throughout the century. The transition from village era to the town era commenced from the Elizabethan era itself, accelerated by enclosures.

Tusser's Firsts

At the time of Thomas Tusser's death he was farming a small estate in Cambridgeshire, and Thomas Fuller later noted that he 'traded at large in oxen, sheep, dairies, grain of all kinds, to no profit' and notably that he was unsuccessful in various ventures, in that he 'spread his bread with all sorts of butter, yet none would stick thereon'. Sometime before his death Tusser was a prisoner for debt, in the Poultry Compter (or Counter), a small prison in London. Tusser wrote a book that includes a mix of instructions and observations about farming and country customs, offering insight into life in Tudor times, and his work records many terms and proverbs in print for the first time. He also presented the ten characteristics the perfect cheese must have:

Not like Gehazi, i.e., dead white, like a leper
Not like Lot's wife, all salt
Not like Argus, full of eyes
Not like Tom Piper, "hoven and puffed"
Not like Crispin, leathery
Not like Lazarus, poor
Not like Esau, hairy
Not like Mary Magdalene, full of whey or maudlin
Not like the Gentiles, full of maggots
Not like a Bishop, made of burnt milk.

In Tusser's *A Hundred Good Points of Husbandry* (1557), we first read 'At Christmas play and make good cheer, / For Christmas comes but once a year' and 'Who goeth a borrowing / Goeth a sorrowing'. His 'naught venture, naught have' seems to be the origin of 'nothing ventured, nothing gained'. In another publication, *A Description of the Properties of Wind*, we first read, 'Yet true it is, as cow chews cud / And trees at spring do yield forth bud, / Except wind stands as never it stood, / It is an ill wind turns none to good.'

26

Trade, Business and Money

Trade and Business

Most industrial production was in the home, not in factories, especially in the case of cloth production, the country's main industry and its major export. Wool and the cloth trade came to be centred on East Anglia, mainly because of its Continental links, and its ports grew in importance. The sale of English wool in Flanders had involved the political and economic involvement of the two countries for decades. However, the wool was increasingly worked up to cloth in England, often with Flemings relocating to England. The Merchant Staplers enjoyed a monopoly over the export of wool through Calais, until its loss in 1558. It is impossible to overestimate the value of high-quality English wool and fleeces in this time. The prosperity their export brought the kingdom helped cement the Tudor dynasty in place. Cloth and woollens in 1564–65 accounted for 82 per cent of the value of all exports from England, and perhaps another 13 per cent came from raw wool and woolfell (the skin with the wool attached). There were 8 million sheep in the country, double the human population. The Merchant Adventurers now grew in prominence, trading in the wool throughout Europe. Other important industries included lead mining (Derbyshire), tin mining (Cornwall) and coalmining, especially in the north of England. The phrase 'taking coals to Newcastle', meaning giving someone things they do not need, was first recorded in 1538.

Trade and industry grew rapidly, with England developing its merchant fleet and becoming a more commercial and consequently richer country. To expand their trade, merchants and ships' captains began to seek new business overseas. Fishing fleets crossed the Atlantic for enormous cod catches off Newfoundland. London rapidly rose in importance among Europe's commercial centres through its many small industries, especially weaving. Trade expanded beyond western Europe to Russia, the Levant and the Americas. France was by far the most important country commercially, until the riches of the Americas began to feed into Spain. From Tudor times we see the growth of 'Mercantilism', the theory and practice common in Europe from the sixteenth to the eighteenth century.

Mercantilism promoted governmental regulation of the state's economy, with the aim of augmenting power at the expense of rival national powers. The economic counterpart of political absolutism, mercantilism aims at accumulating monetary reserves through a positive balance of trade. The policy became a cause of frequent European wars and also motivated speedy colonial expansion. Mercantilist theory varied in sophistication from one writer to another and evolved over time. High tariffs upon import, especially of manufactured goods, are characteristic. Other parts of the strategy included building a network of overseas colonies for assured exports and cheap imports; forbidding those colonies to trade with other nations; banning the export of gold and silver, even for payments, to ensure a sound treasury; forbidding trade to be carried in foreign ships; export subsidies; and creating barriers to international trade. France, Spain and the Netherlands, the major trading nations, also followed these policies.

To assist this policy, monopoly trading companies such as the Russia Company in 1555 and the East India Company in 1600 were established by royal charter. Ralph Fitch was one of the first Englishmen to visit India, Burma and Malaya. He published an account of his travels in 1598 that stressed Portuguese corruption and the great wealth of the area. The East India Company was formed by London merchants eager to tap that wealth. By allowing merchants to share the risk on long-distance journeys to India and the Far East, it made access to the highly profitable spice trade viable for businessmen who otherwise would have been afraid to risk everything on one venture. Its main object was to contest Spanish and Portuguese control of the spice trade, by trading directly with the East Indies (modern-day India and Indonesia). The East India Company ultimately came to rule much of India, and became one of the key institutions in Europe.

In 1581 the Turkey Company was formed, and in 1592 it merged with the Venice Company of 1583 to form the Levant Company. It obtained a patent from Elizabeth I for the exclusive right to trade in currants and also purchased wine, cotton and silk from the Eastern Mediterranean. It developed 'factories', trading centres in the already established commercial hubs of Aleppo, Istanbul, Alexandria and Smyrna, all inside the Ottoman Empire. Although initially a joint-stock company, it evolved into a regulated monopoly. In 1585, the Barbary Company (formed in 1551 to trade with North Africa) was granted a monopoly by Elizabeth. The Barbary Coast (modern-day Morocco) was the main source of sugar for the English market, until the development of the West Indies sugar plantations. One area in which English merchants were involved from an early stage was the slave trade, and captains such as Drake and Hawkins were prominent in combining this with privateering.

Sir Thomas Gresham's founding of the Royal Exchange in 1565, the first stock exchange in England and one of the earliest in Europe, was of immense importance for the economic development of England and soon for the world. Gresham's inspiration was the Bourse in Antwerp, where he had been royal agent for both Edward VI and Queen Mary. Gresham was wealthy, owing to a sizeable inheritance and his own financial dealing while in Antwerp. He invested a huge chunk of this fortune in a new London Bourse, which was built between 1566 and 1570 on land between Cornhill and Threadneedle Street in the City of London. The trading floor was open to the elements, with piazzas for wet weather. Although Gresham's aim was to build somewhere to house a trading floor, he realised that it could not be very profitable on its own. He therefore added two more floors on top and moved into the retail business, opening Britain's very first shopping mall. This had about a hundred kiosks or shops, with each shopkeeper paying annual rent, giving Gresham a steady income.

After a slow start, Gresham's retail idea took off following the promise of a visit by Queen Elizabeth I in 1570. She ordered its change of name from the Bourse to the Royal Exchange: 'Proclaime through everie high street of this citie, This place to be no longer cal'd a Burse, But since the building's stately, faire, and strange, Be it for ever cal'd, the Royall Exchange.' Thereafter it was known for the wonderful range of goods on sale as well as for trading. Although its shopping was a pleasant diversion, Gresham's Royal Exchange was the key to the new wealth of the City. Elizabeth I now licensed legal landing quays for goods on the banks of the Thames, ensuring the Crown got its share of the wealth while underpinning London's status as the new centre for trading.

With taxes lower than in other European countries, the economy expanded; however, the wealth was distributed very unevenly, as today. As luck would have it, Gresham's building pre-empted the Spanish sacking of Antwerp in 1576, destroying its position as the financial capital of Europe and allowing London merchants to fill the vacuum.

The sack of Antwerp, or the Spanish Fury at Antwerp, was caused by Spanish troops mutinying over not being paid. Antwerp was the cultural, economic, trading and financial centre of the Netherlands, and its devastation caused Antwerp's decline as a leading city. London now became the leading North Sea port. Importantly, immigrants arrived in London to swell its needs for a greater workforce, not just from all Britain but from the Continent as well. Flemings and French Huguenots arrived in huge numbers, providing needed skills. London's population rose from an estimated 50,000 in 1530 to about 225,000 in 1605.

Economic developments, with general peace and prosperity, allowed the Elizabethan 'Golden Age'. Having inherited a virtually bankrupt state from previous reigns, her frugal policies restored fiscal responsibility. The success of London and Elizabeth's fiscal restraint had cleared the regime of debt by 1574, and ten years later the Crown enjoyed a surplus of £300,000.

The Two Worst Jobs

Apart from the well-paid but gruesome job of executioner, there are a number of claimants. The leech collector waded bare-legged into the shallow waters of reedy marshes waiting for the leeches to latch on, and he could then sell these to the local Barber Surgeon. A gong scourer (also gongfermor or gong farmer) was the man or boy who dug out and removed human faeces from privies and cesspits. Gong is derived from the Old English *gang*, meaning 'to go', and referred to both a privy and its contents. Gong farmers were only allowed to work at night, hence they were sometimes known as nightmen or night soil men. The waste they collected, known as night soil, had to be taken outside the city or town boundary or to official dumps for disposal, from where it might be taken to be spread as fertiliser on fields or market gardens. Larger towns often provided public latrines, known as houses of easement, but they were few and far between. Local regulations were introduced to control the placement of private latrines, and how they should be constructed. Cesspits were often placed under cellar floors, or in the yard of a house, some of which had wooden chutes to carry the excrement from the upper floors into the cesspit, sometimes flushed by rainwater. Cesspits were not watertight, allowing the liquid waste to drain away and leaving only the solids to be collected. The foul odour from cesspits was a continual problem, and the accumulation of solid waste meant that they had to be cleaned out every two years or so. It was the job of the gong scourers to dig them out and remove the excrement, for which in the late fifteenth century they charged two shillings per ton of waste removed.

Those employed at Hampton Court in Elizabeth's era were paid sixpence a day, a good wage, but the working life of a gong farmer was 'spent up to his knees, waist, even neck in human ordure'. They were only allowed to work between 9 p.m. and 5 a.m. and were permitted to live only in certain areas, and because of the noxious fumes produced by human excrement were sometimes overcome by asphyxiation. Gong scourers usually employed a couple of young boys to lift the full buckets of ordure out of the pit and to work in confined spaces. After being dug out, the solid waste was removed in large barrels or pipes, which were loaded onto a horse-drawn cart. In the case of London, much of it was taken to dumps on the banks of the Thames (such as the appropriately named Dung Wharf), from where it was transported by barge to be used as fertiliser on fields or market gardens. One London gong scourer who poured effluent down a drain was put in one of his own pipes, which was filled up to his neck with filth before being publicly displayed in Golden Lane with a sign detailing his crime.

When sheep were sheared, the wool was carded, spun into yarn and then woven. To make the weaving process easier, the natural grease (lanolin) was left in the wool, but this made the resulting cloth coarse, with large holes in the mesh. Thus it was the fuller's job to 'full' or pound and clean off the grease and other impurities from the cloth. Soaking the fabric made it softer, shrank it to close the holes and made it thicker, and trampling meshed the wool fibres together to make them stronger and less likely to fray. The solution in which the loosely woven cloth was soaked needed to be alkaline in order to break down the grease, and the cheapest form of alkaline solution available was stale urine. The fuller had to obtain gallons of urine from the neighbouring farms and private houses. Not only was the job revolting, it was terribly monotonous, taking seven or eight hours of treading on the cloth in urine to produce a piece of finished cloth. Thus if one's surname is Fuller, Tucker or even Walker, one of one's distant ancestors worked in the wool industry and spent every day trudging up to their knees in stale human urine.

Woad is a plant related to the cabbage, and before the importation of indigo from the East at the end of the sixteenth century, it was used to produce the rich blue dyes seen in Tudor tapestries and textiles. However, the process used to extract the blue dye from the plant was so foul that woad dyers, like gong scourers, were forced to live on the outskirts of the society. The woad was fermented and dried into woad balls, which caused particularly noxious fumes. It took fifty pounds of woad to produce five pounds of pigment. The smell became even worse because to extract the dye the woad balls had to be crushed and fermented further in an alkaline solution. The only alkaline solution available was the stale urine mentioned above. The dried woad had to be placed in a vat of the stale urine and kept at 51° C for three days. The trick was maintaining the alkalinity for the solution. Without the aid of special equipment to test pH levels, they had to use a combination of their senses, touch, taste and smell. According to Tony Robinson, this cooked woad smelt and tasted like 'rotting boiled cabbage mixed with sewage'. The stench was so terrible that Elizabeth I not only ordered the woad dyers to stop work completely before she entered a town, but decreed that they could not come within five miles of where she was staying.

Transport

Roads were just dirt tracks. Only around London would one generally find some paved roads. They were paved for a short distance either side of the gates through the city walls, where traffic was densest, as were Holborn High Street and the Strand. On horseback one might travel around forty miles a day, and it normally took a week to travel from London to Plymouth. Goods were sometimes transported by packhorse (horses with bags on their sides). Also carriers with covered wagons carried goods and sometimes passengers. When possible people preferred to transport goods by water, and all around England there was a 'coastal trade'. In Elizabethan times the streets of London were also transformed as coaches took to the streets and caused huge ruts. Each village was supposed to repair its own roads. A law was introduced in 1555 where one man was chosen every year to be 'Surveyor of the Highway'. Rich people were required to provide the materials for repairing the roads and the poorer people were to work unpaid for six days a year to carry out the repairs. Nobody liked having the job of surveyor and quite often the surveyor would only bother to repair those pieces of road they travelled on.

Money

All coins were made of either gold or silver, a coin's value being what its constituent metals were worth. Thus, any foreign coin was also current in England, and the exchange rate was based upon the amount of gold or silver it contained relative to an English coin. 'Money of Account' was a bookkeeper's convention and was not represented by an actual coin. Until 1583 the pound was a Money of Account, and a pound coin was minted in that year for the first time.

In the sixteenth century, goldsmith-bankers across Europe began to accept deposits, make loans and transfer funds. They also gave receipts for gold coins deposited with them. These receipts were known as 'running cash notes', made out in the name of the depositor and promising to pay him 'on demand'. Many also carried the words 'or bearer' after the name of the depositor, which allowed them to circulate in a very limited way. Not until 1694 was the Bank of England established, in order to raise money for William III's war against France.

Tudor coinage was based upon pounds, shillings and pence – *£ s d*. Twelve pence made one shilling and twenty shillings made up one pound. These values were constant and never varied in relation to each other. The exact value of other coins might vary, however. Sovereigns (invented in Henry Tudor's reign), nobles, angels, testoons and royals all had values that fluctuated, depending on their weight and purity at their most recent minting. Gold was always more valuable than its monetary equivalent in silver and tended to be hoarded while silver circulated. A seller would often be willing to accept a lower price for goods if payment was in gold.

Around 1580, the values of currency were as follows. Gold coins included the sovereign (20*s*). Until 1583, the sovereign was the pound coin. When the pound coin was issued, a 30*s* 'fine' sovereign was minted. There was also a half-sovereign (10*s* and then 15*s*). The pound stopped being a 'money of account' and was worth 20*s*, with a half-pound (10*s*). The mark was equivalent to 13*s* 4*d*, or 160*d*, i.e. two-thirds of a pound. It was primarily used in high-level transactions such as buying or selling land or assessing substantial fines. The royal (11*s* 3*d*) had not been minted since Queen Mary's rule but was still in circulation. It was also spelled ryal or rial. The gold angel was worth 10*s* and there was also a half-angel (5*s*) and a quarter-angel (2*s* 6*d*). The noble was worth a third of a pound, 6*s* 8*d*. The crown, worth five shillings, last minted under Henry VIII, was still in circulation under Elizabeth. It was the smallest gold coin, also issued as a silver coin of the same value, and there was a half-crown, which some of us remember in circulation pre-decimalisation.

Silver coins were the shilling (12*d*), sixpence (6*d*), groat (4*d*), and thruppence (3*d*), which this author recalls as a thruppeny bit. Thus the terminology for a three-penny coin passed through four centuries. The silver testoon (2¼*d*) was also called a tester, and was a coin of Henry VIII still in circulation. The half-groat and tuppence (2*d*) were both in circulation, and again this author recalls the tuppeny bit. There was a three-half-penny coin (1½*d*), a penny (1*d*), three-farthing (¾*d*), and half-penny (½*d*) bit. The last was known as a ha'penny (pronounced haypenny), another term which lasted until its demise in 1971's Decimalisation Act. There was no Elizabethan farthing coin (¼*d*), and they were not minted until Victoria's reign, being abandoned in 1961.

27

Architecture and Buildings

The Poor

A poor family would live in what we might consider a hut, one or perhaps two small rooms with a hole in the wall for a window, sometimes with a closing wooden shutter but often just strips of linen soaked in linseed oil. Slits in the walls and a door gave some more light and ventilation. Floors were of hard-beaten earth, and some can still be seen. They slept on straw or straw-filled mattresses with only an old wool blanket to keep themselves warm. Furniture was probably a wooden table, some stools and perhaps one wooden bed, and one or more wooden chests to keep everything in. They would also have an iron cooking pot, to hang/sit over the fire, and some wooden bowls and mugs. The cheapest homes were cob houses, some of which survive, with walls made from a mixture of mud, straw and lime. Cob is durable if plastered over and kept from damp at top and bottom. The earliest standing examples are from around 1300, but these are exceptional. Earth houses generally have a lifespan of 150 to 200 years, although this could be prolonged by casing the walls in brick. Cob was popular in Devon up to the nineteenth century and was also used in Cumbria, the East Midlands, Hampshire and Ireland. The flexibility of the material permitted rounded corners. Another clue to cob construction is the thickness of the walls.

The cheapest wooden frame for house construction was the cruck frame, originally basically a tree which had grown into a 'V' shape, placed upside down, one at each end of the building. The walls of these houses were filled in with 'wattle and daub', basically a mixture of woven branches covered with a plaster made of mud, animal dung and straw. The daub was pushed into and over the wattle to make the walls. Horsehair was also used in daub, with the hair giving extra holding ability. The daub was often painted with protective limewash, making it look white. Better homes in towns were simply timber frames pinned together with wooden pegs, and the spaces in between filled with clay or brick. Cottage roofs were generally made of the cheapest material, straw or reed thatch. Houses were damp and draughty, filled with smoke as there were no chimneys. Smoke went out through a hole in the thatch, or permeated through the thatch.

In the country the poor often shared their home with their animals, this being cheaper than having a separate barn and providing more warmth. The room would be divided by a fence to keep the animals at one end. Farmers developed this into the 'long houses' seen in Wales and the West Country to this day, extending and later adding another storey. The long house suited a peasant or smallholder with a few animals in a climate with long, hard winters. They are found in Cumbria, Dartmoor, the Hebrides, northern and western Ireland and south Wales. The Welsh version is the *tŷ-hir*. Surviving examples are all byrehouses, where the agricultural end sheltered cattle.

The only water would come from a well or stream and would have to be fetched in buckets, and the toilet would be a hedge or an outside hut away from the house. The term for a toilet in Welsh has always been *tŷ bach*, small house, and some readers will remember having a small outside toilet. People often did their washing outside in a stream using homemade soap of fat and ashes. Rubbish was just thrown onto a 'midden', where the pigs and hens would find anything worth scavenging; this practice remained in country areas until the twentieth century. Middens are even now explored for old pottery and bottles. Artificial light was needed on all but midsummer evenings, and some needed it during the day. The most common form of domestic lighting was the rushlight, made by dipping a dried, peeled rush in animal fat. They were cheap and lasted up to an hour, having been used since pre-Roman times.

The Rich

The upper floors of Tudor houses in towns were often larger than the ground floors, which would create an overhang, or jetty. This would create more floor surface above while also keeping maximum street width. Glass was very expensive and difficult to make, so windowpanes were made small and held together in a lead lattice, in casement windows. There were cases of people moving house and taking their glass windows with them. Tall, narrow casement windows with small window panes can be seen. Casement windows hinge outwards so air can be let in. Wealth was demonstrated by the extensive use of glass. Tudor chimneys were tall, thin and often decorated with symmetrical patterns of moulded or cut brick. Mansions were often designed to a symmetrical plan, with 'E' and 'H' shapes being popular. For the first time, rich people's houses were designed for comfort rather than defence. In a wealthy home, furniture was usually made of oak and was heavy and massive. Comfortable beds became more and more common in the sixteenth century. Many rich men had four-poster beds hung with curtains to reduce drafts. In a middle-class Tudor home a mattress was often stuffed with flock (a kind of rough wool).

Chairs were more common than in the Middle Ages but they were still expensive, and even in an upper-class home children and servants sat on stools. In rich people's houses, the walls of rooms were lined with oak panelling to keep out drafts. Some Tudors had wallpaper but it was very expensive. Very wealthy people hung tapestries or painted cloths on their walls. Carpets were usually too expensive to put on the floor, and instead were often hung on the wall or over tables. People covered their floors with rushes or reeds, which were strewn with sweet-smelling herbs. The wealthy people lit their homes with expensive beeswax candles.

Cruck and Box

The most recognisable feature of Tudor buildings is the 'cruck' or 'crook frame', a curved timber, or one of a pair, which supports the roof. This type of timber frame consists of long, generally bent, timber beams that lean inwards and form the ridge of the roof. These posts are then generally secured by a horizontal beam which then forms an 'A' shape. Several of these 'crucks' were constructed on the ground and then lifted into position. They were then joined together by either solid walls or cross beams, which aided in preventing 'racking'. Racking is the action of each individual frame going out of square with the rest of the frame, and thus risking collapse. Crucks were mostly used for houses and barns no more than twenty feet wide. The earliest survivals date from the thirteenth century and most were built before 1600, when the rising demand for two full storeys made crucks obsolete. They are found mainly in Wales, western England and Devon, and only about 4,000 remain.

The box frame overtook the cruck in popularity, for it permitted two (or three) full storeys. Another advantage was the easy addition of wings. The term 'box frame' means that the main vertical posts are held in place by horizontal beams. The upper storeys often overhang the lower, called 'jettying'. Piling storey upon storey, with upper storeys jettied, made the most of the limited space in town centres. The black-and-white effect we see today on Tudor houses was because Victorians coated the beams with tar, whereas before they were left to weather. Tudor houses had steeply pitched roofs covered with thatch, or clay or stone tiles – whichever was available locally. In London, all houses had tiles because of the fear of fire.

The Great Houses

Some of the great houses and palaces, such as Nonsuch Palace (the grandest of Henry VIII's building projects), York Place (which became Whitehall Palace), Greenwich Palace, Sheen Palace and Richmond Palace, have disappeared or been replaced, along with many great abbeys and cathedrals. Sudeley Castle in Gloucester had been owned by Richard III before passing to Jasper Tudor, Duke of Bedford. It was visited by Henry VII, Henry VIII and Anne Boleyn. Elizabeth visited three times, the last occasion being a three-day affair commemorating the defeat of the Armada that has been described as one of the longest parties in history. A stained-glass window depicts Elizabeth, and the castle houses other portraits and textiles relating to the queen. Catherine Parr is buried in its chapel.

Bricks were handmade, expensive and thinner than modern brick, and only the richest households could afford this relatively new building material. The greatest example of Tudor brickwork can be seen at Hampton Court Palace. Hampton Court Palace, on the north bank of the River Thames, was built by Cardinal Thomas Wolsey and Henry VIII between 1514 and 1530. Henry VIII took it off Wolsey, using it as his favourite residence, and began adding to it. Wolsey had fresh water for his new palace running through lead pipes which travelled through Surbiton to get to Hampton Court. Not much of his original building remains due to the remodelling by Henry VIII and later kings. Henry enlarged and rebuilt his own apartments, parts of the kitchens and the Chapel Royal, replaced most of the Great Hall and added tennis courts. Henry also laid out the overall plan for the gardens at Hampton Court, the basic structure of which is still seen today. The astronomical clock was made in 1540 by Nicholas Oursian and shows the hours, days of the week, days of the month, the time of high tide, the phases of the moon, the signs of the zodiac and, in all its pre-Copernican glory, the golden sun travelling around an immobile Earth. Edward VI, Mary and Elizabeth all stayed at Hampton Court at times during their reigns. In 1537, Jane Seymour gave birth to the future King Edward VI at Hampton Court and died there two weeks later. Henry VIII spent three of his honeymoons at Hampton Court, as did his daughter Mary I when she married Philip II. It was at Hampton Court that Henry VIII was told of the infidelity of Catherine Howard, and here he married Catherine Parr.

Penshurst Place in Kent began as a fourteenth-century manor house and was visited by Henry VIII in 1519, when it was held by the 3rd Duke of Buckingham. The duke was executed two years later for treason and the house came into the possession of the Crown. Henry VIII used it as a hunting lodge, and it was given to Anne of Cleves as part of her divorce settlement. In 1552 Edward VI gave the property to Sir William Sidney, and it then passed to his son Sir Henry Sidney in 1554. Sir Henry was married to Mary Dudley, sister of Robert Dudley, Elizabeth's favourite, and Elizabeth visited Penshurst. Sir Henry's son, Sir Philip Sidney, the famed Elizabethan poet and courtier, was born at Penshurst in 1554. The eleven-acre formal walled garden is as it was laid out in Elizabethan times.

The motte of Windsor Castle was constructed by William the Conqueror in about 1080, and the castle has been added to and remodelled almost continually ever since. The Old Chapel, at the east end of St George's Chapel, was remodelled by Henry VII. Henry VII also built a new range to the west of the State Apartments. Edward IV began St George's Chapel, which was finished by Henry VIII, who was buried there along with Jane Seymour. The North Terrace was originally constructed by Henry VIII, although it was later widened. Henry VIII also built a new gate for the lower ward, now known as the Henry VIII Gate. Queen Mary built the Military Knights' Houses in the lower ward. Elizabeth added the Long Gallery to Henry VII's new apartments, and this area now houses the Royal Library.

Hever Castle in Kent is a wonderful sight, seeming to float upon the wide moat that surrounds it, approached across a drawbridge over the moat. Visitors then pass beneath the teeth of two portcullises into the inner courtyard of the castle. Hever was begun in 1270 by William de Hever, though the gatehouse is all that remains of that early fortress. In 1462 the castle passed to the Bullen (Boleyn) family, and Geoffrey de Bullen added wings on each side of the existing gatehouse. Several decades after the Boleyn family took over Hever, its most famous inhabitant, Anne Boleyn, was born. Anne would spend much of her childhood at Hever, and Henry VIII is known to have visited during his courtship. Anne's father, Thomas de Boleyn, expanded Hever still further, adding the Long Gallery, among other features. After Anne's death the castle was given to Anne of Cleves, Henry's fourth wife.

Hardwick Hall in Derbyshire is one of Britain's finest Elizabethan houses, built for Elizabeth Talbot, Dowager Countess of Shrewsbury, who moved there in October 1597. One of the most powerful people in the court of Elizabeth I, 'Bess of Hardwick' married four times, each time gaining more wealth, and her fourth husband was the Earl of Shrewsbury, one of the richest English nobles of the time. For many years the Shrewsburys were responsible for the guardianship of Mary, Queen of Scots. The massive house itself stands in a commanding position overlooking the surrounding countryside next to the ruins of Hardwick Old Hall. The tale is that Bess had a furious dispute with her husband, the Earl of Shrewsbury, and in 1584 had to leave their home at Chatsworth. She came to the Old Hall at Hardwick and largely rebuilt it as a place for herself to live. However, when the earl died in 1590 her finances became much more secure and she immediately began the construction of the 'New' Hall. With its massive windows and fine proportions it is an impressive statement of the power and wealth of its creator, who made sure the statement was made quite clear by having the initials E. S., carved on stone letters at the head of the towers. The hall was notable for the size of its windows and the amount of glass used, which was far more than in similar houses of the period. It was known by the rhyme 'Hardwick Hall, more glass than wall'. Many of the tapestries are original to the hall and were probably chosen by Bess herself.

Burghley House, near Stamford, Lincolnshire, is one of the largest and grandest houses of the first Elizabethan Age. Built and mostly designed by William Cecil, Lord High Treasurer to Queen Elizabeth I, between 1555 and 1587, the main part of the House has thirty-five major rooms on the ground and first floors.

Sixteenth-Century London

London grew enormously in the sixteenth century. In 1500 the town was encompassed by its walls, but by 1600 rich men had extended the city and built houses along the Strand, joining London to Westminster. The Church had owned about a quarter of the land in London. When Henry VIII dissolved the monasteries it released a great deal of land for new buildings. Along the walls of Tudor London were several gates: Aldgate, Bishopsgate, Moorgate, Cripplegate, Aldersgate, Newgate and Ludgate. Two of the gates, Ludgate and Newgate, were used as prisons. At night the streets of London were dark and dangerous. At 9 p.m. in summer and at dusk in winter, church bells rang the curfew and the city gates were locked.

South of the Thames was the large suburb of Southwark. The Thames was a major transport route as Tudor London was the largest port in England. Sailing ships sailed to quays just before London Bridge and there were also smaller boats owned by watermen for transporting people along the Thames. Tudor monarchs and other rich people had their own barges. There were also many fishermen in London and the river teemed with fish like salmon, trout, perch, flounder and bream. However, the Thames sometimes froze over and on these occasions fairs were held on it. The heads of traitors were stuck on spikes on London Bridge for all to see. National triumphs were marked by gorgeous processions over the water. The bridge was the focal point of the city and for all England.

In 1176, after successive wooden bridges were destroyed by fire, Henry II commissioned the building of a permanent stone crossing. It took thirty-three years to complete London Bridge, which lasted over 600 years. It was around 1,000 feet long, supported on twenty Gothic arches. It featured a central chapel, a host of shops and houses (the rent from which funded its construction and upkeep), gates, a drawbridge – even waterwheels and a mill. The houses were up to seven storeys high and jutted over the river by as much as seven feet on either side. Many practically touched in the middle, making the bridge more of a pedestrian tunnel in places. Although the bridge was about twenty-six feet wide, buildings reduced the space for traffic to just twelve feet, room for only one narrow lane north and one south. These were shared by horses, carts, livestock and pedestrians, and crossing the bridge could take as long as an hour.

The crossing was also difficult by ferry or skiff. The narrowness of the arches and the later addition of waterwheels created a dam effect. The water level on one side of the piers could be several yards below that on the other, and shooting the rapids connecting the two was a dangerous game played only by the most skilled watermen. Drowning was common.

'The Most Complete Medieval Town in Britain'

'The most complete medieval town in Britain' is Lavenham in Suffolk, with a superb collection of medieval and Tudor architecture. Most of its buildings date from the fifteenth century, and in the medieval period it was among the twenty wealthiest towns in England. Suffolk is a county with many colour-washed and timber-framed buildings. Bull's blood, chalk, soot and charcoal were traditional pigments used to colour the limewash on Tudor houses. Lavenham prospered from the wool trade in the fifteenth and sixteenth centuries, with the town's blue broadcloth being an export of note. By the late fifteenth century, the town was paying more in taxation than considerably larger towns such as York and Lincoln. The church, completed in 1525, is excessively large for the size of the village and, with a tower standing 141 feet high, lays claim to being the highest village church tower in Britain. Other buildings also demonstrate the town's medieval wealth, such as the Guildhall of 1529. When visiting the town in 1487, Henry VII fined several Lavenham families for displaying too much wealth. However, during the sixteenth century Lavenham's industry was badly affected by Dutch refugees settling in Colchester, who produced cloth that was cheaper and lighter than Lavenham's, and also more fashionable. Cheaper imports from Europe also aided the settlement's decline, and by 1600 it had lost its reputation as a major trading town. This sudden and dramatic change to the town's fortune is the principal reason for so many medieval and Tudor buildings remaining unmodified in Lavenham, as subsequent generations of citizens did not have the wealth required to rebuild in the latest styles. A similar happening can be seen in Charleston, South Carolina. It was not destroyed in the American Civil War, and people could only afford to repair, not build, leaving us with superb antebellum architecture.

Henry's New Castles

When invasion by Spain and France threatened, Henry VIII developed his famous chain of coastal fortresses. He took a close interest in their design and at Deal in Kent there is a castle at the cutting edge of Tudor military architecture: squat, multiple bastions cluster around a central keep, their low walls minimising the target available to enemy fire. The tiered layout allowed for sixty-six guns to be mounted and it was virtually impregnable, one of England's finest Tudor artillery fortresses.

28

Religion, Reformation, Martyrs and Relics

England was divided into around 10,000 local parishes, with the minister or priest of each parish being the rector or vicar. A curate, or deputy, often conducted services on the behalf of an absentee vicar. The parish also acted as an administrative unit; for instance, poor relief was organised on a parish level. Higher Church officers included archdeacons and deans, and at the top there were twenty-one (later twenty-six) bishops. Each bishop controlled a diocese from a cathedral town. There were two English archbishops, of Canterbury and of York, who led the two archdioceses of England. Ecclesiastical courts summoned and punished people for offences such as fornication, adultery, failure to attend church and malicious gossip. The most severe penalty was excommunication, exclusion from church services. This also meant severe civil liabilities, such as not being able to plead in court. Heretics were handed over to civil authorities for burning, the last person being burnt for heresy being Edward Wightman in 1612. Because of the lack of media and literacy, the clergy from priest to archbishop also acted as the monarch's main propaganda agency, as everyone attended church. If clergymen refused to pass on the monarch's messages, they would usually lose their livings, i.e. their positions and incomes.

While the better-paid posts in the Church usually went to the gentry, most clergy were poorly educated and underpaid, while a small minority of prelates grew wealthy on the profits of pluralism, simony and nepotism. Pluralism was the holding of multiple benefices (Church positions), so a man might be the parish priest of several different parishes and could even collect a living from a parish he had never seen and would never visit. If a clergyman held multiple benefices, he would often appoint poor priests as curates to perform his duties in distant or less desirable locations. Simony was the practice of buying or selling spiritual benefits such as pardons and relics or preferments – promotions and offices within the Church. Nepotism is simply the giving of positions to relatives. The term originated with the assignment of popes' and bishops' nephews to cardinal positions. Over 200 British MPs employ relatives in a variety of office roles, so nepotism still exists.

'Indulgences' were sold by the Church, to remit the punishment of sin in Purgatory after death. In other words, any Catholic could pay money to the Church in exchange for the forgiveness of sins. From the twelfth century onward, the process of salvation was increasingly bound up with money. Reformers of the fourteenth and fifteenth centuries frequently complained about the sale of indulgences by pardoners. As the papacy weakened in this period, secular governments increasingly allowed the granting of indulgences, but only in return for a substantial share of the yield, often as much as two-thirds. Monarchs and princes across Europe accrued a great deal of the proceeds, but the popes received most of the blame. Around 1505, Pope Julius II began the project of creating St Peter's Basilica and commissioning Michelangelo to paint the ceiling of the Sistine Chapel. Both Julius and his successor Leo X were in great need of funds for the completion of the basilica. Both promoted the sale of indulgences in order to help pay for it. This practice was despised by Martin Luther, who argued that only God, not churchmen, could forgive the sins of those who put their faith in Jesus. He also discovered that many of his parishioners felt no need to come to church after they had purchased indulgences. To Martin and his followers, the sale of indulgences was a corrupt practice that was 'irrelevant to divine forgiveness', aimed more at financially benefiting the Pope and the papal headquarters. His disagreement with this practice, among others, led to Luther's Ninety-Five Theses, which inspired the Protestant Reformation.

Monasteries were declining before the Tudor era. Only a few orders still maintained high standards. Renaissance popes were a poor example for monks, living lives of greed, corruption and sensuality, and the taxes to Rome of annates and 'Peter's pence' were often resented. A great deal of money was voluntarily left for funerals and chantries by the endowment of priests to say Masses for the dead. This could be accomplished by prayers to God for the soul of a deceased person, or Masses, or good works offered on behalf of the soul of a deceased person. Monastic incomes from great estates were later seen by Henry VIII's advisers as a method of balancing his overspending.

Reformation and Martyrs

When Henry became king in 1509, the Pope in Rome was the head of the Church *in* England, priests were not allowed to marry and all Church services were held in Latin. By the time of Henry's death in 1547, the monarch was head of the Church *of* England. Priests were still not allowed to marry in general, although Thomas Cranmer, Archbishop of Canterbury from 1533, was a married man. Under Edward VI, priests could marry. Church services were still mostly said in Latin, and there was rapid change to English in Elizabeth's reign, but the Lord's Prayer was always said in English.

Henry VIII's forthcoming break with Rome was caused by non-religious motives, but many of those who supported it were disgusted by the abuses rife in the Catholic Church and at the corruption of the papacy. Some English clerics went further and sympathised with the growing Protestant movement in Europe. They exposed clerical ignorance and promoted educational reform. The traditional starting date for the Reformation is 31 October 1517, when Martin Luther nailed his Ninety-Five Theses to the door of the castle church of Wittenberg. This was a traditional method of inviting debate and discussion among scholars, and over the next few years Luther attacked more and more aspects of established Roman Catholicism. He decried indulgences, clerical power, clerical celibacy, the use of Latin in church worship, the seven sacraments, transubstantiation and eventually papal power. He denounced his monasticism, married a former nun and also translated the Bible into German. It was published in 1534, and sold over 100,000 copies over the next forty years.

His most important doctrines were salvation by faith alone, the rejection of papal power, a reduction in the number of sacraments from seven to two, the rejection of transubstantiation, the use of communion in both bread and wine for laity, the rejection of Purgatory, the rejection of clerical celibacy and the abolition of monasteries. Luther's ideas soon spread throughout and beyond Germany, reaching England quickly. In response, in 1521 Henry VIII published *Assertio septem sacramentorum* (*Defence of the Seven Sacraments*). The Pope rewarded Henry with the title of *Defensor Fidei* (Defender of the Faith), and English monarchs retain the title. However, on the eve of the Reformation in 1529, the Imperial ambassador to England noted that 'nearly all the people here hate the priests', and an Italian diplomat wrote of the English 'raging against the clergy, or would be if the King's Majesty were not curbing their fury'.

Lutheran books were soon brought to England by merchants and travellers, and William Tyndale, Robert Barnes, Miles Coverdale, and Hugh Latimer were early converts to Lutheran views. Tyndale's translation was the first English Bible to draw directly from Hebrew and Greek texts, the first English one to take advantage of the printing press and first of the new English Bibles of the Reformation. It was taken to be a direct challenge to the hegemony of both the Roman Catholic Church and English laws to maintain Church rulings. Tyndale translated the New Testament into English while living in exile. His New Testament was published in part in Cologne in 1525, and in full in Worms in 1526; it was soon banned in England as heretical. Tyndale produced a revised version in 1534. In 1530, Tyndale also wrote *The Practyse of Prelates*, opposing Henry's divorce on the grounds that it contravened Scripture.

In 1535, Tyndale was arrested by imperial authorities and jailed in the castle outside Brussels for over a year. In 1536 he was convicted of heresy and executed by strangulation, after which his body was burnt at the stake. His dying request that the King of England's eyes would be opened seemed to find its fulfilment just two years later with Henry's authorisation of the 'Great Bible' for the Church of England. It was largely Tyndale's own work, and played a key role in spreading Reformation ideas. Notably, in 1611, the fifty-four independent scholars who created the King James Version, drew significantly from Tyndale, as well as translations that descended from his.

One estimate suggests the New Testament in the King James Version is 83 per cent Tyndale's work, and the Old Testament 76 per cent.

Other early Protestants, such as Richard Bayfield, James Baynham, John Frith and Thomas Bilney, met the same fate at Henry VIII's hands. It is important to note that Henry was always a Catholic, and that the holy saint Thomas More was responsible for the burning of some of the first Protestant martyrs. Thomas Hitton is generally considered to be the first English Protestant martyr of the Reformation, although some Lollard followers of John Wycliffe had been burnt at the stake in 1519. Hitton was a priest who had joined William Tyndale and other English religious exiles in the Low Countries. He returned to England on a brief visit in 1529 to contact the supporters of Tyndale and to arrange for the distribution of smuggled books. He was seized and found to be in possession of letters from the English exiles. He was then arrested on grounds of heresy, interrogated and probably tortured. Hitton believed in the supremacy of the Scriptures. He also argued that, while baptism was necessary and marriage was good, neither had to be done by a priest or in a church, and that baptism 'would be much better if it were spoken in English'. Hitton was condemned by Archbishop Warham and Bishop Fisher and burnt at the stake at Maidstone on 23 February 1530. Tyndale blamed More for Hitton's death, as More described Hitton as 'the devil's stinking martyr' and took a personal interest in the case.

Thomas Bilney (*c.* 1495–1531) was a priest who denounced saint and relic veneration, together with pilgrimages to Walsingham and Canterbury. He was orthodox as regards the power of the Pope, the sacrifice of the Mass, the doctrine of transubstantiation and the authority of the Church. However, Cardinal Wolsey was suspicious of him. In 1527, serious objection was taken to a series of sermons preached by Bilney and he was dragged from the pulpit while preaching in Ipswich, arrested and imprisoned in the Tower. He recanted and was eventually released, though banned from preaching in church. He preached openly in the fields, was arrested and was burned at Norwich.

Richard Bayfield was a Benedictine monk who was approached by the Protestant reformer Robert Barnes and given a New Testament in English. As a result he was influenced by Protestant ideas, and was therefore imprisoned and interrogated. He escaped to the Low Countries and assisted William Tyndale. Bayfield then returned to England and was active in circulating the New Testament and other prohibited books, including the works of Luther, Zwingli and Melancthon. Bayfield was discovered, imprisoned and, on the instructions of Thomas More, tortured, before being burnt at the stake at Smithfield on 4 December 1531.

In 1531, the lawyer and Protestant reformer James Baynham was accused of heresy by Thomas More, then chancellor. According to Foxe, More imprisoned and flogged him in his house at Chelsea and then sent him to the Tower to be racked, in the hope of discovering other heretics by his confession. This may be religious propaganda, however. He was interrogated because his approval of the works of Tyndale and Frith was considered sufficient cause for execution for heresy. After considerable hesitation Baynham abjured all his errors, paid a fine and performed penance by standing with a faggot on his shoulder. Within a month he repented, and openly withdrew his recantation during service. He was sentenced as a relapsed heretic and burned in Smithfield on 30 April 1532. In a conversation with Bishop Latimer, the day before his death, Baynham stated, 'I spoke also against purgatory, that there was no such thing; but that it picked men's purses; and against satisfactory masses' (i.e. against the doctrine that the Mass was an atonement or sacrifice for sins).

John Frith (1503–33) was a priest who had joined Tyndale in Antwerp, and pleaded for religious toleration. Sir Thomas More issued a warrant for Frith's arrest on a charge of heresy. Frith was sent to the Tower when he was caught trying to escape to Holland again. More would condemn Frith to death, eventually burning him at the stake. Frith was sentenced to death by fire and offered a pardon if he answered positively to two questions: do you believe in purgatory, and do you believe in transubstantiation? He replied that neither purgatory nor transubstantiation could be proven by Scripture, and thus was condemned as a heretic. Archbishop Cranmer later subscribed to Frith's views on purgatory, and published the Forty-Two Articles which explicitly denied purgatory.

Henry's marriage to Anne Boleyn in 1533 and his annulment from Catherine of Aragon was the overriding reason for the split from Rome, as described in earlier chapters, but the wise Cromwell now seized the opportunity to enrich the Crown. He began to conceive of dissolving the monasteries in about 1534, but the plan was not put into practice until 1536. Henry's government needed money, but knew it would be unpopular to demand new taxes from Parliament. Monasticism had seen a slow decline in numbers and influence. The Black Death and successive epidemics had reduced the number of monks, and travelling friars had become more influential in lay circles. When Cromwell launched his attack on the English monasteries they were poorly placed to defend themselves. Although the population of England was increasing during the sixteenth century, the number of monks and nuns was in decline from the start of the century until the Dissolution. The number of monks fell from about 12,000 to 10,000, and of nuns from 2,000 to 1,600.

Monastic houses varied greatly both in the number of monks and in their revenues. The vast landholdings of the monasteries, however, meant that in total they controlled about a half of the Church's annual income. Cromwell orchestrated a publicity campaign to make monasteries seem corrupt, with commissioners then being sent around to assess their values and report upon abuses. Pamphlets accused nuns of murdering the infants that resulted from their promiscuous lives. Henry tried to justify his actions by stating that priests and nuns had moved away from God, and therefore he had a moral right to dissolve the monasteries. At a monastic house at Bradley the prior was accused of fathering six children. At Lichfield Convent two nuns were found to be pregnant, and at Pershore Monastic House the monks were found to be drunk at Mass. At Lampley Convent, Mariana Wryte had given birth to three children and Johanna Standen to six.

In 1536, Parliament passed an Act dissolving all monasteries with an income of less than £200 per annum. The members of minor monasteries were allowed to move to the larger ones. The only real protest in England against what Henry was doing came in 1536 with the Pilgrimage of Grace. This was led by Robert Aske, a lawyer. Aske, along with several thousands of others, marched to London. Henry promised to look into their complaints and many of the protesters went home satisfied with this. Aske was arrested and hung in chains until he died of starvation. There was little resistance, as local nobles and gentry grew rich from purchasing from the Crown at cheap rates, confiscated valuables and estates. Thus in 1539, another Act was passed dissolving the larger monasteries also. The last English monastery, Waltham Abbey, was closed in 1540.

The immediate effect of the Dissolution of the Monasteries was to transfer vast tracts of land to the Crown. Monastic lands were worth at least three times as much as existing royal landholdings. Henry also acquired vast amounts of gold and silver plate, worth as much as £1 million. The Crown also acquired the monasteries' right to collect tithes (support from the parish to its priest) which had been taken over by the monasteries in exchange for them paying the priest a wage instead. Many monasteries had also held the right to choose which person should become priest of a parish. This right of presenting to a church living was known as an advowson, and about two in five English advowsons were controlled by monasteries. All these fell to the Crown, making it an overwhelmingly powerful patron. The seizure of monastic land gave the Crown the possibility of complete financial independence. Not only the Crown gained by the Dissolution, as many royal administrators and clients gained. The Dissolution involved physical destruction: buildings decayed because the lead was seized from the roofs and libraries were broken up and sold off. Moreover, traditional charitable functions of feeding and housing travellers ceased, leading to the rise of inns offering rooms to travellers. Henry VIII promised to found thirteen new bishoprics on the proceeds from the Dissolution, but only nine were actually created. Henry VIII did found a number of schools and Trinity College, Cambridge, but on balance charity and education suffered for some time afterwards.

Had Henry VIII exploited his massive new incomes, he and his successors might never have needed to call Parliament again. However, from the very beginning, and particularly between 1543 and 1547, Henry sold most of the land to pay for extravagant wars with France and Scotland. The land was bought by merchants, yeomen syndicates and noblemen, but mainly by neighbouring gentry families. Nobles and gentlemen also bought the impropriated tithes and advowsons, and so strengthened their hand in parish affairs. The enrichment of the gentry increased their power and independence relative to both Church and Crown. It also created a powerful pressure group with a vested interest in ensuring that the old Roman Catholic Church was never fully restored.

In 1536 the Ten Articles were issued, sufficiently indefinite and ambiguous to be acceptable to the growing Lutheran community but not so far enough removed from Catholic dogma to alienate Henry. The Thirteen Articles of 1538 were similarly unclear. In 1538, injunctions urged priests to educate their flocks and to keep efficient parish registers, and also commanded the destruction of 'superstitious' images. Cromwell and Cranmer persuaded the king to allow the publication in England of a vernacular Bible. The project came to fruition in Matthew's Bible of 1537. In 1539, it was revised and reissued as the Great Bible. In May 1541, a royal proclamation ordered every parish to comply with Cromwell's instructions and have a copy of the Bible for public use before Ash Wednesday 1541. Henry grew increasingly concerned about the social and political consequences of allowing the lower orders to read the Bible, but his attempts to limit access were ineffectual. In 1539, Henry's fear of invasion by France or the Holy Roman Empire decreased, and with it his desire for good relations with the Lutheran princes. He ensured that Parliament passed the Act of Six Articles, a conservative document that endorsed transubstantiation and clerical celibacy.

The year 1540 demonstrates the religious uncertainty and turmoil of the time. Robert Barnes (1495–1540) had given an openly evangelical sermon proclaiming the gospel and accusing the Church of its heresies in 1525, now sometimes considered to be the first sermon of the English Reformation. Barnes was examined by Wolsey and four other bishops. He was condemned to abjure or be burnt, and took the former option. Barnes escaped to Antwerp in 1528, and met Martin Luther in Wittenberg. In 1531 Barnes returned to England, and in 1535 he was sent to Germany, in the hope of inducing Lutheran divines to approve of Henry's divorce from Catherine of Aragon. In 1539 he was employed in negotiations connected with Anne of Cleves' marriage, but was one of six men executed on 30 July 1540. The Protestants Barnes, William Jerome and Thomas Gerard were burnt for heresy under the Six Articles, whereas the Catholics Thomas Abel, Richard Fetherstone and Edward Powell were hanged, drawn and quartered for treason in denying the Royal Supremacy. Protestants and Catholics in England and on the Continent were shocked.

Becoming more unhealthy and concerned with his afterlife, Henry kept trying to stem the tide of Protestantism. The Bishops' Book was altered to express far more conservative, Catholic doctrine (and this revised version indeed became known as the King's Book). Henry showed a real fear of the social change that Protestant ideas might provoke, and in 1543 again tried to prevent those below the rank of gentry from reading the Bible. In his speech to Parliament of December 1545, Henry complained that he was 'sorry to know and hear how unreverently that most precious jewel, the word of God is disputed, rhymed, sung and jangled in every alehouse and tavern'. Despite his Catholicism, Henry continued to protect major Protestants such as Archbishop Cranmer. Within the English court, the Protestant cause was strongly supported first by Thomas Cromwell and later by Catherine Parr.

Tudor Belief, Superstitions and Assorted Religious Trivia

Hell Must Be a Star

In 1563, Johann Weyer's *Pseudomonarchia Daemonum* was published and accepted across Europe, laying out the constitutional arrangements of Hell. The Emperor of the Demons is Beelzebub, founder of the Order of the Fly. He has deposed Satan, who leads the opposition. Among the great princes of Hell are Moloch, Prince of the Country of Tears and member of the Imperial Council of State; Pluto, Prince of Fire and Superintendent of Punishments; Leonard, Grand Master of the Sabbaths and Inspector-General of Magic and Sorcery; Proserpine, Archduchess of Hades and Sovereign Princess of the Evil Spirits; and Eurynome, Prince of Death. The responsibilities of the minsters of state are outlined, along with lists of the households of the princes and Hell's ambassadors to England, France, Russia, Spain, Turkey, Italy and Switzerland. Excluding Hell's residents, the poor souls sent there for not being Christian enough – that is, not paying the Church enough – are organised into 6,666 legions. Each legion has 6,666 demons, making a total of 44,435,556 demons and hundreds of millions of sinners being perpetually burnt in the fiery flames. One can only come to the modern conclusion that Hell is a star.

The Cleverest Pope

An impoverished pig dealer had a son, Felice Peretti di Montalto, born in 1521. When the boy had become a poor friar, it is said that Nostradamus knelt at his feet, kissed his robe and exclaimed he was kissing the robe of the future Pope. Coming to favour under two popes, di Montalto was an unpopular Inquisitor-General in Venice, and became a cardinal. Prior to the papal election in 1585 he gave the appearance of sickliness and imbecility. Many other cardinals voted for him as they thought they could control him, or that he would not live long and they could plan to succeed him. However, upon being elected, he called himself Sixtus V, threw away his walking sticks and declared that he was seven years younger than he had previously told them, being sixty-four instead of seventy-one. For the five years until his death, he ruled sternly. Sixtus entertained fantastic ambitions, such as the annihilation of the Turks, the conquest of Egypt, the transport of the Holy Sepulchre to Italy, and the accession of his nephew to the throne of France. Sixtus agreed to renew the excommunication of Elizabeth I and to grant a large subsidy to the Philip II's Armada, but would give nothing until the expedition actually landed in England. This way, he saved a fortune that would otherwise have been lost in the failed campaign.

How Constipation Changed the World

Upon 31 October 1517, Martin Luther nailed his Ninety-Five Theses to the door of Wittenberg's castle church. These writings theologically and theoretically underpinned the Protestant Reformation that was to sweep across northern Europe. Luther was a chronic sufferer of haemorrhoids and constipation. He stated that he had come to his radical and world-changing conclusion that salvation is granted through faith, not deeds, while for some time '*in cloaca*'. This means sitting upon a lavatory.

What's Black, White, Grey, Blue and Crutched?

Of the monastic orders, Carthusian monks (and nuns) of the Order of St Bruno lived in silence in cloistered cells like hermits. Living their lives in prayer and silence, their food was passed to them without seeing the bearer. The Cluniac monastic order had thirty-three priories in England and Wales, and its monks did not 'begrime' themselves with physical labour, as the Benedictines were supposed to. The Benedictines, or 'Black Monks' from the colour of their gowns, were the most powerful order, and were probably the most lax in their observance of godliness. The Cistercian order, or Bernadines or 'White Monks', had a white choir robe, and were generally well respected for their work with the people. As well as these monastic orders, based in priories, abbeys, monasteries, convents and the like, there was the military order of the Hospital of St John of Jerusalem, the Knights Hospitallers, suppressed in 1540.

Canons were different to monks in that they followed the teachings of St Augustine of Hippo. They included the Premonstratensians (White Canons) and the Augustinian canons, also known as Austin Canons and Black Austins. The Grandmontine Canons only had three cells for hermits in England, and the Gilbertines, following the Order of St Gilbert at Sempringham, is the only monastic order to be founded in England. Founded in 1130, it allowed monks and nuns to live in a double monastery and worship in the same church. They wore a habit of a black cassock with a white hood and scapular, so that when God viewed them from above, they would appear as a white cross on a black background. The few Crosier Canons in England wore the opposite, appearing as a black cross on a white background. Presumably the Lord then knew whom to miss with his lightning bolts.

Finally, there were the 'mendicant orders', friars who, unlike monks, went out and preached to rich and poor alike. They gave up everything they owned, took a vow of chastity and abstinence and could roam across the country, living on alms and handouts. Some stumbled under the weight of a cross, which they set up to preach near. Often they returned to their friary, priory or hospital to sleep. There were Austin Friars, Franciscans (Grey Friars, or Friars Minor), Dominicans (Black Friars or Friars Preacher) and Carmelites (White Friars). The Friars of the Holy Cross were known as Crutched Friars, Brethren of the Holy Cross, Crossed Friars or Crouched Friars because of the red cross on their blue robes.

Secreted with the Excreted

In 1553, with Mary I's accession, Protestants were forced into subterfuges to conceal their faith. Benjamin Franklin's great-grandfather concealed his family's English Bible by fastening it to the inside of a 'close stool'. This was the wooden cabinet used to enclose a covered chamber pot, which was emptied when full. Franklin wrote that 'one of the children was stationed at the door to give notice if he saw an officer of the Spiritual Court make his appearance; in that case the lid was restored to its place, with the Bible concealed under it as before'.

The Best Bloody Mary

Ferdinand Petiot, bartender at Harry's New York Bar in Paris, mixed vodka and tomato juice in 1920. The American entertainer Roy Barton gave it the name 'bucket of blood' after the club in Chicago. There was also a tavern called the Bucket of Blood in Cardiff's Tiger Bay docks area, as well as one called the House of Blazes. Petiot later spiced up his cocktail with the addition of pepper, salt, lemon and Worcester sauce and called it 'the red snapper'. Popular in the 1930s as 'the Queen of Drinks', it then became known as a Bloody Mary, in regard to Mary I's epithet.

'Bilious' Bale's Magic Members

In 1534, Bishop John Bale, known as 'Bilious' Bale, was preaching against the cult of St Walstan. Walstan's holy well at Bawburgh near Norwich was a place of pilgrimage for farmers and farm labourers who sought a blessing on themselves and their animals, particularly regarding fertility. Bale damned St Walstan in his sermons as a version of the Roman god Priapus, who was rather well endowed in depiction and writing. He claimed that men and beasts 'which had lost their Privy Parts', upon visiting the shrine 'had newe Members restored to them, by this Walstane'. Instead of ridding East Anglia of the superstition, this had the opposite effect as men flocked to the shrine to restore their privy parts to full working order.

Holy Relics

Religious houses used a variety of relics and images to gain incomes from pilgrims. The oldest Benedictine houses in England all possessed a multiplicity of relics from long before the Norman Conquest until their dissolution. In many cases these were the entire bodies of saints, for instance at Christ Church, Canterbury, the bodies of Saints Alphege (d. 1012; translated to Canterbury in 1023) and Dunstan (d. 988) in tombs near the high altar. St Winifred's finger was at Holywell and the rest of her bones at Shrewsbury. Nearly every reliquary in England in the 1530s was taken to be destroyed. The Crown's commissioners visiting each holy place had two reasons for seeking out relics. The first was the Protestant objection to the intercessory role ascribed to saints. The second was the precious metal, marble and gems comprising the reliquaries. Throughout the Middle Ages Europe had hosted a thriving trade in holy relics, the vast majority being counterfeit. The sixteenth-century Protestant reformer John Calvin, who believed the veneration of relics to be a form of false worship, commented that if all the relics were brought together in one place 'it would be made manifest that every Apostle has more than four bodies, and every Saint two or three'.

One church displayed the brain of St Peter until it was accidentally moved and revealed to be a piece of pumice stone. Relics of Jesus or the Virgin Mary were extremely valuable and included the milk of the Virgin Mary, the baby teeth, hair and blood of Christ, pieces of the Cross and samples of the linen Christ was wrapped in as an infant. Their real value of relics lay in their ability to perform miracles. A relic that was an acknowledged fake could become 'real' if it performed a miracle. The European faithful regularly made pilgrimages over hundreds of miles to visit the most powerful relics. This pilgrimage traffic had an enormous impact on local economies, leading towns to go to extreme lengths to obtain the relics that would draw the most pilgrims.

Patrick Geary in *Furta Sacra: Thefts of Relics in the Central Middle Ages* wrote that towns were usually reluctant to simply buy or trade relics. No one would sell a 'miracle-performing' relic unless it no longer possessed its powers. Instead, towns often stole the relics they desired. Geary relates that the Italian town of Bari in 1087 commissioned a team of thieves to obtain the remains of Saint Nicolas from the Turkish town of Myra. The expedition was a success, and for decades Bari made money in the glory of being the town that owned the stolen bones of Santa Claus.

Henry VIII began his reign as a devotee of traditional Catholic piety, even visiting the shrine of the Virgin at Walsingham Abbey in Norfolk. However, in 1541, the king ordered that all saints' shrines should be destroyed. Their bodies were no longer to be venerated and instead buried in common graves. Soon afterwards, the remains of St Cuthbert at Durham Cathedral were extracted from their beautiful shrine. Finding the body incorrupt 900 years after the saint had died, the king's agents hesitated, as they knew incorruptibility was a sign of sanctity. They dumped the corpse in the cloister and sent to London for instructions. Word came back that the shrine should be levelled and the saint reburied under the floor of the cathedral in the same spot. By this time, the saint had been exposed to the elements for a few weeks and was incorrupt no longer. The bones were buried as instructed.

In the reign of Edward VI, almost all remaining religious art in the country was lost. A few wall paintings and painted screens survive, but of the images of Christ crucified that were mounted in the chancel of every parish church, not a single one remains. The English destroyed almost their entire artistic tradition and then suppressed their memory of it. Today, medieval alabaster sculptures hold places of honour in museums across Europe and North America, but few of us recognise them as products of the Midlands.

Two Heads

There is the tale of a traveller to France who, around 1500, visited a monastery which possessed the skull of St John the Baptist. Such pilgrims, of course, were supposed to give alms to the possessors of such relics. The traveller said he had been shown the skull at another monastery. A monk replied that the other foundation had the skull of the saint when he was a young man, whereas 'ours was his skull when he was an older and wiser man'.

The Holy Prepuce and Henry VII

All Jewish boys are required to be circumcised on the eighth day following their birth, and Christ's foreskin began appearing in Europe during the Middle

Ages. The earliest recording came on 25 December 800, when Charlemagne gave it to Pope Leo III when the latter crowned Charles Holy Roman Emperor. Charlemagne claimed that it had been brought to him by an angel while he prayed at the Holy Sepulchre, but it was reported as being a wedding gift from the Byzantine Empress Irene. Its authenticity was later considered to be confirmed by a vision of Saint Bridget of Sweden, but the foreskin was looted during the Sack of Rome in 1527. The German soldier who stole it was captured in the village of Calcata, fifty-five miles north of Rome, and hid the jewelled reliquary in his cell, where it was rediscovered in 1557. Many miracles are claimed to have followed, and it was venerated from that time onwards, with the Church approving its authenticity by offering a ten-year indulgence from sins to all pilgrims. The foreskin was reported stolen by a local priest in 1983. According to David Farley, 'Depending on what you read, there were eight, twelve, fourteen, or even eighteen different holy foreskins in various European towns during the Middle Ages.' Apart from the one in Rome and then Calcata, they were revered in Santiago de Compostela, Antwerp, Le Puy-en-Velay, Coulombs, Chartres, Besançon, Metz, Hildesheim, Charroux, Conques, Langres, Fécamp, Stoke-on-Trent and there were two in Auvergne. The Antwerp prepuce was a gift in 1100 from Baldwin I of Jerusalem, who had bought it in Palestine during the First Crusade. It achieved great fame when the Bishop of Cambrai, during Mass, saw three drops of blood blotting the linens of the altar. A special chapel was constructed which became the goal of pilgrimages. The relic disappeared in 1566, but the chapel still exists, decorated by two stained-glass windows donated by Henry VII and Elizabeth of York in 1503.

Duck Worship

Upon Christmas Eve 1536, Hailes Abbey in Gloucester was dissolved. Henry VIII's commissioners declared that its great relic, a phial of the 'Holy Blood' that drew great incomes from pilgrims, contained the blood of a duck. It was regularly refilled to prevent its congealing.

Pope Alexander VI, Roderic Llançol i de Borja (1431–1503)

Popes were not expected to be perfect, but medieval popes were among the worst examples of Christianity in the world. Basically a syphilitic, greedy sex maniac, a poisoner and a murderer, this particular Borgia became a byword for the debased standards of the papacy of his times. The Spaniard had bribed his way to the papacy and as early as 1460, when he was a cardinal, he had been reported to Pius II for holding obscene dances with naked ladies in a garden at Siena. From the official diary of German chaplain Johann Burchard, Alexander's master of ceremonies, we learn that 'the pope's Christianity was a pretence'. Alexander had at least twelve bastard children, including Cesare, Giovanni, Lucrezia and Jofre, and his numerous mistresses ensured the 'Vatican was again a brothel'

> On Sunday evening, 30 October [1501], Don Cesare Borja gave his father a supper in the apostolic palace, with 50 decent prostitutes or courtesans

> in bright garb in attendance, who after the meal danced with the servants and others there, first fully dressed and then naked ... Following the supper, lampstands holding lighted candles were placed on the floor and chestnuts strewn about, which the prostitutes, naked and on their hands and knees, had to pick up with their mouths as they crawled in and out among the lampstands ... The Pope watched and admired their noble parts. The evening ended with an obscene contest of these women, coupled with male servants of the Vatican, for prizes which the Pope presented. Don Cesare, Donna Lucrezia and the Pope later each took a partner of their liking for further dalliances.

A later pope, Julius II, was forced to flee Italy to avoid assassination attempts ordered by Pope Alexander VI, and stayed in exile for ten years before Borgia's death made it possible for him to return.

29
Witchcraft and Ghosts

Tudor Witchcraft and Sorcery

British attitudes to witchcraft were generally less extreme than those of contemporary Europeans. This produced characters such as the village 'cunning woman', with healing skills, who could be burnt at the stake in places like Denmark or Germany, but also the eccentric gentleman with a library of arcane tomes whose 'experiments' were considered scientific rather than supernatural. Acceptance was not universal, however, and those who attracted the attention of the witchfinder, or even the Inquisition under Mary I's reign, could end up on trial for their lives.

Whereas the Europeans burnt or even boiled their witches alive, the more usual sentence for a British witch was death by hanging. Witches came to trial for crimes such as inflicting death or disease on livestock and humans, souring milk or causing miscarriage and cursing and hurting children. Under torture, the European witch typically confessed to having intercourse with the Devil and suckling demons at her breast. The British witch usually kept a familiar, a cat, dog or toad, which spoke with her and often suckled too, leaving a distinct mark. The accused would be stripped and searched for such tell-tale marks, then tortured to extract a 'confession'. In July 1589, three 'notorious witches' were hanged at Chelmsford, Essex; one of them, Joan Prentice, was later depicted as having suckled familiars, including two rat-like ferrets named 'Jack' and 'Jill'. The discovery of a birthmark or extra nipple was therefore a key factor in determining a witch's guilt, with or without a confession. Attitudes hardened after Elizabeth I's statute of 1563, enforcing the death sentence for the practice of witchcraft. However, it was not until after James I came to the throne in 1603, with his treatise *Daemonologie* and his fear of the supernatural, that the witch-hunting craze in England really took off.

In England, the first Act of Parliament directed specifically against witchcraft was the *De heretico comburendo*, passed at the instigation of Archbishop Thomas Arundel in 1401. It specifically named witchcraft or sorcery as a species of heresy, and provided that, unless the accused witches abjured these beliefs, they were to be burnt at the stake. Elizabeth I in 1563 made witchcraft a felony, removing the accused witches from the jurisdiction of the ecclesiastical courts to the courts of common law. In central Europe, torture inflicted on heretics suspected of magical pacts or demon-driven sexual misconduct led to some alarming confessions, where defendants admitted to flying on poles and animals to attend assemblies presided over by Satan, who usually appeared in the form of a goat or other animal. Some defendants told investigators that they repeatedly kissed Satan's anus as a display of their loyalty, while others admitted to casting spells on neighbours, having sex with animals, or causing storms.

In his papal bull of 1484, Pope Innocent VIII claimed that German Satanists were meeting with demons, casting spells that destroyed crops and aborting infants, and he complained that the clergy were not taking the 'threat' of witchcraft seriously enough. He asked two inquisitors of the Catholic Church to publish a full report on the suspected witchcraft, and in 1486 the friars published *Malleus Maleficarum* (*The Hammer of Witches*), which put to rest the old orthodoxy that witches were powerless in the face of God, and established a new orthodoxy which held that Christians had an obligation to hunt down and kill them. Much of the book offered hints to judges and prosecutors, such as the suggestion to strip each suspect completely and look for a mole, and to have the defendants brought into court backwards to minimise their opportunities to cast dangerous spells on officials. Barbaric torture techniques, and execution by burning, hanging, pressing or drowning became common. In the early sixteenth century, outbreaks of witchcraft hysteria, with subsequent mass executions, began to appear. In 1515, the authorities in Geneva burned 500 accused witches at the stake; in 1526, in Como, Italy, spreading of witchcraft charges led to as many as 1,000 executions; witch hysteria swept France in 1571 after claims were made of over 100,000 witches roaming the country.

Jean Bodin's 1580 book *On the Demon-Mania of Sorcerers* opened the door to the use of testimony by children against parents, entrapment and instruments of torture. Germany saw Europe's greatest execution rates of witches, higher than those in the rest of Europe combined. Over the 160 years from 1500 to 1660, an estimated 50,000–80,000 suspected witches were executed (about 80 per cent of them women), including about 26,000 in Germany and about 10,000 in France. England executed significantly less than 1,000 during the main period of the witch craze, and Ireland just four, due in part to better procedural safeguards for defendants in those countries. However, many more were tried and condemned in Scotland (one estimate giving as many as 4,400 executions overall), which followed the Continental, inquisitorial model. At one point it was not even considered necessary to obtain a confession before conviction and execution in Scotland, a general reputation as a witch being sufficient proof for an indictment and conviction.

The Witch with Three Breasts

Anne Boleyn was beheaded on 19 May 1536, having been accused of adultery, incest and witchcraft. In support of the witchcraft charge, Henry VIII's second wife was said to have not only eleven fingers but also three breasts. Her 'third nipple', supposedly for suckling the Devil, was a mole on her neck.

Mother Shipton's Mother

Agatha Southeil (*c.* 1470–88) died very young, soon after giving birth to a daughter, Ursula Southeil (later known as Mother Shipton), in a cave near Knaresborough now known as Mother Shipton's Cave. She was widely regarded as a witch, mainly due to her status as a social outcast and due to her deformed and hideously ugly child. Southeil was probably an orphan of 'slothful and idle' tendencies, subject to the scorn and derision of local women for her loose morals. While she was pregnant, she may have been tried as a common prostitute. She was expecting a child at the age of fifteen, outside wedlock, and was so victimised that she fled to a cave by the Dropping Well at Knaresborough, on the opposite bank of the River Nidd, to give birth. The petrifying property of the water that runs down the cliff into the well made this a secret place that was regarded with fear by the superstitious. It was believed that Agatha's hideously ugly child was sired by the Devil.

Mother Shipton (c. 1488–1561)

This soothsayer, prophetess and supposed witch supposedly made dozens of unusually accurate predictions, including the Great Plague of London, the Spanish Armada and the Great Fire of London. Ursula Southeil was reputedly born grotesquely deformed and hideously ugly, but was nevertheless taken in by a kindly townswoman. Her head was too large, her 'goggling' eyes glowed like embers, her cheeks were sunken, her limbs were twisted and ill formed, and she was born with a full set of teeth which protruded like the tusks of a boar. According to local accounts she was referred to as 'Hag-Face' and 'Devil's Bastard' as she grew up, and it was believed by many that the father of such an ugly child must be the Devil himself. However, neither her growing reputation as a witch nor her worsening appearance deterred a York carpenter and builder named Toby Shipton from marrying her in 1512. Her early forecasts were to do with local people and events, and people travelled to Knaresborough from some distance around to consult her. She was particularly successful in solving commonplace interpersonal disputes, and it was recorded that under her influence thieves would publicly return stolen goods (apologising to the astonished owners for their sin), wandering husbands would beg forgiveness and mend their ways and corrupt officials would make spontaneous acts of restitution.

But, as time passed, her prophecies became more ambitious and began to relate to the country as a whole, including prominent figures at the court of Henry VIII. For example, she was said to have predicted that Cardinal Wolsey (the 'Mitred Peacock') would see York, but never reach it. The most notable book of her prophecies, edited by Richard Head, was first published in 1684, and Head later admitted to having invented almost all of Shipton's biographical details. Despite the disproofs of many of her prophesies, she was both feared and revered in her own time, and has been remembered by many over the centuries as England's greatest prophetess.

Witch Trials

There were 270 Elizabethan witch trials, of which 247 involved women and only 23 dealt with men. A common witch-hunting method was 'swimming' or 'ducking', based on the ancient 'ordeal by water', whereby the accused was tied hand and foot and immersed in deep water. If the accused witch floated, the water (God's creature) had rejected her and she was deemed guilty. If she sank (and drowned), she was deemed innocent. Sometimes villagers might tie a rope to the woman to pull her in if she sank. 'Pricking' was when the accused was pricked all over with a sharp instrument in the search for insensitive spots where the Devil had (visibly or invisibly) marked them. Torture was routinely used to elicit confessions and accusations against accomplices, including the use of thumbscrews, leg vices, whipping stocks with iron spikes, scalding lime baths, prayer stools furnished with sharp pegs, racks and the strappado (hoisting on a pulley to pull the arms from the sockets). An Elizabethan statute of 1563 ordered that witches were prosecuted under civil, rather than ecclesiastical, law, so were always hanged (usually after torture) in England and Wales, rather than burnt as was the case across the rest of Europe.

The Chelmsford Witches Trial, 1566

The first statute against witchcraft was passed by Parliament in 1542, towards the end of Henry VIII's reign, but revoked in 1547. The first major trial under Elizabeth I's 1563 witchcraft law, which ordered the death penalty for witches, enchanters and sorcerers, was at Chelmsford in Essex in 1566. Charges were made against Elizabeth Francis, Agnes Waterhouse and Agnes' daughter Joan. Elizabeth Francis had allegedly bewitched a child, and her 'confession' makes interesting reading. She stated that she learned witchcraft from her grandmother, aged twelve. Her grandmother taught her to renounce God and gave her a white spotted cat named Sathan, who was the Devil in animal form. Elizabeth fed it with her own blood, plus the more traditional bread and milk, and learned to converse with Sathan. The cat promised, in a hollow voice, that she would be rich. Sathan brought her livestock and promised that one Andrew Byles would marry her. She became pregnant but Byles refused to marry her, and Sathan killed him and taught Elizabeth how to abort the child. Elizabeth then married and had a daughter that annoyed her, so Sathan killed the girl. After sixteen years of enjoying the Devil's favours, she exchanged him for a cake from Agnes Waterhouse. Agnes wished to use the wool lining Sathan's box, and he subsequently turned into a toad. Sathan now helped Agnes kill geese, drown cows and spoil butter to the distress of the community. She fed the toad with her own blood by pricking her body. Blemishes upon the women's bodies when they were stripped proved this had occurred. Agnes was hanged in 1566, and her daughter Joan acquitted. Elizabeth Francis received a lighter sentence but was hanged after a second conviction thirteen years later.

The Essex Trials of 1579 and 1589

At the Essex Assizes in 1579, several women were arraigned for witchcraft. Ellen Smythe's daughter had an argument with a child named Susan Webbe. Ellen gave Susan a clip across the head, and Susan died two days later. Directly after Susan's death, her mother saw 'a thing like a black dog go out of her door'. A black dog was said to be the Devil's 'familiar', so Ellen Smythe was hanged. Margery Stanton was acquitted of making cattle give blood instead of milk, causing a woman to swell up as if pregnant and using magic to kill chickens. In 1589, Jane Prentice was charged because she saw the Devil in the form of a 'dunnish-coloured ferret', while sitting in her chamber. The ferret said, 'Jane Prentice, give me thy soul,' to which she answered, 'In the name of God, what art thou?' The ferret answered, 'I am Satan. Fear me not.' She was hanged.

The Witches of Warboys Trial, 1589–93

The accusation, trial and execution for witchcraft of Alice Samuel and her family in the village of Warboys occurred between 1589 and 1593. The first allegations were made in November 1589 by Jane Throckmorton, the ten-year-old daughter of Robert Throckmorton, the squire of Warboys, when she started suffering from fits. She accused the seventy-six-year-old Alice Samuel of being the cause, and this was soon echoed by Jane's four sisters and some household servants who began exhibiting similar symptoms. The squire was a close friend of Sir Henry Cromwell, one of the wealthiest commoners in England, and when Lady Cromwell came to visit in March 1590 she also accused Alice Samuel of being a witch. Lady Cromwell reportedly grabbed a pair of scissors and cut a lock of hair off Alice Samuel, and gave it to Mrs Throckmorton to burn, a folk remedy believed to weaken a witch's power. That night, Lady Cromwell had nightmares and became ill; she later died, in 1592. The local parson persuaded Alice to confess to witchcraft in 1592, but she recanted the very next day. However, she confessed again when brought before the Bishop of Lincoln, and was taken to Huntingdon where she was imprisoned with her daughter, Agnes, and her husband, John. All three were tried in April 1593 for the murder by witchcraft of Lady Cromwell. Alice's words to Lady Cromwell – 'Madam, why do you use me thus? I never did you any harm as yet' – were used against her at the trial, with 'as yet' being construed as a threat. All three were found guilty and hanged.

Ghosts

Anne Boleyn's ghost has been seen several times at places associated with her. At Blickling Hall, Norfolk, her ghost is said to appear on the anniversary of her execution. Dressed in white and carrying her severed head, she arrives in a coach driven by four headless horses and coachmen. The coach steadily drives up the driveway of Blickling Hall. Upon reaching the front door the coach and drivers vanish, just leaving Anne. She then glides into the hall, where she wanders the rooms until daybreak. Anne's father, Thomas Boleyn, is another spirit at Blickling; Boleyn lost not only a daughter but his only son to execution. It is said that Thomas Boleyn was given a penance after his death in 1539, a task he is required to perform every year for a thousand years. He has to try to cross twelve bridges before cockcrow, which involves going from Blickling to Aylsham, Burg, Buxton, Coltishal and on to Wroxham. Like his daughter he is headless, and again the headless horses are attached to his coach. He too carries his head underneath his arm, but flames rush from his mouth instead of blood.

Anne has been seen standing in the window of the Dean's Cloister at Windsor Castle, and has also been seen at Windsor, running screaming down a corridor, sometimes clutching her head. She has been seen headless at Hampton Court Palace, wearing a blue or black dress. In the Tower of London, a Captain of the Guard saw a light flickering in the Chapel Royal, which had been locked up for the night. To find out what was causing the light, he climbed up a ladder and saw inside a procession in progress, including lords and ladies wearing old clothes. At the head of the procession was a woman whose face the guard never saw but whose clothes he recognised from one of the portraits of the beheaded queen. Then the procession disappeared. Anne Boleyn's ghost has also been seen walking from the queen's house in the Tower of London to the chapel of St Peter ad Vincula and to her grave. The most famous sighting was in 1864, when Major-General J. D. Dundas of the 60th Rifles was quartered in the Tower of London. As he was looking out of the window of his quarters he noticed a guard below in the courtyard, in front of the lodgings where Anne had been imprisoned, behaving strangely. He appeared to challenge something, which to the general 'looked like a whitish, female figure sliding towards the soldier'. The guard charged through the form with his bayonet, then fainted.

Only the general's testimony and corroboration at the court-martial saved the guard from a lengthy prison sentence for having fainted while on duty. In 1960, Canon William Sandford Pakenham-Walsh (1868–1960), Vicar of Sulgrave in Northamptonshire, reported having conversations with Anne. The canon died in that year, having written in his diary that he had for thirty years been in communication with Henry VIII and Anne. Her ghost still visits her childhood home at Hever Castle, where she is seen walking across the bridge over the River Eden. She also appears under the oak where she was courted by Henry VIII.

Catherine Howard was accused of adultery and stripped of her title of queen consort in November 1541. Afterwards, she was confined to her chambers at Hampton Court Palace under house arrest. Catherine was able to escape her rooms and crept down the Long Hall to find the king in order to beg for mercy. The guards found her before she reached him, and they dragged her, screaming, back to her room.

Since 1918, when the Long Gallery has been open to visitors, it has been better known as 'the Haunted Gallery' because the spirit of Catherine is said to walk across the gallery in the direction of the Royal Pew, where Henry was at prayer the night she was looking for him. Then, abruptly, the figure stops, and rushes backwards, screeching. Some visitors of the gallery today still report feeling cold, dizzy or unwell in the gallery. In 2000, two female visitors fainted in the same area of the gallery one hour apart.

At Hampton Court, Queen Jane Seymour's ghost was said to be seen nightly, near the stairway leading to apartments formerly occupied by her. She died of post-natal complications twelve days after giving birth to her only child, Edward VI, in 1537. Her spirit has been reported wandering around Hampton Court Palace, the place where she died. She has been seen in the Silver Stick gallery, the Clock Court and walking down a staircase. Her spirit wears a white gown and carries a candle, and it is thought that she is looking for the son she never came to know. Others say she is trying to find her son to protect him from her brothers. Sightings are most frequent on the anniversary of Edward's birth.

The ghost of Catherine of Aragon has been seen wandering the halls and Queen's Chamber of Kimbolton Castle in Cambridgeshire, where she spent the last years of her life. Her ghost has been observed, apparently unaware of the changes made to the level of the flooring since her time, walking with her legs and lower half descended from the ceiling on one floor and as a head and upper body slowly drifting on the next floor above.

The ghost of Henry VIII's last wife, Catherine Parr, has been seen roaming Sudeley Castle, where she died due to complications from childbirth in 1548. Her ghost is described as a woman dressed in green, seeming to be searching for someone or something, perhaps her only daughter Mary, rumoured to have died as a young child. Catherine's ghost has also been reported at Snape Castle, where she has been seen wearing a blue dress and fills the rooms with an overwhelming sense of calm and peace when her apparition is near.

The Countess of Salisbury, at seventy-two years of age, was the last of the Plantagenets. Her son, Cardinal Pole, had vilified the king's claim as head of the Church of England. However, he was safely hidden in France, so Henry had his mother brought to the block on 27 May 1541. When told by the executioner to kneel, the spirited old lady flatly refused. The executioner raised his axe, taking a swing at her, and she ran in hysterics, pursued by him with his axe in hand. He hacked at her until he had hewn the countess to death. Her screaming phantom continues to be chased throughout eternity by a ghostly executioner. Also, the shadow of a great axe has been witnessed falling across the scene of her murder.

The Tower was home to the Royal Menagerie; lions, leopards, bears, birds, monkeys, and an elephant – a present from the King of France – were kept on display. Rumours persist of acts of abuse against some of the animals, as there have been sounds of animals coming through the brickwork. This could be down to what is known as the 'stone tape theory', where the atmosphere records sounds of the past.

One midnight in January 1815, a sentry heard a low growl behind him. Turning, he witnessed a bear from this menagerie come from a doorway. Lunging at it with his bayonet, his blade passed right through the apparition and embedded itself in the door, and the phantom immediately vanished. The sentry was later found unconscious; it is said he died of fright within two months of this encounter. It is also said that dogs will not enter the Salt Tower, and since one of the Yeoman Warders was nearly strangled by an unseen presence, no one will go inside after dark.

Lady Jane Grey's ghost was last seen at the Tower by two guardsmen on 12 February 1957, the 403rd anniversary of her execution. She was described as a 'white shape shaping itself on the battlements'. Her husband, Guildford Dudley, has been seen in Beauchamp Tower, sobbing. At Temple Newsam, one of her residences, the ghost known as 'the White Lady' is said to be the ghost of the nine-day queen.

30

Heroes and Heroines

Saint John Fisher (1469–1535)

He was one of the very few men who stood up to Henry VIII. Erasmus said of John Fisher that 'he is the one man at this time who is incomparable for uprightness of life, for learning and for greatness of soul'. Fisher was chaplain to Margaret Beaufort, the mother of Henry VII, and Chancellor of Cambridge University (for life) before being elevated to the bishopric of Rochester in 1504, at the personal insistence of Henry VII. Rochester was then the poorest diocese in England and was usually seen as a first step on an ecclesiastical career, but the gifted Fisher stayed there, presumably by his own choice, for the remaining thirty-one years of his life. At this time he is also said to have acted as tutor to Prince Henry, afterwards Henry VIII. Fisher's reputation as a preacher was so great that he was appointed to preach the funeral oration for both Henry VII and Lady Margaret Beaufort, both of whom died in 1509. He counted Thomas More among his friends and was respected for his learning and piety.

John Fisher strongly opposed the divorce between Henry VIII and Catherine of Aragon and the constitution of the so-called Anglican Church. Henry VIII and Cardinal Wolsey had gone to Fisher when they first came up with the idea of annulling the king's marriage. Fisher was widely respected across Europe as a theologian after publishing works decrying Luther's movement to reform the Catholic Church. However, when Henry and Wolsey approached him for advice, he was clear that an annulment would go against the will of God. They proceeded anyway, and Fisher never relented in his opposition. He openly defended Catherine, making great trouble for Henry. When the Supremacy Act passed in 1534, Fisher, with Sir Thomas More at his side, refused to take the required oath because it was a repudiation of papal authority.

Because Fisher refused to swear an oath affirming the supremacy of Henry VIII as Supreme Head of the Church of England, he was imprisoned in the Tower of London. He was to remain there for over a year, and while he was allowed food and drink sent by friends, and a servant, he was not allowed a priest, even to the very end. A long letter exists, written from the Tower by Fisher to Thomas Cromwell, speaking of the severity of his conditions of imprisonment. Like Thomas More, Bishop Fisher believed that because the statute condemned only those speaking maliciously against the king's new title, there was safety in silence. Fisher was dragged in front of the king's council many times during his imprisonment, and he always refused to speak about the Supremacy Act. However, on 7 May 1535 he fell into a trap laid for him by Richard Rich, who was later to perjure himself to obtain Thomas More's conviction. Rich told Fisher that for his own conscience's sake the king wished to know, in strict secrecy, Fisher's real opinion. Fisher, trusting him, declared that the king was not Supreme Head of the Church, to Henry's fury.

Upon 20 May 1535 Fisher received the title of cardinal, granted him by the newly elected Pope Paul III. This was effected apparently in the hope of inducing Henry to ease Fisher's treatment, but had the reverse effect. Henry forbade the cardinal's hat to be brought into England, declaring that he would send the head to Rome instead. In June a special commission for Fisher's trial was issued, and on Thursday 17 June he was arraigned in Westminster Hall before a court of seventeen, including Thomas Cromwell and Anne Boleyn's father. The charge was treason, in that he denied that the king was the Supreme Head of the Church of England. Since he had been deprived of his position of Bishop of Rochester by an Act of attainder, he was treated as a commoner and tried by jury. The only testimony was that of Richard Rich, and the gravely ill and emaciated Fisher was condemned to be hanged, drawn and quartered at Tyburn.

However, there was a public outcry in London. The people saw a parallel between the conviction of John Fisher and that of his namesake, John the Baptist, executed by King Herod Antipas for challenging the validity of Herod's marriage to his brother's divorcée Herodias. For fear of John Fisher living through the great feast day of the Nativity of St John the Baptist on 23 June, Henry commuted the sentence to that of beheading, to be accomplished before that date. Fisher's execution on Tower Hill on 22 June 1535 had the opposite effect from that which King Henry VIII intended. It created another parallel with the martyrdom of St John the Baptist, who was also beheaded, and also happened on the feast day of St Alban, the first martyr of England.

Fisher's last moments were in keeping with his life. He met death with a calm and dignified courage that profoundly impressed those present. His body was treated with particular disrespect, apparently on Henry's orders, being stripped and left on the scaffold until the evening, when it was taken on pikes and thrown naked into a rough grave in the churchyard of All Hallows', Barking. There was no funeral prayer. A fortnight later, his body was laid beside that of Sir Thomas More in the chapel of St Peter ad Vincula in the Tower. Fisher's head had been stuck upon a pole on London Bridge, but its ruddy and lifelike appearance excited talk of a miracle, so after fifteen days it was thrown into the Thames. The head was replaced by that of More, executed on 6 July. Fisher was esteemed throughout Europe and remained so. When fifty-four English martyrs were beatified in 1886 by Leo XIII, the greatest place was given to Fisher. He was later canonised, in 1935, by Pius XI, along with Thomas More, after a petition by English Catholics.

Anne Askew (1520/1521–46)

A Protestant poet and 'gospeler' condemned as a heretic, Askew is the only woman on record known to have been both tortured in the Tower of London and burnt at the stake. She was one of the earliest female poets to compose in the English language and the first Englishwoman to demand a divorce. Her family had close family ties to the court of King Henry VIII. Her father, William Askew, was a significant landowner who served in the court of Henry VIII. His son Edward was cupbearer to Henry VIII, and his eldest son, Sir Francis, was Sheriff of Lincoln in 1545, 1549 and 1554. Anne was forced into marriage as a substitute for her sister Martha, who had died. Her husband, Thomas Kyme, was a Catholic and it was said to be a brutal marriage in which she refused to take his name. Anne had two children with Thomas before he threw her out for being Protestant and trying to divorce him. Anne moved to London, met other Protestants and became a 'gospeler'. The City of London was full of Bible study groups. Members were a mixture of nobility and commoners – anyone who revered the Scriptures, high or low, male or female, could attend. The ban on reading the English Bible had intensified the hunger for it, and those who knew the Bible well became known as 'gospelers', a new breed of lay preacher.

In March 1545, Thomas Kyme had Anne arrested. She was brought back to Lincolnshire, where Thomas demanded she stay. Anne escaped and returned to London to continue preaching. In 1546 she was arrested again, but released. In May 1546 she was arrested again for preaching in London and handing out Protestant leaflets, and tortured in the Tower of London. She was ordered to give up likeminded women, as Henry VIII was looking for grounds for a divorce against the fiercely Protestant Catherine Parr. The Privy Council seized Queen Catherine's estate books a few days before Anne was burned, but fortunately Henry died in the following year, before she could be arrested.

Before being put on the rack, prisoners were usually shown others being tortured. They would often 'give in' without the need for being tortured themselves. Anne was denied this opportunity, as it would have been unsuitable for a lady to see a naked man upon the rack. Her second examination in the Tower took place upon 19 June 1546. She was subject to a two-day-long period of cross examination led by Chancellor Sir Thomas Wriothesley, Bishop of Winchester Stephen Gardiner, John Dudley and Sir William Paget, the king's principal secretary. They threatened her with execution, but she still refused to confess, name fellow Protestants, or convert back to Catholicism. She was then ordered to be tortured. Her torturers were probably motivated by the desire for Askew to admit that Queen Catherine Parr and her ladies were also practising Protestants.

At about ten o'clock in the morning, Anne was taken from her cell to the lower room of the White Tower. She was shown the rack and asked if she would name those who believed as she did. Askew declined to name anyone at all, so she was asked to remove all her clothing except her shift. Askew then climbed onto the rack, and her wrists and ankles were fastened. Again she was asked for names, but she would say nothing. The wheel of the rack was turned, pulling Askew along the device and lifting her so that she was held taut about five inches above its bed and slowly stretched. In her own account written from prison, Askew said she fainted from pain and was lowered and revived. This procedure was repeated twice. Sir William Kingston, Constable of the Tower of London, had been responsible for holding Anne Boleyn and her fellow prisoners. He refused to carry on torturing her, left the tower, and sought a meeting with the king at his earliest convenience to explain his position and also to seek his pardon, which the king granted.

Lord Chancellor Thomas Wriothesley and his future successor Sir Richard Rich personally set to work themselves. They turned the handles so hard that Anne was drawn apart, her shoulders and hips were pulled from their sockets and her elbows and knees were dislocated. Askew's cries could be heard in the garden next to the White Tower, where the Lord Lieutenant's wife and daughter were walking. Askew gave no names, and her ordeal ended when the Lord Lieutenant of the Tower, Sir Anthony Knyvet, arrived and ordered her to be returned to her cell. Anne wrote, 'Then they did put me on the rack because I confessed no ladies or gentlemen to be of my opinion; and thereon they kept me a long time and because I lay still and did not cry, my Lord Chancellor and Master Rich took pains to rack me with their own hands till I was nigh dead.'

Rich and Wriothesley must have presumed that Queen Catherine would soon be arrested and her property confiscated. In response to Anne Askew's execution, the queen hurriedly threw out her most evangelical books. Despite incriminating no one, and with little, if any, evidence against her, Anne was convicted of heresy and was condemned to be burned to death at Smithfield, along with John Lascelles and two other Protestants. She was so incapable from the physical torture she had suffered that she had to be carried to her execution on a chair. She was carried wearing just her shift as she could not walk or dress herself and every movement caused her severe pain. She was dragged from the chair to the stake, which had a small seat attached to it on which she sat. Chains were used to bind her body firmly to the stake at the ankles, knees, waist, chest and neck. Anne refused to recant, and because of her recalcitrance she was burned alive slowly rather than being strangled first or burned quickly. Those who saw her execution were impressed by her bravery, and reported that she did not scream until the flames reached her chest. The execution lasted about an hour, and she was unconscious and probably dead after fifteen minutes or so. Such a large gathering of people assembled to watch her execution that the crowd had to be pushed back far enough in order to make room for her to be burned at the stake.

At her execution there was a sudden thunderstorm and a loud clap of thunder. Protestant bishop John Bale wrote,

> Credibly am I informed by various Dutch merchants who were present there, that in the time of their sufferings, the sky, and abhorring so wicked an act, suddenly altered colour, and the clouds from above gave a thunder clap, not unlike the one written in Psalm 76. The elements both declared wherein the high displeasure of God for so tyrannous a murder of innocents.

She was only twenty-five years of age, and the last martyr in the reign of Henry VIII. Her own account of her ordeal and her beliefs was published by Bale as *The Examinations*. Later it was reprinted in John Foxe's *Acts and Monuments* of 1563, which proclaims her as a Protestant martyr. Several ballads were written in the seventeenth century about her, and in Victorian times an Anne Askew doll was produced, complete with the rack and stake.

Henry VII's Daughter – Margaret, Queen of Scots (1489–1541)

Margaret was the eldest daughter of Henry VII of England and Elizabeth of York, born at the Palace of Westminster a year and a half before Henry VIII. As the first Tudor princess, Margaret was immediately placed on the European marriage market since Henry VII was eager to strengthen foreign support for his new dynasty. Henry and his advisers considered marriages across the Continent, but settled upon England's nearest neighbour, Scotland. Tudor legitimacy would be assisted by marriage into one of the long-established European royal families, the Stewarts. Henry realised that a marriage might lead to a Scottish king in England, but he had two sons so must have felt the chance to be small. Also, he thought that England would be the dominant partner in these circumstances.

By this marriage the dynastic fortunes of Scotland and England would be firmly linked, making the governance of the Borders and the south of Scotland easier for both countries. The alliance would also demonstrate that Scotland no longer depended upon France, its traditional ally against the English. Catherine of Aragon married Prince Arthur of Wales in 1501, and the twelve-year-old Margaret attended the wedding feast at Westminster Hall. Prince Henry became aggressively angry when told that his sister would soon be known as Queen of Scots and that she was now accorded precedence over him at the feast and in other public ceremonies. He seemed to have a resentment of his sister for the rest of his life.

In 1502, Henry VII and James IV signed a Treaty of Perpetual Peace and a marriage treaty was signed on the same day, joining the ruling families of Scotland and England. James IV had begun negotiations for Margaret Tudor's hand, even as his favourite mistress, Margaret Drummond, gave birth to their daughter. James then moved mother and child to his palace of Linlithgow and showed them every favour. There was suspicion that there had been a secret marriage between James IV and Drummond, but the Scots successfully concluded the marriage treaty with Henry VII. James's ministers were concerned that Henry VII would learn of Margaret Drummond and that it might complicate relations, but the problem was solved when Margaret Drummond and her two sisters died, possibly from food poisoning, in spring 1502. James IV was devastated, but no one was arrested. His councillors had seen her as an obstacle, but there was no evidence against any of them. James almost immediately resumed his affair with Lady Janet Kennedy, by whom he had three children, and continued seeing her after his marriage to Margaret Tudor. He had also had three children by an earlier mistress, Marion Boyd. James IV had at least eight illegitimate children with four different mistresses.

Margaret Drummond's death freed the thirty-year-old James to marry Margaret Tudor on 8 August 1503, when she was thirteen. The Scottish poet William Dunbar wrote a poem in praise of the marriage of the Scottish Thistle and the Tudor Rose in 1503, 'To the Princess Margaret on her Arrival at Holyrood'. The last verse goes, 'Welcum the Rose bothe rede and whyte, / Welcum the floure of our delyte!' / Rejoysyng frome the sone beme, / Welcum of Scotlond to be quene; / Welcum of Scotlonde to be quene!'

Henry VIII became King of England after their father's death, when Margaret was nineteen. When France went to war with England, James chose the French side and invaded Northumberland. He was killed at Flodden Field in 1513. Margaret's young son James V was not old enough to rule, so she became Regent of Scotland, and the first Tudor woman to rule a kingdom. However, the Scots Council wanted a military leader, not an English female regent, placing her in danger. The nobles wanted rule to pass to the Duke of Albany, who was next in line to the throne. Margaret feared that meant he might kill her sons and become king, so she needed powerful backing to oppose Albany taking power.

She thus married the Earl of Angus. The earl had a strong following, but when the nation heard of the new marriage her reputation suffered greatly, and under the terms of James IV's will her remarriage meant she lost the regency. Henry VIII advised her to flee Scotland, and Margaret remained in England under his protection before making peace with Albany and returning to Scotland in 1517. However, her marriage with Angus broke down when she found he had taken a mistress while dissipating her Scottish incomes. Margaret next staged a coup d'état to remove Albany as regent in 1524 and place her twelve-year-old son on the throne. The Scottish Parliament removed Albany from power, and recognised Margaret as chief councillor to the boy king.

Restored to power, she managed to secure a divorce from Angus despite strong opposition from her brother Henry VIII. It may well be her success that stimulated him to try and find grounds to divorce Catherine of Aragon soon after. In 1527 Margaret married again, to Henry Stewart, her former treasurer. Margaret's ongoing correspondence with Henry VIII led to her being accused of being an English spy, and caused her son to distance himself from her in her later years. Throughout her life she 'worked in her son's interests', according to de Lisle, trying to improve relations between Scotland and England and bring her Tudor and Stewart relatives closer together. Margaret died of a stroke in 1541, aged fifty-one. Without her influence, war broke out once again between England and Scotland.

Margaret's son was James V of Scotland. James's daughter ruled as Mary, Queen of Scots. Mary's son was James VI, the first king to rule both Scotland and England. He was Margaret's great-grandson. He came to power in 1603, exactly a century after Margaret's marriage to James IV. Margaret had four children and two stillbirths, and James V was the only one to reach adulthood. It seems that some of the Tudors could have been affected by a genetic disorder regarding effective reproduction.

Sir Philip Sidney (1554–86)

He was born at his family's state at Penshurst in Kent, England. From his youth, Sidney was respected for his high-minded intelligence, and frequently provided diplomatic service to Queen Elizabeth I as a Protestant political liaison. His opposition to her possible French marriage earned her displeasure, however, and he later left court and began writing his poetical works. In 1586, Sidney accompanied his uncle, Robert Dudley, Earl of Leicester, to the Low Countries to join the Dutch in fighting for the independence of the Netherlands from Spain.

At Zutphen, Sidney was shot in the thigh:

> The 22nd of September opened gloomily. So thick a mist covered the Flemish lowlands that a man could not see farther than ten paces. Sidney, leading a troop of two-hundred horsemen, pushed his way up to the walls of Zutphen. Chivalrous punctilio caused him to be ill-defended, for meeting Sir William Pelham in light armour, he threw off his cuisses, and thus exposed himself to unnecessary danger. The autumn fog, which covered every object, suddenly dispersed; and the English now found themselves confronted by a thousand horsemen of the enemy, and exposed to the guns of the town. They charged, and Sidney's horse was killed under him. He mounted another, and joined in the second charge. Reinforcements came up, and a third charge was made, during which he received a wound in the left leg. The bullet, which some supposed to have been poisoned, entered above the knee, broke the bone, and lodged itself high up in the thigh. His horse took fright, and carried him at a gallop from the field. He kept his seat, however; and when the animal was brought to order, had himself carried to Leicester's station.
>
> On the way occurred the incident so well-known to every one who is acquainted with his name. 'Being thirsty with excess of bleeding, he called for drink, which was presently brought him; but as he was putting the bottle to his mouth, he saw a poor soldier carried along, who had eaten his last at the same feast, ghastly casting up his eyes at the bottle, which Sir Philip perceiving, took it from his head before he drank, and delivered it to the poor man, with these words, "Thy necessity is yet greater than mine." And when he had pledged this poor soldier, he was presently carried to Arnheim.' At Arnheim he lay twenty-five days in the house ... At first the surgeons who attended him had good hopes of his recovery ... Sidney's death sent a thrill through Europe ... Elizabeth declared that she had lost her mainstay in the struggle with Spain.
>
> Fulke Greville, *Life of Sir Philip Sidney* (1652)

Considered a national hero, the poet-courtier was given a lavish funeral that almost bankrupted his father-in-law, Sir Francis Walsingham, the queen's spymaster. His great state funeral was delayed until February of the following year, just eight days after the beheading of Mary, Queen of Scots; it is thought that this was to draw attention away from that political powder keg. He is buried at St Paul's Cathedral. When his poetry was subsequently published,

Sidney became lauded as one of the great Elizabethan writers. He wrote, 'If you have so earth-creeping a mind that it cannot lift itself up to look to the sky of poetry ... thus much curse I must send you, in the behalf of all poets, that while you live, you live in love, and never get favour for lacking skill of a sonnet; and, when you die, your memory die from the earth for want of an epitaph.'

Sir Richard Grenville (1542–1591)

He was born at Buckland Abbey in Devon, which he later sold to Francis Drake. He fought against the Irish and settled on lands in Munster, Ireland. His father, Roger, died as captain of the ill-fated *Mary Rose*. Grenville gained his early military experience fighting in Hungary against the Turks. In 1574, Grenville proposed sailing through the Strait of Magellan in order to circumnavigate the world, only once achieved, in 1519–22 by Juan Elcano when he took over Magellan's expedition. His proposal was refused, but Francis Drake took up the idea in 1577–80. In 1577, Grenville became Sheriff of Cornwall and was knighted. On 25 March 1584, Walter Raleigh received the patent to explore and settle North America, and Grenville commanded Raleigh's fleet of seven vessels. In June 1584, Grenville and Ralph Lane, with 108 men, reached Roanoke Island. In 1585 he commanded another Raleigh-sponsored expedition, departing for Virginia in the *Tiger*, *Roebuck*, *Lion*, *Elizabeth* and *Dorothy*. In 1586, Grenville took three ships to Roanoke to find the place deserted by its former colonists, except for three men mistakenly left behind by Drake. Grenville re-established it. On his return to England, acting as a privateer, he captured a Spanish ship and pillaged the Azores.

Sir Richard Grenville was appointed vice-admiral of the navy to protect England from the Spanish Armada of 132 ships in 1588. England's navy consisted of only 34 ships and 163 armed merchant vessels. In 1591, Grenville and Lord Thomas Howard sailed to the Azores. In order to impede a Spanish naval recovery after the Armada, Sir John Hawkins had proposed a blockade of the supply of treasure being acquired from the Spanish empire in America by a constant naval patrol designed to intercept Spanish ships. *Revenge* was on such a patrol in the summer of 1591 under the command of Grenville.

Revenge was seen by Spanish contemporaries as 'one of the finest galleons in the world'. Built in 1577 by the leading English shipwright Matthew Baker of Deptford, *Revenge* had a long record of service in Ireland and the West Indies and as Drake's flagship during the Armada campaign, when she had been in the thick of the action. She had been one of the first of the new 'race-built' galleons to be added to the English fleet. These were long, lean vessels, averaging around 500 tons, the high poop decks that had been a feature of older galleons replaced by a lower series of decks stepped down into the waist of the ship and with a much lower forecastle than had hitherto been usual.

The Spanish had dispatched a fleet of fifty-three ships to capture the English fleet at Flores in the northern Azores. In late August 1591 the Spanish fleet came upon the English while repairs to the ships caused the crews, many of whom were suffering an epidemic of fever, to be ashore. Most of the ships managed to slip away to sea. Grenville, who had many sick men ashore, decided to wait for them. When putting to sea he might have gone round the west of Corvo Island, but he decided to go straight through the Spaniards, who were approaching from the east.

The battle began late on 31 August, when overwhelming force was immediately brought to bear upon the ship, which put up a gallant resistance. For some time Grenville succeeded by skilful tactics in avoiding much of the enemy's fire, but they were all round him and gradually numbers began to tell. As one Spanish ship retired beaten another would take her place, and for fifteen hours the unequal contest continued. Attempts by the Spaniards to board were driven off. *San Felipe*, a vessel three times her size, tried to come alongside for the Spaniards to board her, along with the *San Cristóbal*. After boarding *Revenge*, *San Felipe* was forced to break off. Seven men of the boarding party died, and another three were rescued by *San Bernabé*, which grappled her shortly after. The Spanish also lost the galleon *Ascensión* and a smaller vessel by accident that night after they collided with each other. Meanwhile, *San Cristóbal*, which had come to help *San Felipe*, rammed *Revenge* underneath her aftercastle, and later the *San Bernabé* battered the English warship with heavy fire, inflicting many casualties and severe damage. The English crew returned fire from the embrasures below deck.

When morning broke on 1 September, *Revenge* lay with her masts shot away, six feet of water in the hold and only sixteen men left uninjured out of a crew of 250. She remained grappled by the galleons *San Bernabé* and *San Cristóbal*, the latter with her bow shattered by the ramming. The grappling manoeuvre of *San Bernabé*, which compelled the English gun crews to abandon their posts in order to fight off boarding parties, was decisive in securing the fate of the *Revenge*.

'Out-gunned, out-fought, and out-numbered fifty-three to one', in the words of Alfred Tennyson, when the end looked certain the badly injured Grenville ordered *Revenge* to be sunk, as memorably recorded by Tennyson three centuries later: 'Sink me the ship, Master Gunner – sink her, split her in twain! ... Fall into the hands of God, not into the hands of Spain!' His officers could not agree with this order and a surrender was agreed by which the lives of the officers and crew would be spared. After an assurance of proper conduct, and having held off dozens of Spanish ships, *Revenge* at last surrendered. The injured Grenville died of wounds two days later aboard the Spanish flagship.

Raleigh described the battle in a superb piece of anti-Spanish propaganda (spelling modernised):

> All the Powder of the *Revenge* to the last barrel was now spent, all her pikes broken, forty of her best men slain, and the most part of the rest hurt. In the beginning of the fight she had but one-hundred free from sickness, and four score and ten sick, laid in hold among the ballast. A small troop to man such a ship, and a weak Garrison to resist so mighty an Army. By those hundred

> all was sustained, the volleys, boardings, and enterings of fifteen ships of war, besides those which beat her at large. On the contrary, the Spanish were always supplied with soldiers brought from every squadron: all manner of Arms and powder at will ...

The captured but heavily damaged *Revenge* never reached Spain, being lost with her mix of prize and crew numbering seventy Spaniards and English captives along with many of the Spanish ships in a dreadful storm off the Azores. The battle-damaged *Revenge* was cast upon a cliff on the island of Terceira, where she broke up completely. Between 1592 and 1593, fourteen guns of the *Revenge* were recovered by the Spanish from the site of the wreck. Other cannons were driven ashore years later by the tide, and the last weapons raised were salvaged as late as 1625. Four generations of the Grenville family died in the service of their country – Sir Richard's father on the *Mary Rose* in 1545, Sir Richard himself in the Azores in 1592, his son in Guiana in 1595, and his grandson in support of the Royalists in 1643.

The last verses of Tennyson's 'The Revenge: A Ballad of the Fleet' (1878) are,

> 'Sink me the ship, Master Gunner – sink her, split her in twain!
> Fall into the hands of God, not into the hands of Spain!'
> And the gunner said 'Ay ay,' but the seamen made reply:
> 'We have children, we have wives,
> And the Lord hath spared our lives.
> We will make the Spaniard promise, if we yield, to let us go;
> We shall live to fight again and to strike another blow.'
> And the lion there lay dying, and they yielded to the foe.
>
> And the stately Spanish men to their flagship bore him then,
> Where they laid him by the mast, old Sir Richard caught at last,
> And they praised him to his face with their courtly foreign grace.
> But he rose upon their decks and he cried:
> 'I have fought for Queen and Faith like a valiant man and true.
> I have only done my duty as a man is bound to do.
> With a joyful spirit I, Sir Richard Grenville, die!'
> And he fell upon their decks and he died.

Sir Walter Raleigh (*c.* 1552–1618)

A courtier, statesman, chemist, poet, historian, soldier, explorer, colonist and privateer, his final speech was delivered in the Old Palace Yard at Westminster. When Raleigh's head lay on the block awaiting the axe, someone remarked that it ought to be turned to the east. Raleigh responded, 'What matter how the head lie, if the heart be right?' He had told his executioner, 'Let us dispatch. At this hour my ague comes upon me. I would not have my enemies think I quaked from fear.' After he was allowed to see the axe that would behead him, he said, 'This is a sharp Medicine, but it is a Physician for all diseases and miseries.' Raleigh had been involved in Ireland and Virginia, before serving against the Spanish Armada, exploring the River Orinoco in 1594 and commanding a squadron in the defeat of the Spanish fleet at Cadiz in 1596. A favourite of Elizabeth I, he fell out of favour with the Catholic James I, was falsely accused of treason and sent to the Tower in 1603, where he wrote his *History of the World*. He was allowed out of prison to lead an expedition to Guiana in 1616, searching Guiana and the Orinoco again for El Dorado, when his son was killed. An unauthorised attack on the Spanish led to a mock trial and Raleigh's beheading, to appease the king and the pro-Spanish faction in court. Raleigh's head was embalmed and his wife carried it with her for the remaining twenty-nine years of her life.

His last words were,

> I thank my God heartily that He hath brought me into the light to die, and not suffered me to die in the dark prison of the Tower, where I have suffered a great deal of adversity and a long sickness; and I thank God that my fever hath not taken me at this time, as I prayed God it might not ... And now I entreat you all to join with me in prayer, that the great God of Heaven, whom I have grievously offended, being a man full of all vanity, and having lived a sinful life, in all sinful callings, having been a soldier, a captain, a sea captain, and a courtier, which are all places of wickedness and vice; that God, I say, would forgive me, cast away my sins from me, and receive me into everlasting life. So I take my leave of you all, making my peace with God.

31

Discovery and Explorers

Discovery and the Beginnings of Empire

Water transportation was far cheaper and more efficient than land, and England, being an island, was blessed with excellent seamen, many coming from the West Country and Wales and learning their trade on the highest rises and falls of tide in the world outside the Bay of Fundy. English sea power was built up during Tudor times as a deliberate policy by all monarchs, as much to help enrich the country as for defence, and we see a shift of international trade from the Mediterranean to the Atlantic. England came to be the main beneficiary of this shift, with winds and currents enabling its ships to follow a triangular route off the coast of Africa to the coast of Brazil, up through the Caribbean and the coast of eastern America, and keeping on the Gulf Stream and trade winds to sail back to England.

European ships before this time had been single-masted and poor at sailing into the wind. Driven by Henry the Navigator (1394–1460), Portuguese sailors began to sail south down the coast of Africa in the rough Atlantic to bypass the hostile Muslim nations of North Africa and find the source of African gold. One of the problems of sailing south down the coast of Africa was returning against the wind. This was solved in two ways. First was by the development of the three-masted 'lateen-rigged' caravel, which could sail five points into the wind. Second was the discovery of the circular trade winds, which allowed a ship, if sailed due west from the bulge of Africa rather than north, to be blown back in a circular route to Lisbon. They also developed the more stable and navigable three-masted ship known as the carrack. With its much greater tonnage, the design was soon adopted by English traders to ship Newcastle coal to London.

The period spanning the late fifteenth century and the sixteenth century was known as the Age of Discovery, when Spain and Portugal pioneered European exploration of the world. They began establishing great overseas empires and amassing enormous riches. Portuguese ships travelled to the southern Atlantic and the African coast while Columbus headed west in Spanish ships in 1492 to find a path to the trade centres of Asia. The Spanish and Portuguese looked to the Pope, head of the Roman Catholic Church, to legitimise their claims as they expanded their reach. In 1481, a papal bull granted the Canary Islands to the Castilians of Spain and rights to Africa to the Portuguese. When it was revealed that lands lay across the Atlantic (Europeans would soon realise these were the expansive continents of North and South America), disputes arose as to who had rights to these territories. The Treaty of Tordesillas in 1494 split the 'New World' between Spain and Portugal.

Although very little of the new lands had been seen, lines were slashed across the globe, giving most of North and South America to Spain and the easternmost area of what is now Brazil to Portugal. The Treaty was sanctioned by a papal decree, but future bulls moved this meridian back and forth, giving Spain control in Asia and allowing Portuguese expansion in Brazil. The French and the British were restricted from those areas under papal authority, but they soon disregarded the bulls. Those nations not under the treaty launched the search for a Northwest Passage, or engaged in piracy, conflict and trade monopolies in other areas. Those countries which threw off Catholicism came to disregard the Treaty of Tordesillas and attacked Spanish and Portuguese overseas possessions. England, France and the Netherlands desperately tried to catch up by establishing colonies and trade networks of their own in the Americas and Asia. The process, which started under the Tudors, led to England creating the largest empire the world has seen by the nineteenth century, with around a fifth of the world's population and almost a quarter of its landmass.

In June 1494, Columbus had made his crew swear that they had reached the Indies mainland when they returned to Spain. Anyone who recanted was to have his tongue cut out. The 'discoverer of America' had in fact only reached Cuba. Columbus never realised that he had never reached Asia. When the mainland was discovered, Spain quickly established colonies in South and Central America, as well as Florida. Upon Christmas Day 1497, Vasco da Gama sailed past an unknown land on the eastern coast of southern Africa and called it Natal, Portuguese for Christmas. His crew were beginning to suffer from scurvy, for which the standard treatment was trimming dead matter from swollen gums with a knife and rubbing the wound with urine.

The astute Henry VII soon saw the opportunity to enrich his new kingdom. He embarked on a programme of building larger ships and also invested in dockyards. In 1495, Henry VII had Europe's first dry dock built at Portsmouth, still in existence, and five royal warships were built during his reign. This included two four-masted carracks. The foundations of the British Empire were laid when, in 1496, the king commissioned John Cabot to lead a voyage to discover a route to the lucrative Spice Islands (now the Maluku Islands) of Asia, via the North Atlantic. Both John and his son Sebastian Cabot led English ships on voyages of discovery. In 1497, John Cabot sailed west from Bristol hoping to find a shorter route to Asia, a land believed to be rich in gold, gems and other luxuries. After a month he discovered an unknown land, which he called 'new found land', still known as Newfoundland today.

Henry VIII continued expanding and developing the English navy as a standing armed force of the state, building a series of great warships such as the *Mary Rose*, *Peter Pomegranate* and *Henri Grâce à Dieu*. These were equipped with gunports in their sides, an idea copied from the Portuguese and Spanish, making them far more effective than the converted merchant ships which had previously been used. In 1514 the 1,500-ton carrack *Great Harry* was launched, the first English two-decker and one of the earliest warships equipped with gunports and heavy bronze cannon. Henry also initiated the casting of cannon in England, and by the late Elizabethan age English iron workers using blast furnaces developed the technique of producing cast iron cannons which, while not as durable as the bronze cannons, were much cheaper and enabled England to arm its navy more easily. Both kings realised that merchant shipping and growing trade needed to be protected by a strong royal navy. The king also helped with the infrastructure needed for successful shipping, and Trinity House dates from his time. By 1540 the navy consisted of 45 ships, and in 1545 Lord Lisle had a fleet of 80 ships fighting a French force of 130 attempting to invade England at the Battle of the Solent.

Queen Mary maintained the building program, and her marriage to Philip II led to trade with Spain, allowing English shipwrights to copy modern Spanish galleon design to meet the needs of the English navy, as English ports were soon visited by both Spanish warships and merchantmen. This would prove crucial to the growth and development of the race-built galleon of the Elizabethan navy. Mary's government also encouraged trade with Morocco, exchanging English cloth for African sugar and saltpetre, and the Guinea coast, swapping cloth for gold.

Elizabeth made naval strength a high priority, ordering a fleet review on her accession. It showed the navy to consist of thirty-nine ships, and her ministers planned to build another thirty, to be grouped into five categories, foreshadowing the 'rating system' of ships of the line. Elizabeth maintained a steady construction rate throughout her reign. In 1562, she sanctioned John Hawkins and Francis Drake to make slave-raiding attacks on Spanish and Portuguese ships off the coast of West Africa to try and break into the profitable Atlantic trades. Later, while at war with Spain, Elizabeth lent her blessing to further privateering against Spanish ports in the Americas and shipping that was returning across the Atlantic, laden with treasures from the New World. At the same time, influential writers such as Richard Hakluyt and John Dee, the first to use the term 'British Empire', pressed Elizabeth for the establishment of England's own empire. By this time, Spain had become the dominant power in the Americas and was exploring the Pacific eventually colonising California, Portugal had established trading posts and forts from the coasts of Africa to China, and France had begun to settle the Saint Lawrence River, later to become New France and what we now know as Canada.

Hawkins, Drake and other captains were given privateering commissions to attack Spanish galleons carrying gold and silver from the New World. English shipbuilding yards responded to requests from the privateers, who demanded technical innovations to be able to attack the heavily guarded great galleons. It is thought that the 'full-rigged ship' was one of the greatest technological advances of the century and permanently transformed naval warfare. In 1573 English shipwrights introduced designs in the *Dreadnought*, which were copied to allow ships to sail faster, manoeuvre better and carry heavier guns. Previously warships had tried to grapple with each other so that soldiers could board the enemy ship, but now they stood off and fired broadsides that would cripple or sink the enemy vessel. Against the Armada, the poor design of the Spanish cannons meant they were much slower in reloading in a close-range battle, allowing the English to take control. Spain and France still had stronger fleets, however.

The architect behind the increased efficiency and effectiveness of English ships was Plymouth-born John Hawkins (1532–95), who was responsible for developing English sea power. Hawkins was a shipbuilder, naval administrator and commander, merchant, navigator, privateer and slave trader. He was the first English trader to profit from the 'Triangular Trade', selling African slaves in the Spanish colonies of Santo Domingo and Venezuela. He was knighted after the Armada invasion, where he served as vice-admiral. As treasurer (1577) and controller (1589) of the Royal Navy, Hawkins rebuilt older ships and helped design the faster ships that withstood the Armada in 1588. Hawkins worked with Mathew Baker on the production of the race-built galleons, where the fore- and aft-castles were lowered, making a more manoeuvrable ship. The Dutch, Spain's great enemies, developed an independent state based on maritime trade, and there was a significant sharing of knowhow with England. Both nations shared the same religion, and both often found themselves at war with the Spanish Empire, providing the context for the emergence of England as a great naval power. It was realised that any wish to develop an empire and overseas trade needed a strong naval presence. In England's case, privateering commissions were given to captains to attack the monarch's enemies, in return for which the Crown shared any profits but did not have to finance any missions or ships.

Most new English colonies were established in North America and the West Indies, and were proprietary colonies with 'proprietors' appointed to found and govern settlements under mercantile charters granted to joint-stock companies. English merchants were the main promoters of exploration and discovery. They wanted to buy Oriental spices such as cinnamon, peppers and cloves that were needed to preserve and flavour meat. Spices could be obtained through Middle Eastern middlemen, but their massive markup made spices very expensive. Europeans therefore wanted to establish a direct sea route to the Far East so that they could buy directly from China, India and the East Indies. Spanish and Portuguese seamen sailed west to America, or south around the Horn of Africa and then east across the Indian Ocean. English explorers hoped to find a route by sailing north-west around America (the Northwest Passage) or north-east around Europe (the Northeast Passage).

To navigate, Tudor sailors had a compass and 'rutters', which contained details of the shoreline, currents, makeup of the seabed, etc. To measure depth they used a lead weight on a rope with knots tied at intervals. At the bottom of the weight was a recess filled with tallow. It was used to bring up a sample of the seabed. To measure speed a log reel was used, where a rope with knots tied at intervals was wound around a reel. One end was tied to a wooden board which was thrown into the sea. The rope was gradually unreeled and, using a sand timer, the sailors measured how many knots went out in an hour. Tudor sailors spent many days at sea and so had to take food with them that would keep. Hardtack, biscuits made from a mixture of salted flour and wheat, were a staple part of the diet but quickly became infested with maggots. Ferdinand Columbus, describing one of his father's voyages, wrote, 'Food had become so wormy that sailors waited to dark to eat ... so they could not see the maggots.' Water became stale and covered with algae, so sailors drank up to eight pints of beer a day. A ship like Grenville's *Revenge* was called a 'great shippe' but was only 500 tons, and many, many ships were lost in great storms at sea.

The Explorers

John Cabot/Giovanni Caboto (c. 1450 – c. 1499)

Probably born in Genoa, and later a citizen of Venice, Cabot had read of fabulous Chinese cities in the writings of Marco Polo and wanted to see them for himself. He hoped to reach them by sailing west, across the Atlantic. Failing to find financial backing in Spain and Portugal, he was in England around 1495 and sought Henry VII's support. It was believed that Cathay and Cipangu (China and Japan) were rich in gold, gems, spices and silks, and to find a direct route by sea would have made England the greatest trading centre in the world for goods from the east.

Henry gave his permission and helped pay his 'well-beloved John Cabot ... to seeke out, discover and finde whatsoever isles, countries, regions or provinces ... which before this time have been unknown to all Christians'. Cabot's ship, the 50-ton *Mathew*, sailed from Bristol with a crew of eighteen in 1497. The crew would normally have been around ten men, but extra mariners were needed on such a long trip. She carried enough food for eight months, and a replica can be seen in Bristol Docks. After a month at sea, he landed and took the area of 'new found land' in the name of King Henry VII. Like Columbus, he mistakenly believed that he had reached Asia. Cabot had found one of the northern capes of Newfoundland. It was the first European encounter with the mainland of North America since the Vikings of the eleventh century. Cabot's sailors were able to catch huge numbers of cod simply by dipping baskets into the water, which almost immediately saw English ships sailing for the great fisheries, the Grand Banks. Cabot was rewarded with the sum of £10 by the king for discovering a new island 'off the coast of China'. Cabot was also given a pension of £20 a year.

Henry wanted spices, however, and in 1498 Cabot was given permission by the king to take ships on a new expedition to continue west from the point he had reached on his first voyage. The aim was to discover Japan. Cabot made a visit to Spain and Portugal to try to recruit men who had sailed with Columbus, but without much success. He set out from Bristol with 300 men in May 1498. The five ships carried supplies for a year's travelling. Cabot and his crews were supposedly never heard of again, but some researchers posit that at least some men returned and that a settlement was left in America. William Weston, a Bristol merchant and acquaintance of Cabot, may have been the first Englishman to land on American soil in a voyage soon after. Cabot's son Sebastian made another attempt to find the Northwest Passage in 1509, and later became governor of the Muscovy Company.

Richard ap Meuric/Richard Amerika (fl. 1497)

Richard ap Meuric partly financed the Cabot voyages from Bristol to America in 1497, and was Bristol's chief customs official. It seems that the Cabots inscribed their maps as Amerika in his honour. English merchants afterwards referred to the New World as 'Amerik's Land'. The claim of Amerigo Vespucci with his later voyages is possibly more dubious, as it is unknown for a country to be named after its discoverer's Christian name.

Sir Hugh Willoughby (d. 1554) and Richard Chancellor (d. 1556)

On 10 May 1553, Willoughby was put in command of an expedition to find the Northeast Passage to China and the Indies. The trip was sponsored by a group of London merchants who were led by Sebastian Cabot. The merchants fitted out three ships, the *Bona Esperanza* (commanded by Willoughby), the *Edward Bonaventure* (captained by Richard Chancellor), and the *Bona Confidentia* (under Cornelius Durfoorth). Each ship contained trade goods, mostly English wool cloth, in hopes of opening trade with Russia and China. The ships carried provisions for eighteen months, which included sour beer, hard biscuit, salt pork and cheese. As they sailed north past Norway, contact was lost with Chancellor's *Edward Bonaventure*. Willoughby and Durfoorth continued and reached Novaya Zemlya, but the *Bona Confidentia* began having problems. The two ships became trapped in ice in the Barents Sea. Far north of the Arctic Circle, all seventy crew on the *Bona Confidentia* and *Bona Esperanza* were found dead in 1555.

The Venetian ambassador reported how the sailors who found the frozen men aboard the ships 'found some of the dead seated in the act of writing, pen in hand, and the papers before them; others at table, platter in hand and spoon in mouth; others opening a locker, and others in various postures, like statues, as if they had been adjusted and placed in those attitudes'. It seems that the men may have died quickly of carbon monoxide poisoning, by burning coal in a poorly ventilated space. They would have stopped up all the icy draughts to keep warm. Meanwhile, Chancellor, on the *Edward Bonaventure*, continued on to the White Sea, then journeyed overland to Moscow and was given audience with Tsar Ivan IV. The Tsar gave Chancellor permission to trade throughout Russia. He returned to England in 1554. Chancellor then wrote about his travels and, based on his information about Russia and trade possibilities, the Muscovy Company was formed in 1555 and granted a monopoly of trade with Russia. Richard Chancellor wrote of the Muscovites that 'the poor is very innumerable, and live most miserably:

for I have seen them eat the pickle of herring and other stinking fish: nor the fish cannot be so stinking nor rotten, but they will eat it and praise it to be more wholesome than other fish or fresh meat. In mine opinion there be no such people under the sun for their hardness of living.' He travelled again to Moscow on a trading mission, but died in a shipwreck off Aberdeen in 1556.

Sir Martin Frobisher (c. 1535–94)

From Yorkshire, Frobisher's travels began in the 1550s when he explored Africa's north-west coast, particularly Guinea, in 1553 and 1554. The following year he became a privateer, authorised by the Crown to plunder enemy nations' treasure ships. In the 1560s, Frobisher gained a reputation for preying on French trading vessels in the waters off Guinea. Determined to find a Northwest Passage, Frobisher worked for five years to obtain funding for his expedition. He convinced the Muscovy Company, an English merchant consortium, to license him and then raised enough money for three ships. He set sail in 1576 and sighted the coast of what is now Labrador, Canada. In August he landed at Frobisher Bay on Baffin Island and this was marked by the first Church of England service recorded on North American soil. On Baffin Island a group of natives captured several members of Frobisher's crew, and despite several attempts to get them back Frobisher was unable to retrieve them.

He set sail back to England and took with him a piece of black stone that he believed to contain gold. Frobisher's reports of possible gold mines convinced investors to fund a second voyage. In 1577 Frobisher set out to sea again, this time with additional funding, ships and men. He reached Frobisher Bay and spent several weeks collecting ore. He was directed by his commission to defer discovery of the passage to another time and focus on gathering precious metals. Frobisher and his crew brought back to England 200 tons of what they believed to be gold ore.

Elizabeth sent Frobisher back for a third voyage, this time on a much larger expedition, with fifteen vessels and the necessities for establishing a 100-man colony. Frobisher set sail in June 1578, and claimed Greenland for the Crown. He landed at Frobisher Bay in early July. He and his men failed to establish a settlement as a result of dissension and discontent, so they all returned to England with 1,350 tons of ore. Upon their return, it was discovered that the ore was actually iron pyrite and therefore worthless, and it was used for road metaling. In 1585, Frobisher returned to the seas as the vice-admiral of Sir Francis Drake's expedition to the West Indies. Three years later he fought for the English against the Spanish Armada and was knighted for his efforts. In the six years that followed, Frobisher headed several English squadrons, including one that attempted to intercept Spanish treasure ships in the Azores. During a scuffle with Spanish forces in November 1594 during the Siege of Fort Crozon, Frobisher was shot. He died several days later.

Francis Drake (1541/43–96)

Francis Drake was born in Tavistock, Devon, and first started going to sea while living in Chatham at the age of twelve or thirteen. He was an apprentice on a small trading ship which was left to him when the master died. After selling this ship, he returned to Devon and sailed with his relative John Hawkins. Together, Hawkins and Drake made the first English slaving voyages, bringing African slaves to work in the New World.

He also raided Spanish and Portuguese ports in the Americas and the Atlantic. He was only the second man to sail around the world, fifty years after the first. The circumnavigation took three years, from 1577 to 1580, but the voyage was meant to be a raid on Spanish ships and ports. Some 164 seamen on five ships left Plymouth, with Drake sailing in the *Pelican*, and most of the crews thought they were heading for the Mediterranean. After reaching America, Drake was worried that his ships might get separated from each other so he gave orders for two of them to be destroyed. Then the *Marigold* was lost, with all her crew, and the *Elizabeth* turned back and sailed home. By October 1578, as the company sailed the western coast of South America, there were just fifty-eight men left, all on the *Pelican*. Drake renamed his ship the *Golden Hind* and sailed around Cape Horn and into the Pacific. Heading north and keeping to the coast, he plundered Spanish ports in Chile and Peru and captured treasure ships including the *Cacafuego*. He landed in what is now California, naming it Nova Albion (New England) and claiming it for his queen. Drake then sailed across the Pacific to the East Indies, or Spice Islands. Six tons of cloves were loaded onto the ship. Later, half had to be tossed into the sea in order to free the ship from a reef.

His route through the East Indies lay along the uncharted southern coast of Java. Here Drake discovered that Java was an island, not connected to a southern continent as the Dutch believed. Drake returned from his voyage around the world with the *Golden Hind* packed full of spices from the Indies and plundered Spanish silver and treasure. Sailing back into Plymouth Harbour, his first question to a fisherman was, 'Does the Queen still live?' He knew that if she had been succeeded by a Catholic, or if Spain or France had conquered England, he would have to immediately leave English waters due to his attacks upon Spanish ships and possessions.

At Elizabeth's request, Drake sailed the heavily laden *Golden Hind* to Deptford, where she knighted Drake, and they spent £10,000 of looted Spanish silver on a feast on board. Elizabeth's half of the treasure surpassed the Crown's annual income at that time, Drake's booty being variously estimated at between £285,000 and £450,000. The expedition cost its backers £5,000. Drake was involved in several other battles with the Spanish. In 1585 he attacked and burnt Santiago in the Cape Verde islands. In 1586 he captured Santo Domingo in Hispaniola (the Dominican Republic). His attack on the ports of Cádiz and A Coruña in 1587 is known as the 'singeing of the King of Spain's beard'. Between twenty and thirty ships were sunk or captured, and there was the wholesale destruction of supplies intended for the planned Spanish Armada.

Drake's attack delayed the Armada as he captured the Spanish flagship, the *Rosario*, when it collided with another ship. He died from dysentery off the coast of Panama in Nombre de Dios Bay. His circumnavigation led to an increased knowledge of the geography of the world, particularly of the 'southern continent'. As a navigator his skills put him in the same rank as Columbus. Drake's claim of California, or Nova Albion, for England led directly to later plans to send people to live in colonies in America.

Sir Humphrey Gilbert (1539–83)

Another Devon man, he was a half-brother to Sir Walter Raleigh and a cousin of Sir Francis Drake. In 1565, Gilbert petitioned Queen Elizabeth in order to find a Northwest Passage via America to Cathay (China). Between 1575 and 1578 there were three exploratory trips by Martin Frobisher to Labrador in a search for the Northwest Passage. The attempts were backed by Elizabeth I and Gilbert, who had consulted John Dee on maps and possible routes. In 1578, Elizabeth granted Sir Humphrey Gilbert a patent to discover and settle new English colonies 'to inhabit and possess all remote and heathen lands'. After two failed attempts, in 1583 Gilbert left England with five ships for the New World and Newfoundland. Gilbert and the other ships arrived at St John's, Newfoundland, in August and took possession two days later. No settlers were left. Because it was small and could explore harbours and creeks, Gilbert now sailed on *Squirrel*, a ship of 10 tons, rather than *Delight*, his 120-ton flagship. The *Delight* was later wrecked with the loss of 100 lives and many of Gilbert's records. On the return voyage to England, Gilbert remained aboard *Squirrel* to record his claim rather than transferring to the larger *Golden Hinde*, as urged by his men. On 9 September, he was observed on deck reading a book. As the ships drew near he was heard to say, 'We are as near to heaven by sea as by land.' Later that evening the small ship disappeared, swallowed up by the sea. He was succeeded in his attempts by his half-brother, Walter Raleigh.

Sir Walter Raleigh (1552–1618)

The Devonian was an English courtier, explorer, soldier, poet, patron of the arts and writer who was imprisoned in the Tower of London and eventually put to death after being accused of treason by James I. A rival of the Earl of Essex for the queen's favours, he served in Elizabeth's army in Ireland in 1580, distinguishing himself by his ruthlessness and by the plantation of English and Scots Protestants in Munster. Elizabeth rewarded him with a large estate in Ireland, knighted him in 1585 and gave him trade privileges and the right to colonise America.

Before the arrival of the English, the Spanish influence in the New World extended from Chesapeake Bay to the tip of South America. Spanish possessions included the developing cities of Mexico, Peru and Cuba. In March 1584, Elizabeth granted Raleigh a charter for the colonisation of an area of North America that was to be called Virginia in her honour. Raleigh and Elizabeth intended that the venture should provide riches from the New World and a base from which to send privateers on raids against the treasure fleets of Spain. Raleigh never visited North America, although he led expeditions in 1595 and 1617 to the Orinoco River in South America to search for El

Dorado, the 'golden city'. He sent others to found a colony in 1585 on the coast of North Carolina, but lack of supplies caused the colony to fail. Then, in 1587, Raleigh made a second attempt at settling, this time a colony of 117 settlers at Roanoke, Virginia. On 18 August 1587 Eleanor Dare gave birth to a daughter, the first English child born on American soil. When an English ship returned to check on their progress in 1591, all the colonists had disappeared. The lessons learnt from the 'Lost Colony' of Roanoke helped ensure that the next Virginia colony, of 1607, was better funded and organised.

In 1587 he was appointed Captain of the Queen's Guard, and in 1588 took part in the victory over the Spanish Armada. He led other raids against Spanish possessions and returned with much booty. Raleigh forfeited Elizabeth's favour by his marriage to one of her maids-of-honour, and he was committed to the Tower in 1592. Hoping to recover his position, on his release he led an abortive expedition to Guiana to search for El Dorado, the legendary land of gold. Instead, he helped to introduce the potato plant and tobacco use in England and Ireland. Elizabeth's successor, James I, distrusted Raleigh, charged him with treason and condemned him to death, but commuted the sentence to imprisonment in the Tower in 1603. There Raleigh lived with his wife and servants, and wrote his *History of the World* (1614). He was released in 1616 to search for gold in South America. He was forced to return to England without booty, and was arrested on the orders of the king. His original death sentence for treason was invoked, and he was executed at Westminster.

John Davis/Davys (c. 1550–1605)

From Devon, he sailed further north than any previous English sailor, attempting to find the Northwest Passage. In 1585 he began his first expedition, reaching Baffin Island. He attempted again in 1586, and then in 1587. On the last of these voyages he entered Baffin Bay and sailed northward along western Greenland to Disko Island, about 70 degrees north. Davis showed some imagination in his dealings with the Greenland Eskimo. He established cordial relations with the Inuit. In 1588 Davis commanded the *Black Dog* against the Armada, and he sailed with Thomas Cavendish on his last voyage in 1591. In seeking a passage through the Strait of Magellan, Davis discovered the Falklands Islands in 1592. He and his crew lived on a diet of penguins. He next sailed with Raleigh to Cádiz and to the Azores (1596–97) and accompanied expeditions to the East Indies in 1598 and 1601. On a third voyage to the Indies he was killed by Japanese pirates. Davis invented the remarkable device called the backstaff, or Davis quadrant, used until the eighteenth century for determining latitude by reading the angle of elevation of the sun. He also wrote a treatise on navigation, *The Seaman's Secret* (1594), and his *The World's Hydrographical Description* (1595) deals with the Northwest Passage.

Sir Thomas Cavendish (c. 1560–92)

Privateer, mariner and Member of Parliament, Thomas Cavendish was the second Englishman to circumnavigate the globe. He accompanied Sir Richard

Grenville on his voyage to America in 1585. Seeing Drake return from his exploits at sea and against the Spanish, Cavendish was inspired to copy him and in 1586 set out with three ships for Brazil. He made it through the Strait of Magellan and then proceeded to capture Spanish ships, including their treasure galleon the *Santa Ana*. Philip II mourned the loss and the fact that the ship had been taken by 'an English youth ... with forty or fifty companions'. Now in the Pacific, Cavendish sailed to the Philippines, Maluku Islands and Java before he rounded the Cape of Good Hope and returned home. The journey had taken two years and fifty days, cost him two of his own ships and made him the third person to circumnavigate the globe. He was twenty-eight years old and was knighted upon his ship *Desire* by the queen. However, although received with acclaim, his fortune dissipated. He set sail again in 1591 with five ships but heavy storms separated the ships as they attempted to make their way through the Strait of Magellan. The ship Cavendish captained turned back toward Brazil, attempting to make landfall, but he died of unknown causes, believing he had been deserted by his fellow captains.

Will Adams (1564–1620)

Will Adams was born in Gillingham, was apprenticed to a shipbuilder on the Thames at Limehouse and in 1588 was appointed captain of the ship *Richard Driffield*. His remit was to carry supplies to the ships engaged with the Spanish Armada. In 1589 he married Mary Hyn at Stepney, by which time they already had at least two children. On hearing of the plans by the Dutch East India Company to send an expedition to the Far East, Will Adams travelled to Holland with his younger brother Thomas to seek work. Both were appointed to the flagship of a fleet of five ships. The fleet sailed from Holland in June 1598, and only *De Liefde* (*Charity*) completed the journey to Japan. Of its 110 crew only 24 were alive, and of these only six were capable of standing up without assistance. After nine days, the great warlord Tokugawa Ieyasu summoned the captain of *De Liefde*. He was far too ill to obey, so Will Adams and Melchior Standvoort were taken instead by ship to Osaka. After lengthy imprisonment and interrogation in Osaka Castle, Ieyasu befriended the foreigners.

In October 1600, Tokugawa leyasu won a decisive battle over his enemies which gave him the position of Shōgun, in effect the military commander of Japan and its effective ruler. Will Adams was given a house close to Ieyasu's castle in Edo. In 1602 Will Adams asked for permission to repair the *De Liefde* and sail back to England to his wife and children and was denied. However, in 1604 Will Adams was ordered to build a sailing craft like *De Liefde* for the Shōgun. The ship was constructed at Ito, one of the places where Will Adams and his memory are still honoured in Japan by the Anjin Festival. In 1609, the Dutch East India Company made another attempt to open up trade with Japan. They set up a factory in Hirado. It was their intention to manage all trade between Holland and Japan. There was intense rivalry with other European ventures. The merchants from the English East India Company, for example, also set up a trading post at Hirado.

The Honourable (English) East India Company had been founded in London on 21 December 1600. The aim of the company was to navigate the largely uncharted East Indies, Asia and Africa and to open up trade routes. All such activities were to be undertaken at the company's expense. In 1613, the company set up the English Factory at Hirado with Richard Cocks as its manager. Will Adams was employed by the English East India Company as a pilot and captain but it would seem that his advice on trade was not heeded by the directors of the factory. The viability of both the Dutch and English factories was always in doubt. The Japanese were not open to the idea of foreigners living and trading in their country. They were concerned that Christian missionaries would infiltrate the country with the merchants.

In 1616, the English and Dutch were ordered to restrict their trading activities to Hirado and Nagasaki and to make complete reports of all cargoes. Such severe restrictions caused dissent between the English and Dutch and much distress to Will Adams. From 1617, Will Adams was trading independently. He bought a junk from the English Factory and renamed it *The Gift of God*. His testament or will sets out provision for his family in England and his family in Japan. *Shōgun* is a marvellous 1975 novel by James Clavell, loosely based upon Will Adams, and by 1990 the book had sold 15 million copies worldwide.

32
Some Tudor Myths

Henry VIII threw bones over his shoulder
Tudor etiquette at court and in the great houses was to place one's leftovers in a common 'voiding bowl'. Dogs, to which the bones were allegedly thrown, were not allowed in court.

Lady Jane Grey was the 'Nine Days' Queen'
She was the de facto 'thirteen days' queen'. Edward VI died 6 July but his death was not proclaimed until 10 July, when she was announced queen. The Privy Council changed sides and announced Mary I as queen upon 19 July 1553, but Jane had been queen since 6 July unless there was a period where England had no monarch.

Greenwich Palace was in London
The palace was in Kent until 1889, when the county of London was created.

Thomas More was a saint
Not to Protestants – he had forty imprisoned and another six burnt alive. In 1529 More became Lord Chancellor on the fall of Wolsey, and he ruthlessly persecuted Protestants while strongly opposing the proposed relaxation of the heresy laws. In 1530 a Protestant named Thomas Hitton was burned at Maidstone. With characteristic Christian tolerance, More called him 'the Devil's stinking martyr'. According to Samuel Johnson, More 'was the person of the greatest virtue these islands ever produced'.

Elizabeth was the last of the Tudor dynasty
It is always reported that there was no Tudor successor to Elizabeth I. However, Lady Catherine Grey (The Lady Herbert of Cardiff, 1540–68) married Edward Seymour, 1st Earl of Hertford, for which she was confined by Elizabeth I to the Tower until her death. Seymour was fined the enormous sum of £15,000 for seducing a virgin of the royal blood and Elizabeth had their sons officially declared illegitimate, although she had no authority to do so. Catherine Grey

died without the legitimacy of her two sons – Edward and Thomas, who were born in the Tower – ever being proven, but this was later established after the death of Elizabeth I. Catherine Grey being dead, her sons should have succeeded upon Elizabeth's death. Edward Seymour was the elder of her sons. His mother was already pregnant when she entered the Tower and was given poor living conditions, apparently in the hope that she would either miscarry or die. For many years, Edward and Thomas were regarded as illegitimate because no proof could be produced of her legal marriage. Regardless of legal problems, by 1603 Edward Seymour, Viscount Beauchamp, was the senior qualified heir of Henry VII's will, stipulating that the elder line of Stuart, through Margaret Tudor, should be passed in favour of the younger line, through Mary Tudor, his favourite, younger, sister. Edward Seymour's only possible rival under the will was Anne Stanley, Countess of Castlehaven (1580–1647), who would have been heir if Edward and his brother Thomas were considered illegitimate.

Lady Mary Grey (1545–78) was, like her sisters Lady Jane and then Catherine, next in line to the succession under Henry VIII's will as Elizabeth I was childless, but she was persecuted by the queen. Upon Mary Grey's death, Margaret Stanley, Countess of Derby, should have been the heiress to Elizabeth. Her son Ferdinando was probably poisoned in 1594, aged thirty-five, and would have been heir to Elizabeth, giving us a King Ferdinando I.

Henry VIII married Anne Boleyn

There was a secret marriage in Dover Castle in November 1532, and another upon 25 January 1533 in secret at York Place, now Whitehall Palace. Both were bigamous, as Henry's marriage to Catherine of Aragon was not annulled until May 1533. Thus Henry was never officially married to Anne. This is not pedantry. Eric Ives believes that there was a 'commitment' ceremony in November, quite possibly a binding pre-contract, a watertight legal declaration of intent to marry each other. After such a ceremony had taken place, sixteenth-century canon law stated that it was permissible for the couple to commence sexual intercourse with one another. Engagements were thus treated with suspicion by future brides. It was on grounds of such pre-contracts that Henry VIII's subsequent marriages to Anne of Cleves and Catherine Howard were declared invalid. With the pre-contract formally ratified in November, Henry and Anne began sleeping together, and conceived Elizabeth before wedlock.

Anne Boleyn committed adultery

Three days before her execution on charges of adultery, Anne's marriage to Henry was annulled and declared invalid. Thus she could not have committed adultery, or even been executed for the crime if she had never in law been married to the king.

'Bloody Mary' was a deserved epithet

This is Elizabethan propaganda. It should have been ascribed to the far, far bloodier reign of 'Bloody Henry'. The exact figure may never be known, but according to Raphael Holinshed, the English chronicler who died in 1580, the number of executions in his thirty-eight-year reign amounted to 72,000. This is probably an exaggeration, but many thousands of the poor were executed during the reign of Henry VIII, most for what are now regarded as minor crimes such as stealing.

Henry VIII had six wives
As his marriages to Catherine of Aragon, Anne of Cleves and Anne Boleyn were annulled, i.e. declared illegal (Anne Boleyn's marriage being annulled just before her execution), Henry VIII technically only had three wives. The annulment of the marriage to Catherine of Aragon was on the grounds that she had already been married to his brother, although this annulment was never recognised by the Catholic Church and nor were his succeeding marriages, so according to the Catholic Church Henry had one wife. Anne Boleyn was subject to an annulment on the grounds that she had allegedly seduced him with witchcraft and was incestuous and unfaithful. The marriage to Anne of Cleves was annulled as the marriage was unconsummated (and therefore was not legally binding) and because she had previously been engaged to someone else. The marriage to Catherine Howard was never annulled. She had committed adultery with Thomas Culpeper, so on 22 November 1541 it was proclaimed at Hampton Court that she had 'forfeited the honour and title of queen', and was from then on to be known only as the Lady Catherine Howard. Under this title she was executed for high treason three months later.

Henry was loved as 'Bluff King Hal'
This is a far later description of the monarch.

Elizabeth was universally loved by her subjects
Among the known attempts to destroy Elizabeth there were the Northern Rebellion (1569); the Ridolfi plot and assassination attempts (1571); Anthony Tyrrell's plot (1581); the Throgmorton plot (1583); the Somerville plot (1583); Dr Parry's plot (1548) the Babington plot (1586); Dr Rodrigo Lopez' poisoning attempt (1594); and the Essex Plot (1601).

Henry VII murdered the Princes in the Tower
Henry was not in the country and had no power in the realm. The conclusive proof of Richard's murder of the princes can be seen in the Yorkist desertion of his cause when he came to the throne and in this author's biography of Richard III, *The King in the Car Park*.

Only knights were allowed to wear swords
Just as with those wearing of armour, not everyone who carried a sword was a knight. The custom, or even the right, to wear a sword varied according to time, place and changing regulations.

Armoured knights had to be hoisted into their saddles by cranes
Armour worn for jousts, short periods of exertion, was heavier and designed

for maximum defence. However, battle armour had to be lighter and more flexible to allow wearers to fight. Most men-at-arms would have been able to put one foot in a stirrup and mount their horse without assistance. A stool or perhaps the help of a squire would have made the process even speedier for the richer knights. Cranes hoisting up knights is a twentieth-century myth.

Henry VII was a quarter Welsh, a quarter French and half-English

As the genealogies demonstrate, Henry VII was certainly a quarter British (i.e. Welsh) through his paternal grandfather, Owen Tudor. He was also a quarter French through Owen's wife Catherine of Valois. Thus, on the side of his father he was a quarter British and a quarter French. His mother, Margaret Beaufort, was the offspring of the Beauforts and Beauchamps, French families. Many of this family were born in France, for instance the 1st Earl of Somerset at the Chateau de Beaufort in Angers, Anjou. Even Somerset's father, John of Gaunt, was born in Ghent, and the Angevin and Plantagenet royal families had little English blood. In his bloodline, Henry VII was predominantly French.

Peasants feared the Black Death

This term first appeared in 1755, according to the OED. The plague was known as the 'Pestilence' or the 'Great Mortality'.

Henry VIII, Edward VI and Mary I were British rulers

The English were never called British or Britons until Elizabeth's reign, at the suggestion of Dr John Dee, basing claims for an empire overseas upon the legends of British kings over foreign realms. The case of the Celts taking Rome under Brennius (the Welsh for king is *brenhin*, and *brennius* is its Latin equivalent) seems to have been conflated with Arthur's expeditions across Europe. Equally, the legend of Prince Madog ap Owain Gwynedd discovering America in 1170 was used to justify North American expansion.

Chainmail was armour

Defensive garments composed of interlinking rings should correctly be referred to as mail, from *maille armor*. The phrase 'chainmail' is a Victorian misunderstanding.

Tudors were tiny

Henry VII was five feet nine inches, but his son Henry VIII was six feet two inches, probably following his mother's father Edward IV, who was six feet four inches. Catherine Parr was thought to be around five feet ten inches. The hundred or so skeletons of crewmen recovered from the *Mary Rose* indicate an average height of five feet seven inches to five feet eight inches tall.

Henry VIII was fat

He only began to put on weight after being unable to play sports or hunt, from his time with Anne Boleyn. He was then forty-five years old. He lived to be fifty-five, and it was only in his last five years that he grew into obesity. Henry was merely playing at obesity compared to Queen Victoria. She went from a twenty-inch waist aged eighteen (size zero) to something over fifty-six inches (size 38), with her 'spilt drawers' recently auctioned. Having nine children could not have helped. She was just under sixty inches tall, so would have been ball-shaped.

Nine out of ten people died before the age of forty
Statistics can be meaningless, as politicians know full well. Historians believe that average life expectancy at birth was about thirty-five years in the sixteenth century, in other words 50 per cent of people born reached that age. However, high infant and child mortality skews these figures. If one could survive until twenty-one, one had a good chance of living to a good age. A professor of mathematical statistics, H. O. Lancaster, researched mainly aristocratic males in *Expectations of Life* (1990). In 1500–50, for fifty-two males who reached the age of twenty-one, their extra years of life were around fifty, so they would die aged seventy-one. Again, for a hundred adult males from 1550–1600, they could expect to live until they were around sixty-eight years old.

The name of the dynasty was 'the Tudors'
It should have been the Merediths, Maredudds, Meredudds or even Bowens. Henry VII's grandfather was known as Owain ap Maredudd, Owen Meredith and the like from his birth around 1400, through his time in France around 1421 and when granted letters of English denizenship as 'Oweyn fitz Meredyth' in 1432. He was known as Owen Meredith and similar names during his imprisonment in Newgate in 1438. As 'Owen ap Maredudd' he was in the court party that went to France in 1444 to bring back the young Margaret of Anjou, the king's new queen. The Owen or 'Owyn' Meredith in the royal household between at least 1444 and 1453 is almost definitely Owen Tudor. Then again, it easily could have been the Owen or Bowen (ab Owen) dynasty. Neither of Owen's sons are noted in the English records as the 'son of Owen'. Like him, they are called 'ap Meredith ap Tydier' in 1437, whereas they should have been called 'ab Owen ap Meredith'.

Henry VIII was bearded
He was clean-shaven during the early years of his reign and first grew a beard only in 1519 as part of a friendly pact with Francis I of France. He soon shaved it off to please his wife, Catherine of Aragon, but from around 1525 sported a beard, so for only twenty-one years of his fifty-five did he have a beard.

There was a Hundred Years War
Upon 19 October 1453 Bordeaux surrendered, ending a 116-year war that began in 1337. Its end led indirectly to the great barons concentrating upon England and Wales, leading to the Wars of the Roses and the Tudor dynasty.

Stocks are a thing of the past

There are many stocks remaining in villages, such as in Oakham in Rutland. The Statute of Labourers 1531 ordered the punishment of the stocks for unruly artisans, and their last recorded use was in 1865. The use of stocks has never been abolished, thus for litter louts, public drunkenness, foul-mouthed behaviour and graffiti artists they could be used again as a punishment.

Sirloin received its name from Henry VIII

He was said to have knighted a particularly splendid piece of steak and called it 'Sir Loin'. In reality, sirloin is a corruption of the French *sur* (above or on top of) loin.

The Mary Rose sank on her maiden voyage

The warship was built in Portsmouth in 1509–11. She did not sink until 1545 while fighting the French.

'Greensleeves' was written by Henry VIII

A broadsheet ballad by this name was registered by Richard Jones in 1580 as 'A Newe Northen Dittye of ye Ladye Greene Sleves'. It was believed to have been composed by Henry VIII because of the rejection of his attempts to seduce Anne Boleyn, but the piece is based on an Italian style of composition (*romanesca*) that did not reach England until after Henry's death. It is mentioned three times by Shakespeare, one instance being when Falstaff exclaims, 'Let the sky rain potatoes! Let it thunder to the tune of 'Greensleeves'!'

For operations, a barber-surgeon hit you on the head with a wooden mallet until you passed out

There is no evidence for this. Detailed instructions for barber-surgeons survive but there is no mention of such a procedure. Usually alcohol or opiates were involved to dim the pain or help one pass out.

Divorced, beheaded, died, divorced, beheaded, survived

The mnemonic refers to the order of Henry's wives: Catherine of Aragon, Anne Boleyn, Jane Seymour, Anne of Cleves, Catherine Howard and Catherine Parr. Anne of Cleves and Catherine Parr survived him, and Catherine of Aragon died in 1535, having given birth to the future Mary I in 1516. Jane Seymour died two weeks after giving birth to the future Edward VI in 1537. Anne Boleyn was executed in 1536, having given birth to the future Elizabeth I in 1533. Catherine Howard was executed in 1542. Divorce is not the same as annulment. Divorce is a civil law decree from the state, whereas an annulment is a canon law decree from the Church. The state issues a marriage licence, and the state issues a divorce decree. The Church celebrates the Sacrament of Matrimony, and only the Church can issue a Decree of Nullity, otherwise known as an annulment.

The Roman Church, in charge at the time of Henry's annulments, did not believe in divorce. Also, a civil divorce basically says that what was once a marriage is no longer a marriage. The marriage took place but ended. A previously married couple no longer has the legal obligations of husband and wife. An annulment, on the other hand, basically says that the Sacrament of Matrimony never took place to begin with. Civil divorce ends a civil marriage, but a Church annulment declares that the Sacrament of Matrimony never occurred. Church annulments are not a form of divorce and have no effect whatsoever on the legitimacy of children, because that is a purely legal (civil) matter. Annulments do not make the children born of that union illegitimate. Annulments declare that a marriage was never a valid sacrament in the first place, even if both parties entered into it with good faith and intentions. The mnemonic should actually be annulled and survived; annulled and beheaded; died; annulled and survived; beheaded; survived. However, it does not have quite the same ring to it.

Archbishops of Canterbury could not marry

Thomas Cranmer (1489–1527) was training as a priest at Cambridge University when he took a wife named Joan and was forced to give up his residence at Jesus College. Jesus College reinstated his fellowship when Joan died in childbirth and he became a Doctor of Divinity in 1526, having already been named one of the college's preachers. In January 1532, Cranmer was appointed the resident ambassador at the court of the Holy Roman Emperor, Charles V, to try and arrange Henry's annulment of marriage. That summer, in Nuremberg, Cranmer met the leading architect of the Nuremberg reforms, the Protestant Andreas Osiander. They became good friends, and in July Cranmer married Margarete, the niece of Osiander's wife. This was remarkable given that the marriage required him to set aside his priestly vow of celibacy. He did not take her as his mistress, as was the prevailing custom with priests. He was unable to persuade Charles, Catherine of Aragon's nephew, to support the annulment of his aunt's marriage. In 1533 Henry managed to have Cranmer appointed as Archbishop of Canterbury, and he went against Rome by annulling Henry's marriage to Catherine of Aragon. He also crowned the new queen, to the Pope's fury. His family had been exiled to the Continent in 1539. It is not known exactly when they returned to England, but it was soon after the accession of Edward VI in 1547 that Cranmer publicly acknowledged their existence. His daughter, Margaret, was likely born in the 1530s and his son, Thomas, came later, probably during the reign of Edward. Sometime around Mary's accession, Cranmer's wife, Margarete, escaped to Germany, while his son was entrusted to his brother, Edmund Cranmer, who took him also to the Continent. Cranmer was burnt in 1556.

Henry VIII had syphilis

In the sixteenth century the standard treatment for syphilis was mercury, and all ships until the nineteenth century carried mercury for its treatment. Lists of money spent on medicines for Henry VIII exist but mercury is not listed. It is, however, possible that he suffered from some form of depression in the second half of his life, with a severe bout in 1541.

Anne Boleyn had six fingers

She may just possibly have had a small extra fingernail growing at the side of one of her fingers, but no contemporary mentioned it. It was not until almost fifty years later that the story appeared. It is unlikely that any king would marry a woman with an obvious physical deformity, which could be construed as denoting a witch.

Raleigh introduced smoking to England

The Spanish learnt to smoke tobacco from indigenous people. It is believed that English sailors adopted the habit about 1564, but Raleigh was only twelve years old at the time. Smoking tobacco in clay pipes was already quite common in England by the time Walter Raleigh was an adult. However, he is credited with taking the first 'Virginia' tobacco to Europe, referring to it as 'tobah' as early as 1578.

Elizabeth I loved going to the theatre

In fact, the theatre came to the monarch. She never attended the Globe, but its plays were presented at court or her palaces.

Smoking is good for you

In 1571–74 Nicholas Monardes praised the newfound medicinal herb, ensuring that it became a universal remedy for centuries. He claimed that tobacco could cure thirty-six health problems. Even in the mid-twentieth century, the virtues of smoking were explained rationally by doctors and scientists.

There has never been a Spanish King of England

However, under the terms of Queen Mary's marriage act, Prince Philip of Spain was styled 'King of England', and Parliament was to be called under the joint authority of the couple for Mary's lifetime only. If she died, he would become regent.

33

Tudor Superlatives

First Paper
The first paper to be milled in the British Isles was made by John Tate at his mill near Hertford, the earliest example of his paper being on a printed work dated 1494.

First Joke Book
Wynkyn de Worde's collection of riddles, *Demands Joyous*, in 1511.

Greatest Spies
Anthony Spinelly, a Genoese merchant, was used as a factor and spy first by Edward IV and then by Richard III, Henry VII and Henry VIII. Such was Spinelly's notoriety that in 1513 Louis XII blamed the Anglo-French War upon him, yet Louis' successor Francis I called him his good friend. Spinelly served three years in a French gaol, being released upon condition he worked for the French. He thus served six kings that we know of, in England, Flanders and France. The unrelated Florentine Thomas Spinelly acted as an agent for both Henrys at Calais, and controlled at least three agents in France. When a resident in Burgundy, he drew information from the Roman Curia, Antwerp, Bruges, the Italian banking system and directly from the head of Margaret of Savoy's Privy Council. He was intimate with the de Taxis family, who ran the postal service across much of northern and central Europe, who provided him with digests of news from all the monarchs who used their services. He sent spies to entrap Richard de la Pole, Earl of Lincoln. Wolsey had to alter the cipher for his successor in 1522, as so many people were familiar with it.

First British Battle Decided by Cannon and Firepower
The Battle of Pinkie Cleugh on 10 September 1547, where Somerset beat the Scots. Also considered the 'first modern battle' in Britain.

First Protestant Martyr under Mary I
John Rogers (*c.* 1500 – 4 February 1555), a clergyman and Bible translator, was burnt at the stake.

'Most Christian King'
After the Battle of Guinegate, the Pope stripped the French king of this title and awarded it to Henry VIII.

The Only Councillor to Serve Continuously under Four Monarchs
Sir William Paulet (1483/85–1572) was a Privy Councillor for thirty years, the only councillor to serve continuously under Henry VIII, Edward VI, Mary I and Elizabeth I.

First King to be Referred to as 'His Majesty'
The modest Henry VIII.

Biggest Wastrel
The 8th Earl of Northumberland had an annual income of £4,995 in 1582. When he died in 1585 some was left to his widow, leaving the twenty-one-year-old Henry Percy (1564–1632), the 9th earl, with an income of £3,363. In Henry Percy's own words, 'Hawks, hounds, horses, dice, cards, apparel, mistresses; all other riot of expense that follow them were so far afoot and in excess as I knew not where I was or what I did until, out of my means of £3,000 yearly, I had made shift in one year and one half to be £15,000 in debt.' Thus he was spending £10,000 a year, but as a nobleman could not be imprisoned for debt. A tobacco addict, he spent seventeen years in the Tower for his involvement in the Gunpowder Plot.

The Only Noble at the First and Last Battles of the Wars of the Roses
Jasper Tudor, at the First Battle of St Albans in 1455 and the Battle of Stoke Field in 1487.

First English King to Pronounce Himself Prince of Wales
Henry VII issued his first proclamation as king three days after Bosworth, on 25 August 1485, of which the opening words were 'Henry, by the grace of God, King of England and of France, Prince of Wales and Lord of Ireland'. This was the very first time that any king who had not himself been invested as Prince of Wales, as heir apparent, had appropriated the title.

Best Couplet

> Treason doth never prosper, what's the reason?
> For if it prosper, none dare call it Treason.
>
> Sir John Harington (*c.* 1560–1612)

Last Queen Consort of England to be Crowned Separately from Her Husband
Anne Boleyn, upon 1 June 1533. Anne was the only one of Henry's wives, apart from Catherine of Aragon, to have a coronation. She is also the only consort, before or since, to have been crowned with the St Edward crown, which is reserved for the actual monarch. The original of this crown was lost when Oliver Cromwell melted it down during the English Civil War.

Unluckiest Number for Bears

In 1575, Elizabeth's favourite courtier, the Earl of Leicester, entertained her on a visit to his great court at Kenilworth Castle. In the inner courtyard, thirteen bears were tied to stakes and set upon by a pack of mastiffs.

First European to Encounter the Mainland of North America since the Vikings

John Cabot sailed from Bristol and took the area of 'new found land' in the name of King Henry VII in 1497.

Oldest National Flag in the World

On 3 September 1485 at St Paul's Cathedral, Henry offered to God the three main banners his forces had carried in battle – the arms of St George, the Tarteron and Duncow (representing the houses of Lancaster and Beaufort) and the Red Dragon of Cadwaladr (proclaiming his British ancestry). This was, according to Hall, 'a red firye dragon beaten vpon white and grene sarcenet' – the Welsh national flag, the oldest national flag in the world. His new bodyguard, the Yeomen of the Guard, wore the Welsh national colours of green and white.

Last Words

'Pluck up thy spirits, man, and be not afraid to do thine office, my neck is very short.' These were the last words of Thomas More to his executioner on 6 July 1535.

The Only Woman to Have Been Tortured at the Tower of London

Anne Askew, 15 July 1546. She is the only woman to have been both tortured in the Tower and burnt at the stake. Askew is also one of the earliest female poets to compose in the English language and the first Englishwoman to demand a divorce (especially as an innocent party on scriptural grounds). Today's religious misogynist could link the asking for divorce with her punishments.

First English Child Born on American Soil

In 1587 Raleigh made a second attempt at settling a colony, with 117 settlers at Roanoke, Virginia. On 18 August 1587, Eleanor Dare gave birth to a daughter.

First Blast of the Trumpet Against the Monstrous Regiment of Women

John Knox in 1558 published this vehement attack on the 'practice of admitting females to the government of nations'. In the mid-sixteenth century there was intense philosophical debate about the role of women and Knox had discussed with Swiss divines the biblical origins for their role. In essence the *First Blast* was prompted by the activities of Mary I. Mary died soon after its publication and it then came to be regarded as an attack also on Elizabeth I, as well as Mary of Guise, the Queen regent of Scotland (who died in 1560), and then Mary, Queen of Scots. It was a statement that the divine law had expressly assigned to man the dominion over women and commanded her to be subject to him, that female government was not allowed under the Jews, that it was contrary to apostolic injunctions and that it led to perversion of government. In a letter of October 1559, Sir William Cecil, writing from the court, stated that 'of all others, Knox's name ... is most odious here'.

Bishop Aylmer wrote a defence to satisfy Elizabeth, but his language was stronger than Knox's at times. He wrote, 'Some women be wise, better learned, discreeter, constanter, than a number of men.' However, others he describes as 'fond, foolish, wanton, flibbergibs, tattlers, trifling, wavering, witless, without counsel, feeble, careless, rash, proud, dainty, nice, tale-bearers, eavesdroppers, rumour-raisers, evil tongued, worse-minded, and, in everywise, doltified with the dregs of the devil's dung hill'.

England's First Purpose-Built Shopping Centre

The Royal Exchange was designed in 1566–67 by Sir Thomas Gresham as a three-storied building around a courtyard, emulating Antwerp's Bourse. Merchants met to trade and deal in the cloisters on the ground floor. Above, on the floors known as 'the Pawn', were apothecaries, booksellers, goldsmiths, milliners, armourer, haberdashers and glass sellers, all deliberately placed to attract rich merchants and their wives.

First Idea of a Workhouse for the Able-Bodied Poor

The idea offering basic accommodation and employment for the able-bodied poor was first suggested in 1536 by Thomas Cromwell.

Largest Area of Fan-Vaulted Ceiling in the World

King's College Chapel, Cambridge, where work resumed with funds from Henry VII in 1506, was completed under Henry VIII.

First Princess of Wales

Henry VIII invested his daughter Mary as Princess of Wales in 1525, and she was also the first female royal to hold court at Ludlow Castle.

More Last Words

'I heard say the executioner is very good, and I have a little neck.' Anne Boleyn to the Constable of the Tower of London on the day of her execution, 19 May 1536.

First Recorded Use of 'Gloriana' for Elizabeth I

It is recorded that the troops at Tilbury hailed her with cries of 'Gloriana, Gloriana, Gloriana', after the defeat of the Armada in 1588.

Best Anecdote about Shakespeare

The lawyer John Manningham of the Middle Temple kept a diary, and his entry of 13 March 1602 tells of the great actor Richard Burbage playing Richard III. With spelling modernised:

Upon a time when Burbidge played Richard III, there was a citizen grown so far in liking with him, that before she went from the play she appointed him to come that night unto her by the name of Richard the Third. Shakespeare overhearing their conclusion went before, was entertained and at his game ere Burbidge came. The message being brought that Richard the Third was at the door, Shakespeare caused return to be made that William the Conqueror was before Richard the Third.

Best Epitaph

Manningham, mentioned above, records the following epitaph in January 1601: 'If I be not beguil'd / Here lies Mr Child.'

First Wristwatch

Leicester gave Elizabeth a watch placed in a bracelet, possibly the first wristwatch in the world.

Best Disregard for Health and Safety – 'The Show Must Go On'

In the days before 'elf 'n safety', Richard Edwardes, the supposed illegitimate son of Henry VIII, wrote the play *Palamon and Arcite*. In 1566, it was performed before Elizabeth I at Oxford when the stage fell. Three people died and five were injured, but the show continued to play that night.

First Legitimate King of England and Wales

Henry VIII, after Wales was annexed by the Act of Union of 1536.

Europe's First Dry Dock

In 1495, Henry VII had this built at Portsmouth.

Most Anomalous Position

As Supreme Governor of the Church of England, Elizabeth (like Mary) appointed all the archbishops and bishops, but as a woman was debarred from holding any religious office. The monarch traditionally also led troops into battle and exercised the law. Apart from not being trained to fight, she was barred from holding legal office. She was thus barred by her gender from interpreting laws and religion, despite being the sole arbiter of both. In 1576, Mary Cleese of Ingatestone was burnt at the stake for high treason, stating that the queen was baseborn, not rightly queen, and did not have the power to make knights.

First Fagin

In 1585, Wotton trained a school for child pickpockets in Billingsgate.

Most Fatal Letter

This ends, 'Yours as long as life endures, Katheryn.' It was sent by Catherine Howard to Thomas Culpeper in spring 1541.

Scolding First Criminalised
The year 1585, and it remained illegal until 1967, coincidentally with the rise of 'Women's Lib'!

First Appearance of 'the Sweating Sickness'
Previously unknown, this contagious plague or fever broke out in England between Henry Tudor's landing on 7 August and Bosworth on 22 August 1485.

Last Person Burnt for Heresy
This is slightly outside the Tudor timescale, but worth noting. Heretics were handed over to civil authorities for burning, the last person being Edward Wightman at Lichfield in 1612. A radical Anabaptist, he incurred the enmity of James I, who particularly wanted him burnt.

First Woman in England to Smoke Tobacco
This was said to be Moll Cutpurse (see Chapter 14), a cross-dresser who carried on the habit until her death.

Most Ironic Title
Defender of the (Catholic) Faith. Henry asserted his new authority as 'Supreme Head of the Church of England' in official imagery, as seen on official medals. The king is shown wearing a jewelled cap, ermine robe and jewelled collar, with a legend in Latin around the edge divided by royal emblems. This translates as 'Henry VIII, King of England, France and Ireland, defender of the faith, and under Christ, the supreme head on earth of the Church of England and Ireland'.

First Cauliflower
A new vegetable from western Asia reached England in the sixteenth century. It was called cauliflower, from the Latin *caulis* (cabbage) and flower. It was introduced to France from Genoa in the sixteenth century and was mentioned in 1600 as *caulifiori* 'as the Italians call it, which are still rather rare in France; they hold an honourable place in the garden because of their delicacy'. It seems to have been introduced into England from the Cyprus, and it is mentioned by Lyte, in 1586, under the name of 'Cyprus coleworts'. Gerard published an illustration of it in England in 1597. Commercial cultivation in England began in 1619.

First Stock Exchange in England
Sir Thomas Gresham founded the Royal Exchange in 1565, also one of the earliest in Europe.

Most Expensive Cock
A good fighting cockerel would cost over £5 around 1550, around £20,000 in labour value today.

First Standardisation of the Length of a Mile
Precisely 1,760 yards in a royal declaration of 1592. Interpretations of weights, measures and areas still differed across the country.

Only Woman to Have Her Head Displayed on a Spike on London Bridge
Also possibly the maddest woman, and known variously as the 'Nun of Kent', the 'Holy Maid of Kent' or the 'Mad Maid of Kent', Elizabeth Barton (1506–33) was a poor twenty-year-old woman when she began having visions that seemed to come true, and she defended the Catholic faith. In 1532 she had become a nun in the Benedictine order of St Sepulchre in Canterbury, and prophesied that if Henry married Anne Boleyn he would die within the year and go to Hell. In 1533 she was hanged and decapitated for treason at Tyburn alongside four priests.

Fastest Growth of Literacy
At the beginning of the sixteenth century, only 10 per cent of men and 1 per cent of women could read. By 1600, around 25 per cent of men and 10 per cent of women were literate. This progress was aided by the printing press.

First National Lottery
Upon 11 January 1569, the first national lottery was drawn in England. Profits were intended for the repair of harbours and other public works, and state lotteries continued until 1826, when religious feelings caused their abandonment.

Oldest English Companies
1488 Rathbone Candles of Dublin, the oldest candle manufacturer in the world. It still makes a range of candles varying from paraffin wax to pure beeswax, and specialises in church candles.
1498 Shore Porters Society of Aberdeen is a removals, storage and haulage company.
1503 The Golden Fleece Inn, York, is a 'haunted' free house with four guest bedrooms, mentioned in the York City Archives as far back as 1503. There are hundreds of older 'pubs', however.
1514 Hampton Ferry is a private pedestrian and cycle ferry across the Thames in Richmond.
1514 Trinity House Corporation came into being by royal charter granted by Henry VIII under the name 'The Master, Wardens, and Assistants of the Guild, Fraternity, or Brotherhood of the most glorious and undivided Trinity, and of St Clement in the Parish of Deptford-Strond in the County of Kent'. The charter came as a result of a petition put forward by a guild of Deptford-based mariners troubled by the poor conduct of unregulated pilots on the Thames. They asked the king for licence to regulate pilotage. In 1566, Queen Elizabeth I's Seamarks Act enabled Trinity House 'at their wills and pleasures, and at their costs, [to] make, erect, and set up such, and so many beacons, marks, and signs for the sea ... whereby the dangers may be avoided and escaped,

and ships the better come into their ports without peril'. It is still the general lighthouse authority, the deep-sea pilotage authority and a maritime charity.

1515 R. J. Balson and Son is a high street butcher in Bridport, Dorset, and the oldest continually trading family business in the United Kingdom.

1534 Cambridge University Press is both the oldest publishing house in the world and the oldest university press. It originated from letters patent granted by Henry VIII in 1534, and has been producing books continuously since its first book was printed in 1584. Printing did not actually begin until the first practising University Printer, Thomas Thomas, was appointed in 1583.

1541 John Brooke of Huddersfield made woollen clothing and was the oldest manufacturer of uniforms in the world, but because of foreign competition was forced to close in 1987.

1570 Whitechapel bell foundry in London is the oldest manufacturing company in Great Britain. It still manufactures church bells and other bells today.

1586 Oxford University Press – its legal existence was noted by the Star Chamber in 1586. In response to constraints on printing outside London, Oxford University had petitioned Elizabeth for the formal right to operate a press at the university.

1588 Keymer Tiles of Sussex makes traditional red terracotta roof tiles.

1591 R. Durtnell and Sons is Britain's oldest building company, and has been a private family company for thirteen generations, passing from father to son since its foundation. It is still based in Brasted in Kent, and the first building it constructed, Poundsbridge Manor (also called The Picture House), was completed in 1593. Durtnell also restored the house following bomb damage in the Second World War.

1601 Tissimans (originally Slaters) was a tailor, draper and undertaker opposite St Michael's church in Bishop's Stortford. In 2013 Tissimans has claim to being the oldest men's clothing establishment in the world. Part of the premises dates from about 1360, with modern additions around 1545.

First 'King of Ireland'

Henry VIII assumed this title in 1542.

Taking Coals to Newcastle

The phrase, meaning giving someone things they do not need, was first recorded in 1538.

First Recorded Use of the Word 'Football'

In 1487 we see the first recorded the use of the word to describe a game in which the ball is kicked. 'Mob football' was just as popular then as now but now the mob is divided into players on a pitch and those watching.

World's Oldest, Largest and Longest Football Game

This is played every year on Shrove Tuesday in Ashbourne, Derbyshire, over two days and involving thousands of players. The goals are three miles apart and there are only a few rules. A hand-painted, cork-filled ball is used. It is thought that this game has been played for 1,000 years.

First Mention of Whiskey
The earliest form of the word in English was *uskebeaghe* (1581), and it was made all over the British Isles by monks. After the Dissolution, it was made in homes.

Worst Flying Attempt
The alchemist John Damian, Abbot of Tongland Abbey, attempted to fly off the walls of Stirling Castle in 1507. The flying abbot crash-landed and seemingly expired.

First Potato
Potatoes were brought to England in the 1580s, but at first few English people ate them. Potatoes in the UK were brought by adventurers associated with Raleigh and Drake. Potatoes first arrived in Spain in 1570 and were then introduced to Ireland and Britain in 1586. Gerard was already growing potatoes in London in 1597. Sailors returning from the Andes to Spain with silver presumably brought maize and potatoes for their own food on the trip. Historians speculate that leftover tubers (and maize) were carried ashore and planted. Drake, returning from his circumnavigation, and Raleigh's employee Thomas Harriot are both commonly credited with introducing potatoes into England. John Hawkins was also recorded as first importing potatoes to Ireland from the Spanish colonies in either 1563 or 1565. Some scholars also suggest that Hawkins also introduced tobacco from the New World to England.

First Queen Regnant
Mary I was the first queen reigning in her own right rather than being queen through marriage to a king, or acting as regent for an infant son. Empress Matilda (1102–67), Henry I's heir, was never queen.

Best Puritan Advice
Philip Stubbes (1555–1610) in his *The Anatomie of Abuses* attacked the manners, customs, amusements and fashions of the period:

> If you would have your son soft, womanish, unclean, smooth-mouth, affected to bawdry, scurrility, filthy rimes, and unseemly talking; briefly if you would have him, as it were, transnatured into a woman or worse, and inclined to all kinds of whoredom and abomination, set him to dancing school and to learn music, and then you shall not fail of your purpose. And if you would have your daughter riggish, bawdry and unclean, and a filthy speaker, and suchlike, bring her up in music and dancing and my life for yours, you have won the goal.

First Blast Furnace in England

This was developed in Buxted, the Weald, in 1491.

Most Forgetful Husband

In fairness, Henry VIII had six 'wives', but only for those of the foreign nobility – Catherine of Aragon and Anne of Cleves – do we know their birthdates. We do not even know for certain his English wives' birth years, let alone days and months.

Best Innovation

Dr Alexander Nowell was Dean of St Paul's. When a parish priest at Much Hadham, Hertfordshire, he decanted some beer into a bottle for a fishing expedition on the River Ash. According to Thomas Fuller's *History of the Worthies of Britain*, published a hundred years later, when Nowell returned to the riverbank a few days later and came across the still full bottle, 'he found no bottle, but a gun, such was the sound at the opening thereof; and this is believed (causality is mother of more inventions than industry) the original of bottled ale in England'. The ale had undergone a secondary fermentation in the bottle, building up carbon dioxide pressure so that it gave a loud pop when Nowell pulled the cork out. Such high-condition ale must have been a novelty to Elizabethan drinkers, who knew only the much flatter cask ales. The benefits of bottled beer were discovered by accident upon 13 July 1568, but hand-blown bottles were generally not strong enough to handle fermentation until the following century.

First Person to Use the Phrase 'British Empire'

The term appears in John Dee's 1576 book entitled *General and Rare Memorials Pertayning to the Perfect Arte of Navigation.* After England's break with the papacy stabilised, Dee attempted to rationalise a case for colonies across the world by justifying it upon the lineage of the British kings from Troy onwards via Brutus and the British and Welsh kings. Until his book the Welsh were known as the Britons, and henceforth the English also became British.

First Stocking Frame

William Lee of Calverton invented this mechanical knitting machine in 1589, and its use, known traditionally as framework knitting, was the first major stage in the mechanisation of the textile industry, playing an important part in the early history of the Industrial Revolution. The machine imitated the movements of hand knitters, and Lee demonstrated it to Elizabeth, hoping for a patent. Elizabeth refused, fearing the effects on hand-knitting industries. Lee later improved the mechanism with twenty needles to the inch, and by 1598 he was able to knit stockings from silk as well as wool, but was again refused a patent by James I. Lee moved to France with his workers and his machines but was unable to sustain his business, dying in poverty around 1614. Most of his workers returned to England with their frames, and further development led to England leading the world in textile manufacture.

Best College for Producing Prime Ministers
The year 1546 saw the foundation of Christ Church. Like its sister college, Trinity College, Cambridge, it was traditionally considered the most aristocratic college of its university. Christ Church has produced thirteen British prime ministers, which is equal to the number produced by all the other forty-five Oxford colleges put together.

First Use of the Sonnet in English Literature
Sir Thomas Wyatt (1503–42) was an English ambassador and lyrical poet, credited with introducing the sonnet from Italy.

First Patron of Horse Racing
Henry VIII had a stable of 200 horses, and was the first patron of horse racing, despite the Pope's demands for cessation of all racing in England.

Most Married English Queen
Catherine Parr with four husbands.

First Topless Courtesan and Royal Mistress
Outside the Tudor era, but copied by Elizabeth I, Agnès Sorel is credited with starting the fashion in 1440 when she wore deep, square décolleté gowns with fully bared breasts in the French court. Sorel was the favourite mistress of Charles VII of France and is considered the first officially recognised royal mistress.

First Fashion Policewoman
Henry II of France was married to Catherine de' Medici, who enforced a ban on 'thick waists' at court attendance during the 1550s. For this reason, she was credited with the need for corsets and bodices.

'Easiest Disease from Which to Die'
The French ambassador reported this from England of 'the sweating sickness' in 1528.

First English Queen to be Titled 'Queen of Ireland'
Catherine Parr.

The Only Two Queens in History to Be Double-Bastardised
Mary and Elizabeth Tudor were declared illegitimate by Parliament under Henry VIII in 1532 and 1536 respectively. They were later legitimised, and again bastardised by Edward VI in his 'Device for the Succession' in 1552–53.

First Female Ambassador in European History
Catherine of Aragon, in 1507, served as the Spanish ambassador to England.

Most Effective Measure Against the Plague
From 1578 onwards, thick boards were nailed against the doors and windows

of victims where the afflicted person and his or her whole family, including servants if they had any, were isolated inside for at least six weeks. Watchmen kept guard to ensure no one escaped. Many starved to death.

First Black Trumpeter in England

John Blanke (also Blancke or Blak, *fl.* 1501–11) was a black musician in London, probably brought to England as one of the African attendants of Catherine of Aragon in 1501. He is one of the earliest-recorded black people in England after the Roman occupation. Little is known of Blanke's life, but he was paid 8*d* per day by Henry VII, and a surviving document from the accounts of the Treasurer of the Chamber records a payment of 20 shillings to 'John Blanke, the blacke trumpeter' as wages for the month of November 1507.

Blanke was probably the black person depicted twice in the Westminster Tournament Roll, an illuminated manuscript sixty feet long that records the royal procession to the lavish tournament held in 1511 to celebrate the birth of Prince Henry, who died days later.

First Robot

Leonardo da Vinci (1452–1519) studied human anatomy, leading him to design the first known robot around 1495, the humanoid automaton now known as 'Leonardo's Robot'.

Best Long-Range Forecast

Leonardo da Vinci foresaw English as the world's *lingua franca*, writing in his notebooks, 'Men standing in opposite hemispheres will converse and deride each other and embrace each other, and understand each other's language.'

First Law Enabling People to be Boiled Alive

Henry VIII changed the law in an Act passed in 1531, the preamble of which made poisoning a form of petty treason (that is, killing one's husband or master), the penalty for which would be boiling to death. Richard Rouse, a cook, was particularly mentioned in the statute as Henry had some personal reason for wanting him boiled. He was said to have put poisoned yeast in porridge prepared for the household of the Bishop of Rochester and the poor of Lambeth parish, sickening seventeen people and killing a man and a woman. Rouse (or Roos) was found guilty of petty treason and publicly boiled at Smithfield in 1532. They probably had food poisoning. Some months later a maidservant was boiled at King's Lynn for poisoning her mistress, and in 1542 Margaret Davy or Dawes, a servant, was boiled at Smithfield for poisoning her employer. An entry in *Wriothesley's Chronicle* for 1542 is 'This yeare, the 17th of March, was boyled in Smithfield one Margaret Davie, a mayden, which had poisoned 3 householdes that she dwelled in. One being her mistress, which dyed of the same, and one Darrington and his wife, which she also dwelled with in Coleman Street, which dyed of the same, and also one Tinleys which also dyed of the same.' Death did not come quickly – when the victim passed out with pain, he was lifted by chains until he regained consciousness and lowered again, with his flesh peeling off. Because the heart was strong, the torture lasted ages, and much of the flesh could be cooked before the heart, lungs and brain were badly affected by the heat. The law was repealed in 1547 by a horrified Edward VI and replaced by hanging, but Henry's original Act remained in the statute book until 1863.

First Law Enabling the Insane to Be Executed
Again in 1532, Henry VIII was enjoying himself with the legal system, asking for an Act enabling Lady Jane Rochford to be beheaded.

Worst Catch-22
Shortly before her execution on charges of adultery, Anne's marriage to Henry was annulled and declared invalid. Thus she could never have committed adultery – she had never in law been married to the king.

First Bigamist Monarch
Thomas Cranmer, Henry VIII's newly appointed Archbishop of Canterbury, pronounced on 23 May 1533 that Henry's marriage with Catherine was void. However, Henry had secretly wed Anne Boleyn in January 1533, when she was already pregnant. The Pope refused to accept the pronouncement, and in July 1533 he declared the divorce and remarriage void, and prepared to excommunicate Henry. The excommunication was suspended, but it was reaffirmed by Clement's successor, Paul III.

First Lady Groom of the Stool
In 1558 the male domination of royal private quarters came to an end, and Kat Ashley was appointed First Lady of the Bedchamber by Elizabeth, a position that put her in charge of the bedchamber, a duty formerly performed by the Groom of the Stool. The office effectively came to an end in 1559.

Most Unreported Wrestling Match
At the Field of the Cloth of Gold in 1520 the carefully established rules of the tournament stated that the two kings would not compete against each other, but the six-foot-two-inch Henry surprisingly challenged the six-foot-four-inch Francis I in a wrestling match. However, it turned sour for Henry when he was quickly thrown. No one on the English side found it remotely amusing, and it was not publicised in England.

First and Last Archbishop of Canterbury to Be Burnt at the Stake
Thomas Cranmer, by Mary I, on 21 March 1556.

First English Queen of Jerusalem
Upon her marriage in 1554, Mary I became Queen of Naples and titular Queen of Jerusalem.

Most Historic Pearl

La Pelegrina, a teardrop pearl given to Mary I by her husband Phillip II. After the death of Mary I the pearl was brought back to Spain, where it became part of the crown jewels. The pearl was bought by Richard Burton for Elizabeth Taylor in 1969 at Sotheby's Auction House. When Elizabeth died in 2011 the pearl, which she had attached to a diamond necklace, was on display; it eventually sold at an auction in 2012 to an anonymous buyer.

First Time the British were Given Equality with the English

By the Acts of Union from 1536, Welshmen were given near-equal rights under English law. The English were never called 'British' until the later years of Elizabeth's reign.

Most Hypocritical Title

Henry VIII chose the nickname 'Sir Loyal Heart' for himself for when he participated in tournaments and jousts. For instance, in 1511, he called himself 'Noble Cueur [*sic*] Loyal'. He invented this name for himself during his marriage to Catherine of Aragon, whom the 'loyal-hearted' Henry abandoned after over twenty years of marriage.

Worst Kiss of a Queen

Catherine of Valois, the grandmother of Henry VII, died in 1437. Henry VII made major alterations to Westminster Abbey, which involved moving her embalmed body. She was temporarily placed in a crude coffin and left above ground. Henry died before a proper tomb could be constructed and she remained a public spectacle for over 200 years. Samuel Pepys went to the abbey on his thirty-sixth birthday in 1668 and opened the coffin. Pepys takes up the story here: 'I had the upper part of her body in my hands, and I did kiss her mouth, reflecting upon that I did first kiss a Queene.' Her body was not removed from public view until 1776.

Most Pointless Liaison

In 1560, the English were besieging Leith in Scotland. Some of its French garrison disguised themselves as women and slipped out of a side gate. An English scout, seeing the 'ladies', left his post to talk to them, possibly in the hope of something more. Probably after pumping him for information, the demoiselles decapitated him and placed his head on the church spire in full view of the besiegers.

Most Sarcastic Epitaph

Ben Jonson's epitaph of Robert Dudley, Elizabeth's favourite and 1st Earl of Leicester, reads, 'Here lies a valiant warrior, / Who never drew a sword; / Here lies a noble courtier, / Who never kept his word; / Here lies the Earle of Leister, / Who govern'd the Estates; / Whom the Earth could never living love, / And the just Heaven now hates.'

First Nucleus of an English Standing Army

The Yeomen of the Guard, the distinct corps of royal bodyguards formed by Henry VII in 1485, is still in existence. It seems that Henry formed this bodyguard, composed mainly of Welshmen, for Bosworth. By surrounding his person with guards, copying the King of France, Henry emphasised his special royal dignity. The bodyguard was increased by Henry and maintained until his death, and became a permanent perquisite of the king or queen. It was also the first nucleus of an English standing army. Under Henry VII they fought at Stoke Field in 1487, Boulogne in 1492 and Blackheath in 1497.

Greatest Villain

There are enough villains in Tudor times to fill several books, such as Richard Rich and Thomas Wriothesley for their duplicity and torture, or Henry VIII himself for the destruction of the great monasteries and abbeys and their irreplaceable stained glass and treasures. However, one man stands out for this author, a man who made a career of torturing people: Richard Topcliffe (1531–1604). A landowner and MP, Topcliffe became notorious as a priest hunter and torturer and was often referred to as the queen's principal 'interrogator'. Topcliffe gained a reputation as a sadistic torturer who claimed that his own instruments and methods were better than the official ones, and was authorised to create a torture chamber in his London house, which he boasted contained a personally designed machine for torture – 'compared with which the rack was mere child's play'. He repeatedly raped and impregnated at least one prisoner, and took great pleasure in prolonging the disembowelling of Jesuits.

More Last Words

'Treason! Treason! Treason! Treason! Treason!' Traditional last words of Richard III, 22 August 1485

First Apricot

Apricots were introduced from Portugal and grown in England from the sixteenth century, but the climate cooled. Now there are once more commercial orchards in England, as climatic changes are nothing new.

Biggest Letter

In the Vatican, there is a 1530 parchment sent by members of the House of Lords to Pope Clement VII to support the divorce of Henry VIII. It measures three feet by six feet six inches, and has more than eighty original red wax seals. In the letter, written in Latin, the lords urge the Pope to annul the marriage to help give the kingdom an heir and prevent a bloody fight between successors. Henry 'will surely guarantee stability to the kingdom if he will be able to entrust its government to a male heir', the letter says. The noblemen also foreshadow the coming schism by threatening that should the Pope 'neglect the needs of the English, they would feel authorised to solve the issue on their own and find remedies elsewhere'. Officials said that, while the original document will remain in the Vatican Secret Archives, they plan to put a copy on display.

Greatest Understatement of Tudor Times

'I've finished that chapel I was painting. The Pope is quite satisfied.' Michelangelo (1475–1564) wrote this in a letter to his father in October 1512 upon the completion of the ceiling of the Sistine Chapel in the Vatican. Michelangelo resented this commission for Pope Julius II, as he believed that it was serving the aggrandisement of that Pope. From 1508 to 1512 he painted 12,000 square feet of ceiling, including the iconic image of God creating Adam with touching fingertips at its centre. He said, 'After four tortured years, more than 400 over-life-sized figures, I felt as old and as weary as Jeremiah. I was only thirty-seven, yet friends did not recognise the old man I had become.' Michelangelo had completed his astonishing *Pieta* sculpture, showing Jesus with his head on his mother Mary's lap after the Crucifixion, when he was just twenty-four. His statue *David* was finished before he was thirty, and is the most admired sculpture in the world. Another sculptor had tried and failed to work the solid block of Carrera marble before Michelangelo, who commented, 'I saw the angel in the marble and I carved until I set him free.' Michelangelo was not only possibly the greatest painter and sculptor of all time but also an architect and poet, his thirty-eighth sonnet including the lines, 'Love is a beautiful image / Imagined or seen within the heart, / The friend of virtue and gentility.' His fifteenth sonnet tells us about his ideas on sculpture: 'The marble not yet carved can hold the form / Of every thought the greatest artist has.'

First British Colony

If we discount Wales and Ireland, this was founded by Walter Raleigh at Roanoke in North Carolina in 1584.

Last English Monarch

Elizabeth was the last English monarch to be 'English'. She was followed by the Scottish Stuarts, and then the German Hanoverians, and so on. Even the present royal family had to change its name from Saxe-Coburg-Gotha to Windsor to sound less German in 1917.

First Equals Sign

In 1557, appeared *The Whetstone of Witte*, Robert Recorde's textbook of elementary algebra. In this he invented the = sign using two parallel line segments, 'because no two things can be more equal' and to 'avoid the tedious repetition of "equals to"'.

Earliest Image of a Man Smoking a Pipe

In 1595, Anthony Chute published *Tabaco*, which repeated earlier arguments about the benefits of the plant and emphasised the health-giving properties of pipe smoking.

First Coachbuilder

In 1564 Guilliam Boonen came from the Netherlands to be Elizabeth's coachbuilder, introducing the new European invention of the spring-suspension coach.

Last Letter

'Tonight, after dinners, I have been advised of my sentence. I will be executed like a criminal at eight in the morning.' Mary, Queen of Scots, to her brother-in-law Henri III of France on 7 February 1587.

First Use of the 'Sacred Herb'

The Spanish introduced tobacco to Europeans in about 1528, and by 1533 Diego Columbua had mentioned a tobacco merchant of Lisbon in his will, showing how quickly the traffic had sprung up. Jean Nicot (1530–1600), the French ambassador in Lisbon, sent samples to Paris in 1559. The French, Spanish and Portuguese initially referred to the plant as the 'sacred herb' because of its valuable medicinal properties.

First Smoker

Rodrigo de Jerez sailed to the Americas on the *Santa Maria* with Columbus in 1492. He is credited with being the first European smoker.

First Chocolate and Chili

Columbus and his son Ferdinand encountered the cacao bean on Columbus's fourth mission to the Americas on 15 August 1502, when he and his crew seized a large native canoe that proved to contain cacao beans among other goods for trade. The conquistador Hernán Cortés may have been the first European to encounter it, as the drink was part of the after-dinner routine of Montezuma. Jose de Acosta, a Spanish Jesuit missionary who lived in Peru and then Mexico in the later sixteenth century, wrote of its growing influence on the Spaniards:

> Loathsome to such as are not acquainted with it, having a scum or froth that is very unpleasant taste. Yet it is a drink very much esteemed among the Indians, where with they feast noble men who pass through their country. The Spaniards, both men and women that are accustomed to the country are very greedy of this Chocolate. They say they make diverse sorts of it, some hot, some cold, and some temperate, and put therein much of that 'chili'; yea, they make paste thereof, the which they say is good for the stomach and against the catarrh.

Chilies are from Central America, where they have been grown for thousands of years. The Aztecs were fond of chilies and the Spanish brought them back to Europe. Chilies came to England in 1548. After the Spanish conquest of the Aztecs, chocolate was imported to Europe. There, it quickly became a court favourite. It was still served as a beverage, but the Spanish added sugar, as well as honey, to counteract the natural bitterness. Hernán Cortés is also credited with introducing vanilla to Europe in the 1520s.

Most Unsympathetic Announcement upon Hearing of a Death

On 19 May 1536, Henry was having breakfast under the shade of a large tree, preparing for hunting. He heard the sound of a cannon being fired, telling him that Anne Boleyn had been executed. According to Moray's *History of Essex*, the king then cried out, 'Away! Unkennel the dogs!' The next day he became engaged to Jane Seymour.

More Last Words

'Thy necessity is yet greater than mine.' Sir Philip Sidney, dying from wounds and giving his water to a wounded soldier in 1586.

First Turkey

Turkeys were introduced into England about 1525. When Europeans first encountered turkeys in America, they incorrectly identified the birds as a type of guineafowl (*Numididae*). Guineafowl were also known as turkey fowl (or turkey hen and turkey cock) because they were imported to Central Europe through Turkey. The name turkey fowl, shortened to just the name of the country, stuck as the name of the North American bird. In 1550, the English navigator William Strickland, who had introduced the turkey into England, was granted a coat of arms including a 'turkey-cock in his pride proper'.

First Reference to Cricket

John Derrick gave evidence in a 1598 lawsuit that he and his friends had played 'creckett' fifty years earlier, on land in Guildford.

Shortest Reigning Monarch

Lady Jane Grey, who ruled for thirteen days from 6 July until 19 July 1553 (although she was only proclaimed queen by the Lords of the Council on 10 July).

First Pomegranates

Pomegranates were known in Europe in the Middle Ages and they were mentioned by Shakespeare. Pomegranate is believed to be a corruption of the Old French words *pome garnete*, seed apple. Catherine of Aragon's emblem of the pomegranate can be seen on an altar cloth made by Catherine, in St Peter's Church, Winchcombe, Gloucestershire. Queen Mary used the pomegranate as a badge in memory of her mother Catherine. Following each of his six marriages, Henry ordered that the new emblems and badges of his latest wife replace those of his previous one in his palaces. Courtiers tried to keep up, but Sir Richard Clement, owner of Ightham Mote, clearly fell behind. One of the king's favourite servants, Sir Richard officiated at the royal wedding with Anne Boleyn. However, at his mansion near Sevenoaks, one will still find the

Tudor Rose and pomegranate of Aragon in the stained glass of the Great Hall and the barrel-vaulted roof of the New Chapel.

Oldest Female Monarch at Time of Accession

Mary I, aged thirty-seven years and 151 days when she became queen in 1553.

More Last Words

'Here lies one who neither feared nor flattered flesh.' John's Knox's epitaph from the Earl of Morton, 26 November 1572.

Oldest Queen at Time of First Marriage

Mary I was aged thirty-eight years and157 days when she married Philip of Spain in 1554.

First Appearance of 'the Tudor Rose'

Shortly after Henry VII's marriage to Elizabeth of York in 1486 – the red petals of the Lancastrian rose enclose the white petals of the York rose.

Last Words of Mary I

'When I am dead and opened, you shall find Calais lying in my heart.'

Ruffest Ruffs

Ruffs for men and women being popular, they became increasingly more elaborate and larger after the introduction of starch in 1564 when a Flemish refugee set up as a linen starcher in London. At the height of the fashion in the 1580s and 1590s, ruffs were made with up to eighteen feet of starched material, with up to 600 pleats, stretching eight inches or so from the neck. Ben Jonson described wearing them as pretending to be a head on a plate.

Best Beauty Advice

From *Book of the Courtier* (1513–18) by Baldasarre Castiglione:

> Haven't you noticed how much prettier a woman is if, when she makes up, she does so with so little that those who see her cannot tell whether she is made up or not? But others are so bedaubed that it looks like they are wearing a mask and dare not laugh because they fear it will crack. Such women never change colour except when they dress in the morning, and must spend the rest of the day like motionless wooden images ... How much nicer it is to see a woman, a good looking one I mean, who obviously has nothing on her face, neither white nor red, but just her natural colour, which may be pale or sometimes slightly tinged with a blush caused by embarrassment or the like, maybe with her hair tousled and whose gestures are simple and natural, without working at being beautiful?'

Youngest British Monarch at Start of Reign

Mary, Queen of Scots, who became queen aged six days in 1542.

Most Married Monarch
Henry VIII, six times (or less, depending upon how one interprets mediaeval legality).

Last Words at the Stake
'I see Heaven open and Jesus on the right hand of God.' Thomas Cranmer, Archbishop of Canterbury, on 21 March 1556.

First Beans and Sprouts
Kidney beans are native to South America, and were common in England by the mid-sixteenth century. Runner beans are native to Central America and were discovered by Europeans in the sixteenth century, being first grown in England in the seventeenth century. Brussels sprouts were developed in Belgium from the thirteenth century and became popular across most of Europe in the sixteenth century.

Most Married Queen
Mary, Queen of Scots, with three husbands.

Most Married Queen Consort
Catherine Parr, with four husbands.

Most Prophetic Last Words
'You will not find me alive at sunrise.' Nostradamus, 2 July 1566.

First Love Apple
Tomatoes came to England from Mexico. Tomatoes originate from the Andes in South America, where they grow wild in what is now Peru, Bolivia, Chile and Ecuador. They were first cultivated by the Aztecs and Incas as early as AD 700. The English word 'tomato' comes from the Aztec word *tomatl*. Tomatoes first arrived in Europe in the sixteenth century, although how they got here is unclear. Some say that they were brought back from Central America by Spanish Conquistadors, while another legend suggests that two Jesuit priests brought them to Italy from Mexico. The first cultivated tomatoes were yellow and cherry-sized, earning them the name golden apples; *pommes d'or* in French, *pomi d'oro* in Italian and *goldapfel* in German. The Italian for tomatoes today is *pomodoro*. Soon after the tomato's arrival in Europe it also became known as the Peruvian apple. Tomatoes were originally grown in Britain and the rest of Europe as ornamental climbers and were cultivated for their decorative leaves and fruit. The first known British tomato grower was Patrick Bellow in 1554. The Elizabethans thought the bright red colour of tomatoes was a danger signal and the fruit poisonous. Popular sixteenth-century English herbalists such as John Gerard saw no contradiction in writing that, while Spaniards and Italians ate tomatoes, the plant was nevertheless 'of ranke and stinking savour'. The French were convinced tomatoes had aphrodisiac properties and began calling them *pommes d'amour* or love apples.

First Recorded Reference to 'Publish'
With regard to issuing a book, this first appears in Thomas More's *Dialogue* of 1528, attacking William Tyndale.

Best Will
'I have nothing, owe a great deal, and the rest I leave to the poor.' Single statement in the last will and testament of François Rabelais, 1533.

Most Popular Botany Book
John Gerard (*c.* 1545–1612) was a botanist and herbalist who maintained a large herbal garden in London. His 1,480-page, heavily illustrated *Herball, or Generall Historie of Plantes*, first published in 1597, was the most widely circulated botany book in English in the seventeenth century.

First Stock Market Flotation
The Dutch East India Company in 1602. It was dissolved in 1800.

First Gold Sovereign
Issued in 1489, a statement of unity and power by Henry VII.

Last Words of Henry VIII
'Monks! Monks! Monks!' 28 January 1547.

First Bananas, Figs, Gooseberries, Peaches and Pineapples
Bananas were known in the sixteenth century, but the first recorded sale of bananas in England was not until 1633. Figs were also introduced to England in the sixteenth century. Gooseberries are native to Europe and western Asia. They were first mentioned in England in the sixteenth century when they were grown as a medicine. The name gooseberry may simply imply they were eaten with goose, or it may be a corruption of the Dutch word *kruisbes*, which means cross berry. Peaches were grown in England by the late sixteenth century, but they were rare and expensive until the twentieth century. Pineapples originally grew in South America and Columbus discovered them in 1493. However, during the sixteenth and seventeenth centuries pineapples were very expensive in Europe as they had to be imported.

Last Charge of Mounted Knights in Britain
Richard III and his bodyguard at Bosworth Field in 1485.

Last English King to Die in Battle
Richard III at Bosworth in 1485.

Oldest Woman
In 1499, Agnes Skuner died. According to the inscription on her grave in Camberwell church, she was 119 years old, having outlived her husband Richard by ninety-two years.

Most Poignant Memento

Elizabeth I had a locket ring which spells the initial E in table-cut diamonds and contains two miniature busts, one of her mother Anne Boleyn and one of Elizabeth herself. Elizabeth constantly wore the ring and it was removed from her finger after her death and sent to James VI of Scotland as evidence of her death, showing how important the ring and her mother were to Elizabeth. The ring is often referred to as the 'Chequers ring' because it now belongs to the Trustees of Chequers.

First Systematic Exposition of the Inductive Method in Science

The lawyer Francis Bacon (1561–1626) in 1603 was the first scientist to receive a knighthood. In order to test potential truths, or hypotheses, Bacon devised a method whereby scientists set up experiments to manipulate nature, and attempt to prove their hypotheses wrong, known as the 'scientific method' or 'Baconian method'.

Last Successful Foreign Invasion of England

Henry VII brought a mainly Welsh, French, Scottish and Breton force in 1485. Most people are taught that England has not been conquered by a non-English force since Hastings in 1066, which is an egregious error.

Most Brilliant Word Inventor

Of the 17,677 different words in Shakespeare's collected writings, around 10 per cent are first recorded by Shakespeare and thus can be argued to have been coined by him. These include words such as courtship, extract, accommodation, horrid, premeditated, excellent, obscene, lonely, frugal, reliance, critical and majestic. He thus invented over 1,700 of our common words by changing nouns into verbs, changing verbs into adjectives, connecting words never before used together, adding prefixes and suffixes, and devising words wholly original. As well as inventing wholly new words, Shakespeare also had something of a disregard for the usual rules of written English, which enabled him to play with grammar. He used the un- prefix to create a number of new words such as unlock, unveil and unhand as well as more than 300 others. He also combined existing words to make new compound words, such as blood-stained and barefaced. According to Bill Bryson in his Shakespeare biography, about one-tenth of the quotes contained in the *Oxford Dictionary of Quotations* come from Shakespeare, a few of which are 'the milk of human kindness' (*Macbeth*); 'vanish into thin air' (*Othello*); 'cold comfort' (*The Taming of the Shrew*); 'in a pickle' (*The Tempest*); 'flesh and blood' (*Hamlet*); 'foregone conclusion' (*Othello*); 'in my mind's eye' (*Hamlet*); 'a laughing stock' (*The Merry Wives of Windsor*); 'one fell swoop' (*Macbeth*); 'lie low' (*Much Ado About Nothing*); 'a sorry sight' (*Macbeth*); and 'be cruel to be kind' (*Hamlet*).

List of Illustrations

1. Courtesy of the Yale University Art Gallery, Edwin Austin Abbey Memorial Collection
2. Courtesy of Elizabeth Norton
3. Courtesy of Amy Licence
4. Courtesy of Elizabeth Norton
5. Courtesy of David Baldwin
6. Courtesy of Josephine Wilkinson
7. Courtesy of Jonathan Reeve JR982b20p837 15001600
8. Courtesy of Patrick Williams
9. Courtesy of Stephen Porter
10. Courtesy of Jonathan Reeve JRCD2b20p961 15501600
11. Courtesy of Elizabeth Norton
12. Courtesy of Elizabeth Norton
13. Courtesy of Jonathan Reeve JR1177b2p167B 15001550
14. Courtesy of Elizabeth Norton
15. Courtesy of Jonathan Reeve JR1169b2p7 15001550
16. Courtesy of Elizabeth Norton
17. Courtesy of Jonathan Reeve JRCD2b20p929 15001550
18. Courtesy of Jonathan Reeve JRCD3b20p913 15001550
19. Courtesy of Jonathan Reeve JR1018b5fp204 15001550
20. Courtesy of Jonathan Reeve JRCD2b20p769 15501600
21. Courtesy of Jonathan Reeve JR779b46fp192 14501500
22. Courtesy of Elizabeth Norton
23. Courtesy of Elizabeth Norton
24. Courtesy of Stephen Porter
25. Courtesy of Stephen Porter
26. Courtesy of Stephen Porter
27. Courtesy of Jonathan Reeve JRpc219 15001550
28. Courtesy of Elizabeth Norton
29. Courtesy of Elizabeth Norton
30. Courtesy of Stephen Porter
31. Courtesy of Jonathan Reeve JRCD2b20p987 15001550
32. Courtesy of Elizabeth Norton

33. Courtesy of Elizabeth Norton
34. Courtesy of Jonathan Reeve JRCD2b20p1005 15501600
35. Courtesy of Yale Center for British Art, Paul Mellon Collection
36. Courtesy of Elizabeth Norton
37. Courtesy of Jonathan Reeve JR1003b66fp112 15001600
38. Courtesy of Jonathan Reeve JR1009b66fp181 15501600
39. Courtesy of Stephen Porter
40. Courtesy of Jonathan Reeve JR216b5p148 15501600
41. Courtesy of Jonathan Reeve JR204b5p9 15501600
42. Courtesy of Jonathan Reeve JR1719b89fpiii 16001700
43. Courtesy of Jonathan Reeve JR996b66fp681 15001600
44. Courtesy of Elizabeth Norton
45. Author's collection

Select Bibliography

Ackroyd, P., *Tudors: A History of England, Volume II* (Pan, 2013)

Alexander, M., *The First of the Tudors: a Study of Henry VII and His Reign* (Rowman and Littlefield, 1980)

Allanic, J., *Le prisonnier de la tour d'Elven ou la jeunesse du Roy Henri VII* (Vannes, 1909)

Arthurson, I., 'Espionage and Intelligence from the Wars of the Roses to the Reformation', *Nottingham Medieval Studies*, XXXV (1991)

Blakman, J., *Henry VI, King of England 1421–1471*, ed. M. R. James (Cambridge University Press, 1919)

Breverton, T., *Owain Glyndŵr: The Last Prince of Wales* (Amberley, 2013)

Breverton, T., *Richard III: The King in the Car Park* (Amberley, 2013)

Breverton, T., *The Physicians of Myddfai* (Cambria, 2013)

Breverton, T., *Breverton's Encyclopedia of Inventions* (Quercus, 2012)

Breverton, T., *Jasper Tudor: Dynasty Maker* (Amberley, 2014)

Breverton, T., *Immortal Last Words* (Quercus, 2010)

Breverton, T., *Breverton's Complete Herbal* (Quercus, 2011)

Breverton, T., *Breverton's Nautical Curiosities* (Quercus, 2010)

Chapman, Hester W., *Lady Jane Grey* (Macmillan, 1972)

Chrimes, S. B., *Henry VII* (Eyre Methuen, 1972)

Christie, M. E., *Henry VI* (Houghton Mifflin, 1922)

Cunningham, S., *Henry VII* (Routledge, 2007)

Davies, J. S. (ed.), *An English Chronicle of the Reigns of Richard II, Henry IV, Henry V and Henry VI 1377–1461* (Camden Society, 1856)

Dockray, K., *Henry VI, Margaret of Anjou and the Wars of the Roses: A Source Book* (Sutton, 2000)

Dodd, A. H., *Life in Elizabethan England* (John Jones, 1998)

Domville, M., *The King's Mother: Memoir of Margaret Beaufort, Countess of Richmond and Derby* (London, 1899)

Drayton, M., 'Englands Heroicall Epistles (1597)' in J. W. Hebel (ed.), *The Works of Michael Drayton* (Oxford, 1961)

Ellis, H. (ed.), *Polydore Vergil's English History [1525], Comprising the Reigns of Henry VI, Edward IV and Richard III* (Camden Society, 1844)

Elton, G. R., *England under the Tudors* (Routledge, 1991)

Evans, H. T., *Wales and the Wars of the Roses* (Alan Sutton Publishing, 1995)
Fabyan, R., *The Chronicles of England and France*, ed. H. Ellis (London, 1811)
Foarde, G. and A. Curry, *Bosworth 1485: A Battlefield Rediscovered* (Oxbow, 2013)
Gairdner, J., *Henry the Seventh* (1889)
Gairdner, J. (ed.), *The historical collections of a citizen of London in the fifteenth century (Gregory's Chronicle)* (Camden Society, 1876)
Gairdner, J. (ed.), *A Short English Chronicle in Three Fifteenth Century Chronicles* (Camden Society, 1809)
Gairdner, J. (ed.), *The Paston Letters 1422–1509* (London, 1900)
Griffith, R. A. and R. Thomas, *The Making of the Tudor Dynasty* (St Martin's Press, 1985)
Guy, J., *Tudor England* (Oxford Paperbacks, 1990)
Haigh, P. A., *The Military Campaigns of the Wars of the Roses* (Sutton Publishing, 1995)
Hall, E., *Chronicle containing the History of England from Henry VI to Henry VIII*, ed. H. Ellis (London, 1809)
Halliwell-Phillipps, J. (ed.), *Warkworth's Chronicle of the first thirteen years of the reign of King Edward IV* (London, 1839)
Halsted, C., *Life of Margaret Beaufort, Countess of Richmond and Derby* (London, 1839)
Harriss, G. L. and M. A. (eds), 'John Benet's Chronicle for the years 1400 to 1462', *Camden Miscellany*, 24 (Camden Society, 1972)
Holland, H., *Pancharis: the love between Owen Tudyr and the Queen* (1603)
Jones, E. W., 'Bosworth Field: A Selective Historiography', *National Library of Wales Journal*, Summer 1979
Jones, W. G., 'Welsh Nationalism and Henry Tudor', *Transactions of the Honourable Society of Cymmrodorion*, 1917–18
Jones, Michael K., *The King's Mother: Lady Margaret Beaufort, Countess of Richmond and Derby* (Cambridge University Press, 1992)
Kingsford, C. L., *Chronicles of London* (Oxford, 1905)
Lewis, Brenda Ralph, *A Dark History: The Kings and Queens of England* (Allen Lane, 2008)
Lin, M., *The Mirror for Princesses: the Fashioning of the English Queenship 1553–1603* (Unpub. PhD thesis, Edinburgh University, 2000)
Loades, D., *Mary Tudor* (Amberley, 2012)
Loades, D., *Henry VIII* (Amberley, 2011)
Loades, D., *The Tudors: History of a Dynasty* (Continuum, 2012)
Marshall, R. K., *Mary I* (National Portrait Gallery, 1993)
Meyer, G. J., *The Tudors: The Complete Story of England's Most Notorious Dynasty* (Amberley, 2011)
Major, J., *A History of Greater Britain* (*c.* 1517), ed. A. Constable (Scottish Historical Society, 1892)
Mortimer, I., *The Time Traveller's Guide to Elizabethan England* (Vintage, 2009)
Prestwich, M., *Armies and Warfare in the Middle Ages: The English Experience* (Yale University Press, 1996)
Rees, D., *The Son of Prophecy: Henry Tudor's Road to Bosworth* (Black Raven Press, 1985)

Rex, R., *The Tudors* (Amberley, 2012)

Roberts, P., 'The Welsh-ness of the Tudors', *History Today*, January 1986

Roberts, G., 'Wyrion Eden: the Anglesey descendants of Ednyfed Fychan in the fourteenth century', *Transactions of the Anglesey Antiquarian Society and Field Club*, 1951

Roberts, G., 'Teulu Penmynydd', *Transactions of the Honourable Society of Cymmrodorion*, 1959

Routh, E. M. G., *Lady Margaret, A Memoir of Lady Margaret Beaufort Countess of Richmond and Derby Mother of Henry VII* (Oxford University Press, 1924)

Scarisbrick, J. J., *The Reformation and the English People* (Wiley-Blackwell, 1985)

Simons, E. N., *Henry VII, the First Tudor King* (Muller, 1968)

Skidmore, C., *Bosworth: The Birth of the Tudors* (Weidenfeld & Nicolson, 2013)

Starkey, D., *Henry, Virtuous Prince* (Harper Press, 2008)

Starkey, D., *Six Wives: The Queens of Henry VIII* (Vintage, 2004)

Temperley, G., *Henry VII* (London, 1917)

Thomas, R. S., *The Political Career, Estates and 'Connection' of Jasper Tudor, Earl of Pembroke and Duke of Bedford* (Unpub. PhD thesis, Swansea University, 1971)

Vergil, Polydore, *English History* (Camden Society, 1844)

Warkworth, J., *A Chronicle of the First Thirteen Years of the Reign of King Edward the Fourth 1461–1474*, ed. J. O. Halliwell (Camden Society, 1839)

Watts, J., *Henry VI and the Politics of Kingship* (Cambridge University Press, 1999)

Waurin, J., *Recueil des Chroniques, etc., Vol. V.*, ed. W. Hardy (London: Rolls Series, 1864–91)

Weir, A., *Children of England: The Heirs of Henry VIII* (Vintage, 2008)

Weir, A., *Elizabeth the Queen* (Vintage, 2009)

Weir, A., *Henry VIII: The King and His Court* (Vintage, 2008)

Weir, A., *The Six Wives of Henry VIII* (Vintage, 2007)

William of Worcester, *Annales Rerum Anglicarum*, ed. J. Stevenson (London: Rolls Series, 1864)

Williams, G., 'The Bardic Road to Bosworth: A Welsh View of Henry Tudor', *Transactions of the Honourable Society of Cymmrodorion*, 1986

Williams, G., *Harri Tudur a Chymru (Henry Tudor and Wales)* (Cardiff: Gwasg Prifysgol Cymru, 1985)

Williams, G., *Renewal and Reformation: Wales, c. 1415–1642* (Oxford University Press, 1993)

Williams, N., *The Life and Times of Henry VI* (Weidenfeld & Nicolson, 1973)

Williams, N., *Henry VIII and His Court* (Weidenfeld & Nicolson, 1971)

Williams, N., *The Life and Times of Elizabeth I* (Weidenfeld & Nicolson, 1972)

Williams, N., *The Life and Times of Henry VII* (Weidenfeld & Nicolson, 1973)

Wolffe, B., *Henry VI* (Methuen, 1983)

Websites

thetudorenthusiast.weebly.com; thetudorswiki.com is the site associated with the TV series and is informative; tudorhistory.org; royal.gov.uk; henrytudorsociety.wordpress.com; theanneboleynfiles.com; onthetudortrail.com